W9-AZF-640

Investing in the Disadvantaged

Selected Titles from the American Governance and Public Policy Series

Series Editors: Gerard W. Boychuk, Karen Mossberger, and Mark C. Rom

After Disaster: Agenda Setting, Public Policy, and Focusing Events
Thomas Birkland

Ambiguity and Choice in Public Policy: Political Decision Making in Modern Democracies
Nikolaos Zahariadis

Branching Out, Digging In: Environmental Advocacy and Agenda Setting
Sarah Pralle

Brussels Versus the Beltway: Advocacy in the United States and the European Union
Christine Mahoney

Budgeting Entitlements: The Politics of Food Stamps
Ronald F. King

Collaborative Public Management: New Strategies for Local Governments
Robert Agranoff and Michael McGuire

Controlling Technocracy: Citizen Rationality and the NIMBY Syndrome
Gregory E. McAvoy

Dam Politics: Restoring America's Rivers
William R. Lowry

The Education Mayor: Improving America's Schools
Kenneth K. Wong, Francis X. Shen, Dorothea Anagnostopoulos, and Stacey Rutledge

Expert Advice for Policy Choice: Analysis and Discourse
Duncan MacRae Jr. and Dale Whittington

Federalism and Environmental Policy: Trust and the Politics of Implementation, Second Edition,
Revised and Updated
Denise Scheberle

Federalism in the Forest: National versus State Natural Resource Policy
Tomas M. Koontz

Fenced Off: The Suburbanization of American Politics
Juliet F. Gainsborough

Globalization and the Politics of Pay: Policy Choices in the American States
Susan B. Hansen

The Government Taketh Away: The Politics of Pain in the United States and Canada
Leslie A. Pal and R. Kent Weaver, Editors

Healthy Voices, Unhealthy Silence: Advocacy and Health Policy for the Poor
Colleen M. Grogan and Michael K. Gusmano

How Governments Privatize the Politics of Divestment in the United States and Germany
Mark Cassell

Improving Governance: A New Logic for Empirical Research
Laurence E. Lynn Jr., Carolyn J. Heinrich, and Carolyn J. Hill

Lessons of Disaster: Policy Change after Catastrophic Events
Thomas Birkland

Making Policy, Making Law: An Interbranch Perspective
Mark C. Miller and Jeb Barnes, Editors

Metropolitan Governance: Conflict, Competition, and Cooperation
Richard C. Feiock, Editor

National Health Insurance in the United States and Canada: Race, Territory, and the Roots of Difference
Gerard W. Boychuk

Policy Entrepreneurs and School Choice
Michael Mintrom

The Politics of Automobile Insurance Reform: Ideas, Institutions, and Public Policy in North America
Edward L. Lascher Jr.

The Politics of Ideas and the Spread of Enterprise Zones
Karen Mossberger

The Politics of Unfunded Mandates: Whither Federalism?
Paul L. Posner

Power, Knowledge, and Politics: Policy Analysis in the States
John A. Hird

Preserving Public Lands for the Future: The Politics of Intergenerational Goods
William R. Lowry

School's In: Federalism and the National Education Agenda
Paul Manna

The Shadowlands of Conduct: Ethics and State Politics
Beth A. Rosenson

Taking Aim: Target Populations and the Wars on AIDS and Drugs
Mark C. Donovan

Ten Thousand Democracies: Politics and Public Opinion in America's School Districts
Michael B. Berkman and Eric Plutzer

Terra Incognita: Vacant Land and Urban Strategies
Ann O'M. Bowman and Michael A. Pagano

Transatlantic Policymaking in an Age of Austerity: Diversity and Drift
Martin A. Levin and Martin Shapiro, Editors

Virtual Inequality: Beyond the Digital Divide
Karen Mossberger, Caroline J. Tolbert, and Mary Stansbury

Welfare Policymaking in the States: The Devil in Devolution
Pamela Winston

David L. Weimer
Aidan R. Vining
Editors

Investing in the Disadvantaged
Assessing the Benefits and Costs of Social Policies

Georgetown University Press ∽ Washington, DC

Georgetown University Press, Washington, D.C.
www.press.georgetown.edu

© 2009 by Georgetown University Press. All rights reserved. No part of this book may be reproduced or utilized in any form or by any means, electronic or mechanical, including photocopying and recording, or by any information storage and retrieval system, without permission in writing from the publisher.

Library of Congress Cataloging-in-Publication Data

Investing in the disadvantaged : assessing the benefits and costs of social policies / David L. Weimer and Aidan R. Vining, editors.
p. cm. — (American governance and public policy series)
Includes bibliographical references and index.
ISBN 978-1-58901-257-8 (pbk. : alk. paper)
1. United States—Social policy—1993—Cost effective-ness. 2. People with social disabilities—Services for—United States—Cost effectiveness. I. Weimer, David Leo. II. Vining, Aidan R.
HN59.2.I68 2009
361.6'1—dc22

2008029502

⊗ This book is printed on acid-free paper meeting the requirements of the American National Standard for Permanence in Paper for Printed Library Materials.

15 14 13 12 11 10 09   9 8 7 6 5 4 3 2

First printing

Printed in the United States of America

Contents

List of Illustrations   ix

Foreword   *Michael A. Stegman*   xi

Preface   xv

1

Assessing the Costs and Benefits of Social Policies   1
Aidan R. Vining and David L. Weimer

2

Early Childhood Interventions   17
Barbara Wolfe and Nathan Tefft

3

Elementary and Secondary Schooling   31
Clive R. Belfield

4

Health Care for Disadvantaged Populations   49
David J. Vanness

5

Adults with Serious Mental Illnesses   67
Mark S. Salzer

6

Illicit Substance Abuse and Addiction   83
Jonathan P. Caulkins

7

Juvenile Crime Interventions   103
Jeffrey A. Butts and John K. Roman

8

Prisoner Reentry Programming   127
John K. Roman and Christy Visher

9
Housing Assistance to Promote Human Capital   151
Lance Freeman

10
Encouraging Work   163
Robert Lerman

11
Next Steps in Welfare-to-Work   187
Michael Wiseman

12
Welfare-to-Work and Work-Incentive Programs   205
David Greenberg

13
Overview of the State-of-the-Art of CBA in Social Policy   219
Aidan R. Vining and David L. Weimer

14
An Agenda for Promoting and Improving the Use of CBA in Social Policy   249
David L. Weimer and Aidan R. Vining

List of Contributors   273
Index   277

Illustrations

FIGURES

1.1   Program Evaluation, Policy Analysis, and CBA   5

7.1   Typical Teen Court Process   110

7.2   Juvenile Drug Courts Expanded Quickly   113

TABLES

1.1   Monetization Methods   10

6.1   Gaps between Traditional Focus and Information Needed   88

7.1   Change in Indices of System Quality, by Percentage   119

9.1   Costs and Benefits of Housing Assistance Programs   157

11.1   Financial and Nonfinancial Gains and Losses   200

12.1   U.S. AFDC Random Assignment Welfare-to-Work Evaluations   207

13.1   Overview of CBA in Social Policy Areas   224

13.2   Overview of Monetization of Impacts in Social Policy CBAs   226

Foreword

Congratulations to David L. Weimer and Aidan R. Vining and their expert contributors for creating such an incisive and critical review of the use of cost-benefit analysis in the making and evaluation of social policies. The editors' critical essays and accompanying literature reviews present a comprehensive picture of the state of the art across a wide range of policy domains, a valuable discussion of methodological challenges, and a research agenda to help advance the use of this important analytical tool for social policymaking.

This volume is a product of the first MacArthur Foundation grant under an initiative called *The Power of Measuring Social Benefits*. A starting point for this multiyear initiative is America's increasingly challenging fiscal condition and the harder choices that lie ahead for lawmakers about how to meet society's most urgent social needs with shrinking resources. The drift toward more ideologically grounded social policymaking, and lack of evidence-of-effectiveness also seems to feed a sense in some quarters that a vast array of social programs are generally wasteful, neither benefiting the individuals they were intended to assist nor the larger society.

Although a growing body of literature strongly supports the proposition that the interests of those in need may not always be at odds with the interests of the larger society and economy, evidence on which policies and programs work best to achieve these mutual net benefits is more scarce. Even when rigorous program evaluations do exist, they may not always inform policymakers as well as they might because they either fail to compare program benefits with costs, or translate positive program impacts into returns on public investment. Lacking such a common metric also makes it harder for policymakers to rank-order programs that purport to attack the same or similar problem or compare program payoffs across different policy domains.

A motivating hypothesis that will be tested over the course of this project is that effective social policies that invest in individuals in need or at risk may not only improve their life chances, but in many instances benefit the larger society and economy and generate public returns long after assistance has ended. The goal is to strengthen the case for social policymaking that is more firmly grounded in evidence-of-effectiveness and complementary benefits to recipients and society.

The empirical and methodological precedent for *The Power of Measuring Social Benefits* is the widely recognized Perry Preschool study, which was among the first carefully controlled social experiments to quantify the costs and benefits of early childhood education well into adulthood, looking at things like better education outcomes that led to better jobs and higher incomes, more taxes paid, less involvement in the criminal justice system, and lower demands on welfare, and all the rest. The economic return to participants and society of the Perry Preschool program was more than $17 per dollar invested (Schweinhart 2004, 3; Schweinhart et al. 2006). According to the accounting system employed in the cost-benefit analysis of Perry Preschool, about 75 percent of total benefits accrued to the general public. As fiscal constraints grow more severe, being able to quantify the indirect benefits that accrue to taxpayers who pay for effective social programs, even though they may not directly benefit from them, may be as important to their ultimate political survival as evidence of the impacts of those benefits.

Some would argue that there is something unseemly about a social policy system that requires safety net programs to yield measurable and monetizable returns. I agree that not all social programs should be subject to a cost-benefit test, but I would also argue that policymakers routinely dismiss many effective social programs as wasteful welfare spending when, in reality, they may turn out to be worthy investments. In this context, the judicious use of cost-benefit analysis in social policymaking supplements rather than displaces the values of compassion, conscience, and morality in the formulation of American social policy; and may help protect rather than threaten critical social programs. This may be especially true with regard to early intervention programs whose costs are known and may be relatively large, whereas their payoffs may not be evident until the children reach adolescence.

According to one literature review, "five major studies have shown that these programs reduce the incidence of social problems by large amounts when the children reach adolescence and adulthood . . . and the effects seem to be larger for more severe problems. Cost-benefit analyses were done for four of the five programs . . . and benefit exceeded costs in each case, and the ratio was as high as 7:1 in one study" (Crane and Barg 2003, 2).

In covering such broad ground and featuring studies that vary widely in scope, rigor, and time horizons, and singling out the "best from the rest," Weimer, Vining, and their colleagues not only provide the Foundation with a solid understanding of the state of the field and critical research needs, but also, more important, have created a valuable resource for graduate public policy programs across the country that are training the next generation of social policy analysts and managers. I agree with Greg Duncan and Katherine Magnuson that though a "detailed accounting of the costs and benefits is beyond the scope" of most social program evaluations, "the policy value of studies is enhanced by providing even very rough estimates of the likely costs and benefits" (2007, 46).

Michael A. Stegman, PhD
Director of Policy and Housing
The John D. and Catherine T. MacArthur Foundation
Chicago, Illinois

REFERENCES

Crane, Jonathan, and Mallory Barg. 2003. "Do Early Childhood Intervention Programs Really Work?" Washington, DC: Coalition for Evidence-Based Policy. www.excelgov.org/admin/FormManager/filesuploading/ Do_Early_Intervention_Programs_Really_Work7.pdf.

Duncan, Greg J., and Katherine Magnuson. 2007. "Penny Wise and Effect Size Foolish." *Child Development Perspectives* 1(1): 46–51.

Schweinhart, Lawrence, J. 2004. "The High/Scope Perry Preschool Study through Age 40, Summary, Conclusions, and Frequently Asked Questions." Yipsilanti, MI: High/Scope Press.

Schweinhart, Lawrence J., Jeanne E. Montie, Zhonping Xiang, Steve W. Barnett, Clive R. Belfield, and Milagros Nores. 2006. *Lifetime Effects: The High/Scope Perry Preschool Study through Age 40*. Yipsilanti, MI: High/Scope Press.

Preface

As researchers seeking to contribute to better public policy, we have long had an interest in promoting cost-benefit analysis (CBA). Our graduate school days coincided with the end of its first wave of use, which was primarily in assessing proposed infrastructure projects. In the years that followed, we witnessed a second wave, which applied it to rulemaking by federal agencies in response to presidential orders during the Reagan and Clinton administrations. A third wave, facilitated by the development of stated preference surveys to help measure costs and benefits that could not be measured by the more familiar and comfortable revealed preference techniques, extended CBA to environmental damage assessment and natural resource policy more generally. Throughout these years, we continued to see a trickle of CBAs, some very high quality, applied to social policy issues such as supported work programs for parolees, job training programs for disadvantaged youths, and community-based services for the severely mentally ill. The trickle has grown into a rising tide, but it has not yet become a wave. We took on the project of assessing the state of the art of CBA applied to social policy with the hope that we would help to make the rising tide more wavelike.

We report here on the results of that project. We believe our report will interest several audiences. First are students of social policy. We asked the social policy experts we recruited to write eleven of these chapters to tell us what policy interventions in their areas of specialization are widely believed to be effective by those working in the area, what additional interventions look promising, and the CBAs important in terms of either influence or quality that have attempted to assess the efficiency of the interventions. Despite the interrelationships among the social policy areas, few policy researchers have the time to keep up with all of them. We hope they will find these chapters a valuable resource. Because the experts were careful to write to a general audience, we also believe that their chapters will be useful both in graduate and undergraduate courses and to thoughtful practitioners.

Second are the policy researchers we hope to encourage to use CBA in their work. Although CBA requires sometimes heroic efforts to monetize impacts as costs or benefits, applying it imposes a discipline on researchers to be comprehensive in comparing policies. Assessing impacts precisely is certainly desirable, especially from an intellectual perspective. However, considering the full range of costs and benefits is important to good public policy. We intend that our overview encourage the application of CBA to social policy, offer examples of exemplary CBAs to serve as models, and identify some of the pitfalls to avoid.

Third is the community of researchers interested in CBA. If CBA is to be used more appropriately and more widely, then a number of conceptual issues need to be better resolved and a number of commonly required shadow prices need to be provided. Most policy researchers do not have the resources to make their own estimates of important shadow prices, such as the nonmarket benefits of schooling or the nonmonetary costs of crime. Their capacity for doing CBA would increase greatly if a larger number of these shadow prices were available for their analyses. We believe that the CBA community can make a valuable contribution to public policy by following the research agenda we sketch.

This project would not have been attempted without the encouragement of Michael Stegman and the financial support of the John D. and Catherine T. MacArthur Foundation. It would not have been possible to execute without the help of the experts who generously responded to our request for reviews: Barbara Wolfe and Nathan Tefft on early childhood development, Clive Belfield on elementary and secondary education, David Vanness on health care for disadvantaged populations, Mark Salzer on mental health, Jonathan Caulkins on substance abuse, Jeffrey Butts and John Roman on juvenile justice, John Roman and Christy Visher on prisoner reentry, Lance Freeman on affordable housing, Robert Lerman on work incentives, Michael Wiseman on welfare-to-work, and David Greenberg on welfare-to-work CBAs. We benefited from research assistance by Elizabeth Drilias and Marc Ratkovic, from comments by Scott Farrow, Robert Haveman, and Richard Zerbe, and from logistical support by Barbara Prigge. We also thank Don Jacobs at Georgetown University Press. Of course, the opinions expressed are solely those of the chapter authors. Similarly, the assessments in the introductory and concluding chapters are ours alone.

Assessing the Costs and Benefits of Social Policies

Aidan R. Vining and David L. Weimer

If everyone started life healthy in supportive families and communities, the scope of social policy would be fairly narrow. Unfortunately, we do not live in such a world. Not everyone starts life with physical and mental health, and unfortunate events can take good health from those who do. Not all families provide enough support to enable children to gain educations that prepare them well for effective participation in labor markets. Limited legitimate opportunities and adverse influences from communities may lead to substance abuse, births to unwed teenage mothers, delinquency, and crime. Those who succumb to these maladies hurt their own life prospects and likely those of their own children as well. They may also inflict costs on the rest of society in terms of crime victimization, dependency, and forgone positive contributions to their communities. Social policy seeks to help people make greater investments in their own human capital—health, skills, knowledge, and experience—so that they have attractive legitimate economic opportunities and are less likely to impose costs on the rest of society.

Social policy requires more than resources to achieve these goals. It requires interventions that effectively use the resources. Identifying and assessing such interventions are primary tasks for policy researchers. Structuring interventions into viable policy alternatives and assessing the desirability of alternatives are important tasks for policy analysts.

More generally, policy analysts can play a valuable role, not only in specifying and predicting the consequences of alternative policies, but also in speaking for interests not articulated or represented in the arenas of collective choice. People who are concerned with efficiency, which basically means maximizing the total value to the members of society obtained from the use of scarce resources, are one such interest. At least in western democracies, we normally regard this concern as primarily the responsibility of governments, though it is also borne by philanthropic and not-for-profit organizations. We think it is possible to make a strong case that efficiency concerns are underrepresented in representative democracies for a number of reasons (for a full discussion, see Weimer and Vining 2006). The underrepresentation suggests that analysis that focuses on the efficiency consequences of actual or proposed policies, whether as cost-benefit analysis

(CBA) or related methodologies such as cost-effectiveness analysis (CEA), will be valuable in its own right. CBA provides a framework for comprehensively taking account of the full range of social benefits and costs. Applying CBA requires predicting the effects of investments of scarce resources by governments, philanthropies, or other members of society, and the valuation of these effects in a money-metric, normally present-value dollars. It is important to emphasize that a focus on efficiency per se is agnostic with respect to the level of government intervention. Although it might well encourage new programs, it might equally suggest that many existing programs should be abandoned or substantially redesigned.

Although efficiency should not necessarily dominate other social values, such as equity and human dignity, we believe that it should be considered seriously even when some nonefficiency goal is the primary goal. In a variety of circumstances, it may be worth bearing some inefficiency from the social perspective to achieve these other social goals. Most important, decision makers—responding to people's narrow interests as well as their broader concerns about equity—usually care about the distributional consequences of policies, whether in terms of socioeconomic, racial, or other status characteristics. Unfortunately, sometimes balancing efficiency and equity involves a straightforward trade-off. Choosing among policies with different degrees of trade-off is likely to generate political controversy when viewed from a normative perspective because conservatives primarily concerned with efficiency battle liberals primarily concerned with equity.

Nonetheless, efficiency and equity do not always involve a trade-off. Under certain conditions, which very broadly can be described as market failures, redistributive policies may enhance efficiency (Aghion, Caroli, and Garcia-Penalosa 1999; Rogers 2003). For example, subsidizing vaccination of children from low-income families to protect them against a communicable disease may increase the consumption of a good with a positive externality (vaccination against the disease not only protects oneself but also reduces the risk of disease to others) and promote a fairer distribution of preventive health care. Indeed, policies that narrowly target the level of human capital of disadvantaged racial or socioeconomic groups could be more efficient than those that are less well targeted. It might very well be, for instance, that a program that substantially reduces school class sizes offers positive net benefits only in schools with a disproportionate number of children from low-income families—the marginal gains from the small class size are much greater for these children than for those from more advantaged backgrounds. In such cases, the well-targeted program, which promotes equity, is efficient and the less focused one is not. Similarly, it may be that only well-specified groups of low-income drug abusers impose significant crime costs (negative externalities) on the public; in such a case, remediation policies focused on this low-income group would have higher net present values than those aimed at broader groups. The range of social policies for which there may be an efficiency-equity double dividend is potentially wide.

An added bonus of proposed policies that can be demonstrated to combine efficiency and equity is that they are likely to be politically appealing to broad coalitions with different normative perspectives. In view of the roles of both interests and values in the politics of representative government, one should not be too optimistic about the influence of normative considerations. Nonetheless, analysis that makes the normative attractiveness of policies clearer to multiple constituencies increases the chances that these policies will be adopted.

In some contexts, the absence of efficiency gains does not preclude desirable government intervention: gains in other goals are valuable enough that losses in efficiency are acceptable. However, even in situations in which we wish either exclusively or primarily to pursue some other goal (such as assistance to the poor as a matter of principle), efficiency is socially desirable because it can help identify better choices among the possible means for advancing that goal. For example, consider a policy with the primary purpose of raising the disposable income of the poorest families. If analysis could identify two policies that would produce identical gains, then it would be sensible to choose the one that involved the lowest net cost so that society would have more resources available for other uses. If expending some fixed budget on reducing poverty, one would want to choose the redistributional policy that provides the maximum payments with the least leakage of funds—in other words, the greatest gains for the families (Gramlich and Wolkoff 1979; Olsen 2006). Thus, efficiency enters such an analysis at least by the back door. This same logic applies to all policy analyses, including CBAs only putatively concerned with redistribution or equity. Policies involving inefficiencies are obviously not as normatively attractive as those policies that can be credibly shown to increase efficiency and equity. Nonetheless, identifying the least costly approach to increasing equity facilitates better public policy.

A proper accounting of public expenditures may also make a contribution to the political feasibility of efficient policies. Socially desirable policies often require government expenditures. Sometimes, however, especially if all relevant public expenditures are considered, socially desirable policies also reduce total government expenditures. For example, an after-school program may involve an increase in expenditures for the school district that sponsors it. The district is likely to weigh this expenditure against the benefits it perceives as accruing through impacts directly relevant to its educational mission. If the program also reduces delinquency and adult crime (when the student has left school), then it may produce savings for the criminal justice and social welfare systems. A comprehensive analysis that identified net savings in terms of government expenditures might pave the way for some sort of fiscal arrangement in which the city, county, or state governments share program costs with the school district.

Concerns about efficiency, equity, and the trade-off between them are central to a wide range of social policies that involve investments in individuals' human capital: the stocks of knowledge, skills, experience, and health that enable them to participate fully in economic, social, and political life. The list of programs or policies that fall under this umbrella include juvenile justice, mental health, affordable housing, prisoner reentry, welfare-to-work, early childhood development, substance abuse and addiction, work incentives, a variety of health-care interventions, and primary and secondary education.

We can go a long way toward crafting better social policies if we can answer two questions: First, which policies and programs are, or are likely to be, efficient? Second, for those programs that are deemed valuable for redistributive reasons (that is, they improve equity) despite being inefficient in terms of measured net benefits, which alternatives involve the smallest net costs? A major goal of this book is to assess the extent to which the existing body of research provides answers to these questions for the major areas of social policy.

CBA IN ANALYTICAL CONTEXT

Most social policy is delivered through client-oriented programs, such as job training to make welfare recipients more employable, support programs to enable the mentally ill to live safely in communities, and counseling to help juvenile delinquents avoid becoming adult offenders. Because particular programs rarely enroll the entire eligible population of clients in a particular location, researchers often have an opportunity to assess their effectiveness by comparing outcomes of interest (such as employment earnings, avoided institutionalizations, and avoided crimes) for participants vis-à-vis non participants.

Program evaluation of this sort is shown schematically at the top of figure 1.1. The object of evaluation may be an ongoing program, in which case the basis of the evaluation is likely to be a quasi-experimental design, such as a before-to-after comparison of participants. Sometimes it involves a comparison of participants with observationally similar nonparticipants. Alternatively, the object of evaluation may be a newly created program intended to demonstrate (or, more appropriately, determine) the effectiveness of some new approach. For either ongoing or demonstration programs, it may be possible to conduct a true experiment with random assignment of potential participants into treatment and control groups, the so-called gold standard of evaluation.

Program evaluations usually focus primarily on assessing outcomes, sometimes concentrating on one outcome of particular interest to an initiating agency. An evaluation of an employment training program, for example, may focus exclusively on changes in earnings, ignoring changes in criminal activity or family stability. Additionally, such program evaluations often do not thoroughly document the resources used to produce the outcomes. A comprehensive program evaluation would measure all impacts and all the resources used to produce them.

Including CBA as a component of the program evaluation forces a comprehensive approach. The arrow in figure 1.1 going from program evaluation directly to CBA represents the inclusion of CBA within the program evaluation. The CBA uses an ex post perspective: The analyst goes back to the initiation of the program and looks forward. Did the program offer positive net benefits? The answer to this question (whether asked implicitly or explicitly) informs the question of whether this particular program is a good candidate for replication. It may also inform the decision of the continuation of this particular program. Negative net benefits do not necessarily support discontinuation, however, because costs of some of the resources used to implement the program may be sunk in the sense that, having been expended, they could not be used elsewhere.

Figure 1.1   Program Evaluation, Policy Analysis, and CBA

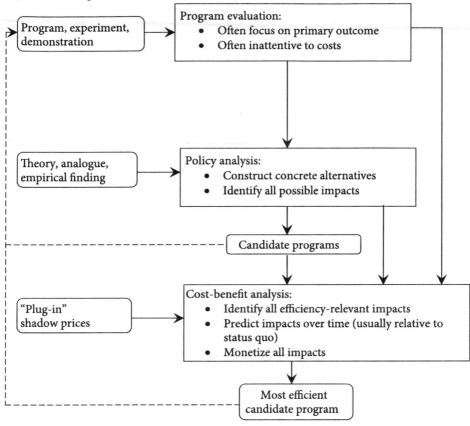

Source: Authors.

The middle level of figure 1.1 introduces policy analysis. Usually conducted in response to some undesirable condition, policy analysis seeks to construct concrete policy alternatives and assess all of their possible impacts. Especially in the social policy area, program evaluations are a primary source of information for constructing alternatives and predicting their consequences. Sometimes, however, policy analysts propose new programs based on social science theory, programs designed to deal with analogous conditions in other policy areas or in other jurisdictions, or empirical findings from natural experiments that suggest promising avenues for intervention. Policy analysis usually makes a recommendation based on an assessment of trade-offs among impacts for each of the constructed policy alternatives. It may also identify candidate programs and pose the question: Which among them is most efficient?

As indicated by the next level in figure 1.1, CBA tries to answer this question. Assuming that the policy analysis was comprehensive in identifying possible impacts, CBA focuses on all the efficiency relevant impacts. So, for example, where the policy analysis may have assessed distributional consequences and political feasibility, the CBA would not consider these impacts unless they could be assessed in terms of individuals' willingness to pay for changes in policy. The CBA would consider all individually valued impacts (benefits) and all resources used to produce them (costs). As discussed shortly, it would typically begin with quantitative predictions of the efficiency-relevant impacts of each candidate program relative to the status quo policy. This would be done over a time span long enough to capture all the important impacts of the candidate programs relative to the status quo policy. The CBA would then convert these impacts to dollars using information about the markets in which the impacts occur or applying shadow prices. The process of applying shadow prices is helped by the availability of estimates of commonly encountered shadow prices that can be plugged into the analysis, such as the willingness of an average person to pay for reductions in mortality (the statistical value of a life).

The CBA identifies the most efficient among the candidate programs. It may also lead to redesigned programs as ways to favorably change trade-offs become apparent after monetization. Good CBA also conveys the uncertainty in the estimate of net benefits, which in turn may prompt new experiments and demonstrations to facilitate better estimates of program effects and therefore more confident predictions in future CBAs. This is shown in figure 1.1 by the arrow from the CBA back to a program or experiment to be evaluated.

OVERVIEW OF CBA

CBA provides the theory and practice for assessing the efficiency of alternative policies. In practice, this means predicting the costs and benefits of each considered alternative, calculating the net benefits of each alternative as the difference between benefits and costs, and then identifying the alternative, or set of alternatives, offering the largest net benefits. Choosing the alternatives that maximize net benefits creates the potential, through accompanying redistribution, to make everyone in society better off than they would be with any other set of considered alternatives.

Although the idea behind CBA is simple, underlying it are extensive conceptual foundations drawn from microeconomics and welfare economics as well as a variety of widely accepted techniques for actually estimating costs and benefits. An exposition of these conceptual foundations and techniques requires a book-length treatment (see, for example, Boardman et al. 2006). Here we provide only a brief overview of the nine basic steps involved in conducting a CBA for readers who are not already familiar with them. In doing so, we use the term *policy* broadly, to include any form of government intervention, including projects, programs, pilot programs, or experimental programs.

Specify the Complete Set of Alternative and Status Quo Policies

The alternatives to be assessed must be clearly identified and described in enough detail to permit predicting their impacts. A program to provide supported work for parolees, for example, must therefore make clear which parolees will be eligible to participate, the services they will receive, and the period over which they will receive them. Additionally, the relevant status quo policy—the baseline or counterfactual should be made clear to allow for the possibility that none of the alternatives offer greater efficiency. This first step provides the basis for assessing the incremental impacts of the alternatives. That is, the impacts of an alternative are assessed relative to what they would be in the absence of any policy change. Although specifying the status quo sounds simple, it is often difficult in practice: In a world of many jurisdictions with different policies which is the sensible counterfactual? The appropriate answer requires one to determine the policy that would be in place in the absence of the adoption of any of the alternatives being considered. In practice, in many social policy arenas, there are only two alternatives: the program (which may be, or may be described as, a pilot program, or an experiment) and no program (the counterfactual). However, sometimes the with-program alternative is described as the status quo, whereas in other studies the no-program alternative is. This confusion may arise from the difference between retrospective evaluation (what the effects of a program put in place were) and prospective policy analysis (what the effects of changing the program already in place would be).

Determine Standing

Determining whose costs and benefits should count is referred to as standing (Whittington and MacRae 1986). CBA takes a social perspective. Nonetheless, the definition of society is sometimes relevant in assessing policies. One obvious consideration is society's jurisdictional extent. Usually analysts deem a national perspective as most appropriate on economic and political grounds. Economically, national economies have their own fiscal and monetary policies. Politically, the rules for collective decision making, the written or unwritten constitutions, operate at the national level. In federations, however, such as the United States, conflicts sometimes arise for analysts doing CBA for subnational governments, especially states, or for specific agencies. In these cases, the clients will nearly always try to reject national standing. For example, a $1 million grant to a city from the national government would be a benefit to the city but a cost to the federal government. CBA from the national perspective would show no net benefit, but one limited to the city would. In practice, where the potential program funds come from (or are funneled through) the state budget, there will be pressure to consider costs and benefits from the state perspective. Similarly, even federal and state agencies often push analysts to consider only the fiscal impacts that show up in their budgets. Although analysts may, and probably should, note these impacts, they should be clear that such exercises overly limit the definition of society for CBA purposes. Indeed, analyses from these limited perspectives are not CBAs.

A more conceptually complex consideration is who within a jurisdiction should have standing. Citizens and legal residents certainly should. Treating legal constraints like technical constraints, illegal immigrants probably should not (Trumbull 1990; Zerbe 1998). Should the U.S.-born children of illegal immigrants have standing? Because they are citizens, it would seem the answer should be yes, though it may not be practical to separate their impacts from those of their households. How to count impacts on prisoners is also likely to be controversial. Should what they consume while incarcerated count as a benefit? When such issues cannot be confidently resolved, prudent analysts may decide to conduct their analyses under other resolutions of standing.

Catalog All the Impacts

It is important to identify all the impacts that might result from each policy, including the resources required to implement it. Quantification begins with specifying the units for measuring the impacts. In general, impacts are identified in comparison to the status quo. That is, they are the valued changes, either positive or negative, that might occur if an alternative were adopted. For example, consider a program to support and treat the severely mentally ill within a community setting rather than leaving them to fend for themselves. Implementing it would require personnel time, space, and medications. The program would possibly have impacts on the participants (reduced morbidity and mortality, increased labor market participation, and improved quality of life), their families (time spent in care giving), their communities (reduced crime), and taxpayers (reduced hospitalizations and criminal justice system costs). The units in which each of these impacts is measured should be chosen to facilitate prediction. For example, measuring reduced mortality from lower suicide risk would be naturally done in terms of either the number of deaths avoided or the number of life-years gained. Note that, as in this example, many social programs produce important benefits that are best thought of as avoided costs: delinquency and crime or morbidity and mortality. Other social programs produce a mix of avoided costs and incremental benefits, such as gains in productivity. Social interventions often generate more varied and complex impacts than other interventions. Identifying and measuring the full range of impacts is difficult but necessary. A roughly measured impact is a better starting point for analysis than one that is ignored and therefore implicitly assumed to be zero.

Project Impacts over Time

The time span for the analysis should be long enough to cover any differences in impacts between the alternative and the status quo. For infrastructure projects like roads or bridges, this is usually the predicted useful life of the facility. Engineers may be able to predict the scrap value of the project at the end of its useful life as well. Analysts rarely have such clear guidance for social policies. Some policies, such as investments in children through preschool programs, may have significant impacts not only beyond participation in the program but also well into adulthood. Others, such as drug intervention programs involving forced abstinence, may deliver most of their impact during the relatively short period of participation.

Unfortunately, the empirical evidence for predicting the impacts of social programs often covers only a few years. Heroic extrapolations are therefore sometimes necessary, either in assuming no impacts beyond the period over which evidence has been collected (the common and usually conservative assumption) or projecting according to some assumed decay rate (the less common and bolder assumption). As we discuss, long-term impacts can sometimes be taken into account in monetizing the more confidently predicted short-term impacts.

Monetize the Impacts

The purpose of monetizing is to value all impacts in the same metric. Willingness to pay is the most common. Imagine a policy with a single impact and no expenditure, whether of money or of resources. If one could elicit truthful statements from each person with standing about the maximum he or she would be willing to pay to have the policy in place, then the algebraic sum of those amounts would represent society's willingness to pay for the policy and assign its total dollar value. The summation is algebraic because some people may in effect demand to be paid to accept the policy. It corresponds to a measure of change in consumer welfare called compensating variation. If one instead elicited truthful answers about how much people would have to be paid to return to the status quo after the policy were implemented, then the negative value of the algebraic sum of these amounts would be an alternative measure of willingness to pay corresponding to a measure of change in consumer welfare called equivalent variation. Table 1.1 presents the common approaches economists use to estimate willingness to pay.

Social Surplus Analysis

The first entry in table 1.1 considers situations in which the impact to be monetized occurs in an operational, undistorted market (one that is competitive and without externalities) for which estimates of supply and demand schedules are available. The first impact to analyze is one that changes the quantity or price of some good available in the market. For example, a housing subsidy may increase the supply of housing available to low-income families in a city. The aggregate willingness to pay for the additional units would be estimated as the change in consumer surplus in the low-income housing market—the difference between the valuation consumers place on the units consumed (the areas under the demand schedule as traditionally drawn) and the amount consumers have to pay to obtain the units (price times quantity at the market equilibrium) plus any payments to the program available to offset program costs. The consumer surplus measured this way, which is based on a demand schedule that can be estimated from observed prices and quantities, lies between the compensating and equivalent variations measures just described. When income effects in the market are small (either because the amount demanded is not sensitive to income levels or the amount consumed is small relative to income), the market-derived measure is a reasonable approximation of either willingness-to-pay measure (Willig 1979).

Turning to the resources—such as labor, land, raw material, and equipment required to implement a policy, the guiding principal for monetization is opportunity cost, the value of the resource in its next best use. When resources are purchased in undistorted markets and the purchases do not increase the market price, the opportunity cost is simply expenditure (the market price times the quantity purchased). If the purchases do increase the price, then the opportunity cost will be somewhere between the pre- and postpurchase prices. The actual calculation involves summing changes in producer surplus (the difference between the total revenue generated and the cost of production) and program expenditures. For example, hiring nurses as part of a community mental health

Table 1.1   Monetization Methods

Method	Circumstance	Comments
Social surplus analysis	Change in quantity or price of a private good traded in an operational market	Requires empirical estimates of supply and demand schedules, textbook valuation of benefits
	Change in quantity or price of resources traded in an operational market	Requires empirical estimates of supply and demand schedules, textbook valuation of opportunity cost
Computable general equilibrium models	Changes in quantities and prices of multiple goods and resources traded in operational markets	Requires assumptions about consumer utility and production technology, most often used to assess trade policy
Travel cost method	Change in nontraded private good with differential cost of access	Price paid by users approximated by travel costs to facility, such as recreational site or mammography clinic
Avoided cost method	Change in quantity of an externality with identifiable dimensions of harm	Prominent example: cost of crime based on victim injury and property loss and criminal justice system costs
Hedonic methods	Change in nontraded private good relevant to other markets	Prominent example: statistical value of life based on wage and risk trade-offs
	Change in the quantity of an externality capitalized into land value	Prominent example: cost of noise based on land values and noise levels
Contingent valuation	Change in nontraded private good	Prominent example: cost of commuting time as a fraction of the prevailing wage rate
	Change in quantity of pure public good	Prominent examples: existence and option values of environmental goods

Source: Authors.

program may drive up the wages of nurses in the local market, increasing their producer surplus. (They are producing hours of skilled labor.) The opportunity cost of the hired labor would be more than the preprogram wage but less than the postprogram wage. If the supply and demand schedules were linear, then the appropriate opportunity cost would use the average of the two wages (Boardman et al. 2006, 96).

It is important to note that opportunity costs do not always (or even usually) correspond to budgetary outlays. For example, even if a program is not charged by its sponsoring agency for the office space it uses, the opportunity cost is not zero if there is some other valued use for the space—which there almost always is. Similarly, the waiting time imposed on clients does not show up in the program's budget, but the lost time requires a nonzero shadow price because it has value to the clients in some other use, such as leisure.

General Equilibrium Analysis

The textbook analyses described are partial equilibrium in that they assume each impact can be assessed in a single market, ignoring any changes in related markets for substitutes and complements. Policies, however, often have impacts that ripple through many markets. Regulations to induce greater production of ethanol may affect the markets for grain and livestock, for example, or an import tariff on an intermediate good may affect exports of the final goods that use it as an input. An increasing number of economists are using multimarket models (so-called computable general equilibrium models) to analyze these sorts of situations in trade and other areas. The major social policy application has been to education, where policy interventions to change schools may also change residential choice and the composition of student bodies (Nechyba 2003). Unfortunately, computational difficulty and high information demands make these models largely impractical for most social policy CBA.

Travel Cost Method

Estimating demand schedules requires variation in price. Normally this variation comes over time or across markets. For some goods, however, the dollar price seen by consumers does not vary. A park may have a fixed entrance fee, for example. The travel cost method recognizes that people living at different distances from a good at a fixed location effectively pay different prices to consume the good because of their travel costs may vary. Although the travel cost method has been used extensively to value recreation sites, it has not generally been used in the social policy area. One exception is Philip Clarke's analysis demonstrating how the method could be used to value greater access to mammography for women living in rural areas (1998).

Avoided Cost Method

The benefits of many social programs are the avoided costs of harms—prison reentry programs to reduce crime, for example. The cost of a crime includes direct harm to victims (lost or damaged property, physical and psychological injury, lost productivity, or even death), direct criminal justice system costs (police, courts, corrections), and possibly additional indirect costs to society (fear and related defensive expenditures). Recognizing the importance of avoided crime as a benefit category in social policy CBA, researchers have attempted to monetize some or most of these categories to provide shadow prices for common crimes (Miller, Cohen, and Wiersema 1996).

The avoided cost method has much wider applicability. Consider, for example, an effective program to help schizophrenics live safely in their communities. It would reduce the number and lengths of commitments to mental hospitals and prevent suicides. Commitments could be monetized by applying the per diem cost of treatment in the relevant mental hospital and prevented suicides could be valued using a shadow price for the value of life. CBAs of most social programs involve monetizing through some combination of directly estimated avoided costs and plug-in shadow prices.

Hedonic Methods

Many impacts cannot be valued as changes in operational markets because, for a variety of reasons, there may be no such market. Nonetheless, sometimes the impacts appear as measurable attributes in other markets. Hedonic methods involve statistical analyses to impute prices for various characteristics of traded goods. No market, for example, allows people to purchase reductions in mortality risk directly. Quite a few, however, do force people to make trade-offs between money and mortality risk. In some labor markets, people receive higher wages for more risky jobs. In some product markets, safer products are more expensive. These trade-offs reveal valuations of risk. It appears that middle-aged people of average income in the United States behave as if they value their life at between about $2 million and $6 million (Boardman et al. 2006 based on Miller 2000; Mrozek and Taylor 2002; Viscusi and Aldy 2003).

Hedonic methods can also be used to value spatially varying externalities or nonmarketed goods that affect property values. A fairly large and consistent literature estimates the effect of highway noise on residential property (Bateman et al. 2001). Hedonic methods have also been used to estimate the social cost of crime and willingness to pay for improvements in school quality (Lynch and Rasmussen 2001; Weimer and Wolkoff 2001).

Contingent Valuation

Rather than estimating from observed behavior, contingent valuation surveys attempt to estimate willingness to pay from the stated preferences of respondents to hypothetical or contingent choices. The most common approach is to describe a change in some good and ask respondents if they would favor that change if it cost them some randomly assigned amount in either higher taxes or prices. The varying costs provide a statistical basis for estimating the average willingness to pay for the change. If the sample is representative of the general population, then the amount can be taken as the average for the population.

Contingent valuation is widely used by environmental economists to value public goods, such as the preservation of wilderness areas. Some people are willing to pay because they want the option of visiting it in the future (option value) even if they never anticipate visiting (existence value). Applications of contingent valuation have spread into other areas. For example, numerous studies have estimated how people value savings in commuting time, leading to a widely accepted estimate of about 50 percent of the after-tax wage rate (von Wartburg and Waters 2004). More directly related to social policy, contingent valuation and other methods, such as those that elicit utilities for various states of health, have become common in health policy research. Researchers have also used it to determine the social costs of crime (Cohen et al. 2004).

Although contingent valuation surveys are difficult to conduct well—they involve all of the problems normally encountered in survey research as well as those that arise in effectively posing the hypothetical choices—they provide an approach for measuring willingness to pay, and developing useful shadow prices, when behavioral data do not support other methods.

Convert Costs and Benefits to Present Values

If the time span is longer than about a year, the monetized values of each of the projected impacts in future years should be converted to their present value equivalents using the social discount rate. If calculations are in real dollars (that is, current-year prices and shadow prices), then a real discount rate is used. Economists (and philosophers) continue to debate the appropriate value of the real social discount rate; their debate has practical implications for the estimated net benefits of investment projects that have initial costs preceding long streams of benefits. For most social policies, we recommend a real social discount rate of about 2 to 3 percent (Moore et al. 2004).

Compute Net Present Values

Net present value is simply the difference between the sum of discounted benefits and the sum of discounted costs (finally, a step involving simple arithmetic). It is common to refer to this difference simply as the policy's net benefits. Benefit-cost ratios can also be computed to provide comparative assessments of exclusive alternatives, though they should be used with caution because the alternative with the largest benefit-cost ratio is not always the alternative that maximizes net benefits.

Perform Sensitivity Analysis

Sensitivity analysis explores the consequences of uncertainty in predicted impacts and their shadow prices on net benefits. It should be clear from the discussions of prediction and monetization that neither can be done with great certainty. Although there are a variety of methods for assessing the resulting uncertainty in net benefits, perhaps the most informative approach is Monte Carlo analysis, which replaces the point estimates of uncertain parameters (such as $4 million for the statistical value of a life) with random draws from appropriate ranges (such as $2 million to $6 million) many times to generate many estimates of net benefits. The distribution of these estimates conveys the overall uncertainty in the net benefits resulting from the uncertainty in parameters. Because applying CBA to social policies typically involves numerous uncertain parameters, assessing the sensitivity of net benefits to uncertainty in the parameters with Monte Carlo analysis is especially important.

Identify the Most Efficient Choice

The most efficient choice is the policy, or set of compatible policies, offering the largest net benefits. CBA identifies the efficient choice and conveys the level of certainty in its net benefits.

CBAs of social policies often consider a limited set of alternatives. When the net benefits of a single alternative are measured relative to the status quo, that alternative increases efficiency if it offers positive net benefits. If CBA were the decision rule, then the identified project or projects would be adopted. In democratic societies, however, the findings of CBA are merely informative. It is therefore important that their results be presented in ways that honestly inform the policy debate.

UNDERDEVELOPMENT OF CBA IN SOCIAL POLICY EVALUATION

CBA is, compared to infrastructure investments and economic and environmental regulation, relatively underdeveloped in application to social policy. Some of the reasons for this are understandable, but not obvious, and thus worthy of enumeration. First, many academic researchers most interested in social policy are not economists and are therefore unfamiliar with both the theory and practice of CBA. Those who are economists often focus narrowly on measuring particular impacts of policy interventions rather than attempting to make comprehensive assessments. Scholarly journals are also generally more receptive to more sophisticated measurement of a particular impact than to the more comprehensive, but methodologically uninteresting, cataloging of all the impacts.

Second, many relevant impacts of social policy interventions are not well monetized with readily observable market prices and therefore require shadow prices. It is extremely difficult, for example, to find a unit cost for a reduced score on a standardized cognition test. Even dedicated cost-benefit analysts have neither the time nor resources to derive monetized values for these impacts from scratch. Yet, without these shadow prices— essentially plug-in values—it is impossible to conduct reasonably comprehensive CBAs, except at the very high cost of developing de novo estimates.

Third, ex ante CBA requires reasonably accurate projections of future impacts. In some policy areas, these impacts are relatively straightforward and reasonably uncontroversial. This is generally not the case in social policy areas. The (potential) impacts can be broad (some mix of cognitive, behavioral, employment, and social dimensions), long term (perhaps the rest of the lives of participants), and variable over time (either increasing or decreasing with time from an initial intervention). Additionally, the degree to which positive or negative impacts accrue to participants or nonparticipants can vary quite widely. Some welfare-to-work programs appear to leave program participants worse off or no better off, but deliver significant benefits to the rest of society. Others leave participants better off, but are costly to the rest of society. In either case, the aggregate net social benefits can be positive or negative. Only a few programs seem able to deliver the sweet spot of net benefits to participants, the rest of society, and positive net social benefits. In sum, the impacts are complex and therefore difficult to assess. Although there has been much progress in the science underlying these tasks of monetization and prediction, applying CBA in these areas still requires enough judgments that even otherwise bold economists are often hesitant to attempt comprehensive assessments.

Fourth, the impacts of programs often fall across a variety of institutional, political, and professional divides. These divides reduce the incentives of particular levels of government, or specific agencies within a level of government with widely different mandates, to engage in the required research. For instance, a CBA of a potential program for which benefits might be roughly divided between cognition improvements (falling within education), reduced obesity (falling within health care) and reduced delinquency (falling within criminal justice policy) would likely be difficult to sell to any one agency. Consequently, evidence about the desirability of such cross-cutting interventions may either not accumulate or do so only fortuitously if there happen to be nongovernmental sources of support for conducting research and analysis.

Fifth, applying CBA to social policies raises a number of important conceptual issues that have not yet been clarified. Some have received considerable attention if not complete resolution. Economists, for example, continue to debate the appropriate way to value changes in productivity, one of the commonly important impacts of investments in human capital. Other issues are narrower but nonetheless important, such as how to assess the costs of volunteer time, reductions in addictive consumption, and the intangible costs of crime. Not surprisingly, social policy analysts have been somewhat fearful to rush in where economists have feared to tread (or, alternatively, have trampled wildly!).

CBA AND SOCIAL POLICY—WHAT DO WE KNOW?

The last decade has seen some progress in CBA being applied to social policies. Prediction for CBA is facilitated by the emerging availability of evidence from demonstrations, pilot programs, quasi-experiments, and sometimes even true experiments with randomized assignment into treatment and control groups. Analysts are increasingly able to draw on accepted shadow prices for nonmarket effects, such as reductions in mortality, morbidity, and crime. To what extent do these promising signs signal the appropriate and widespread use of CBA in the assessment of social policies? The eleven chapters that follow seek to answer this question.

In these chapters, experts in substantive policy areas answer three important questions. First, what interventions are generally viewed by researchers in the field as socially desirable? Second, what other interventions look promising? And, third, what are the important CBAs, in terms either of influence or quality, in the area? The first two establish the potential demand for CBA in confirming or overturning common beliefs and assessing the desirability of promising approaches. The third considers the extent to which the supply of CBA meets the demand.

The final two take a broader perspective. Chapter 13 draws on the expert reports and our own review of available CBAs to assess the state of the art of the application of CBA to social policies. Chapter 14 considers how research could help overcome the institutional, conceptual, and practical barriers to greater use of CBA in assessing social policies.

REFERENCES

Aghion, Philippe, Eve Caroli, and Cecilia Garcia-Penalosa. 1999. "Inequality and Economic Growth: The Perspective of the New Growth Theories." *Journal of Economic Literature* 37(4): 1615–60.

Bateman, Ian, Brett Day, Iain Lake, and Andrew Lovett. 2001. *The Effect of Road Traffic on Residential Property Values: A Literature Review and Hedonic Pricing Study*. Edinburgh: Report to the Scottish Executive Development Department.

Boardman, Anthony E., David H. Greenberg, Aidan R. Vining, and David L. Weimer. 2006. *Cost–Benefit Analysis: Concepts and Practice*, 3rd ed. Upper Saddle River, NJ: Prentice Hall.

Clarke, Philip M. 1998. "Cost–Benefit Analysis and Mammographic Screening: A Travel Cost Approach." *Journal of Health Economics* 17(6): 767–87.

Cohen, Mark A., Roland T. Rust, Sara Steen, and Simon T. Tidd. 2004. "Willingness–to–Pay for Crime Control Programs." *Criminology* 42(1): 89–109.

Gramlich, Edward G., and Michael Wolkoff. 1979. "A Procedure for Evaluating Income Distribution Policies." *Journal of Human Resources* 14(3): 319–50.

Lynch, Allen K., and David W. Rasmussen. 2001. "Measuring the Impact of Crime on House Prices." *Applied Economics* 33(15): 1981–89.

Miller, Ted R. 2000. "Variations between Countries in Values of Statistical Life." *Journal of Transport Economics and Policy* 34(2): 169–88.

Miller, Ted R., Mark A. Cohen, and Brian Wiersema. 1996. *Victim Costs and Consequences: A New Look*. Washington, DC: National Institute of Justice.

Moore, Mark A., Anthony E. Boardman, Aidan R. Vining, David L. Weimer, and David H. Greenberg. 2004."'Just Give Me a Number!' Practical Values for the Social Discount Rate." *Journal of Policy Analysis and Management* 23(4): 789–812.

Mrozek, Janusz R., and Laura O. Taylor. 2002. "What Determines the Value of Life: A Meta–Analysis." *Journal of Policy Analysis and Management* 21(2): 253–70.

Nechyba, Thomas J. 2003. "What Can Be (and What Has Been) Learned from General Equilibrium Simulation Models of School Finance?" *National Tax Journal* 54(2): 387–414.

Olsen, Edgar O. 2006. "Achieving Fundamental Housing Policy Reform." In *Promoting the General Welfare*, eds. Allan S. Gerber, and Eric M. Patashnik. Washington, DC: Brookings Institution Press.

Rogers, Mark. 2003. "A Survey of Economic Growth." *Economic Record* 79(244): 112–35.

Trumbull, William N. 1990. "Who Has Standing in Cost–Benefit Analysis?" *Journal of Policy Analysis and Management* 9(2): 201–18.

Viscusi, W. Kip, and Joseph Aldy. 2003. "The Value of Statistical Life: A Critical Review of Market Estimates throughout the World." *Journal of Risk and Uncertainty* 27(1): 5–76.

Weimer, David, and Aidan R. Vining. 2006. "Policy Analysis in Representative Democracy." In *Promoting the General Welfare*, eds. Allan S. Gerber and Eric M. Patashnik. Washington, DC: Brookings Institution Press.

Weimer, David, and Michael Wolkoff. 2001. "School Performance and Housing Values: Using Non-Contiguous District and Incorporation Boundaries to Identify School Effects." *National Tax Journal* 54(2): 231–53.

Whittington, Dale, and Duncan MacRae Jr. 1986. "The Issue of Standing in Cost-Benefit Analysis." *Journal of Policy Analysis and Management* 5(4): 665–82.

Willig, Robert D. 1979. "Consumer's Surplus without Apology." *American Economic Review* 66(4): 589–97.

Zerbe, Richard O. 1998. "Is Cost-Benefit Analysis Legal? Three Rules." *Journal of Policy Analysis and Management* 17(3): 419–56.

Chapter 2

Early Childhood Interventions

Barbara Wolfe and Nathan Tefft

In recent years, interest in early childhood intervention programs has been rising. Childhood has long been recognized as an important period in the development of individuals as healthy, productive, and socially active members of society. Researchers have begun to understand that in many cases, earlier is better. Young children, especially age five and younger, who are exposed to positive experiences appear to fare better than their counterparts, and this advantage appears to persist and grow over time (Carneiro and Heckman 2003). As a result, researchers in this area believe that, by intervening with the goal of lessening the differences in experiences at younger ages, public policy can most effectively address disparities later in life.

In this chapter, we identify a variety of early childhood investments that are viewed as increasing human capital, review the current state of research on these early childhood interventions (ECIs), and discuss possible ways that cost-benefit analysis could improve our knowledge of interventions in this arena. We identify categories of program studies, each with a different, if sometimes overlapping, approach to improving outcomes in childhood and the subsequent adolescent and adult years. Some of these categories have been more thoroughly studied than others, suggesting differences in the potential for new research. Some have also been more rigorously studied than others, creating the opportunity for improved study design. As an example, early childhood education (preschool) is believed to be an effective approach to increasing human capital, and a good deal of research provides evidence for this. Alternatively, though providing better nutrition and health care in the early years is also believed to be an effective and important intervention, it is supported by less existing evidence. This is also the case for high quality child-care settings compared to alternative child care, including grandparent care. Next, we focus on selected ECIs to draw attention to promising research that might be less well known. Again, this focus has two dimensions, first on categories of early childhood intervention research that are as yet less well understood, and second on specific programs in any category that have notable promise. This attention is important, we believe, because future research initiatives are best served by a broad understanding of the body of research.

Finally, we turn our attention to cost-benefit analysis (CBA) and cost-effectiveness analysis (CEA) insofar as they can be applied to ECIs. Previous researchers have successfully applied these techniques—which continue to be widely used for policy decisions in many contexts—in evaluating ECIs (Aos et al. 2004). Here we explore which of the ECI categories and programs we believe would be most fruitful if analyzed using these techniques. To the extent that researchers can identify ECIs and their categories that yield a high benefit (effectiveness) to cost ratio, the more socially desirable they will be relative to other similarly analyzed government programs.

ECIs AND ECI CATEGORIES WIDELY VIEWED AS SUCCESSFUL

As already noted, researchers have recently become more interested in ECIs because of the understanding that interventions at younger ages will have a greater overall effect across an individual's lifetime. The human capital literature in economics explains this phenomenon in terms of an individual acquiring and nurturing skills, which might include education, health, and positive social behaviors. The process is both cumulative and reinforcing, so that a greater level of each attribute is believed to allow an individual to be even more successful at enhancing that attribute. In other words, skill begets skill (Carneiro and Heckman 2003).

In addition to describing the process, human capital theory often breaks down the concept of overall skill into a number of categories, where each is viewed as a particular attribute of an individual that contributes to his or her productivity. Researchers have effectively adopted this view by focusing ECIs on specific categories, intending to improve on a particular aspect of a child's experience. Examples include school, family, or health interventions.

Perhaps the most often studied and widely recognized ECI category is early schooling (defined as preschool for three- and four-year-olds). School is an extremely important public institution in childhood development, both in terms of the amount resources devoted to it and, more important, in its relevance to career outcomes. Education is highly valued because of its robust correlation with many indicators of success, including wages, crime rates, and other variables.

In the context of ECIs, experimental preschool programs are a prominent area of research. One is the Chicago Child-Parent Center Program (CPC), the oldest federally funded preschool program in the country. Begun in 1965, the program focused on disadvantaged families with the goal of improving the child's educational outcomes as well as parental involvement in the education process. It also featured participation in small classes during preschool and kindergarten (Reynolds, Ou, and Topitzes 2004). CPC has been shown to significantly affect outcomes, including school achievement, dropout rates, juvenile delinquency, and college attendance. One of the reasons it is widely viewed as successful is the long duration of available outcome measures. In contrast to that on many other intervention evaluations, evidence indicates that the effects of CPC persist until early adulthood, and ongoing studies may yet show continuing impacts on wages and other important measures.

We agree with the general perception of CPC, namely that the length of its outcome measurement duration (with relatively low attrition) sets it apart from other programs. There is a limitation to the program, however, that must be accounted for and should be improved upon in future research, where possible. That is, the program was nonrandomly implemented in relation to its comparison groups. Five other low-income Chicago neighborhoods were selected for comparison only after the program was implemented, so the initial program locations may have been idiosyncratic. Overall, though, this drawback could prove to be a minor concern.

Another preschool program held in high regard among researchers is the Perry Preschool Program, which serves as a useful comparison. Similar to the CPC program, Perry consisted of a preschool and kindergarten program implemented for children of low-income families during the 1960s. In addition, the teacher made weekly home visits for the duration of the program (Karoly et al. 1998). Perry, like CPC, is considered highly successful because it has been shown to improve significantly outcomes of program participants over a long follow-up period. A striking example of this is that, at age twenty-seven, program participants enjoyed earnings that were 60 percent higher than earnings in the control group. Such a large program effect at such a long follow-up period is difficult to match in the research literature.

Relative to CPC, Perry has clear strengths and weaknesses. Participants in Perry were randomly assigned to the treatment and control group, a strong advantage relative to CPC. On the other hand, CPC is an improvement over Perry in terms of sample size. Where Perry included only fifty-eight participants in the treatment group and sixty-five in the control group, CPC's sample of more than 550 children increases confidence that the evaluation results may be replicable. Again, we agree that both CPC and Perry are high quality programs showing very promising results, but there are caveats to their success.

The two preschool ECIs mentioned are among the most popular programs in their focus area, and the evidence supports that popularity. Others commonly viewed as successful include the Carolina Abecedarian Project, Early Head Start, and the Early Training Project. We do not discuss details of any of these, but instead note overall the number of successful evaluations in the preschool field. In fact, we argue later in more detail that, because of the relatively large number of successful preschool evaluations, researchers and society could benefit from expanding research into other, less explored areas.

A related area with less available evidence is center-based child care. There is widespread belief that sending a child to a high quality preschool (low child-teacher ratio with little teacher turnover, for example) would lead to improved cognitive and behavioral outcomes. Yet evidence on this is mixed, as is evidence on the optimal number of hours for a young child to spend in such care.

A set of programs receiving a great deal of attention involve home visits by professionals to pregnant women or mothers of infants. Generally speaking, the aim is to enhance care for infants through education both directly and indirectly. As these programs attempt to improve outcomes for very young children, they take to heart the idea that early interventions are likely to yield the most benefit. They take on the burden of tracking and evaluating the children over a longer period, however, until they reach ages at which the program benefits are quantitatively realized.

Perhaps the most well-known home visit program is the Nurse Family Partnership. This program featured visits of nurses to homes of disadvantaged women who were either pregnant or mothers of infants. During the visits, the nurses helped mothers improve their prenatal caretaking skills. After birth, they helped mothers with infant care, in some cases for up to two years. We focus on the Elmira site because of its long follow-up (Olds et al. 1998). Other evaluations have been implemented in Memphis and Denver, with generally consistent results.

Again, one of the advantages of this program is its follow-up. After fifteen years, attrition had reached only a relatively low 22 percent. Children whose families were assigned visits by nurses reported fewer arrests, convictions, and probation violations, but more frequent stops by police. They also reported fewer sexual partners, lower rates of cigarette use, and fewer days of alcohol use. On the other hand, the same children reported higher illegal drug use and their teachers reported more problem behavior, so the program did not show entirely consistent positive results. Finally, lower income families reported relatively stronger results.

In our view, the popularity of Nurse Family Partnership has some research basis because of its successes in follow-up surveys. Not only were children tracked over a relatively long period, but researchers were also able to retain a significant proportion of the original study group in follow-up evaluations. In addition, the expansion of the program to other sites is helping alleviate concerns that the evaluation results were idiosyncratic to a particular location. Some caution should be taken when interpreting the results of the program, however. They seem to be driven by the lowest income segment of an already low-income sample, perhaps limiting the scope of potential benefits to a small overall population. This is not to say that the program is inappropriate to implement, but merely that it may yield large-enough benefits only to be put into practice for a small group. Additionally, the selection of nurses may be a concern. Although the families were randomly sorted, the process of hiring and assigning nurses is not clear. To the extent that more skilled or enthusiastic nurses were recruited for the evaluation than would be hired in a permanent implementation, the results may be biased toward the program's success.

Other well-known home visit programs include the Infant Health Development Project, Project CARE, and the Houston Parent-Child Development Center. These programs, though similar in some ways to Nurse Family Partnership, were limited by their smaller sample sizes (fewer than 200 participants in some cases), shorter follow-up durations (evaluations do not continue beyond elementary school in some cases), and attrition levels (attrition was held only just below 50 percent in some cases). As a result, we cannot confidently classify them as highly as Nurse Family Partnership, which continues to be the most widely recognized home visit program.

Overall, a large number of home visit programs (and other similar programs targeting the first years after birth) have been evaluated, but they appear to be underrepresented in the collection of highly successful programs. According to the theoretical motivations behind the recent interest in ECIs, this is precisely the age at which we are likely to see the greatest benefits in the long term. Yet unanimously successful demonstrations, in the sense of providing convincing findings, remain scarce. Although the reasons for this remain unclear, it is possible that the costs of longer follow-up periods have to this point prevented some potentially successful programs from being fully analyzed. Then again, it may be that the research field needs time to catch up with theoretical developments because of the time required for full program evaluations. It could also be that only a small subset of programs have long-term positive consequences. In any case, given the widespread belief that ECI are likely to have long-term positive consequences for children, we believe that it would be valuable to increase evaluations in this area.

Supplemental or enhanced nutrition programs have also played a significant role in the area of early childhood investments. Although these programs may be considered a subset of investments in child health in general, they are perhaps the most visible of all such investments. Inasmuch as food may be considered health care at its most basic level, nutrition as an issue warrants close attention because of the potential to fundamentally affect the development of a child's health.

A prominent example of nutrition interventions is WIC (Special Supplemental Nutrition Program for Women, Infants, and Children). First implemented in 1972, WIC aims to improve the nutritional quality of low-income women and their young children, mainly through food vouchers and instructional programs. It is different from other interventions in that most analyses of the program have been done without the benefit of a controlled environment, because most research has been done after its nationwide implementation. However, its large size (fewer than 1 million participants in 1977, but up to 7.6 million per month in 2003) requires that it be carefully and accurately studied in spite of these difficulties (Bitler and Currie 2005).

Much of the research on WIC has pointed to significant savings on health care for mothers and children involved in the program. A major driver of this effect is reduced medical care for both mother and infant surrounding birth. This saving is of direct concern to states that provide health care to many WIC participants through Medicaid. The tie to health itself is not known and has not been demonstrated. That WIC has not been studied in a controlled environment has opened the door to criticism on the grounds of selection bias. In particular, if more motivated women or those with higher incomes are more likely to be enrolled in the WIC program than those who are not, it may be these other factors driving the observation that women in WIC have better outcomes in terms of infant health. In this case, the positive correlation between health outcomes and WIC participation would be spurious because WIC would in truth have no effect, on average.

Marianne Bitler and Janet Currie refute these criticisms by showing that there is, in fact, a predominantly negative selection into the WIC program (2005). That is, they find that the characteristics of WIC participants, in categories such as education, age, marital status, father involvement, smoking behavior, obesity, and the like, predict poorer health outcomes across the board. Their main result, then, is that WIC has in the past been shown to be effective despite the overall impoverishment of participants relative to nonparticipants. In addition, they find that these effects are strongest in the lowest socioeconomic groups.

Other widely known nutrition programs include the School Breakfast Program (SBP) and the National School Lunch Program (NSLP). These programs, like WIC, aim to improve the nutrition of low-income children, but are instead school based. Although for the most part these programs do not fall under the category of ECIs, children can participate as soon as they are old enough to start school. Again, studies of these programs occur in uncontrolled settings, so accurate measurement of program effects is challenging. However, there has been some evidence that they have positive effects on dietary outcomes, including a lower percentage of calories from fat, higher intakes of magnesium, and a lower probability of low serum levels of vitamin C and folate (Bhattacharya, Currie, and Haider 2006). This study implements a difference-in-differences approach using cross-sectional data from the National Health and Nutrition Examination Survey (NHANES), which has the advantage of medical tests but the disadvantage that it lacks long-term outcome measures.

In general, we view the results of nutrition program interventions as mixed when considered in the context of ECIs. The programs mentioned are perhaps the largest and most studied, and their immediate effects on child health and diet are well established. Clearly, however, analysis with respect to long-term outcomes associated with the programs is scant. Because the theory motivating attention to early interventions predicts that the greatest effects will be seen later in a child's development, it is imperative to continue evaluations over a long period. In this sense, we view child nutrition programs as having great promise, but more research is needed to determine their overall, long-term effects and to provide analysis suitable for public determination of the level and type of investment most likely to promote child well-being and future health and productivity.

ECIs AND ECI CATEGORIES PROMISING SUCCESS

We now turn to other areas of ECIs that we believe hold promise in terms of improving child outcomes but that have not been as prominently featured. Our aim is somewhat modest, in the sense that we do not stray far from areas traditionally studied; we hope more to flesh out the same basic features of childhood development that ECIs such as those mentioned earlier initially target. This contrasts with another potential approach, which is to expand the consideration of childhood development into entirely new categories.

In particular, we argue that many of the most popular ECIs already target two important pathways to success in adulthood, namely, education and health. Preschool programs aim to extend the duration of the formal education process by beginning earlier, whereas home visit and nutrition programs target specific aspects of child health. We describe lesser-studied programs with the potential to expand the scope of ECIs devoted to education and health, with the intent of broadening the toolset that parents and child development professionals have at their disposal. Another education intervention approach is to change the way in which education is formally delivered. Broadly speaking, this is to change the structure of schooling, which can be accomplished in many ways. One example is the Tennessee STAR (Student Teacher Achievement Ratio) program, which was implemented to explore the effects of varying class sizes on education outcomes. In 1985 and 1986, kindergarten students and teachers were randomly assigned to either small classes (thirteen to seventeen students), regular-size classes (twenty-two to twenty-five), or regular-aide classrooms (twenty-two to twenty-five, but with a teacher's aide) within their school. The program intended that students remain in the same class type for four years, but approximately 10 percent of students switched class sizes between grades because of behavior problems or parent complaints.

The STAR program has been shown to have a significant effect on achievement outcomes including math, reading, and word recognition tests during the years in which the children participated in the program. Performance increased by four percentile points, on average, in the first year of participation in the program, and the performance gap widened by about one percentile per year, even after attempts to control for attrition and transition between class sizes. Finally, teacher characteristics appear to have had no detectable effects on student outcomes, and overall outcome differences were larger for minority and low-income students (Krueger 1999). More recent evidence suggests that these gains did not last in later grades, but children in smaller classrooms were more likely to attend postsecondary school, suggesting some lasting influence.

Overall, findings from the STAR project are consistent with our expectations. A smaller class size presumably creates a more intimate atmosphere, allowing for easier student interactions, and—perhaps more important— allows for greater teacher attention per student. Next, the impact of the study appears to be greater with a longer period of participation, which is expected when viewing ECIs as cumulative processes. Also, as in other interventions, it is reasonable to expect a greater return to participation for students in low-income families, because those students presumably have access to fewer resources that would function as substitutes for the intervention.

We view the results of this study as promising but, as in other cases, more follow-up studies of participant outcomes are needed to have a sense of the long-term benefits. In this case, follow-up studies may be difficult if attrition is high. It is nonetheless useful to consider the STAR program because it offers an alternative dimension (other than time) along which to change the structure of education for children. Although the STAR program is administered slightly later than the more popular preschool interventions, the same techniques could be implemented in a preschool setting as well. The STAR program represents one of many possible ways to restructure education programs, and thus it should be viewed merely as a reasonably well-designed example of one possible research path.

We turn next to opportunities for ECIs in the area of health and health care. We have identified early home visit programs and mother and child nutrition programs as among the most prominent interventions related to the health of young children. We argue that health interventions have a twofold impact; first, that improved health continually improves an individual's productivity in education and in his or her working years and, second, in reducing the future costs of remedial health care. Studies in this area have not clearly documented a tie to health itself, however, and it is only health, rather than health-care use, that can be characterized as human capital. We therefore believe that health interventions deserve special consideration in any review of ECIs.

One example of a health-focused ECI evaluation is the Healthy Kids (HK) program, which was launched in 2001 to address unmet need in health-care coverage in Santa Clara County, California. HK provides health, dental, and vision insurance coverage for children in families who earn less than 300 percent of the federal poverty line (FPL) and are not eligible for the two state-funded programs. Citizens who earn less than 250 percent of the FPL are eligible for at least one of the programs. The majority of the HK participants, then, are not otherwise covered because they are not citizens. In addition, many of the children participating in HK are between age six and twelve, and most of the remainder are younger than six.

The evaluation design of HK compared two groups of participants separated by timing of coverage (Trenholm et al. 2005). In particular, established-enrollee children were participants who had been involved in the program for approximately one year and had completed the renewal process, and recent-enrollee children were those who were interviewed at the time they became eligible for HK. The total number of respondents was 1,235 and the survey response rate was a high 89 percent.

HK reduced the proportion of children with unmet need in the previous six months from 22 percent to 10 percent, and the reduction was uniform across all categories of care. In addition, access to health care significantly improved, as evidenced by the fact that the proportion of children participating in Healthy Kids with a usual source of primary care increased from 50 percent to 89 percent. Finally, the proportion of children who had received health care in the previous six months increased from 30 percent to 54 percent, indicating that actual health-care use rose. Again, these increases were relatively uniform across all categories but the direct link to health has not been established.

Although states provide many health-care interventions aimed at young children, including Medi-Cal and Healthy Families in California, we are aware of only a small number of controlled studies of program impacts. A major barrier to implementing this type of program is the set of ethical concerns in withholding care from those who become the control group. The HK evaluation, through a clever program design, successfully overcame this barrier, effectively randomizing yet having a minimal impact on children not receiving care. The success of HK is limited, however, most obviously by the fact that its design allowed for only one year of follow up and that most of the evaluation statistics are secondary to measures of future benefits and costs.

As mentioned, a large body of research used nonexperimental techniques to examine health-care programs that affect young children. Although these methods have yielded a great deal of valuable information about the impacts of such programs, they inevitably suffer from selection biases of varying degrees. To the extent that health-care-based ECIs can be designed in an ethical but broadly informative way, we can hope to learn a great deal from their findings. As a result, evaluations of health-care interventions are uniquely challenging to design but promise to yield fruitful results.

We have provided just a few examples of interventions that expand on the motivations of the most prominent strains of research in ECIs. We consider education and health the most prominent features of childhood development and therefore also see much opportunity to flesh out their study. In the future, concepts analogous to human capital (roughly, education) and health capital (roughly, health status) may yield other features of child development from which to start new strains of research. For example, the concept of social capital (roughly, social skills and an individual's network of social relationships) may yield promising results in the context of ECIs (Borghans, ter Weel, and Weinberg 2006). For practical reasons, however (because of the availability and quantitative constraints of this research), we have limited our discussion to ECIs related to education and health.

ECIs, CBA, AND CEA

The policy analysis tool of choice for determining the relative value of ECIs is cost-benefit (CBA), or in cases where the monetization of benefits is not possible, cost-effectiveness analysis (CEA). Because ECIs are not unlike investments in the business or real estate sectors, policymakers need a practical way to determine what areas most deserve political and financial support. For this reason, it is often not enough to show that an ECI produces positive and significant results. It is also important to identify those programs that are most readily comparable to other government interests, in that they are measurably beneficial or effective. Although many decisions about the provision of public support include elements of subjective discretion, it is nevertheless valuable to be able to identify quantitative measures with confidence.

A number of CBAs and CEAs have been carried out with respect to ECIs, many in the context of a single program, but others as part of meta-analyses. Lynn Karoly and her colleagues focused on a small number of highly regarded programs, and Steven Aos and his colleagues opened up analysis to a large number of programs, both to begin a process of wide-ranging cross-program comparisons (Karoly et al. 1998; Aos et al. 2004). Karoly and her colleagues provided a detailed discussion of the process of applying CBA and CEA to the area of early child development, and illustrate their discussion with a specific application to the inclusion of behavioral health services in the context of primary care (2001). Their presentation attempted to familiarize the reader with CBA and CEA procedures in general and the issues surrounding their application to ECIs in particular.

Overall, then, the use of CBA–CEA in evaluating ECIs is becoming more established as the recent surge of interest in early childhood development matures. Two important questions arise. First, to what existing programs would applying CBA and CEA be most advantageous? Second, what sort of content and design in newly piloted ECIs would most likely yield strong results when subjected to CBA and CEA?

To answer the first question, we consider characteristics of existing programs that argue for or against including them in a CBA–CEA study. We believe the most important applications of CBA–CEA to be those likely to identify the greatest benefits (or effectiveness) with the most confidence, because such programs make the most convincing case for political and financial support. Features that suggest these strengths include those that target categories of childhood development already shown to yield high returns (measures of cognitive skill, such as IQ or achievement test scores), those affecting outcomes that are likely to be significant in large subsets of the population (such as improving the nutritional content of school lunches), and those with rigorous statistical design and analysis.

From a theoretical perspective, the overarching concern in designing and evaluating a program is that the causal mechanisms are identifiable. In other words, programs that most clearly demonstrate a cause and effect relationship between intervention and child outcome (and under what conditions) are promising for CBA-CEA. A design feature associated with well-identified causal mechanisms is randomization into experimental and control groups across as many characteristics as possible or appropriate. This leads to unbiased estimates of outcome differences when the results are applied to another similar population. Additionally, program administrators should limit the treatment of the experimental and control groups to vary only to the extent of the intervention so that the program's effects can be isolated.

Confidence in the results of CBA-CEA analysis, a significant concern for policy makers, is directly related to the statistical confidence of outcome estimates for a given program. The most important factor is sample size. Although it is usually more expensive to include more participants, a larger sample size yields greater statistical confidence and allows for more detailed sample stratification if effect estimates for specific subgroups are desirable. Related to sample size is attrition, because high attrition leads to a smaller ultimate sample with which to make longitudinal comparisons. Attrition can lead to more than just a weakening of statistical confidence, however; to the extent that attrition is attributable to selective departure from the sample, the effects estimates may suffer from bias as well.

With respect to the set of individuals targeted by an ECI, CBA-CEA yields stronger results for larger populations because both techniques aggregate benefits and costs over individuals. Larger is not always better, however. This is true when targeted populations differ in important ways, including income distribution or racial composition. For example, society may value ECIs that target health outcomes among uninsured populations more strongly. CBA-CEAs could include explicit weights that favor ECIs aimed at disadvantaged groups, and these ECIs might be considered more favorably when deciding to conduct a CBA-CEA in the first place.

We have outlined issues to consider when selecting existing programs for CBA-CEA. Of course, these issues are also important when formulating new pilot programs, because the decision to move on to a fuller implementation also depends on the initial confidence and strength of measured outcomes. The question remains, however, how one formulates a pilot study in the first place. The analogous question for existing programs is, when considering multiple programs that are equally well designed, what kinds of programs will lead to convincing results in CBA-CEA? Although a full discussion of ECI content categories is beyond the scope of this chapter, we briefly outline the issue here.

As noted, ECIs have perhaps been most visible in the area of education, but health, behavioral skills, and other areas have also played prominent roles. The theoretical basis for expecting some of these areas to yield stronger results rests on the idea that some features of child development are more cumulative and reinforcing over time, and that earlier intervention is significantly more productive than later. The conclusion is that programs that are cumulative and reinforcing over time will also be those most likely to yield the greatest returns later on. We are not, though, aware of research that comprehensively analyzes the differential human capital accumulation of categories in childhood development.

Regarding specific areas of investment, education has received significant attention, and for good reason. Economists consistently identify strong positive associations between education (and, similarly, cognitive skills) and variables such as lifetime income and health indicators. In addition, the returns to education continue to grow, most likely due to the changing structure of the economy (Juhn, Murphy, and Pierce 1993). It is likely that the importance of education will further increase when the next generation of children reaches the job market. Applying CBA–CEA to education interventions, with the hope of bringing successful programs to full implementation, is therefore an urgent task.

Health, like education, is an especially important area in the context of ECIs. Some research has focused on aspects of health, such as in evaluations of pre- and postnatal home visits for mothers and their infants. We have found the literature relatively scant in other areas, however, such as access to health care for young children, which could potentially yield large benefits. A primary task is to study whether improved access (for particular types of children and providers) leads to better health. As mentioned earlier, the body of research with respect to existing state health-care programs for children is large, but experimentally controlled programs are few.

We argue that the area of health is particularly important when considering CBA-CEA because health-related ECIs yield a double benefit: improved labor market outcomes and reduced future health-care costs. Better health has consistently been associated with greater income and employment outcomes, both because of increased job productivity and because of more healthy time available for training and work (Grossman 1972). In addition, greater access to preventive care for young children may reduce future health-care costs in the form of public assistance, which is a rapidly growing problem for national and state governments.

CONCLUSION

We have outlined the broad categories, detailed by specific examples of ECIs, that make up the current state of research in early childhood development. These include education, family (home visit), and health-based interventions, but this is by no means an exhaustive list. We also described the categories and specific interventions within those categories that we feel to have been strongly emphasized over the past few years, as well as those that have received less attention. Many promising programs in the field would benefit from more analysis, most significantly in improving their original evaluation design in subsequent replications. Other possible interventions have been far less studied or less successfully studied including, in particular, the tie between high quality child care and improved access to health care to increased human capital.

In addition, nearly all of these programs need more attention in the form of CBA-CEA to catalogue their overall value to society. We have discussed features of good program design not only to increase the rigor of the program evaluations, but also to improve confidence in outcome measures as inputs. We also considered categories of program content that would likely score well in long-term CBA-CEAs. The criterion for this selection should be to identify programs that are both cumulative and reinforcing over time. Finally, we note that, as with all CBA-CEA, care must be taken to weight programs according to their political value, so that programs targeting disadvantaged groups receive extra attention.

REFERENCES

Aos, Steve, Roxanne Lieb, Jim Mayfield, Marna Miller, and Annie Pennucci. 2004. *Benefits and Costs of Prevention and Early Intervention Programs for Youth.* Olympia: Washington State Institute for Public Policy.

Bhattacharya, Jayanta, Janet Currie, and Steven J. Haider. 2006. "Breakfast of Champions? The School Breakfast Program and the Nutrition of Children and Families." *Journal of Human Resources* 41(3): 445–66.

Bitler, Marianne P., and Janet Currie. 2005. "Does WIC Work? The Effects of WIC on Pregnancy and Birth Outcomes." *Journal of Policy Analysis and Management* 241:73–91.

Borghans, Lex, Bas ter Weel, and Bruce A. Weinberg. 2006. "People People: Social Capital and the Labor Market Outcomes of Underrepresented Groups." *NBER* Working Paper No. 11985. Cambridge, MA: National Bureau of Economic Research.

Carneiro, Pedro, and James J. Heckman. 2003. "Human Capital Policy." In *Inequality in America: What Role for Human Capital Policies?,* eds. James J. Heckman, Alan B. Krueger, and Benjamin M. Friedman. Cambridge, MA: MIT Press.

Grossman, Michael. 1972. "On the Concept of Health Capital and the Demand for Health." *Journal of Political Economy* 80(2): 223–55.

Juhn, Chinhui, Kevin M. Murphy, and Brooks Pierce. 1993. "Wage Inequality and the Rise in Returns to Skill." *Journal of Political Economy* 101(3): 410–42.

Karoly, Lynn A., Peter W. Greenwood, Susan S. Eviringham, Jill Hoube, M. Rebecca Kilburn, C. Peter Rydell, Matthew Sanders, and James Chiesa. 1998. *Investing in Our Children: What We Know and Don't Know about the Costs and Benefits of Early Childhood Intervention.* Santa Monica, CA: RAND.

Karoly, Lynn A., M. Rebecca Kilburn, James H. Bigelow, Jonathan P. Caulkins, Jill S. Cannon, and James Chiesa. 2001. *Assessing Costs and Benefits of Early Childhood Intervention Programs: Overview and Application to the Starting Early Starting Smart Program.* Santa Monica, CA: RAND.

Krueger, Alan B. 1999. "Experimental Estimates of Education Production Functions." *Quarterly Journal of Economics* 1142:497–532.

Olds, David, Peggy Hill, and Elissa Rumsey. 1998. *Prenatal and Early Childhood Nurse Home Visitation.* Washington, DC: Office of Juvenile Justice and Delinquency Prevention.

Reynolds, Arthur J., Suh-Ruu Ou, and James W. Topitzes. 2004. "Paths of Effects of Early Childhood Intervention on Educational Attainment and Delinquency: A Confirmatory Analysis of the Chicago Child-Parent Centers." *Child Development* 755:1299–328.

Trenholm, Christopher, Embry Howell, Dana Hughes, and Sean Orzol. 2005. *Santa Clara Healthy Kids Program Reduces Gaps in Children's Access to Medical and Dental Care.* Princeton, NJ: Mathematica Policy Research.

Chapter 3

Elementary and Secondary Schooling

Clive R. Belfield

Education is an important component of human capital. Here I draw on the wealth of literature in the economics of education to consider public policy from the perspective of the costs and benefits of incremental investments in primary and secondary education. I first identify the additional investments perceived to be socially desirable and offer a general evaluation of the evidence for them. I then divide them into three types—policies, programs, and reforms—and discuss the most important applications to date of cost-benefit analysis (CBA) in primary and secondary education in the United States. Finally, I suggest investments that might be promoted as socially desirable, based on my reading of the evidence interpreted through a simple value function that incorporates efficiency and equity criteria.

To begin, and taking a general overview of the large body of evidence, it is important to set out a number of points about economic analysis of human capital investments. One conclusion stands out: The private benefits to investing in additional education are substantial.

The private earnings advantage from extra years of schooling is clear. Pedro Carneiro and James Heckman stated that "by now there is a firmly established consensus that the mean rate of return to a year of schooling, as of the 1990s, exceeds 10% and may be as high as 17 to 20%" (2004, 148–49). This return is not significantly biased by endogeneity or confounding, nor does it appear to differ much by race, ability level, or gender (Card 1999; Barrow and Rouse 2005). This fact has led researchers to conclude that an additional year of education would convey benefits to almost any student, particularly for an education system where 20 percent of students do not graduate from high school.

Furthermore, those with higher test scores earn more in the marketplace. The impact on earnings of a one standard deviation increase in test scores, for example, is roughly equivalent to that of one more year of schooling. The magnitude of the gain from higher achievement is open to debate, however, in part because test score advantages in elementary school do not perfectly correlate with advantages by graduation. Eric Hanushek argued that the link is strong, reporting estimates that the earnings premium from a one standard deviation increase in test scores is 12 percent (2006). Heckman and Eric

Vytlacil contended that the link is weak (2001). More recent estimates by Rose showed an almost-zero effect for males, with females gaining a 9 percent advantage where test scores are one standard deviation higher (2006).

Yet income gains are only a fraction of the private advantages from education. A number of studies have identified both monetary and nonmonetary advantages from being more highly educated (for examples, see Wolfe and Zuvekas 1997; for the range of powerful health-related effects, see Cutler and Lleras-Muney 2006). Offsetting these benefits are the illiquidity and irreversibility of human capital investments, but little is known about the importance of either. At issue is the cost of generating achievement and attainment gains, not whether there will be significant economic benefits from so doing. In view of the high levels of public subsidy for education, private economic calculations are relatively simple: A successful investment in elementary or secondary education should yield a net positive return.

There are several perspectives from which to evaluate educational investments. Individuals weigh only the costs they incur (tuition fees, for example) and the benefits they receive (such as extra income). From society's perspective, all the educational costs should be accounted for (including fees and subsidies) and these should be compared to the full economic benefits (including increases in economic growth). A third perspective is the taxpayer's, that only the fiscal costs and governmental benefits are counted. Yet economic analyses may yield different conclusions depending on which perspective is adopted. From the fiscal perspective, for example, the costs are higher (schools are largely publicly funded) and the benefits are lower (income tax gains rather than income gains). An investment that has a high return for the individual may have a low return from the taxpayer's perspective. Also, calculation of the social benefits is much less precise: The costs of crime to a community are not easily bounded, for example, and estimates of how education raises economic growth are sensitive (Taylor 1999). The social benefits may be as high as or higher than the private benefits (for the social costs of a high school dropout, see Cohen 1998). Finally, there is no consensus on whether to refer to the strictly fiscal gains or the social for policy purposes.

Consequently, most research at least supports current levels of public funding for schools. Some libertarian economists might argue that—given the weak progressiveness of the tax code and leaving aside some redistribution on equity grounds—income transfers or tax relief should be given to parents so that they can invest in education independently. However, short-term changes in income do not strongly influence educational attainment and the effect of higher permanent income is not much greater (Taylor, Dearing, and McCartney 2004). More often, the tendency is for proposals to increase public funding, if only to meet equity goals such as equitable or adequate funding for all families.

Beyond these conclusions, it is necessary to acknowledge that cost-benefit analysis and research on the economic value of specific educational investments is far from compelling. Put simply, the available evidence does not give much guidance on what investments are optimal under any particular set of circumstances (Mervis 2004).

Three quotations from economists are illustrative of the thinness of the research base. Hanushek maintained that "estimating the costs of achieving improvements in the teacher force is generally impossible based directly on current data. We simply have limited experience with any policies that alter the incentives for hiring and retaining high-quality teachers (and which also evaluate the outcomes)" (2006, 459). Carneiro and Heckman concluded that "there is no shortage of policy proposals. There is, however, a shortage of empirical evidence on the efficacy of the proposed policies" (2004, 87). Finally, David Neumark observed that "the evidence generated from local providers may fall far short of standards for convincing evidence . . . raising questions about the decision-making of local providers based on this evidence, and the quality of the evidence provided to policymakers" (2006, 315).

One reason for this thinness of evidence is that economic analysis is often not wanted. Policymakers (and ideologues) do not want studies that undermine reforms that look effective but might not be cost-effective or cost-beneficial. Another reason is that genuine economic analysis is often not done (at the supranational level, economic analysis is also far from complete, see Vawda et al. 2003). Henry Levin described the methods used in the vast majority of educational studies that claim to be about cost-effectiveness—they make claims with no data on costs or effects—as rhetorical (2001). Most studies focus on the impacts of an educational investment, presuming that positive impacts will mean positive net returns (King Rice 2002).

In defense, researchers might perhaps argue that cost-benefit analysis is more complex in practice than in theory (on theory, see Levin and McEwan 2002). Data on costs are often confidential and information on marginal costs is often unavailable. Some resources are provided in-kind and from various funding sources. Also, the costs of specific educational interventions often differ across the sites where they are implemented. A year of attainment can be approximately bounded at $6,000 to $10,000 (at least as an average cost), but the cost of raising achievement scores by one standard deviation is unknown and may vary dramatically according to how it is produced.

Identifying impacts is also problematic. Educational programs have diverse benefits, including cognitive and noncognitive skills, and weighing their relative values is not straightforward (Heckman, Stixrud, and Urzua 2006). Educational outcomes are primarily a function of family background, and school effects are secondary (Levin and Belfield 2002). Again, marginal impacts are needed but average impacts are most commonly the only ones available. Resources to perform research trials on education programs that adjust appropriately for all biases are often not available (Mosteller and Boruch 2002). Furthermore, the effects of such interventions will vary across student groups and depend on whether students are willing to participate (Grissmer 2002). An effective program may easily be ineffective if it is not implemented properly. For example, case studies of career academies and high school reforms show significant variance in implementation (Stern et al. 1989). A targeted program will be much more effective than a universal one, delivered to students who would have prospered regardless, but programs may vary in how accurately they are or can be targeted.

Consequently, there are very few studies with clearly reported rates of return or net present values, and even fewer where different investment opportunities are compared directly (for the exceptions, see Aos et al. 2004; Levin, Glass, and Meister 1987).

Disappointingly, there is not only a paucity of rigorous cost-benefit studies but also uncertainty as to the external validity and generalizability of any findings. Research on the High/Scope Perry Preschool program, which scores well on many methodological criteria, includes only samples of at-risk African American children in Michigan in the 1960s. The pertinence of any findings to, say, an early education program for immigrant children in California in the 2000s is an open question. This leads to the unavoidable conclusion that the selection of educational investments is based on criteria other than whether they yield a high rate of return.

For some, the failure to apply economic criteria may be desirable. Yet most evaluations do not make their values implicit. This makes applying CBA more difficult. If, say, one places a heavy weight on raising the academic achievement of disadvantaged children, public funding for a range of programs even if they are very costly might be justified. The achievement is valued at more than the cost of raising funds from taxpayers. Indeed, most educational investments appear to be advocated for on grounds of equity rather than efficiency. Without any information on the costs of such programs, however, it is impossible to say how much weight is being placed on raising achievement levels for disadvantaged children.

Efficiency and equity are distinct criteria. Economic analysis depicts efficiency and equity as subject to a trade-off. For example, from the public perspective, if one adopts a simple CBA approach where the highest return investment is selected, greater educational investments should be made for boys over girls. Boys commit more crime, earn more, and work more (and so pay more taxes). Yet most educational programs are gender neutral.

Notwithstanding these caveats, I offer some conclusions about which elementary and secondary school investments might be shown to be socially desirable using CBA. I then consider what other investments might appear to offer as high or higher returns.

DESIRABLE INVESTMENTS IN HUMAN CAPITAL

In reviewing investments that may pass cost-benefit tests, I distinguish among three types: general policies, programs, and reforms. General policies are changes that influence the technology of education in a broad way and are not linked to a specific program or template, such as reducing class size. Programs are more narrowly focused interventions or treatments that could be applied to some children or in some settings, such as summer school. Reforms are systematic and large-scale changes to the educational organizations or institutions with the intention of affecting many aspects of the education process. Examples of reforms would be rigorous exit-based exams or school choice.

In reviewing the empirical evidence, I appraise studies according to the methodology they used and give priority to experimental research but include other methods as well (otherwise, the review would be extremely brief). I consider quasi-experimental research more valid than controlled observational studies. Consequently, this review is general, rather than a narrow investigation of a few promising interventions (see also Heckman 2000).

General Policies
Review of the literature shows several general policies that are commonly cited as desirable educational investments.

Raising Teacher Quality
Research evidence clearly establishes that some teachers are more effective than others at raising student achievement (Wayne and Youngs 2003; King Rice 2003) and that the cumulative effect of having more effective teachers over the K-12 years is significant (Hanushek and Rivkin 2004; Nye, Konstantopoulos, and Hedges 2004; Rivkin, Hanushek and Kain 2005). From this evidence, researchers have concluded that investing in high-quality teachers is worthwhile.

It is not certain that investing in high-quality teachers would pass a cost-benefit test, however. Because the characteristics of first-rate teachers are not easily identified, the practical policy is to pay teachers a higher baseline salary. Higher salaries will presumably generate a more talented teaching force (Temin 2003). Susanna Loeb and Marianne Page estimated the effects of raising teacher salaries on high school graduation using state data with a ten-year time lag (2000). A 10 percent increase in teacher salaries across the K–12 years would raise the high school graduation rate by 5 percentage points. Given the economic benefits of graduating from high school, this investment is likely to pass a cost-benefit test. An alternative to paying teachers more is to hire better quality teachers and fire lower quality ones (or wait for them to retire). Performance-related pay has been less than successful, for various reasons (Ballou 2001). Allocating teachers to schools is also far from straightforward (Lankford, Loeb, and Wyckoff 2002). Hanushek estimated that this alternative would generate significant economic benefits even though it would take a long time for the teaching pool to become high quality (2004).

Reducing Class Size
Perhaps the most commonly mentioned educational policy is that of reducing class size. Such reductions were evaluated by Fred Mosteller as a large-scale experimental trial named Project STAR (1995). Students were randomly assigned to larger classes that averaged twenty-two students or to smaller ones that averaged about fifteen students for up to four years, kindergarten to third grade. Tests were administered on word skills, reading, and math. Longitudinal follow-up of students found that those in smaller classes for more years had higher test scores and were more likely to graduate from high school than students assigned to larger classes. The largest effects were found for minorities and students from the lowest socioeconomic backgrounds (Finn and Achilles 1999; Finn, Gerber, and Boyd-Zaharias 2005). Minority students gain most from smaller classes in reading (but not math). Girls gain most in math (but not reading). The effects do not vary by ability (Nye, Hedges, and Konstantopoulos 2002). The effects are cumulative—that is, each year of smaller classes produces a boost in test scores such that, by fifth grade,

those in smaller classes were about five months ahead (Nye, Hedges, and Konstantopoulos 2001). Implementing this class size reduction policy would increase the high school graduation rate by 11 percentage points (from a base rate of just under 70 percent), suggesting that the policy would pass a cost-benefit test.

An economic evaluation by Alan Krueger found that the internal rate of return to Project STAR is around 6 percent (2004). This is above a threshold rate of return that might be used to evaluate public projects (Moore et al. 2004). It is a social rate of return (adding public and private returns together), however, though it counts only labor market returns. Other economists have questioned whether the estimate of 6 percent is overly optimistic (Carneiro and Heckman 2004). A national analysis of the cost implications of reduced class size by Dominic Brewer and colleagues (1999) found that costs would increase by approximately $250 per student (2005 dollars) to reach class sizes of twenty or $1,400 to reach class sizes of fifteen. Compared to average per-pupil spending, this represents a 3 percent to 18 percent increase in funding. This study considered only operational costs (instruction), and not facilities costs (reorganization to accommodate more classrooms). It also assumed new teachers could be hired without raising wages. Each of these assumptions understates the costs of class size reduction.

Certainly, the organizational changes required to simulate the circumstances of the STAR treatment are extremely large. (The experiment itself cost $12 million.) For a school district, going from twenty-two to fifteen students per class would increase the numbers of classes by 47 percent, with a corresponding increase in expenditures. Expenditures may not rise proportionally: Some costs are independent of class size. Most costs are for teachers' salaries, however, and if these costs are only 60 percent of total costs, expenditures would still be increased by 27 percent. This ratio does not account for the strong likelihood that, to attract extra teachers of equivalent quality, salaries will have to rise. Finding new teachers may be expensive: Newly recruited teachers in California's class size reduction initiative were less experienced and less qualified (Ogawa, Huston, and Stein 1999). It does not include planning and administration costs. Finally, this change must be sustained: The average duration for a participant in STAR was 2.3 years.

Researchers are divided as to whether such an investment is worth making, both in absolute terms and relative to other educational investments. The Krueger estimate of 6 percent is a moderately good return on investment, though such a return should be considered in light of the magnitude of the initial outlay. Additionally, the costs are incurred by the school district (public costs) and the benefits are reaped by the students (private benefits). Because benefits are greater for students from more disadvantaged backgrounds, a targeted class size reduction would appear most efficient. In contrast, Stephen Prais argued that the academic gains from STAR could be achieved by adding two to three extra days to the academic year, and that this would be considerably less expensive than reducing class size (1996). A simpler comparison is that class size reduction would raise achievement by approximately one-half year in grade equivalence, but require approximately 1.1 years of expenditures (= 2.3 × 0.47). Relative to other investments, reducing class size appears to be expensive.

Reducing School Size

A newly popular educational policy is to reduce school size. The rationale is that students are not engaged and motivated to learn in large, impersonal settings and that academic achievement will be enhanced through higher quality and more focused instruction, increased student engagement, and more parental involvement. Evidence is scant, however, that small schools are more effective than larger ones, controlling for factors such as urban location or demographics (Darling-Hammond, Milliken, and Ross 2006).

Existing evidence shows inconsistent results, but most of this is from simple cross-sectional comparisons that do not control for endogeneity. A high-quality study for elementary schools in Indiana by Ilyiana Kuziemko, however, found statistically significant academic advantages for smaller schools (2006). Kuziemko reported that larger schools have lower attendance rates and lower math scores and slightly lower language scores (tables 5–7). However, doubling the size of each elementary school would reduce math scores by only 4 percentage points. Whether this would pass a cost-benefit test will depend on the economies of scale, that is, whether large schools have lower or higher unit costs.

Programs

Programs are educational interventions involving a specific technology and implementation plan. They may be large scale or small scale. I exclude interventions that are either behavioral but are education-related insofar as they may raise achievement or attainment, or school-based but not strictly educational (for example, drug education classes). On the latter, see Aos et al. (2004) for a full tabulation. Yet if these reduce public expenditures on crime or health they may be more socially desirable than interventions that raise achievement (see Caulkins et al. 2004).

Publicly Funded Preschool

Expanding preschool provision is possibly the most compelling investment on economic grounds. The evidence is based on high-quality research methods with full CBAs from both the private and public perspective; and it is almost completely consistent in identifying impacts (see the review of evidence in Barnett and Belfield 2006). The three most frequently cited programs are the High/Scope Perry Preschool program, the Chicago Child-Parent Centers, and the Abecedarian program (Belfield et al. 2006; Reynolds et al. 2002; Masse and Barnett 2002). Each yields returns over the lifetimes of participants that easily exceed costs. The Perry program generates total benefits that are 8.8 times the costs, with public benefits 7.2 times the costs. Ratios for the Chicago program are 10.1 (total benefits) and 6.9 (public benefits) and those for the Abecedarian program are 3.8 and 2.7, respectively.

Each of these model programs was targeted to at-risk children, but cross-sectional research indicates that all children benefit from preschool (Magnuson and Waldfogel 2005). Even if the benefits for advantaged families are dramatically below those for at-risk children, there would still be economic gains from expanded pre-school programs (Karoly and Bigelow 2005).

Head Start

Head Start, the federal government's largest comprehensive child development intervention, is intended to improve children's cognitive, social, emotional, and physical development, as well as offer support to parents. Early analyses raised the possibility that the program would have only transitory effects (Currie and Thomas 1995). The best estimates of its actual effects are provided by a recent national randomized trial of Head Start. The magnitude of estimates for immediate effects of one year is fairly small, from less than 0.10 to 0.24 for standardized measures of language and cognitive abilities. This echoed the Early Head Start trial findings, in which cognitive and language effects were about 0.10 or less. Both Head Start and Early Head Start trials yielded small decreases in antisocial behavior, about 0.10, and there is no evidence of negative effects on social and emotional development.

Head Start does appear to generate long-term gains. Erica Garces and colleagues found increased rates of high school graduation and college attendance for whites, with no clear effect on earnings by age twenty-three (2002). African American children in Head Start were less likely to be booked or arrested for a crime. However, it is not clear whether these benefits are enough to offset the costs of the Head Start. Jens Ludwig and Douglas Miller found slight improvement in educational achievement from participation (2007). More significantly, they also identified an improvement in mortality which, given the economic value of a life, would be enough to justify investment in Head Start.

Other Programs

A range of other programs have been considered. One is summer school (see Carneiro and Heckman 2002). Summer school's promise is based partly on the same arguments used for more attainment and partly on the fact that children lose ground during the time away from school. However, the economic case for summer school investments has not been established. Using an experimental field trial in Baltimore, Geoffrey Borman and N. Moritza Dowling showed that summer school is effective: After two successive summer schools, with the treatment group approximately 0.5 standard deviations ahead of the control group in test scores (2006). These effects are close to the effect size of 0.19 reported in a meta-analysis of summer school Harris Cooper and colleagues conducted (2000). Annual costs for the Baltimore program are estimated at $815 per student, with an additional $700 in in-kind resources. Back-of-an-envelope calculations suggest that this program is probably cost-effective.

A second example is grade retention. Here, perhaps, there is the most agreement: Grade retention is an inefficient investment. It imposes additional costs on a school system. And it generates adverse effects on the retained students (Temple, Reynolds, and Ou 2003); a recent study by Guanglei Hong and Stephen Raudenbush found that those held back in kindergarten learn less than they would have done had they been promoted (2005; see also Jimerson 2001).

A final example is peer tutoring, which scores well on cost-effectiveness grounds. Barbara Wolfe and Nathan Tefft list this as a "most promising" intervention in their review

(2004). It is attractive primarily because it encourages children to teach others, however, and thus imposes low public costs. If children's time as tutors is valued at zero, any peer-tutoring program that is at all effective will yield a favorable rate of return.

Reforms

Policies and programs are proposed with the expectation of increased funding. Reforms, by contrast, are proposed with the intention of changing how existing resources are allocated. Such reforms are predicated on the belief that simply throwing more resources at the existing system will not yield high returns. Rather, organizational and institutional change is necessary. To quote again from Carneiro and Heckman: "Marginal improvements in school quality are likely to be ineffective in raising lifetime earnings and more fundamental changes are required if we hope to see a significant improvement in our educational system" (2004, 159).

School Choice and Competition

School choice and competition are reforms that seek to foster markets for educational services. Believers in school choice argue that it is a revolutionary change to the education system and that the effects will be dramatic (Hoxby 2003). However, the effects of school choice and competition, though positive, have been found to be only modest (Teske and Schneider 2001). Positive but very moderate results have been found from introducing competitive pressures into education markets (Belfield and Levin 2002). Voucher programs also yield only slight achievement gains for participants (Greene, Peterson, and Du 1998; Rouse 1998; Witte 1999). The randomized field trials for vouchers in New York, Dayton, and Washington, DC, found small test score gains after three years (Howell and Peterson 2002, table 6-1). There are no effects in New York and Dayton, with achievement gains for voucher users in Washington, DC, in the second (of three) years, and the effects are not cumulative (rising with the duration of participation). There are, however, strong impacts for African American children across all three years in New York and the second year in Dayton and in Washington.

Most evidence from expanded public school choice points to the same conclusion of small achievement gains from placement in a choice school. The Chicago lotteries analyzed by Julie Cullen, Brian Jacob, and Steve Levitt show no gains from winning the lottery in terms of any of the following educational outcomes across ninth and tenth grades: dropping out, reading, algebra, English, geometry, course credits, and absences; but they do find lower involvement with the criminal justice system (2005, table 6). For charter schools, there is no gain and possibly even some fall in achievement.

Competition and choice convey slight positive benefits, but may not be enough to justify the costs of reorganization. These costs are not easily identified. Typically, the voucher payments are lower than the per-student expenditure in the schools. Thus, if there are any positive benefits, voucher programs would immediately pass a cost-benefit test. There are other costs as well as the voucher payment that should be taken into account, however, and these reduce the returns to voucher reforms (see Levin and Driver 1997).

Accountability Standards and Exit Exams
One reform typically considered a good investment is rigorous exit-based exams. It appears attractive because it might be low cost: Schools already impose some form of assessment so a replacement should not be expensive, and tougher exams require students to work harder (and their time is not a cost to the public purse).

In their evaluation of the A+ Accountability Program in Florida, David Figlio and Cecilia Rouse found modest results (2005). Using data on more than 180,000 students, they compared the performance of students in schools eligible for vouchers against those in schools that just avoided being eligible (such as the schools were graded F in one or two subjects rather than all three). They found achievement gains for voucher students from low-performing schools but with much of the improvement attributable to teaching to the high-stakes test and to student characteristics. An analysis of state-level scores by Hanushek and Margaret Raymond also found positive impacts from stricter accountability regimes (2005).

Accountability frameworks may therefore help in raising achievement for some students. However, the benefits of exit-based exams vary significantly across student groups (Dee and Jacob 2006). Furthermore, imposing exit-based tests may discourage students from accumulating attainment, reducing education levels for those who expect to fail the test. The net effect is likely to be gains for those pushed to study harder and losses for those who drop out early. It is significant that Thomas Dee and Brian Jacob found only very small impacts on labor market outcomes (earnings and employment) as a result of stronger exit-based exams (2006). The aggregate effect is thus likely to be small.

Whole-School Reform
Whole-school reforms are often advocated as a way to change the culture and organization of schools to ensure greater learning. Overall, economic analysis of whole-school reform is incomplete, despite the substantial cost involved in implementing them. Many of the challenges in conducting the economic analysis just identified are especially pertinent to whole-school reform (see Levin 2002).

One example of evaluated whole-school reform is Success for All. This focuses on promoting early school success among educationally at-risk students. Success for All includes materials, training, and professional development to implement a school-wide program for grades K–5 to ensure every child will reach third grade on time. It serves approximately 1 million children in 2,000 schools. The evaluation by Borman and Hewes showed that Success for All might be a good investment because it raises test scores by eighth grade, reduces special education placement, and reduces rates of grade retention (2002). For a per student investment of approximately $3,100 over four years of schooling, the effect size gains in reading and math were 0.29 and 0.1, respectively.

An example of reform at the high school level is First Things First, which emphasizes small learning communities, instructional improvement, and teacher advocacy for each student (Quint et al. 2005). Small learning communities require that schools or subunits of schools with which students and faculty are affiliated are limited to no more than 350 students. Key teachers remain together for several years and each student is matched with a staff member who meets with the student regularly, monitors the student's progress, and works with parents to support the student's success. Instructional improvement focuses on high expectations and rigorous curriculum. In a research study using interrupted time-series data First Things First generated higher graduation rates as well as benefits in terms of student attendance and test scores in mathematics and reading. The high school graduation rate was increased by 16 percentage points as a result of the intervention. Although costs data are not available, this improvement in graduation rates is large enough that the reform is likely to pass a cost-benefit test.

IMPORTANT EDUCATIONAL INVESTMENTS

On this reading of the literature, there appears to be a reasonable evidence base justifying investments in high-quality preschool, with other investments described as promising. Beyond this, researchers have focused on identifying a common set of features that lead to increased high school graduation rates and educational success: (1) small school size where students and staff are known to each other, (2) high levels of personalization such that students' personal and academic needs are addressed, (3) high academic expectations with a rigorous curriculum and assessment, (4) strong counseling for students facing personal and educational challenges, (5) parental engagement to support school programs, (6) extended-time school sessions so that learning is maintained, and (7) competent and appropriate personnel with both credentials and commitment to the school and its mission. The cost of educational programs with such features is unknown, however.

Giving a list of desirable investments would be mere speculation and is therefore inappropriate. But it is reasonable to speculate about areas where researchers might find high returns. This approach to identifying desirable investments is to look for low-hanging fruit, that is, where a lot of money is spent but relatively little evaluation is performed. An alternative approach is to consider investments that force students to work harder. From the public perspective, this is very low cost because students are not compensated for their effort.

Clearly, a lot of educational investment must be spent on teaching personnel, and thus reforms to the teaching profession should be investigated further. What makes teachers more productive (for example, how absenteeism and turnover rates can be reduced, or how job satisfaction can be enhanced) should also be considered.

A second priority area is special education. Approximately 15 percent of students are in special educational programs and the vast majority of them do not have severe disabilities. Special education expenditures represent one-quarter of all public expenditures. Almost no research is conducted on which types of special education services are most cost-effective or on whether students are appropriately enrolled in special education programs. Yet, one of the arguments for preschool is that it reduces placement in special education programs, yielding a considerable public saving that alone offsets about half the cost of preschool (Conyers, Reynolds, and Ou 2003). It is unlikely that preschool is the only intervention with such impacts.

Finally, it is necessary to recognize that the returns will vary across different student groups and that those with the least education are likely to benefit the most from additional educational investments. The U.S. population now has a large proportion of immigrants with relatively low education levels (a large fraction have not completed high school and a nontrivial proportion have less than ninth grade schooling by age twenty). In view of the high economic returns to basic skills, more research should be performed on interventions that help those with very low levels of education.

CONCLUSION

Although this review does not identify many policies, programs, or reforms that have support from economic evaluation, some conclusions are possible. First, a general presumption is that it is more efficient to invest early (preschool and elementary school) rather than late (high school and remedial training). This presumption has two parts. One is that, simply abstracting from the technology of education and how public funds are allocated, the returns will be higher for early investments. Human capital accumulation is dynamic such that higher level skills cannot be obtained without the foundation of earlier, lower level skills. The other is that many researchers would argue that existing investments are not sufficiently allocated to the early years (Carneiro and Heckman 2004, 90). These presumptions give further credibility to preschool programs, which currently have some of the strongest (and positive) economic evaluations.

Second, educational investments must have long-term impacts to yield a positive return. This persistence has been established for years of attainment, which are correlated with earnings over decades. The persistence of achievement gains has not been fully established, however. A program that boosts test scores in elementary school by one standard deviation may not necessarily convey impacts in later adulthood. Also, programs that affect multiple dimensions, beyond the labor market, such as health effects or welfare dependency, see higher returns. Although public investments in education can pass a cost-benefit test based only on income tax gains, the margin for investment is considerably smaller if this is the only source of gain.

Third, in view of the empirically identified economic benefits to the state of high school graduation (higher tax payments, lower expenditures on criminal justice, health, and welfare), a large fraction of investments that are effective in this domain are likely cost-effective. This is not a blank check to invest in programs to reduce the number of dropouts, but there is probably a lot of room to be generous in public funding of education and to experiment with multiple approaches simultaneously (for example, smaller classes with high-quality teachers).

Fourth, because of the heterogeneity in students' learning proficiency, it is unlikely that a single type of investment will yield the highest returns in each situation. Some economists, such as Eric Hanushek, have gone further, raising the question of whether there are in fact no best practices? This appears to confuse the search for the most efficient investments with the search for investments that yield a positive return. Some practices will be better than others. Little is known about whether to invest in new programs or simply to invest more in existing programs. Nonetheless, it is likely that the highest returns will be found in situations where students currently have the least resources.

Finally, improvements should be made in the economics of evaluating education reforms. CBA is an important evaluative method. Indeed, it may be a superior method, given the ad hoc elements included in other methods (for a discussion, see Adler and Posner 2000). More CBAs should be performed and more economic metrics (such as the monetary value of achievement gains) should be developed and systematized. Such analysis is not a substitute for making decisions on equity grounds, but a desirable complement.

REFERENCES

Adler, Matthew, and Eric Posner. 2000. *Cost-Benefit Analysis. Legal, Economic and Philosophical Perspectives*. Chicago: University of Chicago Press.

Aos, Steve, Roxanne Lieb, Jim Mayfield, Marna Miller, and Annie Pennucci. 2004. *Benefits and Costs of Prevention and Early Intervention Programs*. Olympia: Washington Institute for Public Policy.

Ballou, Dale. 2001. "Pay for Performance in Public and Private Schools." *Economics of Education Review* 20(1): 51–61.

Barnett, Steve, and Clive Belfield. 2006. "Early Childhood Education." *Future of Children* 16(2): 73–98.

Barrow, Lisa, and Cecilia Rouse. 2005. "Do Returns to Schooling Differ by Race and Ethnicity?" *American Economic Review* 95(2): 83–87.

Belfield, Clive, and Henry Levin. 2002. "The Effects of Competition on Educational Outcomes: A Review of the U.S. Evidence." *Review of Educational Research* 72(2): 279–341.

Belfield, Clive, Milagros Nores, Steven W. Barnett, and Lawrence J. Schweinhart. 2006. "The Perry Pre-School 40-Year Follow-Up Cost-Benefit Analysis." *Journal of Human Resources* 42:215–46.

Borman, Geoffrey D., and Gina M. Hewes. 2002. "The Long–Term Effects and Cost–Effectiveness of Success for All." *Educational Evaluation and Policy Analysis* 24(4): 243–66.

Borman, Geoffrey D., and N. Moritza Dowling. 2006. "Longitudinal Achievement Effects of Multi-year Summer School: Evidence from the Teach Baltimore Randomized Field Trial." *Educational Evaluation and Policy Analysis* 28(1): 25–48.

Brewer, Dominic, C. Krop, Brian Gill, and R. Reichardt. 1999. "Estimating the Costs of National Class Size Reductions under Different Policy Alternatives." *Educational Evaluation and Policy Analysis* 21(2): 179–92.

Card, David. 1999. "Causal Effect of Education on Earnings." In *Handbook of Labor Economics*, eds. O. Ashenfelter and D. Card. Amsterdam: North-Holland.

Carneiro, Pedro, and James Heckman. 2004. "Human Capital Policy." In *Inequality in America. What Role for Human Capital Policies?*, eds. James Heckman and Alan Krueger. Cambridge, MA: MIT Press.

Caulkins, Jonathan P., Rosalie Liccardo Pacula, Susan Paddock, and James Chiesa. 2004. "What We Can and Cannot Expect from School-Based Drug Prevention." *Drug and Alcohol Review* 23(1): 79–87.

Cohen, Mark. 1998. "The Monetary Value of Saving a High-Risk Youth." *Journal of Quantitative Criminology* 14(1): 5–33.

Conyers, Liza M., Arthur Reynolds, and Suh-Ruu Ou. 2003. "The Effects of Early Childhood Intervention and Subsequent Special Education Services: Findings from the Chicago Child–Parent Centers." *Educational Evaluation and Policy Analysis* 25(1): 75–95.

Cooper, Harris, K. Charlton, Jeff C. Valentine, and Laura Muhlenbruck. 2000. "Making the Most of Summer School: A Meta-Analytic and Narrative Review." *Monographs of the Society for Research in Child Development* 65, serial no. 260.

Cullen, Julie, Brian Jacob, and Steve Levitt. 2005. "The Effect on School Choice on Student Outcomes: Evidence from Randomized Lotteries." *Journal of Public Economics* 89(5): 729–60.

Currie, Janet, and Duncan Thomas. 1995. "Does Head Start Make a Difference?" *American Economic Review* 85(3): 341–64.

Cutler, David, and Adreanna Lleras-Muney. 2006. "Education and Health: Evaluating Theories and Evidence." *NBER* Working Paper 12352. Cambridge, MA: National Bureau of Economic Research.

Darling-Hammond, Linda, Michael Milliken, and Peter Ross. 2006. "High School Size, Structure, and Content: What Matters for Student Success?" Working Paper. Washington, DC: Brookings Institution Press.

Dee, Thomas, and Brian Jacob. 2006. "Do High School Exit Exams Influence High School Achievement and Labor Market Performance?" *NBER* Working Paper 12199. Cambridge, MA: National Bureau of Economic Research.

Figlio, David, and Cecilia Rouse. 2006. "Do Accountability and Voucher Threats Improve Low-Performing Schools?" *Journal of Public Economics* 90(1-2): 239–55.

Finn, Jeremy, and Chris Achilles. 1999. "Tennessee's Class Size Study: Findings, Implications, Misconceptions." *Educational Evaluation and Policy Analysis* 21(2): 97–109.

Finn, Jeremy, Susan Gerber, and Jayne Boyd-Zaharias. 2005. "Small Classes in the Early Grades, Academic Achievement, and Graduating from High School." *Journal of Educational Psychology* 97(2): 214–23.

Garces, Erica, Duncan Thomas, and Janet Currie. 2002. "Longer-Term Effects of Head Start." *American Economic Review* 92(4): 999–1012.

Greene, Jay, Paul Peterson, and Jiangtao Du. 1998. "School Choice in Milwaukee: A Randomized Experiment." In *Learning from School Choice*, eds. Paul Peterson and Brian Hassel. Washington, DC: Brookings Institution Press.

Grissmer, David. 2002. "Cost-Effectiveness and Cost-Benefit Analysis: The Effect of Targetting Interventions." In *Cost–Effectiveness Analysis and Educational Policy*, eds. Henry Levin and Patrick McEwan. Larchmont, NJ: AEFA Yearbook, Eye on Education.

Hanushek, Eric. 2004. "What If There Are No 'Best Practices'?" *Scottish Journal of Political Economy* 51(2): 156–72.

———. 2006. "Alternative School Policies and the Benefits of General Cognitive Skills." *Economics of Education Review* 25(4): 447–62.

Hanushek, Eric, and Margaret Raymond. 2005. "Does School Accountability Lead to Improved Student Performance?" *Journal of Policy Analysis and Management* 24(2): 297–327.

Hanushek, Eric, and Steve Rivkin. 2004. "How to Improve the Supply of High-Quality Teachers." In *Brookings Papers on Education Policy 2004*, ed. Diane Ravitch. Washington, DC: Brookings Institution Press.

Heckman, James, and Eric Vytlacil. 2001. "Identifying the Role of Cognitive Ability in Explaining the Level of and Change in the Return to Schooling." *Review of Economics and Statistics* 83(1): 1–12.

Heckman, James, Joel Stixrud, and Sergio Urzua. 2000. "Policies to Foster Human Capital." *Research in Economics* 54(1): 3–56.

———. 2006. "The Effects of Cognitive and Noncognitive Abilities on Labor Market Outcomes and Social Behavior." *NBER* Working Paper 12006. Cambridge, MA: National Bureau on Economic Research.

Hong, Guanglei, and Stephen P. Raudenbush. 2005. "Effects of Kindergarten Retention Policy on Children's Cognitive Growth in Reading and Mathematics." *Educational Evaluation and Policy Analysis* 27(3): 205–24.

Howell, William, and Paul Peterson. 2002. *The Education Gap. Vouchers and Urban Public Schools.* Washington, DC: Brookings Institution Press.

Hoxby, Caroline. 2003. *The Economics of School Choice.* Chicago: University of Chicago and NBER Press.

Jimerson, Shane R. 2001. "Meta-Analysis of Grade Retention Research: Implications for Practice in the 21st Century." *School Psychology Review* 30(3): 420–37.

Karoly, Lynn, and James Bigelow. 2005. *The Economics of Investing in Universal Pre-School Education in California*. Pittsburgh, PA: RAND.

King Rice, Jennifer. 2002. "Cost Analysis in Education Policy Research: A Comparative Analysis Across Fields of Public Policy." In *Cost-Effectiveness Analysis and Educational Policy*, eds. Henry Levin and Patrick McEwan. Larchmont, NJ: AEFA Yearbook, Eye on Education.

———. 2003. *Teacher Quality: Understanding the Effectiveness of Teacher Attributes*. Washington, DC: Economic Policy Institute.

Krueger, Alan. 2004. "Inequality: Too Much of a Good Thing?" In *Inequality in America. What Role for Human Capital Policies?*, eds. James Heckman and Alan Krueger. Cambridge, MA: MIT Press.

Kuziemko, Ilyiana. 2006. "Using Shocks to School Enrollment to Estimate the Effect of School Size on Student Achievement." *Economics of Education Review* 25(1): 63–75.

Lankford, Hamilton, Susanna Loeb, and James Wyckoff. 2002. "Teacher Sorting and the Plight of Urban Schools." *Education Evaluation and Policy Analysis* 24(1): 37–62.

Levin, Henry. 2001. "Waiting for Godot: Cost–Effectiveness Analysis in Education." In *Evaluations that Surprise*, ed. Richard Light. San Francisco, CA: Jossey-Bass.

———. 2002. "Issues in Designing Cost-Effectiveness Comparisons of Whole-School Reforms." In *Cost-Effectiveness Analysis and Educational Policy*, eds. H. M. Levin and P. J. McEwan. Larchmont, NJ: AEFA Yearbook, Eye on Education.

Levin, Henry, and Clive Belfield. 2002. "Families as Contractual Partners in Education." *UCLA Law Review* 46(6): 1799–824.

Levin, Henry, and Cyrus Driver. 1997. "Costs of an Educational Voucher System." *Education Economics* 5(3): 303–11.

Levin, Henry, Gene V. Glass, and Gail R. Meister. 1987. "Cost-Effectiveness of Computer-Assisted Instruction." *Evaluation Review* 11(1): 50–72.

Levin, Henry, and Patrick McEwan. 2001. *Cost-Effectiveness Analysis*, 2nd ed. New York: Sage Publications.

———. eds. 2002. *Cost–Effectiveness Analysis and Educational Policy*. Larchmont, NJ: AEFA Yearbook, Eye on Education.

Loeb, Susanna, and Marianne Page. 2000. "Examining the Link between Teacher Wages and Student Outcomes: The Importance of Alternative Labor Market Opportunities and Non-Pecuniary Variation." *The Review of Economics and Statistics* 82(3): 393–408.

Ludwig, Jens, and Douglas L. Miller. 2007. "Does Head Start Improve Children's Life Chances? Evidence from a Regression Discontinuity Design." *Quarterly Journal of Economics* 122(1): 159–208.

Magnuson, Katherine, and Jane Waldfogel. 2005. "Early Childhood Care and Education: Effects on Ethnic and Racial Gaps in School Readiness." *Future of Children* 15(1): 169–88.

Masse, Len, and Steve Barnett. 2002. "A Benefit-Cost Analysis of the Abecedarian Early Childhood Intervention." In *Cost-Effectiveness and Educational Policy*, eds. Henry Levin and Patrick McEwan. Larchmont, NJ: AEFA Yearbook, Eye on Education.

Mervis, James. 2004. "Education Research—Meager Evaluations Make It Hard to Find Out What Works." *Science* 304(5677): 1583.

Moore, Mark A., Anthony E. Boardman, Aidan R. Vining, David L. Weimer, and David H. Greenberg. 2004. "Just Give Me a Number! Practical Values for the Social Discount Rate." *Journal of Policy Analysis and Management* 23(4): 789–812.

Mosteller, Fred. 1995. "The Tennessee Study of Class Size in the Early School Grades." *The Future of Children* 5(2): 113–27.

Mosteller, Fred, and Robert Boruch. 2002. *Evidence Matters: Randomized Trials in Education Research*. Washington, DC: Brookings Institution Press.

Neumark, David. 2006. "Evaluating Program Effectiveness: A Case Study of the School-to-Work Opportunities Act in California." *Economics of Education Review* 25(3): 315–26.

Nye, Barbara, Larry Hedges, and Spyros Konstantopoulos. 2001. "The Long-Term Effects of Small Classes in Early Grades: Lasting Benefits in Mathematics Achievement at Grade 9." *Journal of Experimental Education* 69(3): 245–57.

———. 2002. "Do Low Achieving Students Benefit More from Small Classes? Evidence from the Tennessee Class Size Experiment." *Educational Evaluation and Policy Analysis* 24(3): 201–17.

Nye, Barbara, Spyros Konstantopoulos, and Larry Hedges. 2004. "How Large Are Teacher Effects?" *Educational Evaluation and Policy Analysis* 26(3): 237–57.

Ogawa, Rodney T., Deborah Huston, and Deborah E. Stine. 1999. "California's Class Size Reduction Initiative: Differences in Teacher Experience and Qualifications across Schools." *Educational Policy* 13(5): 659–73.

Prais, Stephen. 1996. "Class Size and Learning: The Tennessee Experiment—What Follows?" *Oxford Review of Education* 22(4): 399–414.

Quint, Janet, Howard S. Bloom, Alison Rebeck Black, and LaFleur Stephens, with Theresa M. Akey. 2005. *The Challenge of Scaling Up Educational Reform: Findings and Lessons from First Things First*. New York: MDRC.

Reynolds, Arthur, Judy Temple, Dylan L. Robertson, and Emily A. Mann. 2002. "Age 21 Cost-Benefit Analysis of the Title I Chicago Child–Parent Centers." *Educational Evaluation and Policy Analysis* 24(4): 267–303.

Rivkin, Steve, Eric Hanushek, and John Kain. 2005. "Teachers, Schools, and Student Achievement." *Econometrica* 73(2): 417–58.

Rose, Heather. 2006. "Do Gains in Test Scores Explain Labor Market Outcomes?" *Economics of Education Review* 25(4): 430–46.

Rouse, Cecilia. 1998. "Private School Vouchers and Student Achievement: An Evaluation of the Milwaukee Parental Choice Program." *Quarterly Journal of Economics* 113(2): 553–602.

Stern, David, Charles Dayton, Il-Woo Paik, and Alan Weisberg. 1989. "Benefits and Costs of Dropout Prevention in a High School Program Combining Academic and Vocational Education: Third Year Results from Replications of the California Peninsula Academies." *Educational Evaluation and Policy Analysis* 11(4): 405–16.

Taylor, Beck A., Eric Dearing, and Kathleen McCartney. 2004. "Incomes and Outcomes in Early Childhood." *Journal of Human Resources* 39(4): 980–1007.

Taylor, Lori. 1999. "Government's Role in Primary and Secondary Education." *Federal Reserve Bank of Dallas Economic Review* First Quarter: 15–24.

Temin, Peter. 2003. "Low Pay, Low Quality." *Education Next* 3(3): 8–13.

Temple, Judy, Arthur Reynolds, and Suh-Ruu Ou. 2003. "Grade Retention and School Dropout: Another Look at the Evidence." In *Can Unlike Students Learn Together?: Grade Retention, Tracking, and Grouping*, eds. Herbert J. Walberg, Arthur J. Reynolds, and Margaret C. Wang. Greenwich, CT: Information Age.

Teske, Paul, and Mark Schneider. 2001. "What Research Can Tell Policymakers about School Choice." *Journal of Policy Analysis and Management* 20(4): 609–32.

Vawda, Ayesha Yaqub, Peter Moock, J. Price Gittinger, and Harry Anthony Patrinos. 2003. "Economic Analysis of World Bank Education Projects and Project Outcomes." *International Journal of Educational Development* 23(6): 645–60.

Wayne, Andrew J., and Peter Youngs. 2003. "Teacher Characteristics and Student Achievement Gains: A Review." *Review of Educational Research* 73(1): 89–122.

Witte, John. 1999. *The Market Approach to Education*. Princeton, NJ: Princeton University Press.

Wolfe, Barbara, and Nathan Tefft. 2004. "Child Interventions that May Lead to Increased Economic Growth: A Report to the Pew Charitable Trusts." Washington, DC: Pew Charitable Trust.

Wolfe, Barbara, and Samuel Zuvekas. 1997. "Non-Market Outcomes of Schooling." *International Journal of Education Research* 27(6): 491–502.

Chapter 4

Health Care for Disadvantaged Populations

David J. Vanness

Health is a fundamental part of being a productive human being. "Economists regard expenditures on education, training, medical care, and so on as investments in human capital," Gary Becker notes. "They are called human capital because people cannot be separated from their knowledge, skills, health, or values in the way they can be separated from their financial and physical assets" (2002, para II.3.2). As the saying goes, even if you lose your money, at least you've got your health. But for how long?

In attempting to explain why some people are rich and others are poor, the earliest formal economic models of human capital focused on establishing a causal arrow in one direction only—from human capital to income (Mincer 1958). The relationship between income and health, however, has long been recognized to be much more complex. In her 1962 paper, "Health as an Investment," Selma Mushkin explained it this way: "Health services are similar to education, too, in that they are partly investment and partly consumption, and the separation of the two elements is difficult. An individual wants to get well so that life for him may be more satisfying. But also when he is well he can perform more effectively as a producer" (131). Michael Grossman was among the first to attempt this difficult separation: formally modeling health as both a means to productivity and a direct source of individual utility (1972). The key implications from Grossman's model include that in a model of rational individual behavior, health-care consumption increases with wages and health itself is a normal good.

So, where the first studies of health as human capital focused on variations in health as a determinant of income inequality, Grossman's model allowed the causal arrow to be drawn both ways. Indeed, in recent research, much greater attention has been focused on income as a determinant of health—at both individual and population levels (Evans and Stoddart 2003; Lynch et al. 2004; van Doorslaer et al. 2006). In the Eight Americas Study, Christopher Murray and his colleagues divided the U.S. population into eight groups by mortality and epidemiological patterns: Asians (America 1), below-median-income whites living in the Northland (America 2), middle America (America 3), poor whites living in Appalachia and the Mississippi Valley (America 4), Native Americans living on reservations in the West (America 5), black middle-Americans (America 6), poor blacks living in the rural South (America 7), and blacks living in high-risk urban environments (America 8) (Murray, Kulkarni, and Ezzati 2005). The health disparities among those groups are enormous. For example, men in America 8 have a life expectancy at birth that is 16.1 years lower than men in America 1, a gap "as large as the gap between Iceland with the highest male life expectancy in the world and Bangladesh" (4).

In 2000, the U.S. Department of Health and Human Services drew special attention to the health of the disadvantaged, making its second broad goal to eliminate health disparities in the United States by the year 2010 (2000). The Healthy People 2010 report outlined specific objectives, identifying a number of health interventions at both the clinical and community levels considered likely to both improve health overall and reduce health disparities. A 2006 Commonwealth Fund report titled "Why Not the Best?" emphasized that "variation in the way Americans experience the health care system" in large part underlies the relatively poor performance of the United States in obtaining good health outcome value for its enormous health expenditures (5). The report claimed that by raising performance across thirty-seven key indicators in a National Scorecard on U.S. Health System Performance to the level achieved by the best nations, "we could save at least $50 billion to $100 billion per year in health-care spending and prevent 100,000 to 150,000 deaths" (12). In the language of cost-effectiveness analysis, the new health-care system would dominate the old—providing better health outcomes at a reduced cost.

In addition to providing a bridge between income and health, Michael Grossman's model of health capital has also served as the theoretical foundation for using cost-effectiveness analysis (CEA) and cost-benefit analysis (CBA) to evaluate health-care interventions (Garber and Phelps 1998; Meltzer 1997). Great debate among researchers persists over the theoretical and practical equivalence (or lack thereof) between CBA and CEA (Donaldson 1998; Dolan and Edlin 2002), but CEA has become the dominant mode of formal economic evaluations of health interventions. In 1996, the U.S. Public Health Service Panel on Cost-Effectiveness in Health and Medicine issued recommendations that practitioners use CEA rather than CBA as the basis for so-called Reference Case analyses: "CBA adds an additional difficulty in that it presumes to put a dollar figure on the value of human life and uses controversial methods to do so. The panel has shared the dominant bias of the health sector—that monetizing the price of life in these ways introduces ethical concerns that are avoided by CEA, albeit at some sacrifice of generalizability" (Gold et al. 1996, xxii). It should be noted, however, that the Reference Case practice involves calculating an incremental cost-effectiveness ratio (ICER) in terms of additional dollars spent per quality-adjusted life year (QALY) gained and accepting the intervention if it falls below a cutoff—a practice that itself implies a value for health (Kenkel 1997). Regardless of whether CEA or CBA is used, some notion of optimal investment in human capital under a budget constraint underlies economic analyses of health-care interventions.

Recognizing that resources for investing in human capital are limited, the $64,000 (per QALY?) question becomes this: If we want to maximize the health of our population and eliminate disparities, what health interventions should we promote? (Hoerschelmann 2006). This review and commentary addressed that question in three parts, identifying interventions the author believes are most widely perceived to be beneficial, the intervention the author believes has the potential to be most beneficial, and the applications of CBA-CEA that the author believed have been most important to date.

INTERVENTIONS WIDELY PERCEIVED TO BE NET BENEFICIAL

To get an idea of which interventions are most widely considered net beneficial, it is useful to consider two high-profile, government-sponsored publications that considered the cost-effectiveness of a wide range of clinical and community interventions likely to have direct impact on disadvantaged populations. In a 1999 report titled "An Ounce of Prevention . . . What Are the Returns?," the Centers for Disease Control and Prevention (CDC) sponsored assessment of the cost-effectiveness of clinic and community-based health interventions in nineteen areas (Messonier et al. 1999). In 2006, the CDC and the U.S. Agency for Healthcare Research and Quality (AHRQ) cofunded the nonprofit, public-private collaborative National Commission on Prevention Priorities (NCPP) to produce a report titled "Priorities among Effective Clinical Preventive Services" explicitly prioritizing twenty-one clinical interventions recommended as highly effective by the U.S. Preventive Services Task Force (USPSTF) in its *Guide to Clinical Preventive Services* (Maciosek et al. 2006; U.S. Preventive Services Task Force 2005). In a commentary to that report, the NCPP chair, former Surgeon General David Satcher, drew direct attention to the role of using CEA-guided prioritization in addressing health disparities (Satcher 2006).

This chapter considers a subset of recommended health-care interventions from the reports outlined above that the author believes are widely perceived to be net beneficial, particularly for economically disadvantaged populations: chlamydia screening, routine prenatal care for prevention of low birth weight, childhood vaccination, screening and brief clinical intervention for problem drinking, screening and brief intervention for tobacco use, cervical cancer screening using Pap smears, colorectal cancer screening using a variety of methods, and breast cancer screening using mammography.

Chlamydia Screening

Infection with Chlamydia trachomatis is extremely common in the United States (Groseclose et al. 1999), with higher prevalence in populations of nonwhite women and women of lower socioeconomic status (Klausner et al. 2001). Chlamydia infection can result in pelvic inflammatory disease (PID), leading to reduced fertility and increased rates of ectopic pregnancy, all of which present a substantial preventable disease burden (Brunham et al. 1985; Chow et al. 1990).

The NCPP "Priorities" document concluded that DNA-based urine screening of young, asymptomatic women is highly cost-effective (between $0 and $14,000 per QALY gained over no screening) and that for a hypothetical birth cohort of 4 million persons, increasing screening from the current 40 percent level of adherence to 90 percent would yield an additional 19,000 undiscounted QALYs (Shults et al. 2001). A 2002 systematic review of CEAs by Honey and colleagues identified ten simulation-based studies, all of which considered cost per clinical outcome, such as cost per case of PID prevented

(Honey et al. 2002). Perhaps the most compelling evidence was a simulation study by Rene Howell and colleagues that found that under moderate prevalence rates, screening asymptomatic women under thirty is both less expensive and more effective than other approaches, including no screening and screening symptomatic women, reducing both cases of PID and costs (Howell, Quinn, and Gaydos 1998).

Prenatal Care for Low Birth Weight

Low birth weight contributes substantially to infant mortality and is associated with a number of severe conditions such as cerebral palsy, mental retardation, and blindness that cause persistent, long-term disability (Hack et al. 1995). Both direct medical costs and indirect costs (such as special education) are substantial (Petrou et al. 2001) and the incidence of low birth weight in the United States is higher among populations with lower socioeconomic status (Parker, Schoendorf, and Kiely 1994).

The "Ounce of Prevention" document recommended prenatal care and maternal nutrition through the Women, Infants and Children (WIC) program as highly net-beneficial interventions (Messonnier et al. 1999). An early report by the Institute of Medicine concluded that the prenatal care for prevention of low birth weight was net beneficial, with a benefit-cost ratio of 3.38 (Behrman 1985). Subsequent reviews of the literature on prenatal care, however, generally found slim support for its effectiveness in reducing the incidence of low birth weight (Lu et al. 2003; Fiscella 1995; McCormick and Siegel 2001). On the other hand, more recent evidence from the National Longitudinal Survey of Youth suggested that the effectiveness of WIC in increasing birth weight was, if anything, underestimated in previous studies (Kowaleski-Jones and Duncan 2002).

Childhood Immunization

Immunization has substantially reduced the incidence of serious childhood diseases. The CDC and USPSTF recommend childhood immunization for polio, measles, mumps and rubella (MMR), diphtheria, tetanus and pertussis (DTP), haemophilus influenza type b (Hib), hepatitis b, and varicella (chicken pox) (U.S. Preventive Services Task Force 2005; Atkinson et al. 2002). In 2004, pneumococcal conjugate vaccine (PCV) and influenza vaccine were added to the list of recommended screenings (Committee on Infectious Diseases 2004). Although eventual rates of vaccination by the time the child is thirty-five months old exceed 80 percent for polio, DTP MMR, Hib, varicella, and hepatitis b, small but significant differences persist by race and income—particularly for DTP and PCV (National Center for Health Statistics 2005). Furthermore, receipt of all vaccinations on time or acceptably early (by nineteen months) varies substantially by state, ranging from 2 percent in Mississippi to 26 percent in Massachusetts (Luman et al. 2005).

The NCPP "Priorities" document lists childhood vaccination as one of its top priorities, based on clinically preventable burden of disease and dominant cost-effectiveness, that is, both cost-reducing and outcome-improving (Shults et al. 2001). Generally, simulation-based economic analysis of both individual and combined vaccination programs demonstrate strong evidence of both cost savings and outcome improvement, regardless of perspective (Zhou et al. 2005; Lieu et al. 1994). However, in 2000, Lieu and his colleagues performed a simulation-based CEA that PCV vaccination alone would cost $80,000 per life-year saved—a borderline range for cost-effectiveness (2000). The study captured a comprehensive societal measure of costs (including work loss productivity for parents), but quality of life was not considered.

Screening and Brief Intervention for Adult Problem Drinking
In 1998, a Lewin Group study commissioned by the National Institute on Alcohol Abuse and Alcoholism estimated the comprehensive societal cost of alcohol abuse (including direct medical expenditures, lost earnings due to premature death, illness, fetal alcohol syndrome and costs to the public safety and criminal justice infrastructure) to be nearly $185 million per year (Harwood 2000). A great deal of public attention is paid to alcohol dependence, but less severe but more widespread alcohol misuse poses a serious threat to public health—both as a possible precursor to alcohol dependence and as a direct cause of morbidity and mortality (Reid et al. 1999). A recent meta-analysis found that average volume of alcohol consumption is associated with several types of cancer (particularly liver and breast), unipolar major depression, hypertension, stroke, cirrhosis of the liver, and both intentional and unintentional injuries (Rehm 2003). The USPSTF recommends screening and behavioral counseling to reduce alcohol misuse (2005). Use of screening tools such as the Alcohol Use Disorders Identification Test has been demonstrated to be effective in identifying disorders of alcohol misuse among adults in primary care settings (Babor et al. 2001; Fiellin et al. 2000). A review of evidence for the USPSTF concluded that while 10 to 20 percent reductions in drinking from problem to safer levels have been demonstrated for a range of behavioral interventions, no studies to date have identified improved health outcomes (Whitlock et al. 2004).

The NCPP "Priorities" document lists primary-care-based screening and brief counseling for problem drinking in adults as a high priority based on high clinically preventable burden of disease and strong evidence of cost-effectiveness, between $0 and $14,000 per QALY (Shults et al. 2001). A number of economic analyses of inpatient, outpatient, and community-based interventions have been conducted, including societal perspective CBAs and CEAs that indicate social desirability (French and McGeary 1997). A randomized, controlled trial of brief physician advice for problem drinkers by Michael Fleming and colleagues demonstrated not only reduced alcohol consumption, but also substantial reductions in hospital and emergency room use, encounters with the criminal justice system and motor vehicle accidents (Fleming et al. 2000). Although changes in morbidity were not observed or economically valued, Fleming and colleagues demonstrated that the societal cost savings from reduced medical use, crime, and accidents more than offset the cost of the intervention, yielding an estimated benefit-cost ratio of 5.6 at the end of twelve months and 4.3 at the end of forty-eight months (Fleming et al. 2002).

Screening and Brief Intervention for Tobacco Use
Cigarette smoking is considered the largest single cause of preventable morbidity and mortality in the United States (CDC 2002). Rates of smoking are strongly related to

low socioeconomic and racial-ethnic minority status (U.S. Department of Health and Human Services 1998). Consequently, the burden of smoking-related illness is substantially higher for economically disadvantaged populations (U.S. Department of Health and Human Services 1998; Fernander et al. 2006). Screening for tobacco use combined with brief (less than five-minute) counseling in primary care is widely considered highly effective (Anderson et al. 2002), earning the highest recommendation from the USPSTF (2005).

The NCPP "Priorities" document lists repeated tobacco-use screening and brief intervention (that is, offered at each primary care visit) as one of its top priorities, based on clinically preventable burden of disease and dominant cost-effectiveness (both lower cost and improved outcomes) (Shults et al. 2001). The NCPP published a technical report outlining its review and simulation-based economic analysis, concluding that repeated tobacco screening and intervention in a hypothetical birth cohort of 4 million individuals would save 190,000 undiscounted QALYs and $500 per smoker treated (discounted) when comprehensive societal costs are considered (Solberg et al. 2006).

Colorectal Cancer Screening

Colorectal cancer is the second most deadly cancer in the United States after lung cancer and was expected to cause more than 56,000 deaths in 2005 (Jemal et al. 2005). Age-adjusted incidence rates are highest among African Americans and lowest among Hispanics (Ward et al. 2004). Indeed, higher colorectal cancer mortality for the African American population has been one of the major drivers in overall cancer-related disparities by race, particularly for women (Ward et al. 2004). The relationships among race, income, and colorectal cancer incidence are complex. For whites, living in a county with higher rates of poverty is associated with higher cancer incidence, but the trend is reversed for Hispanics and indeterminate for African Americans (Howe et al. 2006). Overall, rates of colorectal cancer and attributable mortality have declined from 1998 to 2003, partially due to increases in screening (Howe et al. 2006). Systematic reviews of evidence on the effectiveness of colorectal cancer screening in reducing cancer-related mortality are generally positive (Pignone et al. 2002). The USPSTF strongly recommends adults over age fifty be screened regularly using one or more of three modalities: annual fecal occult blood tests, sigmoidoscopy every five years, or colonoscopy every ten years (U.S. Preventive Services Task Force 2005). The overall rate of population adherence to recommended screening is low, particularly so for nonwhites and those with lower socioeconomic status (Swan et al. 2003).

The NCPP "Priorities" document lists screening for colorectal cancer as a high priority, based on clinically preventable burden of disease and cost-effectiveness (Shults et al. 2001). The NCPP published a technical report outlining its review and simulation-based economic analysis, concluding that colorectal cancer screening in a hypothetical birth cohort of 4 million people would save 338,000 undiscounted years of life, costing $11,900 per year of life saved (discounted) (Solberg et al. 2006). The NCPP ignored effects of colorectal cancer (and screening) on quality of life because of a lack of available evidence.

Cervical Cancer Screening

Cervical cancer is the twelfth most commonly diagnosed cancer among women and was predicted to cause more 3,700 deaths in 2005 (Jemal et al. 2005). Age-standardized incidence rates for African Americans and Hispanics are 30 percent and 80 percent higher than for whites, respectively, and mortality rates more than twice as high for African Americans and 37 percent higher for Hispanics than for whites (Ward et al. 2004). Cervical cancer incidence is 18 percent higher for whites in counties with more than 20 percent of individuals living under the poverty line than for whites in counties with less than 10 percent in poverty; for African Americans, the poverty differential in incidence is 30 percent and for Hispanics, it is 39 percent (Howe et al. 2006). The USPSTF strongly recommends screening for cervical cancer using Pap smears at least every three years, beginning within three years of the onset of sexual activity or age twenty, whichever comes first (U.S. Preventive Services Task Force 2005). Rates of adherence to Pap testing within three years are higher for African American women (compared to whites and Hispanics), women of higher socioeconomic status, and those who have a usual source of care; rates are substantially lower for recent immigrants than for those in the United States for more than 10 years or for women born in the United States (Swan et al. 2003).

The NCPP "Priorities" document lists screening for cervical cancer as a high priority, based on high clinically preventable burden of disease and modest cost-effectiveness (Shults et al. 2001). An NCPP technical report concluded that cervical cancer screening in a hypothetical birth cohort of 4 million women would save 228,000 undiscounted years of life, costing $17,600 per year of life saved (discounted) (Maciosek et al. 2006). The NCPP ignored effects of cervical cancer (and screening) on quality of life due to a lack of available evidence.

Breast Cancer Screening

Breast cancer is the most commonly diagnosed cancer among women and was predicted to cause more than 40,000 deaths in 2005 (Jemal et al. 2005). Examining breast cancer incidence rates alone might lead to the likely but erroneous conclusion that breast cancer has a lower burden among disadvantaged populations. Age-standardized breast cancer incidence rates for African American and Hispanic women are approximately 31 percent and 36 percent lower, respectively, than for white women (Ward et al. 2004). Higher county level poverty rates are also associated with lower breast cancer incidence for all race-ethnicity groups (Howe et al. 2006). However, the likelihood of breast cancer being detected at a distant stage (that is, after the cancer has metastasized and when chances for a cure are substantially reduced) increases with the county-level poverty rate: Comparing counties with more than 20 percent in poverty to those with fewer than 10 percent, the proportion detected at a distant stage is 16 percent higher for whites, 27 percent higher for African Americans, and 56 percent higher for Hispanics (Howe et al. 2006). Although the ratio of breast cancer incidence to mortality is approximately the same for white and Hispanic women, approximately 20 percent, it is alarmingly higher for African American women, approximately 30 percent (Ward et al. 2004). Racial disparities in breast cancer mortality are a significant contributor to disparities in cancer-related mortality overall (Ward et al. 2004).

These conflicting patterns of incidence, detection, and mortality point to a role for disparities in rates of screening. The USPSTF recommends screening for breast cancer using mammography every one to two years, beginning at age forty (U.S. Preventive Services Task Force 2005). Despite substantial controversy over the benefit of screening for women aged forty to forty-nine and the potential for overdetection of ductal carcinoma in-situ, which may or may not progress to invasive cancer in individuals, the perception of the societal benefit of mammography overall is widespread (Fletcher 1997; Ernster and Barclay 1997; Humphrey et al. 2002). Rates of adherence to mammography screening within three years are moderately lower for African American and Hispanic women than for whites; rates are substantially lower for women with lower socioeconomic status, those who do not have a usual source of care, and less than ten-year immigrants (Swan et al. 2003).

The NCPP "Priorities" document lists regular screening of women over age fifty for breast cancer with mammography and discusses screening risks and benefits for those age forty to forty-nine as a priority, based on high clinically preventable burden of disease but borderline cost-effectiveness (Shults et al. 2001). The NCPP report concluded that mammography screening over age fifty in a hypothetical birth cohort of 4 million women would save 356,000 undiscounted years of life (not quality-adjusted), costing $48,000 per QALY saved (discounted) (Maciosek et al. 2001). The incremental cost-effectiveness ratio was highly sensitive to assumptions about quality of life, in particular the hypothetical disutility caused by anxiety and discomfort associated with mammography and biopsy of suspicious findings.

THE INTERVENTION WITH THE POTENTIAL FOR HIGHEST NET BENEFIT

None of the specific clinical prevention efforts mentioned can be successful in improving the health capital of disadvantaged persons and reducing health disparities if they don't have access or the ability to pay for them. Both the Healthy People 2010 report and the Commonwealth Fund National Scorecard identified increasing health insurance coverage and improving access to care as critical policy issues for improving health and reducing health disparities (U.S. Department of Health and Human Services 2000; Commonwealth Fund Commission 2006). The Census Bureau estimates that 46.6 million people in the United States went without health insurance at some time during 2005 (DeNavas-Walt, Proctor, and Lee 2006). A comprehensive, systematic review by Jack Hadley concluded that, though the quality of studies varied substantially, forty-three of the fifty-four studies indicated statistically significant, positive relationships between having health insurance and having better health across a wide range of health conditions (Hadley 2003). The consequences for health and human capital are substantial. According to the Institute of Medicine, lack of health insurance causes approximately 18,000 deaths annually, with $65 billion to $130 billion in health capital lost due to avoidable morbidity and early mortality (Institute of Medicine 2004). Because of the strong relationships among income, race, and health-insurance status (DeNavas-Walt, Proctor, and Lee 2006; Holahan and Cook 2005), an excess of this burden falls on the economically disadvantaged.

The pathways from lack of insurance to poor health are complex. Disparities in use and access to a usual source of health care, however, are widely considered important determinants of socioeconomic and racial-ethnic disparities in health (U.S. Department of Health and Human Services 2000; Commonwealth Fund Commission 2006; Weinick, Zuvekas, and Cohen 2000; Andrulis 1998). Recent reviews of the literature have concluded that providing health insurance would most likely reduce health disparities by increasing the number of individuals who have a usual source of care (Lillie-Blanton and Hoffman 2005; Starfield and Shi 2004). In a telephone survey of enrollees in New York State's SCHIP program, Laura Shone and her colleagues found that extending insurance to previously uncovered children was associated with an increase in access, continuity, and quality of care and a reduction (but not elimination) in racial-ethnic disparities (2005). Thomas Buchmueller and his colleagues' comprehensive, systematic review of the literature found substantial evidence that extending health insurance coverage to the uninsured would increase health-care use for adults and children (2005).

In the absence of national health-care reform, the boldest initiatives to expand access to health care through health insurance recently have come at the state level. From 2003 to 2006, Massachusetts, Vermont, and Maine implemented comprehensive health insurance reform, each providing substantial subsidies for the purchase of insurance for families under 300 percent of the federal poverty level (Burton, Friedenzohn, and Martinez-Vidal 2007). The most widely discussed of the three initiatives, Massachusetts' new system combines both individual and employer mandates with creation of a new administrative entity called the "Commonwealth Health Insurance Connector Authority," designed to "(1) reduce the health insurance administrative burden for small businesses; (2) make it easier for small businesses and individuals to find affordable policies; (3) allow individuals to buy insurance with pretax dollars; (4) allow part-time and seasonal employers to combine employer contributions; and (5) enable individuals to keep their coverage when they change jobs" (McDonough et al. 2006, w424). These reforms are too recent to allow for comprehensive program evaluation using cost-benefit analysis. Notably, the governors of California, Illinois, and Pennsylvania also recently introduced comprehensive health-insurance reform proposals modeled on that of Massachusetts, although the likelihood of passage is a matter of debate (Sack 2007).

Other less-comprehensive state reform initiatives include proposed legislation in Illinois, Pennsylvania, Tennessee, Oregon, and Wisconsin to substantially increase coverage for children by expanding eligibility under the federally funded, but state-administered, State Children's Health Insurance Program (SCHIP) (Burton Friedenzohn, and Martinez-Vidal 2007). Notably, the 2007 congressional reauthorization of the SCHIP program (S.1224) includes a proposed budget increase of $35 billion over five years, with the goal of increasing enrollment by 3.3 million children. However, the proposal faces the threat of a veto by President George W. Bush, who said, "my concern is that when you expand eligibility . . . you're really beginning to open up an avenue for people to switch from private insurance to the government" (Lee 2007, A03).

Interestingly, the state of Maryland attempted to directly legislate against the so-called crowding out of private benefits by public benefits by passing the Fair Share Act in 2006, which required employers with more than 10,000 employees (notably only one employer in the state—Wal Mart) to spend at least 8 percent of payroll on health insurance. However, a federal district court ruled that the law was pre-empted by the Employee Retirement Income Security Act (ERISA), which gives broad latitude for large, multistate employers to set uniform, nationwide benefits (Abelson and Barbaro 2006). Indeed, ERISA preemption has been and will continue to be a major impediment to the implementation of state initiatives for health-insurance reform (Butler 2006).

AN IMPORTANT APPLICATION: THE OREGON HEALTH PLAN

Depending on whom you ask, the Oregon Health Plan conjures images of either a government run amok—withholding life-saving health care and interfering with the doctor-patient relationship—or the boldest attempt to date to merge rational decision making and evidence-based medicine with health-care policy. In 1989, the state of Oregon adopted a plan to extend Medicaid coverage to all individuals between 50 and 100 percent of the federal poverty level without increasing program expenditures or reducing payments to health-care providers (Jacobs, Marmor, and Oberlander 1999; Conviser 1995). To accomplish this task, the state enacted two broad forms of cost-containment: first, requiring (with limited exceptions) that new enrollees enter health-maintenance organizations (HMOs) and, second, restricting covered health services to a list of rank-ordered diagnoses and procedures above a threshold determined by expected expenditures relative to an assigned budget (Jacobs, Marmor, and Oberlander 1999).

An initial prioritized list was determined by a simplified form of CBA that rank-ordered treatments and conditions according to cost, duration of benefit, physician determination of the likelihood of symptom relief or prevention of death, and the quality of life impact of the medical condition as assessed by a telephone poll of state residents and a series of community meetings (Jacobs et al. 1999; Garland 1992). Measurement of quality-of-life impacts proved to be quite controversial—both practically, because data on the clinical effectiveness for many interventions was rather limited, and theoretically, because the QALY is, in essence, an interpersonally comparable, cardinal utility measure (LaPuma 1992; Nord 1993; Kaplan 1992). Interestingly, the Health Care Financing Administration refused to grant a waiver to the State of Oregon on the grounds that assigning health-state utilities based on perceived morbidity violated the Americans with Disabilities Act, and the state was forced to rank-order diagnoses and procedures only on the basis of cost and mortality prevention (Jacobs, Marmor, and Oberlander 1999). In the first year of the program, 745 diagnoses and procedures were rank-ordered, and on the basis of expected expenditures relative to a preassigned budget, the Oregon Health Plan determined that it could afford to cover the top 606 (Jacobs, Marmor, and Oberlander 1999). Because of the expanded eligibility criteria, an additional 120,000 individuals enrolled in Medicaid in the first year of the program (Jacobs, Marmor, and Oberlander

1999). The program is credited with long-run reductions in Oregon's overall uninsured rate (Leichter 2004).

Some have argued that, in large part due to the requirement that measures of health-state utilities be excluded from the prioritization mechanism, the Oregon Health Plan does not represent a successful application of true cost-benefit analysis (Jacobs, Marmor, and Oberlander 1999). Nevertheless, the Oregon Health Plan represents a truly important innovation in health policy (Weimer 2007): the first explicit attempt by a public health program in the United States to maximize the health capital returns of a fixed investment. To date, it remains the only such attempt.

CONCLUSION

In comparison to other countries, such as the United Kingdom (Claxton, Sculpher, and Drummond 2002) and Canada (Menon and Topfer 2000) where cost-effectiveness plays a key role in health policy, formal applications of CEA and CBA are relatively uncommon in the United States (Perry, Gardner, and Thamer 1997; Neumann 2004). To some extent, concern with a lack of rigor and uneven application of methodological standards underlies the skepticism of U.S. policymakers, at clinical, health system, and societal levels (Carande-Kulis et al. 2000). But surely other countries face the same challenges, and yet they are far ahead of the United States. In an article titled "Why Don't Americans Use Cost-Effectiveness Analysis," Peter Neumann offered another explanation:

CEA's proponents have always assumed that increased spending and the public's appetite for medical technology will eventually force us to recognize limits more directly and that inevitably we will embrace CEA as the best solution to our dilemma. But Americans' reluctance to acknowledge limits—and their resistance to CEA—has proven remarkably durable. In many ways, CEA has emerged as a technical success but a political failure (Neumann 312).

Until a more rational approach toward investing our limited health-care resources is adopted, future reports will continue to proclaim that the U.S. health-care system misallocates resources, with public health consequences reaching into the millions of years of healthy life lost—a disproportionate share of which will come from disadvantaged populations.

REFERENCES

Abelson, Reed, and Michael Barbaro. 2006. "Judge Gives Wal-Mart Reprieve on Benefits." *New York Times*, July 20, 2006, C1.

Anderson, Jane E., Douglas E. Jorenby, Walter J. Scott, and Michael C. Fiore. 2002. "Treating Tobacco Use and Dependence: An Evidence-Based Clinical Practice Guideline for Tobacco Cessation." *Chest* 121(3): 932–41.

Andrulis, Dennis P. 1998. "Access to Care Is the Centerpiece in the Elimination of Socioeconomic Disparities in Health." *Annals of Internal Medicine* 129(5): 412–16.

Atkinson, William L., Larry K. Pickering, Benjamin Schwartz, Bruce G. Weniger, John K. Iskander, and John C. Watson. 2002. "General Recommendations on Immunization: Recommendations of the Advisory Committee on Immunization Practices (ACIP) and the American Academy of Family Physicians (AAFP)." *Morbidity and Mortality Weekly Report* 51(RR 2): 1–35.

Babor, Thomas F., John C. Higgins-Biddle, John B. Saunders, and Maristela G. Monteiro. 2001. "The Alcohol Use Disorders Identification Test. Guidelines for Use in Primary Care." Geneva, Switzerland: World Health Organization Department of Mental Health and Substance Dependence.

Becker, Gary S. 2002. "Human Capital." *The Concise Encyclopedia of Economics*. Library of Economics and Liberty. www.econlib.org/library/Enc/HumanCapital.html.

Behrman, Richard. 1985. "Preventing Low Birth Weight." Washington, DC: National Academy Press.

Brunham, R. C., I. W. Maclean, B. Binns, and R. W. Peeling. 1985. "Chlamydia Trachomatis: Its Role in Tubal Infertility." *Journal of Infectious Diseases* 152(6): 1275–82.

Buchmueller, Thomas C., Kevin Grumbach, Richard Kronick, and James G. Kahn. 2005. "Book Review: The Effect of Health Insurance on Medical Care Utilization and Implications for Insurance Expansion: A Review of the Literature." *Medical Research and Review* 62(1): 3–30.

Burton, A., I. Friedenzohn, and E. Martinez-Vidal. 2007. "State Strategies to Expand Health Insurance Coverage: Trends and Lessons for Policymakers." New York: The Commonwealth Fund.

Butler, Patricia A. 2006. "ERISA Implications for State Health Care Access Initiatives: Impact of the Maryland 'Fair Share Act' Court Decision." Portland, ME: National Academy for State Health Policy. http://statecoverage.net/SCINASHP.pdf.

Carande-Kulis, Vilma G., Michael V. Maciosek, Peter A. Briss, Steven M. Teutsch, Stephanie Zaza, Benedict I. Truman, Mark L. Messonier, Marguerite Pappaioanau, Jeffrey R. Harris, and Jonathan Fielding. 2000. "Methods for Systematic Reviews of Economic Evaluations for the Guide to Community Preventive Services." *American Journal of Preventive Medicine* 18(1 Suppl): 75–91.

Centers for Disease Control and Prevention. 2002. "Annual Smoking-Attributable Mortality, Years of Potential Life Lost, and Economic Costs—United States, 1995–1999." *Morbidity and Mortality Weekly Report* 51(14): 300–303.

Chow, J. M., M. L. Yonekura, G. A. Richwald, S. Greenland, R. L. Sweet, and J. Schachter. 1990. "The Association between Chlamydia Trachomatis and Ectopic Pregnancy: A Matched-Pair, Case-Control Study." *Journal of the American Medical Association* 263(23): 3164–67.

Claxton, Karl, Mark Sculpher, and Michael Drummond. 2002. "A Rational Framework for Decision Making by the National Institute for Clinical Excellence (NICE)." *The Lancet* 360(9334): 711–15.

Committee on Infectious Diseases. 2004. "Recommended Childhood and Adolescent Immunization Schedule—United States." *Pediatrics* 113(1):142–43.

Conviser, Richard. 1995. "A Brief History of the Oregon Health Plan and Its Features." Salem: Office of Oregon Health Policy and Research.

DeNavas-Walt, Carmen, Bernatte D. Proctor, and Cheryl Hill Lee. 2006. "Income, Poverty, and Health Insurance Coverage in the United States: 2005." Washington, DC: U.S. Census Bureau.

Dolan, Paul, and Richard Edlin. 2002. "Is it Really Possible to Build a Bridge between Cost-Benefit Analysis and Cost-Effectiveness Analysis?" *Journal of Health Economics* 21(5): 827–43.

Donaldson, Cam. 1998. "The (Near) Equivalence of Cost-Effectiveness and Cost-Benefit Analyses: Fact or Fallacy?" *PharmacoEconomics* 13(4): 389–96.

Ernster, Virginia L., and Barclay John. 1997. "Increases in Ductal Carcinoma In Situ (DCIS) of the Breast in Relation to Mammography: A Dilemma." *Journal of the National Cancer Institute Monograph* (22): 151–56.

Evans, Robert G., and Greg L. Stoddart. 2003. "Consuming Research, Producing Policy?" *American Journal of Public Health* 93(3): 371–79.

Fernander, Anita F., Christi A. Patten, Darrell R. Schroeder, Susanna R. Stevens, Ivana T. Croghan, Kenneth P. Offord, and Richard D. Hurt. 2006. "Characteristics of Six-Month Tobacco Use Outcomes of Black Patients Seeking Smoking Cessation Intervention." *Journal of Health Care for the Poor and Underserved* 17(2): 413–24.

Fiellin, David A., M. Carrington Reid, and Patrick G. O'Connor. 2000. "Screening for Alcohol Problems in Primary Care: A Systematic Review." *Archives of Internal Medicine* 160(13): 1977–89.

Fiscella, Kevin. 1995. "Does Prenatal Care Improve Birth Outcomes? A Critical Review." *Obstetrics and Gynecology* 85(3): 468–79.

Fleming, Michael F., Marlon P. Mundt, Michael T. French, Linda Baier Manwell, Ellyn A. Stauffacher, and Kristin Lawton Barry. 2000. "Benefit-Cost Analysis of Brief Physician Advice with Problem Drinkers in Primary Care Settings." *Medical Care* 38(1): 7–18.

———. 2002. "Brief Physician Advice for Problem Drinkers: Long-Term Efficacy and Benefit-Cost Analysis." *Alcoholism Clinical and Experimental Research* 26(1): 36–43.

Fletcher, Suzanne W. 1997. "Whither Scientific Deliberation in Health Policy Recommendations? Alice in the Wonderland of Breast-Cancer Screening." *New England Journal of Medicine* 336(16): 1180–83.

French, Michael T. and Kery Anne McGeary. 1997. "Estimating the Economic Cost of Substance Abuse Treatment." *Health Economics* 6(5): 539–44.

Garber, Alan M., and Charles E. Phelps. 1998. "Economic Foundations of Cost-Effectiveness Analysis." *Journal of Health Economics* 16(1): 1–31.

Garland, M. J. 1992. "Rationing in Public: Oregon's Priority-Setting Methodology." In *Rationing America's Medical Care: The Oregon Plan and Beyond*, eds. M. A. Strosberg, J. M. Wiener, R. Baker, and I. A. Fein. Washington, DC: Brookings Institution Press.

Gold, Martha R., Joanna E. Siegel, Louise B. Russell, and Milton C. Weinstein, eds. 1996. *Cost-Effectiveness in Health and Medicine*. New York: Oxford University Press.

Groseclose, Samuel L., Akbar A. Zaidi, Susan J. DeLisle, William C. Levine, and Michael E. St. Louis. 1999. "Estimated Incidence and Prevalence of Genital Chlamydia Trachomatis Infections in the United States." *Sexually Transmitted Diseases* 26(6): 339–44.

Grossman, Michael. 1972. "On the Concept of Health Capital and the Demand for Health." *Journal of Political Economy* 80(2): 223–55.

Hack, Maureen, Nancy K. Klein, and H. Gerry Taylor. 1995. "Long-Term Developmental Outcomes of Low Birth Weight Infants." *Future Child* 5(1): 176–96.

Hadley, Jack. 2003. "Sicker and Poorer—the Consequences of Being Uninsured: A Review of the Research on the Relationship between Health Insurance, Medical Care Use, Health, Work, and Income." *Medical Care Research and Review* 60(2 Suppl): 3S–112S.

Harwood, Henrick. 2000. *Updating Estimates of the Economic Costs of Alcohol Abuse in the United*

States: Estimates, Update Methods and Data. Report prepared by the Lewin Group. Washington, DC: National Institute on Alcohol Abuse and Alcoholism.

Hoerschelmann, Olaf. 2006. "U.S. Quiz Shows: The $64,000 Question. The Museum of Broadcast Communications." www.museum.tv/archives/etv/S/htmlS/$64000quest/$64000quest.htm.

Holahan, John, and Allison Cook. 2005. "Changes in Economic Conditions and Health Insurance Coverage, 2000–2004." *Health Exclusive* W5: 498–508.

Honey, E., C. Augood, A. Templeton, I. Russell, J. Paavonen, P.-A. Mardh, A. Stary, and B. Stary-Pedersen. 2002. "Cost Effectiveness of Screening for Chlamydia Trachomatis: A Review of Published Studies." *Sexually Transmitted Infections* 78(6): 406–12.

Howe, Holly L., Xiaocheng Wu, Lynne A. G. Ries, Vilma Cokkinides, Faruque Ahmed, Ahmedin Jemal, Barry Miller, Melanie Williams, Elizabeth Ward, Phyllis A. Wingo, Amelie Ramirez, and Brenda K. Edwards. 2006. "Annual Report to the Nation on the Status of Cancer, 1975–2003, Featuring Cancer among U.S. Hispanic/Latino Populations." *Cancer* 107(8): 1711–42.

Howell, M. Rene, Thomas C. Quinn, and Charlotte A. Gaydos. 1998. "Screening for Chlamydia Trachomatis in Asymptomatic Women Attending Family Planning Clinics: A Cost-Effectiveness Analysis of Three Strategies." *Annals of Internal Medicine* 128(4): 277–84.

Humphrey, Linda L., Mark Helfand, Benjamin K. S. Chan, and Steven H. Woolf. 2002. "Breast Cancer Screening: A Summary of the Evidence for the U.S. Preventive Services Task Force." *Annals of Internal Medicine* 37(5): 347–60.

Institute of Medicine. 2004. "Insuring America's Health: Principles and Recommendations." *Academic Emergency Medicine* 11(4): 418–22.

Jacobs, Lawrence, Theodore Marmor, and Jonathan Oberlander. 1999. "The Oregon Health Plan and the Political Paradox of Rationing: What Advocates and Critics Have Claimed and What Oregon Did." *Journal of Health Politics, Policy, and Law* 24(1): 161–80.

Jemal, Ahmedin, Taylor Murray, Elizabeth Ward, Alicia Samuels, Ram C. Tiwari, Asma Ghafoor, Eric Feuer, and Michael J. Thun. 2005. "Cancer Statistics, 2005." *CA: A Cancer Journal for Clinicians* 55(1): 10–30.

Kaplan, R. M. 1992. "A Quality-of-Life Approach to Health Resource Allocation." In *Rationing America's Medical Care: The Oregon Plan and Beyond*, eds. M. A. Strosberg, J. M. Wiener, R. Baker, and I. A. Fein. Washington, DC: Brookings Institution Press.

Kenkel, Don. 1997. "On Valuing Morbidity, Cost-Effectiveness Analysis, and Being Rude." *Journal of Health Economics* 16(6): 749–57.

Klausner Jeffrey D., Willi McFarland, Gail Bolan, Maria T. Hernandez, Fred Molitor, George F. Lemp, Barbara Cahoon-Young, Scott Morrow, and Juan Ruiz. 2001. "Knock-Knock: A Population-Based Survey of Risk Behavior, Health Care Access, and Chlamydia trachomatis Infection among Low-Income Women in the San Francisco Bay Area." *Journal of Infectious Diseases* 183(7): 1087–92.

Kowaleski-Jones, Lori, and Greg J. Duncan. 2002. "Effects of Participation in the WIC Program on Birthweight: Evidence from the National Longitudinal Survey of Youth." *American Journal of Public Health* 92(5): 799–804.

La Puma, J. 1992. "Quality-Adjusted Life-Years: Why Physicians Should Reject Oregon's Plan." In *Rationing America's Medical Care: The Oregon Plan and Beyond*, eds. M. A. Strosberg, J. M. Wiener, R. Baker, and I. A. Fein. Washington, DC: Brookings Institution Press.

Lee, Christopher. 2007. "Bush: No Deal On Children's Health Plan." *Washington Post*, July 19, 2007, A3.

Leichter, H. M. 2004. "Obstacles to Dependent Health Care Access in Oregon: Health Insurance or Health Care?" *Journal of Health Politics, Policy and Law* 29(2): 237–68.

Lieu, Tracy A., S. L. Cochi, S. B. Black, M. E. Halloran, H. R. Shinefield, S. J. Holmes, M. Wharton, and A. E. Washington. 1994. "Cost-Effectiveness of a Routine varicella Vaccination Program for U.S. Children." *Journal of the American Medical Association* 271(5): 375–81.

Lieu, Tracy A., G. Thomas Ray, Steven B. Black, Jay C. Butler, Jerome O. Klein, Robert F. Breiman, Mark A. Miller, and Henry Shinefield. 2000. "Projected Cost-Effectiveness of Pneumococcal Conjugate Vaccination of Healthy Infants and Young Children." *Journal of the American Medical Association* 283(11): 1460–68.

Lillie-Blanton, Marsha, and Catherine Hoffman. 2005. "The Role of Health Insurance Coverage in Reducing Racial/Ethnic Disparities in Health Care." *Health Affairs* 24(2): 398–408.

Lu, M. C., V. Tache, G. R. Alexander, M. Kotelchuck, and N. Halfon. 2003. "Preventing Low Birth Weight: Is Prenatal Care the Answer?" *Journal of Maternal-Fetal and Neonatal Medicine* 13(6): 362–80.

Luman, Elizabeth T., Lawrence E. Barker, Mary Mason McCauley, and Carolyn Drews-Botsch. 2005. "Timeliness of Childhood Immunizations: A State-Specific Analysis." *American Journal of Public Health* 95(8): 1367–74.

Lynch, John, George Davey Smith, Sam Harper, Marianne Hillemeier, Nancy Ross, and George A. Kaplan. 2004. "Is Income Inequality a Determinant of Population Health? Part 1. A Systematic Review." *Milbank Quarterly* 82(1): 5–99.

Maciosek, Michael V., Ashley B. Coffield, Nichol M. Edwards, Thomas J. Flottemesch, Michael J. Goodman, and Leif I. Solberg. 2006. "Priorities among Effective Clinical Preventive Services: Results of a Systematic Review and Analysis." *American Journal of Preventive Medicine* 31(1): 52–61.

Maciosek, Michael V., Nichol M. Edwards, Margaret Davis, Amy Butani, D. A. McGree, and Leif I. Solberg. 2006. "Cervical Cancer Screening: Technical Report Prepared for the National Commission on Prevention Priorities." Minneapolis, MN: HealthPartners Research Foundation and Partnership for Prevention.

McCormick, M. C., and J. E. Siegel. 2001. "Recent Evidence on the Effectiveness of Prenatal Care." *Ambulatory Pediatrics* 1(6): 321–25.

McDonough, John E., Brian Rosman, Fawn Phelps, and Melissa Shannon. 2006. "The Third Wave of Massachusetts Health Care Access Reform." *Health Affairs* 25(6): w420–w431.

Meltzer, David. 1997. "Accounting for Future Costs in Medical Cost-Effectiveness Analysis." *Journal of Health Economics* 16(1): 33–64.

Menon, Devidas, and Leigh-Ann Topfer. 2000. Health Technology Assessment in Canada. *International Journal of Technology Assessment and Health Care* 16(3): 896–902.

Messonnier, Mark L., Phaedra S. Corso, Steven M. Teutsch, Anne C. Haddix, and Jeffrey R. Harris. 1999. "An Ounce of Prevention . . . What Are the Returns? Second Edition." *American Journal of Preventive Medicine* 16(3): 248–63.

Mincer, Jacob. 1958. "Investment in Human Capital and Personal Income Distribution." *Journal of Political Economy* 66(4): 281–302.

Murray, Christopher J. L., Sandeep Kulkarni, and Majid Ezzati. 2005. "Eight Americas: New Perspectives on U.S. Health Disparities." *American Journal of Preventive Medicine* 29(5, Supplement 1): 4–10.

Mushkin, Selma J. 1962. "Health as an Investment." *The Journal of Political Economy* 70(5, Part 2: Investment in Human Beings): 129–57.

National Center for Health Statistics. 2005. *Health, United States, 2005.* Washington, DC: U.S. Government Printing Office.

Neumann, Peter J. 2004. "Why Don't Americans Use Cost-Effectiveness Analysis?" *The American Journal of Managed Care* 10(5): 308–12.

Nord, E. 1993. "Unjustified Use of the Quality of Well-Being Scale in Priority Setting in Oregon." *Health Policy* 24(1): 45–53.

Parker, J. D., K. C. Schoendorf, and J. L. Kiely. 1994. "Associations between Measures of Socioeconomic Status and Low Birth Weight, Small for Gestational Age, and Premature Delivery in the United States." *Annals of Epidemiology* 4(4): 271–78.

Perry, S., E. Gardner, and M. Thamer. 1997. "The Status of Health Technology Assessment Worldwide: Results of an International Survey." *International Journal of Technology Assessment in Health Care* 13(1): 81–98.

Petrou, Stavros, T. Sach, and L. Davidson. 2001. "The Long-Term Costs of Preterm Birth and Low Birth Weight: Results of a Systematic Review." *Child: Care, Health, and Development* 27(2): 97–115.

Pignone, Michael, Melissa Rich, Steven M. Teutsch, Alfred O. Berg, and Kathleen N. Lohr. 2002. "Screening for Colorectal Cancer in Adults at Average Risk: A Summary of the Evidence for the U.S. Preventive Services Task Force." *Annals of Internal Medicine* 137(2): 132–41.

Rehm, Jurgen, Robin Room, Kathryn Graham, Maristela Monteiro, Gerhard Gmel, and Christopher T. Sempos. 2003. "The Relationship of Average Volume of Alcohol Consumption and Patterns of Drinking to Burden of Disease: An Overview." *Addiction* 98(9): 1209–28.

Reid, M. Carrington, David A. Fiellin, and Patrick G. O'Connor. 1999. "Hazardous and Harmful Alcohol Consumption in Primary Care." *Archives of Internal Medicine* 159(15): 1681–89.

Sack, Kevin. 2007. "A State Finds No Easy Fixes on Health Care." *New York Times*, July 10, 2007, A1.

Satcher, David. 2006. "Priorities among Effective Clinical Preventive Services: A Commentary." *American Journal of Preventive Medicine* 31(1): 97–98.

Shone, Laura P., Andrew W. Dick, Jonathan D. Klein, Jack Zwanziger, and Peter G. Szilagyi. 2005. "Reduction in Racial and Ethnic Disparities after Enrollment in the State Children's Health Insurance Program." *Pediatrics* 15(6): e697–705.

Shults, Ruth A., Randy W. Elder, David A. Sleet, James L. Nichols, Mary O. Alao, Vilma G. Carande-Kulis, Stephanie Zaza, Daniel M. Sosin, and Robert S. Thompson. 2001. "Reviews of Evidence regarding Interventions to Reduce Alcohol-Impaired Driving." *American Journal of Preventive Medicine* 21(4, Supplement 1): 66–88.

Solberg, Leif I., Michael V. Maciosek, Nichol M. Edwards, Hema S. Khanchandani, and Michael J. Goodman. 2006. "Repeated Tobacco-Use Screening and Intervention in Clinical Practice: Health Impact and Cost Effectiveness." *American Journal of Preventive Medicine* 31(1): 62–71.

Starfield, Barbara, and Leiyu Shi. 2004. "The Medical Home, Access to Care, and Insurance: A Review of Evidence." *Pediatrics* 113(5 Suppl): 1493–98.

Swan, Judith, Nancy Breen, Ralph J. Coates, Barbara K. Rimer, and Nancy C. Lee. 2003. "Progress in Cancer Screening Practices in the United States: Results from the 2000 National Health Interview Survey." *Cancer* 97(6): 1528–40.

The Commonwealth Fund Commission on a High Performance Health System (Commonwealth Fund Commission). 2006. "Why Not the Best? Results from a National Scorecard on U.S. Health System Performance." New York: The Commonwealth Fund.

U.S. Department of Health and Human Services. 1998. "Tobacco Use among U.S. Racial/Ethnic Minority Groups—African Americans, American Indians and Alaska Natives, Asian Americans and Pacific Islanders, and Hispanics: A Report of the Surgeon General." Atlanta, GA: U.S. Department of Health and Human Services, Centers for Disease Control and Prevention, National Center for Chronic Disease Prevention and Health Promotion, Office on Smoking and Health.

———. 2000. *Healthy People 2010, Second Edition.* Washington, DC: U.S. Government Printing Office.

U.S. Preventive Services Task Force. 2005. "Guide to Clinical Preventive Services, 2005." Rockville, MD: Agency for Healthcare Research and Quality.

van Doorslaer, Eddy, Cristina Masseria, and Xander Koolman. 2006. "Inequalities in Access to Medical Care by Income in Developed Countries." *Canadian Medical Association Journal* 174(2): 177–83.

Ward, Elizabeth, Ahmedian Jemal, Vilma Cokkinides, Gopal K. Singh, Cheryll Cardinez, Asma Ghafoor, and Michael Thun. 2004. "Cancer Disparities by Race/Ethnicity and Socioeconomic Status." *CA: A Cancer Journal for Clinicians* 54(2): 78–93.

Weimer, David L. 2007. "Medical Governance: Are We Ready to Prescribe?" *Journal of Policy Analysis and Management* 26(2): 217–29.

Weinick, Robin M., Samuel H. Zuvekas, and Joel W. Cohen. 2000. "Racial and Ethnic Differences in Access to and Use of Health Care Services, 1977 to 1996." *Medical Care Research and Review* 57(1 Suppl): 36–54.

Whitlock, Evelyn P., Michael R. Polen, Carla A. Green, Tracy Orleans, and Jonathan Klein. 2004. "Behavioral Counseling Interventions in Primary Care to Reduce Risky/Harmful Alcohol Use by Adults: A Summary of the Evidence for the US Preventive Services Task Force." *Annals of Internal Medicine* 140(7): 557–68.

Zhou, Fangjun, Jeanne Santoli, Mark L. Messonnier, Hussain R. Yusuf, Abigail Shefer, Susan Y. Chu, Lance Rodewald, and Rafael Harpaz. 2005. "Economic Evaluation of the 7-Vaccine Routine Childhood Immunization Schedule in the United States, 2001." *Archives of Pediatrics and Adolescent Medicine* 159(12): 1136–44.

Chapter 5

Adults with Serious Mental Illnesses

Mark S. Salzer

Serious mental illnesses (schizophrenia-spectrum disorders, bipolar disorder, and major depression) affect approximately 15 million to 21 million Americans (5 to 7 percent of the U.S. population) and are the leading cause of disability in the United States, Canada, and western Europe. The World Health Organization found that schizophrenia, bipolar disorder, and major depression account for 25 percent of all disability worldwide and are among the top ten conditions associated with significant loss of economic productivity and burden of disease (2001). The economic and social impacts of these illnesses result from the large number of people affected, early onset, given that the illnesses often strike in late adolescence and early adulthood, and the extent to which participation is affected in multiple life domains, especially employment.

The social costs in the United States associated with these illnesses are staggering. Thomas Insell, who currently heads the National Institute of Mental Health, estimates that seriuous mental illnesses are associated with more than $317 billion in annual costs—$100 billion in direct health-care expenditures, $193 billion in lost earning, and $24 billion in disability payments (2008). The most recent total annual costs associated with schizophrenia alone were estimated to be $62.7 billion, with direct health-care cost of $7.0 billion for outpatient services, $5.0 billion for drugs, $2.8 billion for inpatient stays, and $8.0 billion for long-term care, unemployment costs adding substantially to indirect costs (Wu et al. 2005). Approximately 40 percent of all individuals receiving SSI and SSDI payments have a psychiatric disability, making them the largest disability group to receive such payments, and fewer than 1 percent of individuals with psychiatric disabilities enrolled in these programs discontinue their involvement, the smallest discontinuation rate among all disability groups (Baron and Salzer 2002).

There is great interest among mental health policymakers, administrators, researchers, practitioners, and consumers in understanding the costs associated with these illnesses, the most effective treatment and rehabilitation interventions to improve the lives of individuals with serious mental illnesses and to ameliorate these costs, and the costs of these interventions relative to their benefits.

This chapter answers three questions: First, what are the socially desirable programs and interventions for adults with serious mental illnesses as viewed by experts? Second, what programs and interventions for adults with serious mental illnesses are potentially socially desirable, but lack a solid research base, are not well known, or are controversial? Third, what are the important adult mental health policy areas in need of cost-benefit or cost-effectiveness analyses?

SOCIALLY DESIRABLE OUTCOMES IN ADULT MENTAL HEALTH

A growing number of interventions have become universally recognized by most key stakeholder groups as effective and desirable. Historically, the justification of their importance in mental health policy has often been argued in terms of their ability to: reduce the costs of institutionalization in long- and short-term hospitals and jails and prisons; increase productivity in terms of achieving and maintaining employment and decreased SSA payments and use of other entitlement programs; and enhance well-being, recovery, and community integration.

The first set have arguably been a main driver in the development of many of the highly researched and established interventions in the adult mental health field. The emphasis on increasing productivity is a relatively newer socially desirable outcome that has generated the development of interventions primarily in the employment domain. The evolution in emphasis has emerged over the past twenty years or so as it has become increasingly recognized that individuals with serious mental illnesses can work, should work, and could work (Baron and Salzer 2002). Finally, there is a growing interest in a third set of outcomes—enhancing well-being, recovery, and community integration—that has been discussed by individuals with mental illnesses for many years, but has only recently become widely recognized in the last five or ten years. Recovery generally refers to the idea that people with mental illnesses can live satisfying and fulfilling lives with or without psychiatric symptoms.

Promoting recovery has been adopted as the mission of national, state, and local policies. Evidence of these goals can be found in, for example, the President's New Freedom Commission on Mental Health report (2003). Recovery as a socially desirable outcome is generally considered independent of hospitalizations. In other words, positive changes in recovery are important even if hospitalizations do not decrease. Community integration—defined as efforts to increase opportunities for those with psychiatric disabilities to live successfully in the community like everyone else—is a related socially desirable outcome embedded in both the 1990 Americans with Disabilities Act (ADA) and the Supreme Court Olmstead decision that unnecessary institutionalization of persons who could otherwise live in the community with proper supports is a violation of the ADA (Salzer 2006). Recovery and community integration as desirable outcomes underlie a number of the newer and promising practices in the field, though many of these interventions may have a positive impact on costs and enhance productivity. Cost-benefit analyses have almost exclusively focused on examining the impact of interventions on costs and productivity, but it is clear that recovery and community integration are also desired social goals that need more research attention.

SOCIALLY DESIRABLE INTERVENTIONS

There is a current wave of interest in developing evidence-based practices in mental health and policies to implement such practices. The result has been the development of a number of interventions over the last decade or so generally considered socially desirable by experts within the mental health community.

Psychopharmacological interventions and case management delivered in accordance with current evidenced-based practices are widely accepted as a necessary part of a mental health system. Both focus on symptom management and reducing the need for institutional or hospital-based care. Recent research has reasserted the value of psychotherapy as a socially desirable intervention in the treatment of serious mental illnesses. Illness management and other similar psychoeducation approaches and family psychoeducation are viewed as strategies to increase positive coping with the illnesses and reduce stressors associated with acute exacerbations that may lead to hospitalizations. Supported housing is valued as an effective strategy to supporting people remaining in the community and out of institutions. Supported employment is deemed effective in getting people back into the workforce. These interventions are universally accepted as the standard of care for adults with serious mental illnesses.

Many consider psychopharmacological interventions and medication management for psychiatric symptoms the most important interventions in the mental health field. The first generation of medications for schizophrenia, bipolar disorder, and depression were developed in the 1950s through the 1970s and have been consistently shown to reduce symptoms and hospitalizations when taken as prescribed. The National Institute of Mental Health has devoted a large amount of its annual research budget to funding basic biological and genetic research and pharmaceutical companies have been investing millions of dollars to develop new medications that started to become approved by the Food and Drug Administration in the early and mid-1990s. These newer medications have generally been found to have a greater impact on symptoms than the older medications and to have fewer side effects. Concerns are growing, however, about some side effects of these newer medications, such as weight gain and onset of diabetes. Such effects, of course, are considered extremely undesirable. The newer medications were thought to increase treatment adherence and tolerance dramatically for the medications because of reduced side effects. However, initial research from the Clinical Antipsychotic Trials of Intervention Effectiveness (CATIE) study did not find this to be the case (Lieberman et al. 2005). Nonadherence, due to side effects and other factors, has been identified as a major factor in rehospitalizations.

Although medications remain the central focus of treatment for the most serious mental illnesses, new research on cognitive-behavioral (CBT) psychotherapeutic approaches have solidified their position as important and widely accepted treatments. These approaches attempt to modify thoughts and behaviors through interpersonal interactions with a highly trained professional. CBT for depression has been found as effective as short-term psychopharmacological approaches in managing symptoms and distress and more effective in long-term relapse prevention (DeRubeis et al. 1999, 2005). CBT has also been found effective in reducing residual symptoms among those diagnosed with schizophrenia and not completely responsive to medications (Dickerson 2000).

The Surgeon General's 1999 Report on Mental Health mentioned psychiatric rehabilitation approaches as effective in decreasing hospitalizations and enhancing functional outcomes of those who experience mental illnesses (U.S. Department of Health and Human Services 1999). Medications and psychotherapy target symptom reduction and symptom management with the expectation of fewer hospitalizations. Psychiatric rehabilitation involves a wide range of supportive services that enable people to live successfully in the community regardless of symptoms. These programs generally target skills and supports necessary to be successful in specific domains (such as friendships, housing, work, education). Several widely accepted and evidence-based programs fall within the domain of psychiatric rehabilitation services.

A specific type of case management services, Assertive Community Treatment (ACT), has been identified as an evidence-based practice in mental health by the Substance Abuse Mental Health Services Administration (SAMHSA), based on research using rigorous research designs showing a decrease, among other things, in hospitalizations (Mueser et al. 1998). ACT is a multidisciplinary team approach to delivering intensive treatment and community supports to individuals with the most severe mental illnesses. ACT services are relatively expensive because of their low client-to-staff ratio and intensive service approach (frequent contacts). Less intensive and expensive forms of case management have been developed. Results are more mixed for these other forms of case management, however, including a strategy—referred to as brokered case management or resource coordination—of helping people obtain treatment and supports, but not providing the services directly.

Psychoeducational approaches, also referred to as illness management, are a broad set of group and individual teaching programs designed to help individuals with serious mental illness collaborate with service providers, reduce their susceptibility to the illness, and cope effectively with their symptoms. Outcomes associated with these efforts include decreases in relapses, rehospitalizations, and symptoms, and enhanced social functioning (Mueser et al. 2002). Psychoeducation for families is also considered an evidence-based practice and a highly desirable service, though the benefits tend to be found for family members with only weaker indirect effects on the individual with the mental illness (Dixon et al. 2001). These programs generally include emotional support for family members, information and education on the family member's illness, suggestions for managing day-to-day problems and crises, and development of family problem-solving skills during crises. Programs also serve as referral sources and resources during crises.

Supported housing refers to a broad range of case management, psychoeducational, and skills-based services to assist individuals in living in their own home (room, apartment, or other location) and successfully remaining in the community. Supports also include assisting individuals in finding housing and helping address disputes with landlords and others. There is good evidence that supported housing is effective in reducing homelessness and the need for hospitalizations, and increasing community tenure (for example, Rosenheck et al. 2003).

Supported employment refers to programs that help people identify and obtain employment and stay employed in competitive work settings. These programs have been found to be associated with greater rates of employment, increased job tenure, and higher annual wages (Bond et al. 1999, 2001).

NO SOLID RESEARCH BASE, NOT WELL KNOWN, OR CONTROVERSIAL

A number of other policies and interventions fall just below universal acceptance as part of the standard of care in the treatment of serious mental illnesses because of a combination of a minimal research base, unfamiliarity, and controversy resulting from differences in service philosophies.

Policies

One policy worth discussing focuses on continued efforts to support individuals with mental illnesses in the community rather than in institutions. The 1999 Supreme Court Olmstead decision reinforced the policy in their finding that unnecessary institutionalization of persons who could live in the community with proper supports is a violation of the Americans with Disabilities Act. Having begun in the 1960s, deinstitutionalization has continued to this day with consistent yearly decreases in state and county hospital censuses across the nation (Salzer, Kaplan, and Atay 2006). More than sixty hospitals shut down over the past forty years. More than 200 still remain open, however, and at considerable cost. Treating people in communities is far less expensive than treating them in institutions. One study followed persons affected by the closing of a hospital in Philadelphia and found that total treatment costs in the community, including the cost of housing, was $60,000 per person per year compared to $130,000 for institutional care (Rothbard et al. 1999). There are efforts to close even more hospitals and limit admissions, but there is resistance from communities concerned about loss of jobs, family members concerned about the lack of community supports, and providers concerned about the loss of treatment options and potential liability.

Involuntary outpatient commitment refers to a statute that allows judges to require people with mental illnesses to adhere to prescribed treatment or face a variety of consequences, including hospitalization. The Bazelon Center has documented the increase in such statutes across the country. The reviews of research on this highly controversial topic have been mixed. One review by Susan Ridgely, John Borum, and John Petralia found that these statutes, when followed through with proper services, supports, and oversight, could reduce certain negative outcomes and produce good outcomes (2001). Another more recent, extensive review concluded that there is little evidence for positive outcomes (Kisely, Campbell, and Preston 2005). These authors also questioned the social desirability of an approach that takes away citizens' rights with what they believed are very limited positive societal and personal benefits.

Psychiatric advanced directives (PADs) refer to legal documents created by competent individuals with mental illness in which they describe what mental health treatment they would like to receive should they be found incompetent at some point. The document can also include information about guardians who are allowed to make decisions about their mental health treatment. PADs are viewed as important in promoting self-determination. Some research suggests that they are associated with positive psychological benefits, but PADs remain controversial. Those with mental illnesses express concerns about their inability to predict what they want in the future and confusion over legal issues. Providers are in turn concerned that the treatment outlined by the individual in their PAD will prevent providers from providing treatment that they think is most appropriate.

Crisis intervention teams (CIT) refer to prebooking jail diversion programs, like that started in Memphis, Tennessee, involving a specially trained team of police officers with the skills to recognize and respond appropriately to anyone experiencing a psychiatric crisis. The goal is to reduce violent incidents between police and those with mental illnesses, avoid arrests and incarceration, and help provide needed treatment during acute illness episodes. The number of CIT programs across the country is expanding greatly. Limited research suggests that CIT can have many positive effects, including reduced arrests and reduction in violent incidents. Mental health advocates and providers generally accept CIT, but some police departments that fear loss of independence in how they operate do not support them. The research on their effectiveness is also limited. CIT is an example of one of many types of jail diversion programs that have been developed. More research is needed on the entire class of diversion interventions.

Specific Interventions

One of the most exciting developments in mental health services is interest in peer support programs—interventions in which interactions between persons with mental illnesses is the key element. Often at least one of these individuals is someone who is successfully coping, known as in recovery, with his or her illness. Many programs are developed and run by peers, but can also include programs in which peers provide traditional services such as case management and supported housing or employment. There is a growing interest in paid peer specialist positions, but peer support also occurs in self-help and mutual-aid groups. These efforts are considered a best practice based on a solid theory base, policy support, and a consistently favorable research base (Salzer and MHASP Best Practices Team 2002). The research conducted to date, however, has not involved randomized, controlled trials, with the exception of the multisite consumer-operated services program (COSP) funded by Center for Mental Health Services, whose results are promising but have not yet been published. Peer support interventions are now eligible in more than seven states for reimbursement as part of the federal Medicaid program.

Clubhouses refer to places in the community where people with mental illnesses go to develop new skills to live successfully in the community. The structure of clubhouse activities is based around work concepts, and regaining competitive employment is a central goal. A growing number of cross-sectional, longitudinal studies of clubhouses have shown positive effects on employment (for example, McKay et al. 2006). Randomized, controlled trials, however, are lacking. Clubhouses are fairly popular across the country and may grow in popularity as an alternative to partial hospitalization and other similar day treatment programs that are falling out of favor because they are viewed as not providing the supports to help people live successfully in the community. Clubhouse programs are not controversial except to the extent that they may be viewed as relatively expensive, especially compared to other employment-oriented programs.

Drop-in centers are also places in the community where people can come during the day. They focus on general social rehabilitation and psychoeducation, but in a relaxed, relatively unstructured setting. Some longitudinal studies have found positive psychological outcomes associated with participation in drop-in centers, and the results from the randomized, controlled COSP study mentioned earlier suggest that consumer-run drop-in centers have positive psychological outcomes. More rigorous research is needed, however. These programs are not controversial and are numerous across the country, but tend to be thought of as an ancillary program in mental health systems.

Supported education refers to a variety of supports to assist persons with mental illnesses in advancing their education. Education attainment goals can include taking and completing random classes of interest, obtaining a GED, or getting accepted into a postsecondary educational institution and obtaining a degree. Some research supports the benefits of supported education programs (see Mowbray et al. 2002).No randomized, controlled trials have been conducted, however. Interest in supported education is growing across the country, but relatively few programs currently exist. They are without question socially desirable because serious mental illnesses have been found to diminish educational attainment and education is a key factor of success in the labor market.

WHAT MENTAL HEALTH POLICY AREAS NEED CBA?

Studies of pharmacotherapy for various illnesses and possibly Assertive Community Treatment aside, there is a significant need for additional, high quality studies in all other areas. The social costs associated with serious mental illnesses are considerable. Optimism is growing, however, that new treatment and rehabilitation approaches can reduce these costs. Appropriate and efficient investments, including using currently available resources in more cost-effective ways, are needed. However, as in many areas of health care, identifying cost-effective interventions in mental health care does not always lead to their being used. For example, Theo Vos, Michelle Haby, and their colleagues (2005) argued that some treatments have been clearly identified as cost-effective and yet remain underused. They argue that reallocation of funds between disorders and service providers would be needed to ensure that these interventions are used at the appropriate levels.

Psychopharmacological Interventions
Although clearly perceived to be invaluable, the new psychotropic medications cost upward of ten to fifteen times the cost of old medications, raising serious cost-related questions. Much more research is needed in this area and should be considered a high priority, because psychotropic medications are quickly becoming one of the single highest cost

items in public mental health systems. One former administrator reported needing to make a trade-off between expanding his system's formulary to include more of the newer medications and funding other psychosocial programs (Luchins 2006).

A number of studies have examined the efficacy of the newer medications versus the older medications in terms of reducing hospitalizations, especially for schizophrenia, but this topic needs to be much more thoroughly studied, especially given that the savings resulting from bed-day reductions have not often been contrasted with medication costs. There has been some speculation that the newer medications are not cost-beneficial for those who have relatively few hospitalizations but are for those who have frequent and long hospitalizations. Finally, some researchers are also touting the social benefits of increased productivity and ability to work offered by some of these medications, mostly resulting from reduced side effects and improved cognitive benefits. Few studies that adequately document this socially desirable outcome and no cost-benefit analyses have been conducted. One item to keep in mind about studies in this area is that cost-benefit and cost-effectiveness expectations of any particular antipsychotic medication, new or old, are seriously hampered by the recent findings that very few people—fewer than 25 percent—stay on any particular medication for more than eighteen months (Lieberman et al. 2005).

Some specific cost-related studies are worth mentioning. For example, Aileen Roth-bard and her colleagues conducted a descriptive, longitudinal study and found that those on the newer medications for schizophrenia had higher inpatient service use and higher costs than those on the older medications (2005). Over a six-month period, they found average treatment costs (medications and services) of $6,528 for those receiving the newer medications alone and $6,589 for those receiving newer and older medications in combination versus $3,463 for those receiving only the older medications. Attempts to identify the net benefits of the newer medications, however, are often confounded because those receiving the newer medications have often failed on previous older medications and may have more severe illnesses. Stephen Stahl and Meghan Grady found that 17 percent of all patients receiving one of the newer antipsychotics also received at least one other of these medications, driving up costs by more than three times (2006). This practice, referred to as polypharmacy, has not been proven to be more effective than monotherapy.

Frank Gianfrancesco, Jacqueline Pesa, and Ruey-Hua Wang compared the differences in costs between some of the newer atypical antipsychotics in the treatment of bipolar disorder (2005). They reported that one medication (Olanzapine) appeared to be more costly than others per person per month. Dan Chisolm and his colleagues conducted a study examining various pharmacotherapies for the treatment of bipolar disorder (lithium versus valproic acid) combined with hospital and community services (2005). They found that lithium and community-based services were most cost-effective. Overall, very few similar studies have been conducted involving treatment for bipolar disorder.

Psychopharmacological treatments remain the treatment of choice in reducing symptoms of schizophrenia and bipolar disorder. Effective psychopharmacology and psychotherapy have both been developed for the treatment of major depression. However, depression is increasingly being treated with antidepressants, especially the newer, and more expensive, serotonin reuptake inhibitors (SSRIs). Studies have attempted to examine the relative cost-effectiveness of older and newer medications versus psychotherapy in treating depression. Depression has also been identified as a major factor in decreased work productivity. Studies of depression treatment as part of employment assistance programs (EAPs) have been conducted to examine costs and benefits in terms of reducing tardiness, loss of work days due to illness, and increased productivity. Some studies have found that the treatment of depression in general in work settings is associated with a positive return on investment (see Lo Sasso, Rost, and Beck 2006).

One study compared service use and expenses associated with persons with depression treated with the newer and more expensive SSRIs rather than with the older tricyclic antidepressants (TCAs) (Chung 2005). One major issue identified was that antidepressants were frequently prescribed for symptoms other than depression, especially the TCAs, which complicates the analysis of depression-related service use. Overall, when focusing on those persons receiving medications for depression symptoms, he found no differences in inpatient services, one of the largest expenditures for this population.

One of a growing number of recent cost-effectiveness studies compared pharmacotherapy, cognitive behavior therapy (CBT), and community referral to primary care in the community that could be considered usual care for low-income minority women (Revicki et al. 2005). The authors found that both pharmacotherapy and CBT were relatively equally cost-effective compared to community referral. A recent Australian study also found that pharmacotherapy and CBT were both cost-effective using a disability-adjusted life year (DALY) as the outcome measure (Vos, Corry et al. 2005). Pharmacotherapy, however, was somewhat less cost-effective and the authors raised concerns from a societal standpoint about increased dependence on pharmacotherapy treatments as the cornerstone in the treatment of depression.

One review of cost-effectiveness studies of the treatment of depression highlighted the fact that relatively more studies have been done in this area than for psychopharmacological studies of schizophrenia treatment and especially treatment of bipolar disorder (Barrett, Byford, and Knapp 2005). Barbara Barrett and her colleagues concluded that there is evidence for the cost-effectiveness of the newer SSRIs compared to the older medications, but that the evidence for the cost-effectiveness of psychotherapy is weaker, especially compared to medications. Overall, they challenged the quality of studies that have been conducted to date.

Assertive Community Treatment and Intensive Case Management

Case management services are plausibly the second most expensive type of ambulatory service frequently found in a public mental health system. Case management is usually reserved for those with the most serious illnesses who have a history of frequent and recent hospitalizations. These are often the individuals who use the most (and most costly) services. Many forms of case management exist, but only the Assertive Community Treatment (ACT) approach has been documented as an evidence-based practice. ACT has a lower staff-client ratio than most other approaches and is therefore more costly to implement. A few studies have examined the cost-effectiveness of it and other case management approaches. A comprehensive meta-analysis of these studies is desirable, but it is likely that one conclusion would be that much more research is needed to demonstrate the worth of case management services from a societal perspective. One complication in this area is that there is no standard form of intensive case management or standard case management beyond ACT. Clearly, this makes conclusions about their generic value difficult.

One of the early cost-effectiveness studies of ACT found that persons in ACT remained out of the hospital and in the community longer than those receiving other forms of case management, and at no additional costs (Essock, Frisman, and Kontos 1998). Robin Clark and colleagues found that ACT was not more cost-effective than standard case management services in terms of psychiatric symptoms, functioning, quality of life, and social costs (1998). Susan Johnston and her colleague reported results from a study of intensive case management (ICM) versus routine case management in Australia (2000). They found that ICM is more effective in terms of engaging people in treatment and improvement in functioning, but also more costly. They call for more research. Another Australian study also compared ICM and routine case management and report that the additional ICM costs were associated with a significant savings from reduced inpatient bed days and resulted in a cost savings (Preston and Fazio 2000).

Psychoeducational Approaches

Psychoeducational approaches for patients and families are touted as evidenced-based practices and are thought to be relatively inexpensive compared to pharmacotherapy, case management, and supported housing services. Low costs combined with significant quality of life benefits and possible reduced hospitalizations from enhanced treatment adherence could make them quite valuable. Nonetheless, they remain underused. Little is known about their costs and relative value from a societal perspective. Such information could increase the extent to which these types of programs are implemented in public mental health systems.

Supported Housing

A series of studies have recently been conducted on the costs and benefits associated with supported housing. Housing and homelessness are associated with costly inpatient, outpatient, and ancillary service use. These studies all demonstrate that supported housing approaches are associated with cost savings or cost neutrality. What is missing are studies that examine societal benefits in terms of increased community quality of life as a result of reduced homelessness and associated issues such as pandering), reduced crime, and potential increased employment.

Dennis Culhane and his colleagues (2002) conducted a matched control designed study comparing service costs for persons who were homeless in New York City who were placed in supported housing to costs for those who were not. They found that supported housing was associated with significant reductions in shelter use, hospitalizations, length of stay per hospitalization, and time incarcerated. Costs for services before placement were estimated to be $40,451 per person per year (1999 dollars) and were brought down to $16,281 after placement. Supported housing costs were estimated at $17,277, for a net fiscal cost of $995 per housed person per year. Kristine Jones and her colleagues compared service costs for individuals receiving one form of supported housing compared to usual care (2003). They found that the supported housing group had considerably fewer homeless nights at a negligible additional cost per nonhomeless night ($152). Finally, Robert Rosenheck and colleagues conducted a study examining the cost-effectiveness of a supported housing program for homeless veterans (2003). They also found the supported housing group to experience significantly fewer homeless nights at negligible additional costs ($45 per nonhomeless night).

Supported Employment
Cost-related studies of supported employment are incredibly scarce despite the great potential for significant societal benefits in this area in terms of reducing entitlement costs and reducing the disease burden of these illnesses that strike early in life. The issue is in critical need of additional study. Supported employment programs have been found to help people work and increase job tenure. Less discussed, however, are findings that the connection to the labor market remains tenuous (job tenure of four to six months), and income, even in the most promising studies, remains well below the poverty level and does not come close to supporting people in moving off of SSA and other entitlement programs. Maturot Chalamat and colleagues conducted an excellent analysis of supported employment and concluded that the costs associated with one of the most well-documented and effective programs—Individual Placement and Support—are almost twice what can be saved from implementing such a program across the system—10.3 million Australian dollars in costs versus 4.7 million in benefits (2005). They argued that economic disincentives inherent in the entitlement policies in Australia that decrease the willingness of persons to seek full-time employment and move off entitlement programs are signficant. Others have argued that similar disincentives are in the U.S. system as well (Baron and Salzer 2002). Studies of how changes in entitlement structures affect the willingness of persons to seek gainful employment are sorely needed.

PROMISING POLICIES

A number of promising policies that may be socially desirable are either controversial or lack research documenting their effectiveness. The effectiveness and costs associated with community- versus institutional-based care of persons with serious mental illnesses remains a critical question in need of further study, especially through CBA and CEA research. Aileen Rothbard and her colleagues found that treating persons in the community rather than in institutions was associated with a savings of $70,000 per year (1999). One review of studies examining the cost-effectiveness of community-based services found them to be effective and to cost the same or less than institutional care (Roberts, Cumming, and Nelson 2005). That review also identified a number of significant methodological problems in the studies examined, including poorly defined program costs. The authors see a need for determining the most cost-effective programs through additional research. More research, and more rigorous research on community-based services, is critical given that it is associated with potentially significant cost savings and that community-based treatment is considered more consistent with current legal, policy, and state-of-the-art treatment approaches.

Little or no CBA or CEA research has been conducted for the other policies mentioned: involuntary outpatient commitment, psychiatric advanced directives (PADs), and crisis intervention teams (CIT) and other jail diversion program. Studies of involuntary outpatient commitment and jail diversion programs are particularly important because they offer potentially significant cost savings through reduced inpatient bed and jail days.

Research on clubhouses examined their costs (McKay, Yates, and Johnsen 2007), but no CBA or CEA to assess their social desirability were conducted. Similarly, research on drop-in centers also examined costs, and found an average of $8 to support one individual per day, but with a wide discrepancy in terms of costs across thirty-two centers in Michigan (Holter and Mowbray 2005). The research also identified many factors associated with discrepancies in costs and services provided. No cost-effectiveness studies have been conducted involving drop-in centers to date. Some cost data, however, were gathered about drop-in centers and other peer support programs as part of the Center for Mental Health Services' multisite study of consumer-operated services. Data should soon be publicly available for analysis for those interested in these psychosocial interventions. It comes from a pre-post, matched comparison group controlled study comparing bed days for participants in a self-help and mutual-aid group to those not participating in the group. This study was conducted using data from the mid-1980s and found that those in the group experienced significantly fewer bed days in a three-year post-period. Another quasi-experimental study found that participants in a peer support program experienced fewer bed days compared to a similar group of individuals who did not (Min et al. 2007). Both studies suggest that this is a promising area that would benefit from CBA or CEA.

Finally, supported education may increase educational attainment that in turn might provide social benefits in terms of higher productivity resulting from longer job tenure. Further, employment has been found to be associated with lower symptomatology and better functioning, though the causal relationship is unclear. These potential gains make supported education a good candidate for cost-benefit or cost-effectiveness studies.

CONCLUSION

Overall, up-to-date research and data on the costs and benefits associated with mental illnesses are relatively scarce. Current direct and indirect costs estimates use data from the mid-1990s. Substantial structural and service changes have occurred since then that could arguably increase or decrease (or plausibly not change other than through inflation) the costs associated with these illnesses.

A critical first step in conducting cost-related studies is to improve the ability of public mental health systems around the country to track and document costs and service utilization better. This will require creating a more data-driven policy decision-making environment and substantially updating the data infrastructure and management information systems that at the state, county, and local levels are oftentimes antiquated, sometimes even using technology and human resource skills that are decades old. The Center for Mental Health Services (CMHS) with the Substance Abuse and Mental Health Services Administration has been working with states to document service use trends across the country, including the state and county mental institution census, and to make this information available online and in various reports. However, states are not required to provide the information. The result is that states are inconsistent in submitting their data, and the reliability of the data they do submit varies greatly. For example, Mark Salzer and his colleagues used one CMHS dataset to examine state hospital census (point-in-time count) over the past twenty years and found that approximately 10 percent of these most basic data had irregularities and inconsistencies (2006). In conclusion, cost-benefit and cost-effectiveness studies are sorely needed in mental health, but attention should be paid to the infrastructure of management information systems to ensure that cost and service use data of sufficient quality to support analysis are being collected.

REFERENCES

Baron, Richard C., and Mark S. Salzer. 2002. "Accounting for Employment among People with Mental Illness." *Behavioral Sciences & the Law* 20(6): 585–99.

Barrett, Barbara, Sarah Byford, and Martin Knapp. 2005. "Evidence of Cost-Effective Treatments for Depression: A Systematic Review." *Journal of Affective Disorders* 84(1): 1–13.

Bond, Gary, Robert E. Drake, Deborah Becker, and Kim Mueser. 1999. "Effectiveness of Psychiatric Rehabilitation Approaches for Employment of People with Severe Mental Illness." *Journal of Disability Policy Studies* 10(1): 18–52.

Bond, Gary R., Deborah R. Becker, Robert E. Drake, Charles A. Rapp, Neil Meisler, Anthony F. Lehman, Morris D. Bell, and Crystal R. Blyler. 2001. "Implementing Supported Employment as an Evidence-Based Practice." *Psychiatric Services* 52(3): 313–22.

Chalamat, Maturot, Cathrine Mihalopoulos, Rob Carter, and Theo Vos. 2005. "Assessing Cost-Effectiveness in Mental Health: Vocational Rehabilitation for Schizophrenia and Related Conditions." *Australian & New Zealand Journal of Psychiatry* 39(8): 693–700.

Chisholm, Dan, Mark van Ommeren, Jose-Luis Ayuso-Mateos, and Shekhar Saxena. 2005. "Cost-Effectiveness of Clinical Interventions for Reducing the Global Burden of Bipolar Disorder." *British Journal of Psychiatry* 187(December): 559–67.

Chung, Sukyung. 2005. "Does the Use of SSRIs Reduce Medical Care Utilization and Expenditures?" *Journal of Mental Health Policy & Economics* 8(3): 119–29.

Clark, Robin E., Gregory B. Teague, Susan K. Ricketts, Philip W. Bush, Haiyi Xie, Thomas G. McGuire, Robert E. Drake, Gregory J. McHugo, Adam M. Keller, and Michael Zubkoff. 1998. "Cost-Effectiveness of Assertive Community Treatment versus Standard Case Management for Persons with Co-Occurring Severe Mental Illness and Substance Use Disorders." *Health Services Research* 33(5): 1285–308.

Culhane, Dennis P., Steven Metraux, and Trevor Hadley. 2002. *Public Service Reductions Associated with Placement of Homeless Persons with Severe Mental Illness in Supportive Housing.* Washington, DC: Fannie Mae Foundation.

DeRubeis, Robert J., Lois A. Gelfand, Tony Z. Tang, and Anne D. Simons. 1999. "Medications versus Cognitive Behavioral Therapy for Severely Depressed Outpatients: Mega-Analysis of Four Randomized Comparisons." *American Journal of Psychiatry* 156(7): 1007–13.

DeRubeis, Robert J., Steven D. Hollon, Jay D. Amsterdam, Richard C. Shelton, Paula R. Young, Ronald M. Salomon, John P. O'Reardon, Margaret L. Lovett, Madeline M. Gladis, Laurel L. Brown, and Robert Gallop. 2005. "Cognitive Therapy vs Medications in the Treatment of Moderate to Severe Depression." *Archives of General Psychiatry* 62(4): 409–16.

Dickerson, Faith B. 2000. "Cognitive Behavioral Psychotherapy for Schizophrenia: A Review of Recent Empirical Studies." *Schizophrenia Research* 43(2-3): 71–90.

Dixon, Lisa, William R. McFarlane, Harriet Lefley, Alicia Lucksted, Michael Cohen, Ian Falloon, Kim Mueser, David Miklowitz, Phyllis Solomon, and Diane Sondheimer. 2001. "Evidence-Based Practices for Services to Families of People with Psychiatric Disabilities." *Psychiatric Services* 52(7): 903–10.

Essock, Susan M., Linda K. Frisman, and Nina J. Kontos. 1998. "Cost-Effectiveness of Assertive Community Treatment Teams." *American Journal of Orthopsychiatry* 68(2): 179–90.

Gianfrancesco, Frank, Jacqueline Pesa, and Ruey-Hua Wang. 2005. "Comparison of Mental Health Resources Used by Patients with Bipolar Disorder Treated with Risperidone, Olanzapine, or Quetiapine." *Journal of Managed Care Pharmacy* 11(3): 220–30.

Holter, Mark C., and Carol T. Mowbray. 2005. "Consumer-Run Drop-In Centers: Program Operations and Costs." *Psychiatric Rehabilitation Journal* 28(4): 323–31.

Insel, Thomas R. 2008. "Assessing the Economic Costs of Serious Mental Illness." *American Journal of Psychiatry* 165(6): 663–65.

Johnston, Susan, Glen Salkeld, Kristy Sanderson, Catherine Issakidis, Maree Teesson, and Neil Buhrich. 1998. "Intensive Case Management: A Cost-Effectiveness Analysis." *Australian & New Zealand Journal of Psychiatry* 32(4): 551–59.

Jones, Kristine, Paul Colson, Mark C. Holter, Shang Lin, Elie Valencia, Ezra Susser, and Richard Jed Wyatt. 2003. "Cost-Effectiveness of Critical Time Intervention to Reduce Homelessness among Persons with Mental Illness." *Psychiatric Services* 54(6): 884–90.

Kisely, S., L. A. Campbell, and N. Preston. 2005. "Compulsory Community and Involuntary Outpatient Treatment for People with Severe Mental Disorders." *The Cochrane Database of Systematic Reviews* 3. Art No: CD004408.pub2. DOI:10.1002/146518.CD004408.pub2. www.update-software.com/abstracts/AB004408.htm.

Lieberman, Jeffrey A., T. Scott Stroup, Joseph P. McEvoy, Marvin S. Swartz, Robert A. Rosenheck, Diana O. Perkins, Richard S. E. Keefe, Sonia M. Davis, Clarence E. Davis, Barry D. Lebowitz, Joanne Severe, John K. Hsiao, and Clinical Antipsychotic Trials of Intervention Effectiveness (CATIE) Investigators. 2005. "Effectiveness of Antipsychotic Drugs in Patients with Chronic Schizophrenia." *New England Journal of Medicine* 353(12): 1209–23.

Lo Sasso, Anthony T., Kathryn Rost, and Arne Beck. 2006. "Modeling the Impact of Enhanced Depression Treatment on Workplace Functioning and Costs: A Cost-Benefit Approach." *Medical Care* 44(4): 352–58.

Luchins, Daniel J. 2006. "Letter to the Editor." *Psychiatric Services* 57(1): 139–40.

McKay, Colleen E., Matthew Johnsen, Steven Banks, and Reva Stein. 2006. "Employment Transitions for Clubhouse Members." *WORK* 26(1): 67–74.

McKay, Colleen, Brian T. Yates, and Matthew Johnsen. 2007. "Costs of Clubhouses: An International Perspective." *Administration and Policy in Mental Health and Mental Health Services Research* 34(1): 62–72.

Min, So-Young, Jeanie Whitecraft, Aileen B. Rothbard, and Mark S. Salzer. 2007. "Peer Support for Persons with Co-Occurring Disorders and Community Tenure: A Survival Analysis." *Psychiatric Rehabilitation Journal* 30(3): 207–13.

Mowbray, Carol T., Kaaren Strauch Brown, Kathleen Furlong-Norman, and Anne Sullivan Soydan, eds. 2002. *Supported Education and Psychiatric Rehabilitation: Models and Methods*. Linthicum, MD: International Association of Psychosocial Rehabilitation Services.

Mueser, Kim T., Gary R. Bond, Robert E. Drake, and Sandra G. Resnick. 1998. "Models of Community Care for Severe Mental Illness: A Review of Research on Case Management." *Schizophrenia Bulletin* 24(1): 37–74.

Mueser, Kim T., Patrick W. Corrigan, David W. Hilton, Beth Tanzman, Annette Schaub, Susan Gingerich, Susan M. Essock, Nick Tarrier, Bodie Morey, Suzanne Vogel-Scibilia, and Marvin I. Herz. 2002. "Illness Management and Recovery: A Review of the Research." *Psychiatric Services* 53(10): 1272–84.

New Freedom Commission on Mental Health. 2003. *Achieving the Promise: Transforming Mental Health Care in America: Executive Summary*. DHHS Pub. No. SMA-03-3832. Rockville, MD: U.S. Department of Health and Human Services.

Preston, Neil Joseph, and Sam Fazio. 2000. "Establishing the Efficacy and Cost Effectiveness of Community Intensive Case Management of Long-Term Mentally Ill: A Matched Control Group Study." *Australian & New Zealand Journal of Psychiatry* 34(1): 114–21.

Revicki, Dennis, A., Juned Siddique, Lori Frank, Joyce Y. Chung, Bonnie L. Green, Janice Krupnick, Manishi Prasad, and Jeanne Miranda. 2005. "Cost-Effectiveness of Evidence-Based Pharmacotherapy or Cognitive Behavior Therapy Compared with Community Referral for Major

Depression in Predominantly Low-Income Minority Women." *Archives of General Psychiatry* 62(8): 868–75.

Ridgely, M. Susan, John Borum, and John Petralia. 2001. "The Effectiveness of Involuntary Outpatient Treatment: Empirical Evidence and the Experience of Eight States." Los Angeles, CA: RAND Corporation.

Roberts, Evan, Jacqueline Cumming, and Katherine Nelson. 2005. "A Review of Economic Evaluations of Community Mental Health Care." *Medical Care Research & Review* 62(5): 503–43.

Rosenheck, Robert, Wesley Kasprow, Linda Frisman, and Wen Liu-Mares. 2003. "Cost-Effectiveness of Supported Housing for Homeless Persons with Mental Illness." *Archives of General Psychiatry* 60(9): 940–51.

Rothbard, Aileen B., Eri Kuno, Arie P. Schinnar, Trevor R. Hadley, and Roland Turk. 1999. "Service Utilization and Cost of Community Care for Discharged State Hospital Patients: A 3-Year Follow-Up Study." *American Journal of Psychiatry* 156(6): 920–27.

Rothbard, Aileen, Mary Rose Murrin, Neil Jordan, Eri Kuno, Bentson H. McFarland, T. Scott Stroup, Joseph P. Morrissey, Paul G. Stiles, Roger A. Boothroyd, Elizabeth Merwin, David L. Shern. 2005. "Effects of Antipsychotic Medication on Psychiatric Service Utilization and Cost." *Journal of Mental Health Policy & Economics* 8(2): 83–93.

Salzer, Mark S. 2006. Introduction. In *Psychiatric Rehabilitation Skills in Practice: A CPRP Preparation and Skills Workbook*, ed. M.S. Salzer. Columbia, MD.: United States Psychiatric Rehabilitation Association.

Salzer, Mark S., Katy Kaplan, and Joanne Atay. 2006. "State Psychiatric Hospital Census Following the 1999 Olmstead Decision: Evidence of Decelerating Deinstitutionalization." *Psychiatric Services* 57(10): 1501–04.

Salzer, Mark S., and Mental Health Association of Southeastern Pennsylvania Best Practices Team. 2002. "Consumer-Delivered Services as a Best Practice in Mental Health Care and the Development of Practice Guidelines." *Psychiatric Rehabilitation Skills* 6(3): 355–82.

Stahl, Stephen M., and Meghan M. Grady. 2006. "High-Cost Use of Second-Generation Antipsychotics under California's Medicaid Program." *Psychiatric Services* 57(1): 127–29.

U.S. Department of Health and Human Services. 1999. *Mental Health: A Report of the Surgeon General—Executive Summary*. Rockville, MD: U.S. Department of Health and Human Services, Substance Abuse and Mental Health Services Administration, Center for Mental Health Services, National Institutes of Health, National Institute of Mental Health.

Vos, Theo, Justine Corry, Michelle M. Haby, Rob Carter, and Gavin Andrews. 2005. Cost-Effectiveness of Cognitive-Behavioural Therapy and Drug Interventions for Major Depression. *Australian & New Zealand Journal of Psychiatry* 39(8): 683–92.

Vos, Theo, Michelle M. Haby, Anne Magnus, Cathrine Mihalopoulos, Gavin Andrews, and Rob Carter. 2005. "Assessing Cost-Effectiveness in Mental Health: Helping Policy-Makers Prioritize and Plan Health Services." *Australian & New Zealand Journal of Psychiatry* 39(8): 701–12.

World Health Organization. 2001. *The World Health Report 2001—Mental Health: New Understanding, New Hope*. Geneva: World Health Organization.

Wu, Eric Q., Howard G. Birnbaum, Lizheng Shi, Daniel E. Ball, Ronald C. Kessler, Matthew Moulis, and Jyoti Aggarwal. 2005. "The Economic Burden of Schizophrenia in the United States in 2002." *Journal of Clinical Psychiatry* 66(9): 1122–29.

Chapter 6

Illicit Substance Abuse and Addiction

Jonathan P. Caulkins

In this chapter I provide a framework for understanding what is known, what is not known, and what could or should be known about the performance of various illicit drug control interventions from a social planner's return on taxpayer investment perspective. Because the scope of this task is ambitious, all topics must necessarily be covered briefly, with the value in the integrated view of the forest, not the details about any of the trees.

It is common to distinguish among four broad types of drug programs: supply control, prevention, treatment, and harm reduction. Such a simplistic partition has obvious limitations, but in the context of this volume they are outweighed by familiarity and transparency. I also include and discuss interventions that transcend the somewhat artificial boundaries of these four common types. In addition, some literature purports to estimate quantitatively the consequences of legalization.

It is important to note that the size and quality of the evidence base varies enormously across these intervention types (Reuter 2001). In FY 2005, the federal government spent $1.04 billion for research on drug treatment and prevention whereas the National Institute of Justice (the research arm of the Justice Department) funded just $6.4 million in drug-related research, of which the great majority (69 percent) was used to evaluate drug courts and Oxford House treatment programs (ONDCP 2006). Just $1.6 million (24 percent) fell under the heading Drugs and Crime Research, with half of that share going to Mistral Security, Inc. for the project Nontoxic Drug Detection and Identification Aerosol Technology. The remaining 7 percent was for evaluating Indian Alcohol and Substance Abuse Demonstration Programs, which include law enforcement, prevention, and treatment components.

In round numbers, the federal government invests about 500 times as much studying demand-side programs as it does supply-side programs even though the latter account for two-thirds of the U.S. drug control budget. This gross imbalance has two implications. First, relatively modest investments can greatly advance practical understanding about the effectiveness of supply control strategies because much low-hanging fruit remains to be harvested. Second, supply control studies have less research and data on which to build and so may not always meet stringent standards of academic rigor.

It is also important to note that the drug system is complex, and interventions can have many indirect or delayed effects that are important, perhaps even more so than the direct effects. For example, interventions that reduce the spread of infectious disease (HIV/AIDS, HCV, TB, and the like) have spillover effects. Preventing one person from becoming infected can also avert secondary infections the first person would otherwise have caused. Quantifying indirect and lagged effects is often tenuous, so the field wrestles with the choice between more rigorous quantification of a subset of effects and more speculative quantification of the totality of effects.

A third point is that most treatment interventions operate at the individual or family level. Hence it is conceptually if not practically straightforward to imagine collecting data directly on the social costs and benefits of outcomes (employment and earnings, health, for example) and comparing them to corresponding outcomes for a control group. In contrast, many prevention programs (such as media campaigns) operate at the community level, and most supply-control interventions seek to alter market conditions. For them, it is often more natural to evaluate programs in terms of their effect on drug use (such as kilograms of use averted per million dollars), and then perhaps to convert those reductions in use into presumed social benefit using some simple shadow price (for example, an average of $215 in social costs averted per gram of cocaine not consumed).

The cost of illness (COI) studies underpinning such shadow prices are subject to many criticisms, some correctable, such as failure to disaggregate by type of drug or user, and others all but intrinsic to the domain, such as omitting spillover effects on human capital formation (Moore and Caulkins 2006; see also Collins and Lapsley 2002; Harwood, Fountain, and Livermore 1998). Furthermore, crime and violence figure prominently in policy analysis pertaining to drug control in the United States. Notwithstanding some impressive analyses there is no consensus on how to put dollar values on crime reductions (see Miller, Cohen, and Wiersema 1996; Rajkumar and French 1997). A classic conundrum concerns property crime (such as theft or burglary). From an academic perspective, some economists argue that there is no social cost when stolen goods are merely transferred from one citizen (the victim) to another (the offender). Drug policy, however, is the product of a political process beholden to voters who at best roll their eyes at such arguments. Other crimes whose costs are difficult to monetize include homicides, sexual assault, and child abuse. Likewise, it is much easier to calculate the cost to taxpayers per year of imprisonment than it is to estimate the full social cost of imprisonment.

Hence, some return on investment studies avoid using these conversion factors, stopping with a cost-effectiveness result (for example, kilograms averted per million taxpayer dollars). Not surprisingly, it is treatment evaluations for which economists are most likely to monetize all outcomes in a cost-benefit analysis (CBA) that results in a bottom line (for example, French et al. 2002).

The approach here is to emphasize results that appear to be the most important for policymakers, rather than to focus only on those that are most reliable to a scientific purist or only those conducted within what might formally be construed as a CBA frame-work in the sense of monetizing every outcome.

SUPPLY CONTROL

The evidence base does not support rigorous return on investment analyses of sup-ply control programs for at least three reasons. First, it is rarely possible to conduct experiments, let alone randomized controlled trials, particularly of national drug enforcement policies. Second, data systems are weak. Third, supply control is pri-marily the bailiwick of law enforcement, and justice agencies do not have the same scientific culture or evidence-based practice norms as do public health and medical researchers.

Nevertheless, supply control interventions absorb the great bulk of drug control spending in the United States, they set the context (a prohibition framework) within which all other interventions operate, and they generate important side effects. They contribute to the high rates of incarceration among African American males, with atten-dant consequences for human capital formation, prison-based spread of infectious dis-ease, disruption of families and parenting, and in some states even disenfranchisement of significant numbers of potential voters (Mauer 2002). Not attempting some quantifica-tion of supply control programs' performance would thus be like writing a review for an auto magazine that discussed a car's sound system but not its engine.

Beyond some early systems dynamics studies, RAND's Drug Policy Research Cen-ter pioneered attempts to use "risks and prices" equilibrium market models to estimate how effective various supply control programs could be at reducing U.S. cocaine use (Reuter and Kleiman 1986; Rydell and Everingham 1994; Rydell, Caulkins, and Ever-ingham 1996; see also Levin, Roberts, and Hirsch 1975; Gardiner and Schreckengost 1987; Homer 1993). The basic paradigm was that law enforcement imposes costs on drug suppliers that are passed along to users in the form of higher prices. It is well established that drug use is inversely related to price—the demand curve for drugs slopes downward just as it does for essentially all goods (Grossman 2004). So such en-forcement "taxes" ought to reduce drug use. The RAND studies generally found that though it is cheaper to seize large quantities of cocaine in South America than at the borders and easier to seize large quantities by interdiction than by domestic enforce-ment within the United States, the cost-effectiveness in terms of kilograms of cocaine consumption averted per million program dollars was exactly the opposite, in part be-cause cocaine is so much cheaper upstream in the distribution network that it is easy to replace offshore seizures. Within the United States, enforcement against high-level dealers was modeled as having a greater impact on consumption than enforcement against low level dealers, again in part because low-level dealers are so easy to replace Kleiman 1997).

This pessimistic view of interdiction and source country control's effectiveness was unwelcome news to certain supply control hawks, and a competing study soon emerged reaching the opposite conclusions (Crane, Rivolo, and Comfort 1997). Superficially, the studies reach diametrically opposing conclusions, but careful reading reveals that they do not contradict each other as much as address different questions. One difference pertained to assumptions about how cost increases at one market level are passed along to lower market levels. The RAND studies took the traditional view of nearly additive price transmission whereas the study by Barry Crane and his colleagues presumed a multiplicative mechanism, so that a 50 percent increase in the upstream price would lead to a 50 percent increase in the retail price (for clarification of the additive versus multiplicative models, see Caulkins 1990, 1994; for a review of empirical evidence, see Caulkins and Hao 2008). Second, the Crane study looked at short-term disruptions that were not anticipated by the market, whereas the RAND studies considered effects on the long-run equilibrium of ongoing control efforts to which the markets have had time to adjust (Caulkins, Chiesa, and Everingham 2000).

Together the two studies and others like them suggest the following. Those who believe the multiplicative model pertains at higher distribution levels may conclude that interdiction materially increases retail prices of imported drugs and can also be cautiously optimistic about interdiction's and source zone enforcement's ability to create occasional transitory price spikes. Absent that belief, interdiction and—to an even greater extent— source country operations have at most minor effects on drug use. Crop substitution and alternative development programs in particular have never been shown to have any impact on drug use in the United States.

Nevertheless, a National Research Council review commissioned to reflect on these studies dismissed both and argued, as did a companion piece, that the evidence base was at present simply too weak to support scientific evaluation of the benefits and costs of drug law enforcement (Manski, Pepper, and Thomas 1999; Manski, Pepper, and Petrie 2001). The NRC study missed the mark in important respects, but nevertheless clearly put a damper on subsequent efforts to assess quantitatively the performance of drug supply control from a perspective of social costs and benefits (Caulkins, Chiesa, and Everingham 2000).

One of the few studies completed since then addressed what is perhaps the most perplexing observation concerning U.S. drug markets over the last twenty-five years (Kuziemko and Levitt 2004). The number of people incarcerated for drug-law violations has increased more than ten-fold since the beginning of the Reagan-era drug war, and has now reached 500,000. The vast majority of those imprisoned were involved in drug distribution (Caulkins and Sevigny 2005), yet prices of the principal illicit drugs have fallen sharply (Caulkins et al. 2004). Ilyana Kuziemko and Steven Levitt concluded that prices would have fallen even farther had incarceration not expanded (2004). In particular, they credited the 1985–1996 increase in the number of drug-law violators behind bars—which Jonathan Caulkins and Sara Chandler estimated to be from 82,000 to 376,000—with raising cocaine prices by 5 to 15 percent above what they otherwise would have been (Kuziemko and Levitt 2004; Caulkins and Chander 2006). Still, that is far less than risks-and-prices-based models would have predicted (essentially 5 versus 27.5 kilograms per million taxpayer dollars spent, respectively). Furthermore, uncertainty about the social cost per year of imprisonment, as opposed to its budgetary cost to taxpayers, leaves open the question of what the overall cost-benefit ratio of this incarceration is.

PREVENTION

Not surprisingly, people who work in the prevention field are excited about prevention programs with "promising" initial evaluations and believe their field is making progress. They speak of having created a new discipline (Prevention Science), and stress the gap between what they see as proven or model programs and what is implemented in practice (for example, Hawkins, Catalano, and Arthur 2002). A number of scholars, however, are increasingly skeptical that prevention has any material effect on drug use.

To oversimplify, one might distinguish three schools of thought concerning prevention. The optimists believe that prevention works and is cost-effective, and that the main challenge is getting the proven programs adopted in practice. The skeptics are decidedly negative about prevention and explain the small minority of studies that return statistically significant effects as the inevitable result of conducting a very large number of evaluations. After all, 5 percent of evaluations of a placebo will find statistically significant effect when the probability of Type I error is set at the 0.05 level in hypothesis testing. Between these extremes are a few researchers who believe that in certain contexts and for certain behaviors prevention interventions are cost-effective, but that the average performance is far below what the hype or hopes suggest.

The plurality if not outright majority of evaluations pertain to school-based programs, so it is helpful to distinguish school-based programs from all other forms of prevention, which are addressed more briefly later.

School-Based Prevention

An enormous literature evaluates school-based prevention programs but is disappointing in several respects. First, the great majority of studies do not meet standards of quality needed to be trustworthy. Second, many interventions seem to affect knowledge about or attitudes toward drugs, but not actual drug use. Notably poor performers are scare tactics, information-based programs, and affective interventions. Social skills and so-called comprehensive programs seem more promising. In particular, the most widely implemented prevention program (DARE) has fared quite badly in past evaluation studies, though there is some evidence that DARE Plus is better (Perry et al. 2003). Third, most studies have short follow-up periods (one to three years), and few follow subjects beyond the end of high school. These follow-up periods are not necessarily short when compared to treatment evaluations, but a key difference is that treatment clients are already generating substantial social costs. In contrast, the targets of primary prevention are for the most part not yet using heavily, so if prevention is ever to have notable effects, it must have long-term effects, which is not true of treatment. Fourth, most long-term evaluations show decay over time in differences between treatment and control subjects in lifetime prevalence, often disappearing entirely by the end of high school. There is no consensus, nor indeed any empirical basis, for projecting what such delays in initiation portend for lifetime consumption. Historically, those who start earlier in the absence of an intervention tend to consume more over their lifetime. Prevention programs that delay initiation may therefore also cause a reduction in lifetime consumption, but this is an assumption or subjective belief, not an empirically established effect.

A recent review concluded that skills-based programs, as opposed to those that focus on teaching knowledge about drugs, do reduce drug use (Faggiano et al. 2005). However, with some exceptions, true CBA studies of prevention are exceedingly rare because the evaluation literature gives information about effects on self-reported prevalence of risk factors, such as tobacco or marijuana use, among program participants through the end of high school, whereas a CBA needs information about actual amounts, such as kilograms, of use averted of the drugs associated with the greatest social costs throughout the lifetimes of all people affected by the program, including spillover effects on nonparticipants (for exceptions, see Plotnick 1994; Kim et al. 1995; Pentz 1998). A CBA thus has to bridge quite a few gaps between what is known and what is needed, as shown in table 6.1.

RAND's Drug Policy Research Center built models to bridge these gaps and thereby support CBA of school-based drug prevention programs (Caulkins, Rydell, et al. 1999; Caulkins, Paddock, et al. 2002). Some pieces of the bridge were simple, for example, assuming a 40 percent hit to effectiveness when moving from supervision by a charismatic program inventor to large-scale bureaucratic implementation. Some were more complicated, for example, using epidemic models to project a 30 percent social multiplier boost in effectiveness from spillover effects on friends and associates. A critical assumption was that 90 percent of the historical correlation between age of onset and lifetime use carried over to projecting the lifetime consequences of delaying initiation. Collectively, these modeling assumptions generated enormous error bands around projections, to the point that the first book was titled *An Ounce of Prevention, A Pound of Uncertainty* and the analytic framework was explicitly designed to allow readers to type in their own beliefs and recalculate the implications on the bottom line. Nevertheless, to the extent that one is interested in the results of such modeling exercises, there are six conclusions. First, the point estimate of social benefits from reduced substance use per program participant ($840) is larger than the point estimate of the full social cost of implementing the program ($150 per participant). Second, the positive cost-benefit ratio is quite robust with respect to uncertainty about parameters, though of course does depend on struc-

Table 6.1   Gaps between Traditional Focus and Information Needed

Literature Tells Us	What BC Studies Need to Know
self-reported prevalence of marijuana use	actual quantity of all drugs (especially hard drugs)
through twelfth grade	over lifetime
by program participants	by all affected
a past RCT experiment	a future scaled-up program

Source: Author.

tural assumptions such as the ability to use historical correlations between age of onset and lifetime use. Third, the positive cost-benefit ratio comes mostly from prevention being cheap; the absolute effect on lifetime substance use is in the single digit percentage reductions. Fourth, the majority of the social benefits stem from reduced use of alcohol and tobacco. Fifth, spillover effects on people not in the program may be quite large. And, sixth, the social costs are dominated by the opportunity cost of not using classroom time to teach academic subjects.

Other Prevention Programs

However unsatisfying the evidence is concerning school-based prevention's cost-effectiveness, the situation is all the worse for nonschool based programs, in part because the category of nonschool programs includes an extremely heterogeneous mix of interventions. A recent review located only seventeen high-quality articles, and they were limited to four specific types of nonschool interventions: motivational interviewing or brief intervention, education or skills training, family interventions, and multicomponent community interventions (Gates et al. 2006). "There is a lack of evidence of effectiveness of the included interventions," the authors concluded. "Motivational interviewing and some family interventions may have some benefit. Cost-effectiveness has not yet been addressed in any studies, and further research is needed to determine whether any of these interventions can be recommended" (1).

Despite the paucity of evidence, three types of interventions not addressed by the review merit at least brief mention. The first is a media campaign. The logic is appealing: Harness the same social marketing talents that drive consumer trends, but do so in reverse—to discourage rather than encourage consumption. Furthermore, antitobacco campaigns that are in some ways similar have fared well in evaluations (Niederdeppe et al. 2004). The approach has come a long way since the days of the egg-frying ads sponsored by the Partnership for a Drug Free America, for example, with messages targeted at parents encouraging them to talk to their children about drugs. In FY 2006, the Office of National Drug Control Policy invested $99 million in its national media campaign (2006), not including corporate matching contributions. Evaluating such campaigns is extremely difficult because it is hard to know what exposure dose any given individual received. Nonetheless, the evaluations to date of effects on drug use, as opposed to marketing metrics such as recall of having seen the ad, have been negative or inconclusive (Homik et al. 2003).

The second nonschool prevention modality that merits mention is community-level efforts. Perhaps the best known is the Fighting Back initiative begun in 1990 in about fifteen communities around the nation with annual funding provided by the Robert Wood Johnson Foundation of $2 million to $3 million per community. Evaluation results from community-level interventions often are what might be called process evaluation or intermediate outcomes pertaining to whether the community could organize and what actions were taken. Data on drug use and drug-related problems are harder to gather and analyze. For example, the Fighting Back outcomes evaluation made prominent use of alcohol-related fatalities in the Fatal Accident Reporting System database.

Community-based interventions are diverse, and it seems likely that one intervention in one community might perform substantially better or worse than another intervention in another community. Yet, it is sobering that evaluations of Fighting Back, which might be construed as the flagship among community-level interventions, were not terribly positive and, at least in some cases, suggested perverse negative effects (for example, Hallfors et al. 2002).

Finally, some observers note that interventions that are not drug-specific may sometimes have a greater effect on drug use than drug prevention programs per se. Notably, the Good Behavior Game is a first-grade intervention designed to improve classroom management, but evaluations have found substantial reductions in hard drug use for program participants relative to controls at junior high school follow up (Furr-Holden et al. 2004).

TREATMENT

Treatment is the best-studied of the various broad strategies for drug control. The conventional mantra is that treatment works not only for the client, in the sense of improving his or her life outcomes, but also in the sense of being a good societal investment (Cartwright 2000; Harwood et al. 2002). Steven Belenko, Nicholas Patapsis, and Michael French published not long ago a readable and insightful critical review of the economic benefits of drug treatment based on 109 economic evaluations of treatment published between 1990 and 2004 (2005). In view of the size of this literature and the availability of the Belenko review on-line, comments here will focus on a few key points that help explain and qualify the treatment works mantra.

First, it is important to note that, at least for hard drugs, dependent substance abusers create such enormous social costs that even interventions with modest success rates can look great from a return on investment perspective. In round terms, a dependent U.S. cocaine user spends about $10,000 per year on cocaine that costs about $100 per pure gram, implying consumption on the order of 100 pure grams per year. It appears that average social costs are on the order of $215 per pure gram of cocaine (Caulkins et al. 2002). That suggests an annual social cost per dependent cocaine user upward of $20,000 per year. Annual social costs per opiate user may be even higher because of the greater risks of transmitting blood-borne diseases with injected drugs.

Furthermore, residual career lengths are not short, meaning that in the absence of treatment, the approximately $20,000 per year social cost would be incurred for many years to come. Studies that follow treatment clients over extended periods find that many of those who do not die continue using (Hser et al. 2001, 2006). Hence an intervention that managed to persuade a dependent user who would have consumed for another ten years to cease use permanently would generate a social benefit on the order of $200,000. If the average cost per treatment admission is in the vicinity of $2,000, incremental success rates of just a percent or two can be enough to produce a favorable cost-benefit ratio.

Nevertheless, the rosy picture needs to be qualified in certain respects. First, treatment success is not uniform across drugs. We have effective pharmacotherapies and by far the strongest evidence for cost-effectiveness for opiates (such as heroin). There is also reasonably good evidence that treatment works with marijuana dependence, though the cost-benefit calculus for cannabis looks different because the social cost per person-year of dependent use is much lower and the untreated duration of dependent use may be shorter.

In contrast, the technology for treating stimulants (cocaine, including crack, and various amphetamines including methamphetamine) is far less developed, and they account for three-quarters of drug-related social costs in the United States. Considerable funding has been invested in research on pharmacotherapies for cocaine but with no dramatic breakthroughs. So treatment professionals must rely primarily on standard talk therapies or innovative nonpharmacological interventions such as contingency management (or coerced abstinence, which I discuss shortly). Although some authors have reported favorable cost-benefit ratios for cocaine treatment, the NRC was decisively negative concerning the lack of rigorous evidence concerning cocaine treatment efficacy, holding that there is no solid evidence on which one could estimate effectiveness let alone cost-effectiveness (see, for example, Flynn et al. 1999; Manski, Pepper, and Petrie 2001). In particular, before and after studies are vulnerable to regression to the mean and other statistical problems, and there is a dearth of solid evidence from randomized controlled trials. Angela Hawken included a review of cost-benefit ratio studies of treatment, and almost all rest on before and after designs, including such classics as those of Dean Gerstein and colleagues and of Henrik Harwood, Douglas Fountain, and Gina Livermore (Hawken 2006; Gerstein et al. 1994; Harwood, Fountain, and Livermore 1998).

One irony is that within the treatment community belief about the benefits of treatment is so widespread that institutional review boards would generally reject as unethical any study that randomly assigned dependent users to a no-treatment condition. So it is not clear how evidence could ever be produced in the United States that would change the mind of the NRC skeptics.

Instead, many treatment studies look for differences in effectiveness between one program and another. The literature is vast, so no simplistic generalizations can do it justice, but it is not uncommon to find at most modest differences in outcomes across programs (for example, Morral et al. 2006). Skeptics say that is because no program achieves much and apparent benefits are statistical artifacts such as regression to the mean. The more charitable view is that drug dependence is a general condition with a host of correlated social problems, and the purely medical model of matching the right medical technology to the right specific diagnosis is therefore misguided.

One possible exception to this general pattern of failure to develop advanced medical technologies for treating stimulant abuse is immunotherapies, or vaccines, against cocaine and methamphetamine, as well as some other substances, including nicotine. These immunotherapies work by having antibodies bind to and inactivate drug molecules. Animal trials and early research with humans are intriguing (Harwood 2003). Mark Kleiman offered a preliminary cost-benefit projection based on early data and educated guesses, but updating that work based on the recently completed Phase II clinical trials might be valuable (2003).

The second qualification to the treatment works mantra is that many treatment professionals do not like to even think about evaluating programs in terms of proportions of people who become permanently abstinent. They stress that drug dependence is a chronic relapsing condition akin to diabetes, that one should think of managing that chronic condition rather than curing it, and thus that most of the benefits accrue while the client is in treatment, not from changed behavior subsequent to and as a result of treatment (McLellan et al. 2005).

In-treatment effects can cost justify programs. Suppose a program cost $10,000 per year and had 100 percent relapse rate the moment clients left the program, but that during treatment drug-related social costs were reduced by 60 percent. Inasmuch as 60 percent of $20,000 in social costs per user-year is greater than the $10,000 per year program cost, such a program could be cost justified. Indeed, a number of CBA studies (for example, Pollack 2001) have argued that drug treatment can be a good social investment even if it has no effect on drug use, simply by virtue of reducing social harms associated with that use, notably HIV transmission (compare Zaric, Barnett, and Brandeau 2000).

Third, there is no reason to think the return-on-investment for treatment is the same for all subpopulations. The classic example is the possibility of greater social benefits when treating pregnant women, though in view of Harold Pollack's observations about "crack babies" being primarily a pediatric not an obstetric problem, this logic might extend to all drug-dependent parents of young children, not just women who are currently pregnant (2000). On the order of 1 million children live with one or more parents who are dependent on illicit drugs.

Similarly, as a large proportion of the social costs associated with illicit drug use pertains to drug-related crime, the cost-benefit ratio from treating criminally involved dependent users may be higher than that for treating drug dependent users more generally. To be more precise, the key distinction is probably not between those who have or have not ever committed a crime, because some degree of criminal involvement is so common. Rather, the key distinction is between high-frequency and less than high-frequency offenders. The highly skewed distribution of offense rates implies that a small subset of criminals are responsible for a grossly disproportionate proportion of all offending (Blumstein, Canela-Cacho, and Cohen 1993).

HARM REDUCTION

Outside the United States, harm reduction is often seen as a co-equal fourth category of drug control interventions, on a par with enforcement, treatment, and prevention. Three points are important to make with respect to harm reduction. First, it can refer to an overall philosophy of drug control policy. When viewed in that way, rigorous data concerning effectiveness is scant because it tends to be implemented at the jurisdiction level, often for an entire country, and because no relevant comparison group exists. Cross-national comparisons are instructive at the conceptual and qualitative level (MacCoun and Reuter 2001), but rarely provide a solid basis for quantitative estimation of return on investment. The potential for quantitative evaluation is greater for specific harm reduction interventions, as opposed to general philosophies of drug control.

Second, one must distinguish between needle and syringe exchange programs (NSP) on the one hand, and everything else on the other hand. The body of literature evaluating NSPs, including return on investment studies, is large. NSPs are controversial in the United States, with some worry about sending the wrong message or otherwise stimulating drug use, but the predominant consensus in the academic literature is that NSPs are an effective way to reduce the spread of HIV/AIDS and, not surprisingly given the social cost of AIDS, that they are cost-effective. Alison Ritter and Jacqui Cameron's systematic review of harm reduction interventions found NSP cost-effectiveness in the range of $4,000 to $35,000 per HIV infection averted (2005). Ritter and Cameron also described the literature as being "predominantly positive" with respect to Hepatitis C (HCV) control, though Pollack highlighted the marked differences between HIV and HCV control (Ritter and Cameron 2005, 19; Pollack 2001). In brief, the HCV virus is so much more robust that HCV prevalence can be very high even in populations following harm reduction practices sufficient to keep HIV prevalence at very low levels.

Ritter and Cameron described the quantitative, scientific evidence base evaluating all other harm reduction interventions as being much thinner. For example, of the 680 evaluations reviewed, more than half (344) pertained to NSPs. Fewer than 10 percent pertained to the second most frequently evaluated harm reduction intervention, supervised injection facilities (SIFs), which seek to reduce health problems and disorder associated with drug use by allowing drugs obtained elsewhere to be consumed on premises with no risk of arrest and typically with some form of supervision.

Third, Timothy Moore and Henk Rigter showed that even in countries such as Australia and the Netherlands that pursue harm reduction fairly vigorously, the budgetary costs of harm reduction are minor compared to the costs of other forms of drug control (Moore 2005; Rigter 2006). Hence, it may be that if harm reduction is effective at all, and does not produce perverse results, then it would be cost-effective because the costs are so low that large effects are not needed to pass a cost-effectiveness threshold.

INTEGRATIVE INTERVENTIONS

Not all interventions fall neatly into a supply-control, prevention, treatment, or harm reduction bin. For example, there are models of how the cost-effectiveness of interventions vary over the course of a drug epidemic that find that enforcement is relatively most cost-effective early, in the explosive growth stage of an epidemic, whereas treatment and harm reduction may be more useful later, in the endemic stage (Behrens et al. 1999, 2000, 2001; Tragler, Caulkins, and Feichtinger 2001; Caulkins 2005). Employee, athlete, and student drug testing programs are another example. Testing is common, with about half of full-time employees working for firms that drug test. The literature on drug-testing is modestly large, which Robert MacCoun has commented on insightfully (2007). Some strands are quantitative, but, with some exceptions, there are few return-on-investment studies at the societal or even organizational level (see Baker, Lattimore, and Matheson 1996).

Likewise, Lorraine Mazerolle and her colleagues' systematic review of drug law enforcement found that proactive interventions involving partnerships between police and other entities appear to be more promising than traditional policing interventions (2006). In particular, several interventions at the intersection of law enforcement and treatment merit investigation within a CBA framework.

Drug and DWI Courts

Perhaps the best-known partnership between criminal justice and treatment are drug courts, which now number more than 1,200 nationwide. These courts come in many varieties, but generally they allow on a case-by-case basis for nonviolent drug offenders to be sentenced to treatment in lieu of standard prosecution. They typically involve frequent visits before the court and often urinalysis to monitor the defendant's progress, with the judge meting out graduated punishments and rewards in response to progress or backsliding, with poor performance leading to a jail or prison sentence (Shanahan et al. 2004).

Similar to the literature on conventional treatment programs, nonexperimental studies that compare those who complete the program to those who do not, those ineligible for the program, or the clients before the program suggest drug courts offer a very favorable return on investment. However, such nonexperimental studies are vulnerable to biases that undermine the credibility of their conclusions, as Steven Belenko in particular has noted (2001). Christine Eibner and her colleagues reported that experimental and quasi-experimental studies produced mixed results (Eibner et al. 2006; for favorable results, see, Gottfredson et al. 2005; for unfavorable results, see Deschenes, Turner, and Greenwood 1995).

The popularity of drug courts has spawned similar innovations in other areas. Of particular interest are DWI-DUI courts because total deaths (about 17,000 per year) and economic costs (more than $100 billion per year) associated with alcohol-impaired driving are somewhat smaller but still of comparable magnitude to acute deaths and social costs associated with all illicit drug use overall (Freeman-Wilson and Huddleston 1999). Yet, there have been few CBA studies of DWI courts. Eibner and her colleagues may have come the closest, examining a DWI court in Los Angeles for which outcomes were similar to those achieved with standard judicial processing, but at a lower cost for some (specifically, third-time) offenders (2006). The paucity of CBA literature on DWI courts relative to conventional drug courts suggests that there is relatively greater need and potentially greater benefit from additional economic evaluations of DWI courts.

Prison Diversion or Treatment in Lieu of Incarceration

Treatment-in-lieu-of-incarceration policies, such as California's Proposition 36 passed in 2000, are like drug courts in that they divert nonviolent offenders away from prison while being more intensive than probation without treatment. However, they, or at least California's Proposition 36, differ in certain respects. Proposition 36 applies across the board to all eligible offenders, rather than being available at judicial discretion on a case by case basis, and under Proposition 36 any discretion concerning treatment for eligible participants (for example, those without violent prior convictions) is made by medical professionals, not judges. Also, the subsequent monitoring is modest. Indeed, only about 25 percent of offenders complete their treatment (Hawken 2006). Angela Hawken has shown persuasively that Proposition 36 saved the state of California money (2006). However, as of yet there has not been a comparable analysis of Proposition 36 from a social costs and benefits rather than a budgetary perspective.

Coerced Abstinence

Mark Kleiman suggested taking the judge and the individual discretion out of drug courts, replacing them with a simple, well-defined and unyielding system of graduated sanctions for failing drug tests (1997). If the offender thinks he or she needs treatment to stay clean, then treatment can be made available. However, those who can achieve abstinence on their own are welcome to do so. In principle, coerced abstinence can be scaled up to larger sizes than can drug courts because it makes less intensive use of scarce judicial and treatment services. In practice, it is a difficult concept to implement because of the lack of coordination between various agencies (courts, probation, prison, and so on). Nevertheless, Kleiman observed that the great majority of the cocaine and heroin consumed in the United States is used by probationers and parolees who are nominally under criminal justice supervision. Current case loads make that supervision all but vacuous, but if it were made real, for example, by frequent testing with certain and swift but not draconian sanctions, there is at least in principle the potential to eliminate the bulk of the problematic drug use in the United States. No other intervention can credibly make such a claim.

Notable attempts to implement the coerced abstinence principles occurred in Birmingham, Alabama; Jacksonville, Florida; and Tacoma, Washington. The coerced abstinence model was not fully implemented; for example, sanctions for failed drug tests were too mild, primarily because of substantial challenges in coordinating across bureaucratic boundaries. Nevertheless, evaluations found reduced drug use, crime, and family problems, and offered a favorable cost-benefit ratio in all three sites (Harrell et al. 2003; Mitchell and Harrell 2006).

The Hawaii Attorney General's Office has led a similar project called HOPE (Hawaii's Opportunities for Probation with Enforcement) that might have been more successful at integrating the various relevant components of the criminal justice system, but it has not been formally evaluated, let alone subjected to a true CBA.

LEGALIZATION STUDIES

When a nation bans a psychoactive drug, it creates a black market, and black markets generate a variety of harms, notably crime, corruption, and control costs, but also increased health harms, because the drugs contain harmful adulterants or ingestion is more harmful than it otherwise would be (for example, more likely to be injected with nonsterile syringes). So prohibition's benefits of reductions in use that are caused by higher prices, lower purity, lower availability, social stigma, or criminal sanction risk are to some extent offset by a different set of costs or harms. Conversely, legalizing a currently banned substance would avert a great many social costs associated with the black markets but increase use and potentially use-related harms by some unknown extent.

For every important substance except marijuana there is essentially no serious empirical base on which to build a cost-benefit analysis of legalization because no modern, developed nation has ever legalized substances such as cocaine or heroin. Several have decriminalized and most have far less stringent forms of prohibition than the United States, but none have made production, distribution, possession, and use legal for recreational purposes. In 2001, Robert MacCoun and Peter Reuter published the definitive study of what can be learned about legalization by investigating other times, places, and vices, and they are largely agnostic, cautioning against drawing too firm conclusions. Structural assumptions about the nature of the demand curve over price ranges for which we have no empirical data can dramatically affect projected effects on drug use (Caulkins 2001). Although one cannot reliably quantify the benefits and costs of legalizing any of the major drugs except possibly marijuana, that has not stopped people from trying, particularly economists who are predisposed to believe that free markets reliably maximize net social benefits (see, for example, Clark 2003; Becker, Grossman, and Murphy 2006).

CBA of marijuana regime changes, such as decriminalization or de-penalization, as opposed to true legalization, are a different matter altogether. They can be on much firmer ground because various jurisdictions in the United States and abroad have experimented with alternate regimes. Kleiman gave an excellent early analysis, and Wayne Hall and Rosalie Pacula a more current state of the art in the analysis of the social costs and benefits of marijuana regime change (Kleiman 1989; Hall and Pacula 2003). It is possible to overstate what marijuana decriminalization might produce in terms of reductions in incarceration and black market-related social costs more generally, inasmuch as most such costs stem from cocaine, heroin, and methamphetamine markets, not marijuana markets (Caulkins and Sevigny 2005). Still, marijuana is by far the most widely used illicit drug in the United States and it accounts for the plurality of drug arrests, so it is a drug policy question of importance. Furthermore, there is a steady stream of new information whose interpretation is subject to scholarly debate (for example, Arseneault et al. 2004). Also, much past empirical work concerning marijuana decriminalization in the United States may need to be reexamined. Rosalie Pacula, Jamie Chriqui, and Joanna King rebutted the conventional notion that when eleven states decriminalized marijuana in the 1970s, decriminalization meant more or less the same thing in every state. This implies that past studies' modeling of decriminalization dichotomously (that is, as merely present or absent) in statistical anlayses is fundamentally flawed (2003).

CONCLUSION

The literature on CBA or more generally return-on-investment analysis of drug control interventions is modest and growing. Its quality is uneven, reflecting differences in the evidentiary base, data, and funding support across different classes of interventions, most notably, enforcement versus treatment.

Nonetheless, it is in general not possible to say that this or that area is the best topic for the next CBA because what is best can depend considerably on whether one prefers a rough analysis of an important but understudied intervention such as high-level drug enforcement or, at the other extreme, yet another strong analysis of a well-studied intervention such as needle and syringe exchange programs or methadone maintenance.

ACKNOWLEDGMENTS

Many of the ideas in this chapter are due to or were stimulated by discussions with colleagues, notably Keith Humphreys, Martin Iguchi, Mark Kleiman, Rob MacCoun, Lorraine Mazerolle, Rosalie Pacula, Peter Reuter, and Alison Ritter. This work was done with partial support from the Qatar Foundation and a Robert Wood Johnson Foundation Investigator Award in Health Policy Research. The views expressed imply no endorsement by the Qatar or Robert Wood Johnson Foundations.

REFERENCES

Arseneault, Louise, Mary Cannon, John Witten, and Robin M. Murray. 2004. "Causal Association between Cannabis and Psychosis: Examination of the Evidence." *British Journal of Psychiatry* 184(2): 110–17.

Baker, Joanna R., Pamela K. Lattimore, and Lance A. Matheson. 1996. "Cost Effective Drug Testing in the Transportation Industry." *IIE Transactions* 28(9): 735–44.

Becker, Gary S., Michael Grossman, and Kevin M. Murphy. 2006. "The Market for Illegal Goods: The Case of Drugs." *Journal of Political Economy* 114(1): 38–60.

Behrens, Doris A., Jonathan P. Caulkins, Gernot Tragler, and Gustav Feichtinger. 2000. "Optimal Control of Drug Epidemics: Prevent and Treat—But Not At the Same Time?" *Management Science* 46(3): 333–47.

——. 2001. "Why Present-Oriented Societies Undergo Cycles of Drug Epidemics." *Journal of Economic Dynamics and Control* 26(6): 919–36.

Behrens, Doris A., Jonathan P. Caulkins, Gernot Tragler, Josef L. Haunschmied, and Gustav Feichtinger. 1999. "A Dynamic Model of Drug Initiation: Implications for Treatment and Drug Control." *Mathematical Biosciences* 159(1): 1–20.

Belenko, Steven. 2001. *Research on Drug Courts: A Critical Review and Update.* New York: National Center on Addiction and Substance Abuse at Columbia University.

Belenko, Steven, Nicholas Patapsis, and Michael T. French. 2005. *Economic Benefits of Drug Treatment: A Critical Review of the Evidence for Policy Makers.* www.nsula.edu/laattc/documents/EconomicBenefits_2005Feb.pdf.

Blumstein, Alfred, Jose A. Canela-Cacho, and Jacqueline Cohen. 1993. "Filtered Sampling from Populations with Heterogeneous Event Frequencies." *Management Science* 39(7): 886–99.

Cartwright, William S. 2000. "Cost-Benefit Analysis of Drug Treatment Services: A Review of the Literature." *Journal of Mental Health Policy Economics* 3(1): 11–26.

Caulkins, Jonathan P. 1990. *The Distribution and Consumption of Illicit Drugs: Some Mathematical Models and Their Policy Implications.* Doctoral Dissertation. Cambridge, MA: MIT.

——. 1994. *Developing Price Series for Cocaine.* Santa Monica, CA: RAND.

——. 2001. "When Parametric Sensitivity Analysis Isn't Enough." *INFORMS Transactions on Education* 1(3): 88–101.

——. 2005. "Models Pertaining to How Drug Policy Should Vary over the Course of an Epidemic Cycle." In *Substance Use: Individual Behavior, Social Interactions, Markets, and Politics,* eds. Bjorn Lindgren and Michael Grossman Advances in Health Economics and Health Services Research, 16. New York: Elsevier.

Caulkins, Jonathan P., and Sara Chandler. 2006. "Long-Run Trends in Incarceration of Drug Offenders in the US." *Crime & Delinquency* 52(4): 619–41.

Caulkins, Jonathan P., James Chiesa, and Susan S. Everingham. 2000. *Response to the National Research Council's Assessment of RAND's Controlling Cocaine Study.* Santa Monica, CA: RAND.

Caulkins, Jonathan P., and Haijing Hao. 2008. "Modeling Drug Market Supply Disruptions: Where Do All the Drugs Not Go?" *Journal of Policy Modeling* 30(2): 251–70.

Caulkins, Jonathan P., Rosalie Liccardo Pacula, Jeremy Arkes, Peter Reuter, Susan Paddock, Martin Iguchi, and Jack Riley. 2004. *The Price and Purity of Illicit Drugs: 1981 through the Second Quarter of 2003.* Publication NCJ 207768. Washington, DC: Executive Office of the President, Office of National Drug Control Policy.

Caulkins, Jonathan P., Susan Paddock, Rosalie Pacula, and James Chiesa. 2002. *School-Based Drug Prevention: What Kind of Drug Use Does It Prevent?* Santa Monica, CA: RAND.

Caulkins, Jonathan P., C. Peter Rydell, Susan S. Everingham, James Chiesa, and Shawn Bushway.

1999. *An Ounce of Prevention, a Pound of Uncertainty: The Cost-Effectiveness of School-Based Drug Prevention Programs.* Santa Monica, CA: RAND.

Caulkins, Jonathan P., and Eric Sevigny. 2005. "How Many People Does the US Incarcerate for Drug Use, and Who Are They?" *Contemporary Drug Problems* 32(3): 405–28.

Clark, Andrew E. 2003. "The Economics of Drug Legalization. Paris-Jourdan Sciences Economiques." Working paper. Paris: CNRS and DELTA. www.delta.ens.fr/clark/ecleg.pdf.

Collins, David J., and Helen M. Lapsley. 2002. *Counting the Cost: Estimates of the Social Costs of Drug Abuse in 1998-99.* Canberra: Commonwealth of Australia.

Crane, Barry D., A. Rex Rivolo, and Gary C. Comfort. 1997. *An Empirical Examination of Counterdrug Interdiction Program Effectiveness.* Alexandria, VA: Institute for Defense Analysis.

Deschenes, Elizabeth P., Susan F. Turner, and Peter W. Greenwood. 1995. "Drug Court or Probation? An Experimental Evaluation of Maricopa County's Drug Court." *The Justice System Journal* 18(1): 55–73.

Eibner, Christine, Andrew Morral, Rosalie L. Pacula, and John MacDonald. 2006. "Is the Drug Court Model Exportable? An Examination of the Cost-Effectiveness of a Los Angeles-Based DUI Court." *Journal of Substance Abuse Treatment* 31(1): 75–85.

Faggiano, Fabrizio, F. D. Vigna-Taglianti, E. Versino, A. Zambon, A. Borraccino, and P. Lemma. 2005. "School-Based Prevention for Illicit Drugs' Use." *The Cochrane Database of Systematic Reviews* 2. Art. No.: CD003020. DOI: 10.1002/14651858.CD003020.pub2.

Flynn, Patrick M., P. L. Kristiansen, J. V. Porto, and R. L. Hubbard. 1999. "Costs and Benefits of Treatment for Cocaine Addiction in DATOS." *Drug and Alcohol Dependence* 57(2): 167–74.

Freeman-Wilson, Karen, and C. West Huddleston. 1999. *DWI/Drug Courts: Defining a National Strategy.* Alexandria, VA: National Drug Court Institute.

French, Michael T., Kathryn E. McCollister, John Cacciola, Jack Durell, and Raymond L. Stephens. 2002. "Benefit-Cost Analysis of Addiction Treatment in Arkansas: Specialty and Standard Residential Programs for Pregnant and Parenting Women." *Substance Abuse* 23(1): 31–51.

Furr-Holden, C. Debra, Nicholas S. Ialongo, James C. Anthony, Hanno Petra, and G. Kellam Sheppard. 2004. "Developmentally Inspired Drug Prevention: Middle School Outcomes in a School-Based Randomized Prevention Trial." *Drug and Alcohol Dependence* 73(2): 149–58.

Gardiner, Keith L., and Raymond C. Shreckengost. 1987. "A System Dynamics Model for Estimating Heroin Imports into the United States." *System Dynamics Review* 3(1): 8–27.

Gates, S., J. McCambridge, L. A. Smith, and D. R. Foxcroft. 2006. "Interventions for Prevention of Drug Use by Young People Delivered in Non-School Settings." *Cochrane Database of Systematic Reviews* 1. Art. No.: CD005030. DOI: 10.1002/14651858.CD005030.pub2.

Gerstein, Dean R., Robert A. Johnson, Henrick Harwood, Douglas Fontain, Natalie Suter, and Kay Malloy. 1994. *Evaluating Recovery Services: The California Drug and Alcohol Treatment Assessment.* Chicago: National Opinion Research Center.

Gottfredson, Denise C., Brook W. Kearley, Stacy S. Najaka, and Carlos M. Rocha. 2005. "The Baltimore City Drug Treatment Court: 3-Year Self-Report Outcome Study." *Evaluation Review* 29(1): 42–64.

Grossman, Michael. 2004. *Individual Behaviors and Substance Abuse: The Role of Price. NBER* Working Paper 10948. Cambridge, MA: National Bureau on Economic Research.

Hall, Wayne, and Rosalie L. Pacula. 2003. *Cannabis Use and Dependence: Public Health and Public Policy.* Melbourne, Australia: Cambridge University Press.

Hallfors, Denise, Hyunsan Cho, David Livert, and Charles Kadushin. 2002. "Fighting Back against Substance Abuse: Are Community Coalitions Winning?" *American Journal of Preventive Medicine* 23(4): 237–45.

Harrell, Adele, Ojmarrh Mitchell, Jeffrey Merrill, and Douglas Marlowe. 2003. *Evaluation of Breaking the Cycle.* Washington, DC: The Urban Institute.

Harwood, Henrick J. ed. 2003. *Behavioral, Ethical, Legal, and Social Implications of Immunotherapies and Depot Medications for Treating Drug Addiction.* Washington, DC: National Academy Press.

Harwood, Henrick, Douglas Fountain, and Gina Livermore. 1998. *The Economic Costs of Alcohol and Drug Abuse in the United States, 1992.* Washington, DC: U.S. Department of Health and Human Services.

Harwood, Henrick J., Deepti Malhrota, Christel Villarivera, Connie Liu, Umi Chong, and Jawaria Gilani. 2002. *Cost Effectiveness and Cost Benefit Analysis of Substance Abuse Treatment: A Literature Review.* Washington, DC: US Department of Health and Human Services, SAMHSA.

Hawken, Angela. 2006. *The Economics of Alternative Sentencing: Assessing the Substance Abuse and Crime Prevention Act.* PhD dissertation. Santa Monica, CA: RAND Graduate School.

Hawkins, J. David, Richard F. Catalano, and Michael W. Arthur. 2002. "Promoting Science-Based Prevention in Communities." *Addictive Behavior* 27(6): 951–76.

Homer, Jack B. 1993. "Projecting the Impact of Law Enforcement on Cocaine Prevalence: A System Dynamics Approach." *The Journal of Drug Issues* 23(2): 281–95.

Homik, Robert, David Maklan, Diane Cadell, Carlin Henry Barmada, Lela Jacobsohn, Vani Henderson, Anca Romantan, Robert Orwin, Sanjeev Sridharan, Adam Chu, Carol Morin, Kristie Taylor, and Diane Steele. 2003. *Evaluation of the National Youth Anti-Drug Media Campaign: 2003 Report of Findings Executive Summary.* National Institute on Drug Abuse Report. Washington, DC: Westat and the Annenberg School of Communication. www.nida.nih.gov/PDF/DESPR/1203ExSummary.PDF.

Hser, Yih-Ing, Valerie Hoffman, Christine E. Grella, and M. Douglas Anglin. 2001. "A 33-Year Follow-Up of Narcotics Addicts." *Archives of General Psychiatry* 58(5): 503–8.

Hser, Yih-Ing, Maria Elena Stark, Alfonso Paredes, David Huang, M. Douglas Anglin, and Richard Rawson. 2006. "A 12-Year Follow-Up of a Treated Cocaine-Dependent Sample." *Journal of Substance Abuse Treatment* 30(3): 219–26.

Kim, Sehwan, Charles Williams, Shirley D. Coletti, and Nancy Helpler. 1995. "Benefit-Cost Analysis of Drug Abuse Prevention Programs: A Macroscopic Approach." *Journal of Drug Education* 25(2): 111–27.

Kleiman, Mark A.R. 1989. *Marijuana: Costs of Abuse, Costs of Control.* New York: Greenwood Press.

———. 1997. *Coerced Abstinence: A Neo-Paternalistic Drug Policy Initiative.* Washington, DC: Brookings Institution Press.

———. 2003. "Costs and Benefits of Immunotherapies or Depot Medications for the Treatment of Drug Abuse." In *Behavioral, Ethical, Legal, and Social Implications of Immunotherapies and Depot Medications for Treating Drug Addiction,* ed. Henrick Harwood. Washington, DC: National Academy Press.

Kuziemko, Ilyana, and Steven D. Levitt. 2004. "An Empirical Analysis of Imprisoning Drug Offenders." *Journal of Public Economics* 88(9-10): 2043–66.

Levin, Gilbert, Edward B. Roberts, and Gary B. Hirsch. 1975. *The Persistent Poppy: A Computer-Aided Search for Heroin Policy.* Cambridge, MA: Ballinger Publishing.

MacCoun, Robert J. 2007. "Testing Drugs vs. Testing Users: Private Risk Management in the Shadow of the Criminal Law." *DePaul Law Review* 56:507–38.

MacCoun, Robert J., and Peter Reuter. 2001. *Drug War Heresies*. New York: Cambridge University Press.

Manski, Charles F., John V. Pepper, and Carol V. Petrie. 2001. *Informing America's Policy on Illegal Drugs: What We Don't Know Keeps Hurting Us*. Washington, DC: National Academy Press.

Manski, Charles F., John V. Pepper, and Yonette F. Thomas, eds. 1999. *Assessment of Two Cost-Effectiveness Studies on Cocaine Control Policy*. Washington, DC: National Academy Press.

Mauer, Marc. 2002. *Invisible Punishment: The Collateral Consequences of Mass Imprisonment*. New York: The New Press.

Mazerolle, Lorraine, David Soole, and Sacha Rombouts. 2006. "Street-Level Drug Law Enforcement: A Meta-Analytic Review." *Journal of Experimental Criminology* 2(4): 409–35.

McLellan, A. Thomas, James R. McKay, Robert Forman, John Cacciola, and Jack Kemp. 2005. "Reconsidering the Evaluation of Addiction Treatment: From Retrospective Follow-up to Concurrent Recovery Monitoring." *Addiction* 100(4): 447–58.

Miller, Ted R., Mark A. Cohen, and Brian Wiersema. 1996. *Victim Costs and Consequences: A New Look*. Washington, DC: National Institute of Justice Report.

Mitchell, Ojmarrh, and Adele V. Harrell. 2006. "Evaluation of the Breaking the Cycle Demonstration Project: Jacksonville, FL and Tacoma, WA." *Journal of Drug Issues* 36:97–118.

Moore, Timothy J. 2005. *What Is Australia's "Drug Budget"? The Policy Mix of Illicit Drug-Related Government Spending in Australia*. Fitzroy, Victoria: Turning Point Alcohol and Drug Centre.

Moore, Timothy J., and Jonathan P. Caulkins. 2006. "How Cost-of-Illness Studies of Substance Abuse Can Be Made More Useful for Policy Analysis." *Applied Health Economics and Health Policy* 5(2): 75–85.

Morral, Andrew R., Daniel F. McCaffrey, Greg Ridgeway, Arnab Mukherji, and Christopher Beighley. 2006. *The Relative Effectiveness of 10 Adolescent Substance Abuse Treatment Programs in the United States*. Santa Monica, CA: RAND.

Niederdeppe, Jeff, Matthew C. Farrelly, and M. Lyndon Haviland. 2004. "Confirming 'Truth': More Evidence of a Successful Tobacco Countermarketing Campaign in Florida." *American Journal of Public Health* 94(2): 255–57.

Office of National Drug Control Policy (ONDCP). 2006. *National Drug Control Strategy FY2007 Budget Summary*. Washington, DC: U.S. Government Printing Office. www.whitehousedrugpolicy.gov/publications/policy/07budget/partii_funding_tables.pdf.

Pacula, Rosalie L., Jamie F. Chriqui, and Joanna King. 2003. *Marijuana Decriminalization: What Does It Mean in the United States? NBER Working Paper 9690*. Cambridge, MA: National Bureau of Economic Research.

Pentz, Mary Ann. 1998. "Cost, Benefits, and Cost-Effectiveness of Comprehensive Drug Abuse Prevention." In *Cost-Benefit/Cost-Effectiveness Research of Drug Abuse Prevention: Implications for Programming and Policy*, NIDA Research Monograph 176. Washington, DC: U.S. Department of Health and Human Services.

Perry, Cheryl L., Kelli A. Komro, Sara Veblen-Mortenson, Linda M. Bosma, Kian Farbakhsh, Karen A. Munson, Melissa H. Stigler, and Leslie A. Lytle. 2003. "A Randomized Controlled Trial of the Middle and Junior High School D.A.R.E. and D.A.R.E. Plus Programs." *Archives of Pediatric and Adolescent Medicine* 157(2): 178–87.

Plotnick, Robert D. 1994. "Applying Benefit-Cost Analysis to Substance Use Prevention Programs." *International Journal of Addictions* 29(3): 339–59.

Pollack, Harold. 2000. "When Pregnant Women Use Crack." *Drug Policy Analysis Bulletin* (8 February). www.fas.org/drugs/issue8.htm#1.

———. 2001. "Methadone Treatment as HIV Prevention." In *Quantitative Analysis of HIV*

Prevention Programs, eds. Edward Kaplan and Robert Brookmeyer. New Haven, CT: Yale University Press.

Rajkumar, Andrew S., and Michael T. French. 1997. "Drug Abuse, Crime Costs, and the Economic Benefits of Treatment." *Journal of Quantitative Criminology* 13(3): 291–323.

Reuter, Peter. 2001. "Why Does Research Have So Little Impact on American Drug Policy?" *Addiction* 96(3): 373–76.

Reuter, Peter, and Mark A.R. Kleiman. 1986. "Risks and Prices: An Economic Analysis of Drug Enforcement." In *Crime and Justice: An Annual Review of Research* 7, eds. Norval Morris and Michael Tonry. Chicago: University of Chicago Press.

Rigter, Henk. 2006. "What Drug Policies Cost: Drug Policy Spending in the Netherlands in 2003." *Addiction* 101(3): 323–29.

Ritter, Alison, and Jacqui Cameron. 2005. *A Systematic Review of Harm Reduction*. DPMP Monograph Series. Fitzroy, Victoria, AU: Turning Point Alcohol and Drug Centre.

Rydell, C. Peter, Jonathan P. Caulkins, and Susan S. Everingham. 1996. "Enforcement or Treatment: Modeling the Relative Efficacy of Alternatives for Controlling Cocaine." *Operations Research* 44(5): 687–95.

Rydell, C. Peter, and Susan S. Everingham. 1994. *Controlling Cocaine: Supply versus Demand Programs*. Santa Monica, CA: RAND.

Shanahan, Marian, Emily Lancsar, Marion Haas, Bronwyn Lind, Don Weatherburn, and Shuling Chen. 2004. "Cost-Effectiveness Analysis of the New South Wales Adult Drug Court Program." *Evaluation Review* 28(1): 3–27.

Tragler, Gernot, Jonathan P. Caulkins, and Gustav Feichtinger. 2001. "Optimal Dynamic Allocation of Treatment and Enforcement in Illicit Drug Control." *Operations Research* 49(3): 352–62.

Zaric, Greg S., Paul G. Barnett, and Margaret L. Brandeau. 2000. "HIV Transmission and the Cost-Effectiveness of Methadone Maintenance." *American Journal of Public Health* 90(7): 1100–1111.

Chapter 7

Juvenile Crime Interventions

Jeffrey A. Butts and John K. Roman

Economic analysis is increasingly influential in studies of juvenile justice policies and programs. The economic perspective considers the monetized costs and benefits of policies and programs designed to reduce juvenile crime. In other words, do the benefits of implementing a policy or program for juvenile offenders outweigh the costs? What are the costs and benefits of expanding rehabilitation and are they measurable? What are the costs and benefits of enhanced punishment? Are there particular types of offenders for whom one approach is more cost-effective than another? This chapter reviews the cost-benefit literature on juvenile crime reduction programs, proposes four existing program models that should be investigated for their potential cost-effectiveness and recommends four program models for further research in part because early evaluation studies indicate they are promising intervention models, but also because they are extremely popular with policymakers. As such, they are likely to be a part of the juvenile justice system for years to come.

INVESTING IN CRIME REDUCTION

The onset and duration of criminal behavior by young offenders can be affected by a wide range of individual, family, and environmental factors. One of the central goals of the juvenile justice system is to identify and resolve those factors to prevent future crime, restore youth to full citizenship, and ensure the safety of communities. Achieving this goal requires the juvenile justice system to use a variety of intervention strategies. Incarceration is one strategy, but in many cases it is not desirable. For many, even most, youth in the juvenile justice system incarceration is impractical, inappropriate, or ineffective.

Each year in the United States, police make more than 2 million arrests involving youth under the age of eighteen. On any given day, however, only 65,000 youth are in long-term correctional facilities and residential centers (Snyder and Sickmund 2006, 200). Because the average length of stay in long-term juvenile facilities is approximately twelve to eighteen months, the odds of incarceration for the average youthful offender are in the range of forty-six to one (or 65,000 incarcerations for every eighteen months of arrests at 2 million arrests per year). This is not surprising. Most youth in the juvenile justice system have not committed a serious crime that would qualify them for incarceration. According to recent national data, more than half of all juvenile arrests in 2005 involved youth accused of minor assaults, drug offenses, property offenses, and even lesser charges (Butts and Snyder 2006). Juvenile arrests for disorderly conduct in 2005 outnumbered arrests for aggravated assault by more than three to one (201,4000 arrests compared with 61,200). The number of juvenile vandalism arrests was nearly four times larger than the number of robbery arrests (104,100 versus 28,900). More juveniles were arrested for curfew violations (140,800) than for murder, rape, robbery, and aggravated assault combined (95,300).

Less serious crimes are often the first offenses committed by juveniles who then go on to commit serious and violent crime. Not all minor offenders graduate to serious and violent crime, but the majority of youth who do eventually commit serious crimes first come to the attention of law enforcement authorities for less serious offenses (Piper 1985). By the time a young offender has accumulated enough of a criminal record to justify the use of secure confinement the costs of the youth's behavior may be immense. One study estimated that the economy loses up to $2 million for every youthful offender that goes on to become a career criminal as an adult, including actual damages, lost wages, and harm to victims (Cohen 1998).

The juvenile justice system needs to provide a serious and effective response for all youth, including those charged with nonviolent crimes, but how should policymakers target public investments in juvenile crime reduction? Which models and approaches are effective enough to justify their costs? How much should society invest in services for unincarcerated juvenile offenders? Incarceration is a relatively rare event in the juvenile justice system. Thus, most interventions will be implemented in the community. Clearly, community-based intervention for youthful offenders would be cost-effective if it prevented even a small number of young offenders from joining the ranks of career criminals. Failing to intervene could be expensive to society. Overintervening, however, could be costly too. Investing in community-based programs that deliver services to many youth but affect only a small number of future offenders could generate high costs without returning comparable benefits in reduced crime. How should policymakers maximize social investment in juvenile crime reduction? These questions must be answered by research into the costs and benefits of community-based interventions for young offenders.

PREVIOUS RESEARCH

Employing the logic of cost-benefit analysis (CBA) to assess the value of juvenile justice policies and programs is not simple. Many economic benefits that could result from crime-reduction interventions are intangible. It is difficult to calculate their monetary value. There is no crime-reduction marketplace where exchanges between buyers and sellers determine the value of one program versus another. No market exists to set the economic value of crime-related pain, suffering, and fear. Researchers must rely on proxy markets, including expenditures on personal security measures and real estate prices in neighborhoods that may be affected by crime in varying degrees. For these reasons, economic analyses of individual interventions are still relatively rare.

Most crime-related scholarship involves econometric models that estimate the aggregate changes in crime that appear to be associated with the incapacitation or deterrent effects of policy alternatives (Becker 1968; Ehrlich 1973, 1981, 1996; Piehl and DiIulio 1995; Levitt 1996, 1998). These studies are often derived from rational choice theory and usually focus on changes in offender risks and rewards and how those changes affect the incidence and severity of crime (for rational choice theory, see Cornish and Clarke 1986). Most of these models rely on data about adult offenders. There is very little econometric literature on the effects of juvenile justice programs.

Some researchers have applied CBA models to the study of crime policy by linking quasi-experimental or experimental designs with shadow prices to observe the changes in economic efficiency associated with particular interventions (Cartwright 2000; Cohen 2000). There are two key challenges in such studies. The first is developing research designs that limit confounding explanations of observed behavior (Campbell and Stanley 1963; Cook and Campbell 1979; Mohr 1995). The second is developing robust estimates of the shadow price of crime in the absence of real market data. The second challenge has proven the more difficult obstacle to overcome.

It is relatively easy to add up the costs of investigating and adjudicating a crime, and to total the costs of rehabilitation or punishment. It is far more difficult to measure the costs of the harm associated with crime. The first research strategies to estimate the price of crime relied on variations in housing prices and wages. Neoclassical economic theory predicts that prices and wages will vary by the perceived risk of crime, and this variation can be used to infer the value of crime control interventions and the demand for public safety (Thaler 1978; Rosen and Thaler 1975; Clark and Cosgrove 1990). Ted Miller and Mark Cohen pioneered a second approach to estimating the cost of crime to victims, using jury awards and injury costs to tally the costs of crime. Their method used health service use data to estimate the costs associated with crime-related injuries, and applied the estimates to the distribution of injuries. The results were then mapped onto the distribution of injuries in all crimes to estimate the direct costs of crime (Cohen 1988; Miller, Cohen, and Rossman 1993; Miller, Cohen and Wiersma 1996; Rajkumar and French 1997; Cohen 2000; Miller, Fisher, and Cohen 2001; Cohen and Miller 2003). Most published estimates of the social costs of crime have relied on the Miller and Cohen jury-based estimates (Levitt 1996; Cohen and Miller 2003).

A third strategy for estimating the costs of crime relies on contingent valuation techniques, where survey data are used to estimate the public's willingness to pay to avoid crime (Cohen et al. 2004). All three approaches have limitations, however, and the estimates they produce vary widely. For instance, the average social cost of burglary is estimated to be $2,500 using the jury award approach, but approximately $25,000 using willingness-to-pay survey data. Again, almost all of these studies use data about adult crime. Only Miller, Fisher, and Cohen focused specifically on the social cost of crime by juvenile offenders (2001).

Some researchers have focused on the economic return from investments in early childhood programs for disadvantaged youth (Gramlich 1986; Greenwood et al. 1998). These studies have generally found that early intervention programs produce a number of long-term benefits including reductions in future offending, though Ned Gramlich argued that such benefits accrue to the community and not to program participants. Steven Aos and his colleagues reviewed research on early interventions targeting disadvantaged youth in general, including those involving nurse home visitation programs (Aos et al. 2001; for disadvantaged youth generally, see Lally, Mangione, and Honig 1987; Schweinhart, Barnes, and Weikart 1993; Pagani et al. 1998; Reynolds et al. 2000; for visitation programs, see Olds et al. 1998; Moore, Armsden, and Gogerty 1998). They applied a standardized CBA protocol to impute economic effects using findings from the literature on early interventions. Early intervention was cost-beneficial when benefits to both taxpayers and crime victims were taken into account, although most of the apparent benefits were at the community level in the form of reduced victimization.

One analysis of community-based interventions in Minnesota found that juvenile treatment programs based on cognitive-behavioral approaches were more cost-beneficial than programs that provided only monitoring and supervision (Robertson, Grimes, and Rogers 2001). Jonathan Caulkins and his colleagues evaluated the cost-effectiveness of school-based prevention programs in reducing future drug consumption and found the programs to be cost-competitive, but not always cost-effective (1999). In one of the most well-known economic analyses of juvenile justice interventions, Peter Greenwood and his colleagues examined four types of intervention programs for juvenile offenders (graduation incentives, parent training, behavioral supervision, and home visits) and compared their cost-effectiveness in terms of future offending with the cost-effectiveness of three-strikes policies (1998). The results showed that graduation incentives and parent training were more cost-effective than ensuring long sentences for offenders with three strikes laws.

Steve Aos and his colleagues reviewed the economic effectiveness of common program models for juvenile offenders, primarily the costs associated with justice system processing and the harm incurred by victims (2001). Several program models demonstrated positive returns, including juvenile court diversion services, intensive supervision programs, coordinated service-based programs, family-based therapy approaches, and juvenile sex offender programs. They also examined several clinically oriented intervention programs that used fixed protocols, including multisystemic therapy (MST), functional family therapy (FFT), and multidimensional treatment foster care (MFTC). Their review found these programs to be cost-beneficial in terms of reduced crime. In another thorough review of the literature, Peter Greenwood concluded that these same programs were, in fact, the only cost-effective interventions for juvenile offenders (2005).

CONTINUING THE SEARCH

Only a handful of intervention models have survived multiple clinical trials to demonstrate their cost-effectiveness in reducing juvenile crime. This is not to say, however, that these models are the best and only interventions for youthful offenders. In fact, the vast majority of young people in the juvenile justice system may be ill-suited for clinical interventions such as MST and FFT. These models were designed to serve youth with serious behavioral problems. For example, MST was originally intended to address serious antisocial behavior, including chronic and violent offenders already at risk of out-of-home placement. Follow-up studies suggest that MST may be effective for youth involved in violent offenses, but it may not be effective for youth charged with less serious crimes (Henggeler et al. 2002).

Juvenile justice officials must continue to search for new program models and to test the cost-effectiveness of those models. In particular, practitioners should continue to create new interventions for the typical adolescent offender involved in property crime, minor drug use, and other less serious forms of delinquency. Even currently unproven programs may be found one day to be cost-effective for many of these youth.

The absence of evidence for program effectiveness is not proof of ineffectiveness. Developing strong and consistent research findings about particular program models is expensive and complex. Multiple investigators must work for years or even decades to accumulate the high-quality evidence needed to establish a program's impact and then to monetize its costs and benefits. This rarely happens, of course, but it would be foolish to stop the search for crime-reduction methods now simply because a few program models have already been proven effective--especially if previous studies were less than thorough or unbiased or if the existing research agenda was overly narrow. In a best-of-all-possible-worlds scenario where ample research investments followed intervention concepts naturally and without prejudice, using existing research to finalize a list of proven programs might be sensible. In our environment of competitive funding and politically oriented investment, however, relying exclusively on today's research to invest in tomorrow's social programs would stifle innovation and limit the overall impact of crime-reduction policies. Policymakers and researchers must continue to pursue new models.

There are potentially valuable but untested program models in juvenile justice that have not yet attracted the research investment required to generate sound evidence of cost-effectiveness. Many of these models would be difficult to evaluate, especially those that rely on community-based and nonclinical interventions. Funding agencies may be hesitant to invest their limited research budgets in community-based programs that do not take place in office settings and do not have controlled treatment modalities that can be measured with laboratory precision. Some effective programs may happen in courtrooms, community centers, and even neighborhoods where researchers cannot control the sequence and timing of critical events. Many researchers would be reluctant to invest their career capital in complex and constantly evolving community-based programs that depend on nonprofessional staff and volunteers. Researchers need reliable research partners, and programs that employ medical or clinical service providers are more adept at maintaining program fidelity and adhering to rigorous research designs. The resources necessary to generate high-quality research evidence are limited, and few funding agencies are likely to support expensive studies of delinquency interventions falling outside the reassuring environs of the medical model.

For all of these reasons, there is still much work to be done in identifying cost-effective interventions for juvenile offenders, especially community-based interventions that do not involve confinement or incarceration. CBA will play an increasingly important role in the development of new program models in the juvenile justice system. Quantifying the monetary value of policy choices generates compelling evidence for policymakers and for society at large. Given limited resources, CBA helps policymakers identify the amount of resources consumed by a program or policy, how such programs and policies may affect relevant outcomes, and whether any particular program or policy is the most efficient use of resources.

AREAS FOR NEW RESEARCH

Four juvenile justice strategies offer promising opportunities for investment by researchers as well as the policymakers and funding organizations that support research. These strategies are mentoring programs, teen courts, juvenile drug courts, and systemic reform efforts. There are certainly other concepts and program models in juvenile justice that should be explored for their potential cost-effectiveness. These four models were chosen because they are popular interventions that are likely to be part of the juvenile justice system for years to come, and because they represent a broad spectrum of CBA considerations. Mentoring is a low-cost but large-scale program focused on at-risk youth. With so many youth participating in mentoring, even a small behavioral effect could be economically beneficial. Teen courts require more resources to operate, but they are targeted on first-time offenders and may yield significant benefits if successful. Juvenile drug courts require considerable amounts of resources, but they could generate even greater benefits if concentrated on youth involved with serious and harmful drug use. All three of these programs serve a distinct segment of the juvenile offender population. The fourth area of inquiry—systemic reform—focuses on large-scale changes in organization and policy that could affect all youth in the juvenile justice system. The costs of systemic reform could be substantial, but the potential benefits would be significant if such efforts improved the daily operations of the justice system.

Mentoring

Mentoring programs are increasingly popular for youth in the juvenile justice system. The most well-known mentoring program is Big Brothers/Big Sisters (www.bbbs.org). Mentoring programs match at-risk youth with adult volunteers who pledge to provide them with support and a sense of connection. Mentors are not professional service providers; they are friends, confidants, and advisors for youth in need of adult support. Positive relationships with caring and consistent adults may influence youth development in several ways, such as protecting youth from psychosocial risk, enhancing their personal competence, and promoting their social integration into the world of adults and the larger community. Mentoring relationships provide youth with opportunities to acquire academic skills and gain practical knowledge, and to develop a sense of efficacy through participation in joint activities and role modeling (Darling, Hamilton, and Niego 1994). Research supports the common sense notion that young people benefit from having a close, enduring relationship with a caring adult. Youth reporting a positive connection with at least one supportive adult engage in fewer risky behaviors, including substance abuse and delinquency (Aspy et al. 2004; Oman et al. 2004).

Mentoring evaluations suggest that youth who participate in mentoring relationships show improvements in self-efficacy and social competence with measurable reductions in problem behavior (Grossman and Tierney 1998; LoSciuto et al. 1996; Sipe 2002). Experimental evaluations of mentoring for juvenile offenders have found that program participation was associated with significant reductions in youth recidivism (Fo and O'Donnell 1975; O'Donnell, Lydgate, and Fo 1979). Other evaluations have been equivocal, however, possibly because of variations in their definition of risk status, the outcomes they measured, and the quality and duration of the mentoring relationships established by the programs (Jackson 2002; Keating et al. 2002; Royse 1998). Still, youth participants who report better relationships with mentors, as indicated by the frequency and consistency of contact, are generally likely to show more positive outcomes (LoSciuto et al. 1996; Slicker and Palmer 1993). Meta-analytic results support the general effectiveness of mentoring across a range of program types and youth populations (DuBois et al. 2002). Researchers also warn that harmful consequences may result from youth-mentor relationships that are short-lived and characterized by conflict and disappointment (Grossman and Rhodes 2002; Rhodes 2002).

To be effective, mentoring programs have to use proven practices in screening and training participants, making matches, and monitoring the relationships of youth and their mentors. Programs that provide appropriate structure and active support to participants seem to achieve better results. Best practices are particularly important for youth who have already experienced difficult or disrupted relationships with parents and family. Youth with previous relationship problems often harbor fears that others will not accept them, and may be especially sensitive to rejection (Downey et al. 1998; Rhodes 2002). Such youth may interpret even minor relationship difficulties as harbingers of coming rejection.

Mentoring programs appeal to funders in part because they function with largely voluntary labor. In a CBA, the social cost of a resource is measured as the opportunity cost of that resource. In other words, the price of a volunteer's time is equal to the hourly wage a program would have to pay for someone to perform the volunteer's particular task. In this framework, mentoring is not without cost. Mentors give their time and energy to the program, and this is a resource with value. If these costs were included in all CBAs of mentoring programs, it would clarify the true costs of the model. It would also help to test hypotheses about who makes the best mentors—that is, whether volunteers with higher or lower opportunity costs contribute differently to overall program effectiveness.

Teen Courts

Teen courts are another program model that CBA researchers should investigate. Sometimes known as youth courts, peer courts, or peer juries, teen courts are informal diversion programs for young offenders. They are courtrooms in which all (or most) of the principal roles are filled by youth. Teenagers serve as the judges, attorneys, juries, clerks, and even bailiffs. The teen court process is typically used as a nonbinding, informal alternative to the regular juvenile court process. The sanctions a teen court imposes on young offenders do not have the force of law. Youth participate in teen court to avoid prosecution and adjudication in juvenile court. If youth refuse to complete the sanctions imposed in teen court, however, they may be returned to juvenile court to face formal handling and possible adjudication (figure 7.1).

Teen courts have become very popular in the United States. Growing from a handful of programs in the 1970s, there are now more than 1,000 programs in operation across the country, according to the Office of Juvenile Justice and Delinquency Prevention (www .youthcourt.net). The typical case in teen court involves a youth fourteen to sixteen years of age, in trouble with the police for the first time, and probably charged with vandalism, stealing, or another nonviolent offense. Participating in a teen court allows such youth to avoid what might have been the first stain on their legal record. In return, they are almost certain to get a rather stiff sentence compared with what they might have received in a traditional juvenile court. Most teen court defendants are required to do community service and many pay restitution. They may be ordered to write an apology letter to their parent or parents or to the victim or victims of their offense, and they may have to write

Figure 7.1   Typical Teen Court Process

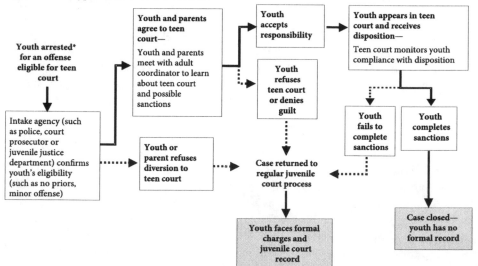

Source: Butts, Buck, and Coggeshall 2002.

* Not all teen court cases are prompted by arrest. Some courts accept school referrals (truancy, fighting, and the like); others accept traffic citations.

an essay about the effects of crime on communities. Some teen courts require defendants to return as jury members in other cases.

Studies of teen court programs have reported low rates of re-offending among former defendants. Researchers have often found rates of postprogram recidivism ranging from 3 to 10 percent within six to twelve months of an appearance in teen court (Butler-Mejia 1998; McNeece et al. 1996; SRA Associates 1995). A few researchers have found higher recidivism rates, but these are often evaluations of teen courts that accept adjudicated, rather than diverted juveniles. Kevin Minor and his colleagues, for example, found that nearly one-third of teen court alumni re-offended within one year, but the Kentucky program involved in that study handled youth referred to teen court as a dispositional alternative after juvenile court adjudication (Minor et al. 1999). The offenders it served could have been from a more delinquent population than would be true of the typical teen court caseload.

Despite their obvious promise, teen courts have not been evaluated with rigorous research designs. Even some of the best studies have relied on data from a single group of teen court cases at a single time, or they have used inadequate comparison groups (Garrison 2001; Harrison, Maupin, and Mays 2001; Minor et al. 1999; LoGalbo and Callahan 2001; Swink 1998; Wells, Minor, and Fox 1998). It is still not possible to reject the hypothesis that teen court outcomes are due to the preprogram characteristics of teen court clients rather than to effects of the program, that is, youth selected for teen court may be less likely to recidivate in the first place.

Some studies, however, have used acceptable comparison groups to measure the effects of teen courts on recidivism and they support the potential effectiveness of the model. Rod Hissong's evaluation of an Arlington, Texas, teen court compared recidivism among teen court defendants with a group of nonteen court participants matched on sex, race, age, and offense (1991). The analysis suggested that teen court participants were significantly less likely to re-offend than the comparison group, 24 percent versus 36 percent. In one of the more rigorous evaluations of teen courts to date, researchers from the Urban Institute studied teen courts in four jurisdictions: Alaska, Arizona, Maryland, and Missouri (Butts, Buck, and Coggeshall 2002). More than 500 teen court cases from the four sites were compared with similar cases handled by the traditional juvenile justice system. The study collected baseline data about youth and their parents or guardians, and tracked each youth for six months, measuring differences in recidivism between teen court youth and those processed in the traditional juvenile justice system. In three of the four study sites, recidivism was lower for teen court. In Alaska, for example, the difference was marked. The six-month recidivism figure for teen court cases was 6 percent, compared with 23 percent for juvenile court cases matched with the teen court sample on age, sex, ethnicity, and offense history. In Missouri, the recidivism rate was 9 percent in teen court and 27 percent in the traditional process, a striking and statistically significant difference.

Teen courts, however, are more than a method of reducing recidivism. The peer-to-peer justice provided by teen courts is believed to promote pro-social attitudes and to encourage civic engagement and social responsibility among young offenders as well as

among youth volunteers. Research suggests that an experience in teen court is associated with high levels of satisfaction with the court process, and enhanced perceptions of
procedural justice (on the court process, see Butts, Buck, and Coggeshall 2002; Colydas
and McLeod 1997; Reichel and Seyfrit 1984; Swink 1998; Wells, Minor, and Fox 1998;
on procedural justice, see Butler-Mejia 1998). One study of a Florida program found that
teen court positively affected defendant attitudes toward authority and understanding of
the legal system (LoGalbo and Callahan 2001). Researchers surveyed 111 youth immediately after their initial interview with teen court staff and again when they completed
the program. The survey asked participants about their knowledge of Florida laws and
the justice system, their attitudes toward authority figures (such as police officers, judges,
parents, teachers), their attitudes toward teen court and toward themselves, and their
perception of the fairness of teen court procedures. The study found that teen court
participation was associated with increased self-esteem and positive attitudes toward
authority. In addition, recidivism was less likely among those defendants with improved
attitudes toward figures of authority.

Strong client satisfaction was also reported by researchers in Kentucky (Wells, Minor,
and Fox 1998). Exit interviews revealed high levels of satisfaction among 123 teen court
participants, with 84 percent indicating that their sentences were fair. Several features of
the teen court experience were cited positively by the Kentucky subjects, including educational advantages (37 percent) and the actual sentences youth received (21 percent).
Teens also consistently indicated that the opportunity to serve as a teen court juror was
an important, positive aspect of the teen court process.

Although no experimental studies have been conducted on the effectiveness of teen
courts, there are many reasons to believe such programs are beneficial for youth participants and their communities. For one, the average annual cost of operating a teen court
is just over $30,000 (Butts and Buck 2000). Even a small effect on subsequent recidivism
could justify the costs of such an affordable program model. Teen courts may be even
more cost-effective because they depend largely on youth volunteers and the opportunity
costs for juveniles involved in teen court are probably smaller than the opportunity costs
for adults in mentoring programs. In addition to measuring recidivism, future CBA efforts should focus on other important teen court outcomes. As noted, teen courts are
designed to improve pro-social attitudes and to encourage civic engagement and social
responsibility among youth. Studies of teen courts could underestimate their benefits if
these other outcomes are not monetized.

Juvenile Drug Courts

Drug courts started twenty years ago and quickly became a prominent part of the justice system both for adults and juveniles. They use a persuasive combination of judicial
authority and interorganizational coordination to motivate drug-involved offenders to
stay in treatment and change their behavior. Drug court programs use case management
to coordinate services, drug tests to monitor offender compliance, and frequent court
hearings to review case progress and establish effective social bonds between offenders, judges, and other court staff. During drug court hearings, judges converse openly

with offenders and their family members. The social dynamics of the courtroom may be a critical component in the effectiveness of drug courts, especially when they support procedural justice, or the visible signs of fairness that encourage offenders to accept the court process and to abide by its rules.

Drug courts are widely praised, from city halls and state capitols to the U.S. Congress and the White House. The National Drug Control Strategy of 2004 described the spread of drug courts as "one of the most promising trends in the criminal justice system" (The White House 2004, 6). The news media lavish even more attention on drug courts. Every month, hundreds of news stories about drug courts appear in American newspapers. On May 28, 2007, a Google News search of the term *drug court* found more than 600 news items published in the previous thirty days alone. Stories often quote judges and other court officials praising the drug court model, and they routinely depict the personal struggles and triumphs of drug court graduates.

First appearing in the mid-1990s, juvenile drug courts (JDCs) grew rapidly in the United States (figure 7.2). Still, only a handful of evaluations of juvenile drug courts had been published by the end of 2006. One of the first studies was a quasi-experimental evaluation in Utah (Parsons and Byrnes 1998). The study matched treatment cases (JDC) and comparison cases (not JDC) and found a statistically significant difference in the number of charges incurred by youth one year after intervention compared with one year before intervention. Participants in JDC had 1.1 fewer charges after intervention, and a comparison group had 0.6 fewer charges. Like many quasi-experimental designs, this study was open to criticism because the matching process failed to control sufficiently for potential bias. Youth in the treatment group turned out to have more extensive criminal histories than the comparison group youth. Thus, some of the difference detected by the study could have been due to a selection-regression artifact (Maltz and McCleary 1977).

The University of Akron conducted one of the first experimental JDC evaluations (Dickie 2002). The study found that youth involved in a JDC had fewer new charges than a comparison group, lower rates of positive drug screens, and higher rates of

Figure 7.2 Juvenile Drug Courts Expanded Quickly

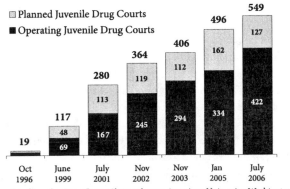

Source: Authors. Based on data from the Drug Court Clearinghouse, American University, Washington, DC.

employment. The strength of the research, however, was compromised by the study's small sample size and high subject attrition. The study began with thirty comparison cases, and after twelve months only nine cases were still available for follow up. The findings were promising, but unpersuasive.

The University of Southern Maine tracked outcomes for 396 youth admitted to JDCs across the state (Anspach, Ferguson, and Phillips 2003; Ferguson, McCole, and Raio 2006). The study measured program completion rates, employment, school attendance, recidivism, and drug use among JDC participants and a matched comparison group. The results suggested that youth who completed JDC programs had lower recidivism rates (33 percent) than those who failed to complete JDC (48 percent), or those in the comparison group (43 percent). The design of the Maine study was similar to the first studies of adult drug courts. Researchers compared offenders in drug court with similar offenders who did not participate in drug court, sometimes including offenders who refused to participate in drug court (Rodriguez and Webb 2004; Thompson 2004). These studies help to underscore the potential of drug courts, but they involve serious threats to validity (selection effects, for example). As important, they rely on a black-box approach to conceptualizing the drug court process and this prevents them from disaggregating the effects of various drug court components (Bouffard and Taxman 2004; Sanford and Arrigo 2005).

In what is arguably the best JDC study published to date, the creators of multisystemic therapy conducted a randomized trial of 161 juvenile offenders assigned to four treatment conditions: (group 1) biannual juvenile and family court hearings with community services, (group 2) weekly drug court with community services, (group 3) drug court with multisystemic therapy (MST), and (group 4) drug court with MST and contingency management or behavioral intervention (Henggeler et al. 2006). The study asked whether JDC improved youth outcomes compared with traditional court, and whether integrating MST into juvenile drug court improved outcomes even further. The apparent answer in both cases was yes. Drug use by youths in groups 2, 3, and 4 decreased more than it did among those in group 1. Furthermore, groups 3 and 4 had stronger results than group 2, suggesting that the addition of MST led to better outcomes. The study was the most elaborate JDC evaluation so far, but it failed to address critical questions about JDC effectiveness. The study showed that JDC with MST is probably more effective than JDC without MST, but this is a test of MST, not JDC. The study's comparison of groups 1 and 2 did address the effectiveness of JDC, but the results showed only that weekly drug court hearings might be more effective than biannual juvenile court hearings. Is this a test of drug court or a test of frequent court appearances?

Researchers still need to address many unanswered questions about juvenile drug courts. If research finds that juvenile drug courts are effective in general, how does this help practitioners identify the specific elements that make effective programs, especially cost-effective programs? What is and what is not part of a juvenile drug court? Does it include the drug treatment provided to youth as part of their participation in JDC? If yes, does this mean that when youth are held in detention for violating drug court rules that detention is also a part of JDC? If JDCs coordinate their efforts with public schools, does this make classroom teachers part of drug court? What are the most important components of JDC programs? Which components are supported by empirical evidence? Are some JDC practices actually counterproductive? Is court-ordered drug treatment for adolescents always better than treatment offered without the backing of judicial authority? Are the benefits of juvenile drug court to be found primarily in the frequency of court hearings? If so, would their cost-effectiveness actually be improved by reducing their use of substance abuse treatment and drug testing, both of which can be very expensive?

Researchers need to develop evidence about JDCs from theoretically informed evaluations that measure the effectiveness of specific procedures and practices. New studies should be guided by theories of how JDCs change youth behavior. Most previous studies have been nontheoretical, black-box evaluations. These studies may help to establish the efficacy of JDCs, but they do not address their effectiveness (Marlowe 2004). Many lessons learned from research on adult drug courts are not directly applicable to juvenile programs. Juvenile drug courts, and evaluations of juvenile drug courts, should fit the juvenile justice environment. Practitioners have made assertions about what they believe are the critical components and strategies in practice for juvenile drug courts (NDCI/NCJFCJ 2003), but researchers should test those assertions with rigorous evaluations.

One critical challenge that faces future economic studies of juvenile drug courts is the possibility that the programs have harmful effects on some participants, particularly youth who are referred to JDC programs for nonserious offenses combined with drug use. Unlike mentoring and teen courts, which are designed to prevent formal involvement in the juvenile justice system and the negative consequences that often accompany that involvement, juvenile drug courts sometimes take relatively minor offenders far deeper into the justice system than their criminal behavior alone would warrant (Butts and Roman 2004). Even assuming that JDC reduces offending and drug use during the period of program participation, researchers should establish whether JDC exposure leads to worse postprogram outcomes for nonserious offenders. A study that does not count these costs would overestimate the net benefits of the JDC intervention.

Systemic Reform

The fourth research area recommended here is not a program or an intervention model for individual youth. Systemic reform is a strategy for improving the impact and efficiency of the juvenile justice system as a whole. Whether it concerns specific system components or all elements of the juvenile justice process, systemic reform is a potentially rich area for further research on the costs and benefits of juvenile justice policy. Systemic reform addresses organizational structures and procedures. By improving the efficiency of the process or the targeting of juvenile justice services, an effective reform strategy can result in large-scale benefits. Just a small increment of improvement—even 1 percent greater crime reduction—could generate significant economic returns. Two recent examples of systemic reform in the juvenile justice system focus on secure detention and the coordination of substance abuse services for youthful offenders.

Juvenile Detention Alternatives Initiative

One of the most well-known systemic reform strategies of the past decade is the Juvenile Detention Alternatives Initiative (JDAI) funded by the Annie E. Casey Foundation of Baltimore, Maryland. The JDAI effort focuses on the use of secure juvenile detention facilities. Detention is analogous to jail in the criminal (adult) justice system. It is used to keep youth out of the community while they wait for juvenile court processing or while they wait to be placed in long-term correctional facilities or other placements after the court process has concluded. The JDAI encourages juvenile justice officials to reserve their costly detention resources for youth who really need to be securely confined, and to use community-based detention alternatives for other youth. Without strict monitoring, local jurisdictions often use juvenile detention for an inappropriately wide array of offenders, including youth charged with nonviolent offenses and those who could be supervised successfully and less expensively in nonconfinement settings.

The JDAI targets the problems that arise when youth are unnecessarily or inappropriately detained at great expense, with long-lasting negative consequences for both public safety and youth development. According to the Casey Foundation (www.aecf .org/Home/OurWork/JuvenileJustice.aspx), the JDAI promotes changes to policies, practices, and programs that reduce reliance on secure confinement, improve public safety, reduce racial disparities and bias, save taxpayers' dollars, and stimulate overall juvenile justice reforms.

The initiative pursues these goals by providing support to state and local officials through direct technical assistance, conferences, and written materials. The areas of focus include the creation and operation of effective community-based programs, detention screening and risk assessment tools, and case flow management techniques to accelerate the legal processing of delinquency cases to minimize the time youth spend in detention awaiting the conclusion of court proceedings.

Starting in just four or five jurisdictions during the 1990s, the JDAI effort was working in more than seventy cities and counties by 2006 (JDAI News 2006). The results of the initiative appeared to be impressive, judging by the reported changes in two principal measures of possible impact—average daily detention populations and average lengths of stay in detention. In many of the state and local jurisdictions participating in JDAI, the size of juvenile detention populations decreased by 30 to 40 percent during the period of implementation, and the average length of stay in detention dropped by 10 to 20 percent (see, for example, JDAI News 2007). If these changes could be attributed to the JDAI effort, and if they could be sustained over time, the cost impact would be profound.

Of course, it is difficult to isolate the empirical results of JDAI. Like most systemic reform initiatives, JDAI was not implemented in a way that would facilitate rigorous evaluation. In addition, the primary implementation period overlapped almost precisely

with the drop in violent crime in the United States from 1995 to 2005 (Butts and Snyder 2006). Many jurisdictions in the United States saw a reduced demand for detention
during that time simply because of the dramatic decline in youth violence. Some JDAI
jurisdictions, however, became active in the initiative only in 2003 or 2004, when most
of the impact of the nationwide crime decline had already occurred. In these jurisdictions, juvenile justice officials reported changes in the use of detention that were just as
dramatic as in the other JDAI sites. For example, juvenile justice officials in New Jersey
began to participate in the JDAI in 2004. By 2005, juvenile detention populations had
dropped 11 percent in Atlantic County, 24 percent in Hudson, 35 percent in Camden,
38 percent in Monmouth, and 43 percent in Essex (JDAI News 2006). If only half the
changes were attributable to JDAI, the economic benefits would easily pay for the costs
of the initiative. Moreover, these reductions in detention occurred while violent crime in
New Jersey remained largely unchanged. According to the FBI Uniform Crime Reports
for 2006, violent crimes in New Jersey's largest cities increased just 1 percent between
2005 and 2006, which was similar to the national average of 1.3 percent (Federal Bureau
of Investigation 2007).

Reclaiming Futures

Another foundation-supported systemic reform effort focused on improving the coordination of substance abuse interventions for young offenders in ten communities across
the United States. The Reclaiming Futures initiative was supported by the Robert Wood
Johnson Foundation and began as a demonstration project in 2002 (Nissen et al. 2006).
The goal was to enhance the integration of services for drug-involved youth in the juvenile justice system. Many youth involved in the juvenile justice system have emerging or
established problems with substance abuse but few receive high-quality substance abuse
services during their time under court supervision. Juvenile justice and drug treatment
agencies do not often collaborate effectively. The top juvenile court officials often do not
know the treatment providers in their own communities. Screening and assessment of
young offenders is rarely consistent or comprehensive. Service providers and court officials do not often share information about specific youth and families. The court system
frequently does not even know whether services are provided to youth as intended because treatment providers are not allowed, or at least they believe they are not allowed to
share clinical information with officials outside their own agencies. Many youth simply
ignore court orders to begin substance abuse treatment and neither the court nor the
treatment agency has any idea that such gaps exist. Not only do many drug-involved
youth fall through the cracks of the juvenile justice system, the entire system could be
described as largely a sequence of cracks.

Reclaiming Futures was designed to address these systemic problems and to make
the juvenile justice and substance abuse treatment systems more accountable to one another, to their mutual clients, and to the entire community. The initiative grew from
previous systemic reform efforts in adolescent treatment, balanced and restorative justice, and children's mental health (Nissen et al. 2006; Bazemore 2006; Pires 2002). It
relied on effective leadership, judicial commitment, active teamwork among treatment

providers and juvenile justice agencies, and broad community partnerships to alter the trajectory of substance abusing youth through (and beyond) the juvenile justice process. The central goal of Reclaiming Futures was to enhance each community's capacity to provide a comprehensive response to substance abuse problems among justice-involved youth by emphasizing interagency, community, and family collaboration.

A performance monitoring approach known as the Reclaiming Futures Model was developed from the ten-site demonstration (see www.reclaimingfutures.org). The model was designed to help communities identify the strengths and weaknesses of their service systems and to create a shared approach for improving systems. The Model was essentially an interorganizational performance measurement framework that encouraged communities to ignore agency boundaries as they created system-level change. It encouraged communities to track youth across six key stages of the juvenile justice and treatment process: initial screening, assessment, care coordination, service initiation, service engagement, and service completion. At most stages, simple performance measures were suggested to assess implementation (process) and performance (outcome).

As part of a national evaluation of Reclaiming Futures, the Urban Institute and Chapin Hall at the University of Chicago conducted biannual surveys of professionals, family advocates, and community members in each of the participating sites. The surveys measured the coordination, quality, and effectiveness of the juvenile justice and substance abuse treatment systems by asking a series of fifty-eight questions that were then combined into thirteen indices of system quality. The pattern of responses suggested that Reclaiming Futures improved the efficacy of court-supervised interventions for youth. Most of the indicators measured by the evaluation improved significantly during the course of the initiative. Improvements were especially strong in the use of screening and assessment tools, treatment effectiveness, the use of client information to support treatment, family involvement in treatment, and overall systems integration. Each of these quality indicators improved between 19 and 28 percent (see table 7.1).

A RESEARCH AGENDA

All four programs and strategies described here have generated some evidence of effectiveness, but none has been subjected to rigorous CBA. The four strategies vary in the amount of investment they require, from very small programs that rely on volunteer labor (mentoring and teen courts), to relatively large programs that demand considerable staff time (juvenile drug courts), to potentially complex organizational change that depends on political skills and long-term effort (JDAI and Reclaiming Futures). The strategies described here also vary in their expected impact. Teen courts are short-term, low-dosage programs that could yield commensurately small behavioral changes, while mentoring and juvenile drug courts require prolonged and sometimes intense participa-

Table 7.1   Change in Indices of System Quality, by Percentage

Index	Possible Improvement Realized
Use of drug and alcohol assessments	28 *
Effectiveness of youth treatment	26 *
Use of client information	24 *
Family involvement	22 *
Overall system integration	19 *
Use of pro-social activities for youth	18 *
Data sharing by agencies	18 *
Resource management by agencies	16 *
Agency collaboration	14 *
Targeting of youth treatment	12 *
Cultural integration	11 *
Access to services by youth and families	9 *
Partner agency involvement	−2

Source: Authors' analysis. Data from National Survey of Reclaiming Futures, Urban Institute, Washington, DC.
Note: Possible improvement on an index is relative to the value of that index in the first of six surveys. Small changes in indices that started with high values could be more significant than larger changes in indices that started with low values. "Possible improvement realized" was calculated by taking the total difference in survey scores (Survey 6 − Survey 1), and then dividing by the possible improvement, or the maximum score minus the first score. Change indices were then rank ordered from largest to smallest percentage of possible improvement realized. For more information, see www.reclaimingfutures.org.
* Amount of change significantly different from zero according to t-test ($p < .05$).

tion but may have strong effects on behavior. Each of the four strategies, however, is a promising area for future CBA work in the juvenile justice system.

Many challenges face CBA in juvenile justice. One significant challenge is that the lives of youth subjected to juvenile justice policies and programs are often closely intertwined with others—specifically, families and peers. If a program causes a youth to change behavior and the behavior in turn affects others outside the study framework, it can be very difficult to evaluate and monetize all program effects. The issue is not as academic as it appears. Consider the social cost of crime. What harm do victims suffer as a result of crime? How much work do they miss? How extensive are their related health costs? What is the value of the pain and fear associated with crime? The textbook approach is to adopt a social welfare perspective in which costs and benefits for all citizens are included in CBA, but this method is far from perfect, especially when programs affect only a few very young offenders charged with relatively minor crimes. Alternatives to this approach, however, present problems of their own. If a CBA counts only costs and benefits associated with the expenditures of public agencies, many of the gains and losses by participants would be excluded. There is a small literature on estimating the true costs of crime, but much more work needs to be done.

CBAs also vary according to their focus—namely, whether they focus on policies that affect groups and organizations or programs that affect individual behavior. The CBA method is generally designed to answer macro policy questions, such as whether overall crime was reduced as a result of some particular action. Ironically, systemic reform strategies such as Reclaiming Futures and the Juvenile Detention Alternatives Initiative are more amenable to this type of analysis, but CBA is more commonly used in studies of programs that are designed to change individual behavior. In studies of individual behavior change, a great deal of attention is focused on issues of internal validity, for example, how to deal with the effects of selection and attrition. Few studies, however, expend much effort on the generalizability of their findings. For example, they rarely if ever use random controlled trial designs. Without rigorous findings on program outcomes, the precision of CBA is jeopardized.

There are two other important implications of these problems. First, programs may affect the behavior of individuals outside the study frame. Suppose juvenile drug courts increased general deterrence as the public learned that JDC programs can be more severe and more intrusive than traditional juvenile court practices. Individuals outside the treatment and comparison groups may change their behavior in important ways, but these changes would not be observed by CBA.

Second, because the sampling frames for many juvenile justice studies are limited, little if anything can be said about the most critical outcomes—reductions in the total amounts of crime and tangible public resources used in response. Many studies use individual recidivism as an outcome, rather than crime in total. A reduction in recidivism, by itself, says very little about reductions in crime. Similarly, a finding that the participants of a program used less detention bed space is not necessarily evidence that public resources were saved, because other juveniles may have used that space. Future CBAs of juvenile justice programs should address these issues directly by explicitly noting whether programs may have substantial costs and benefits that are outside the view of a particular analysis, and then by attempting to measure the effects of programs on crime, not merely recidivism.

Finally, CBA must be very careful in interpreting the effect of an intervention in the presence of rare or extreme events. Even in studies with very small samples, extreme events may occur. Mentoring, for example, is a relatively low-cost intervention. Suppose the evaluation of a mentoring program found that one individual in the comparison group committed a serious assault, was transferred to the adult criminal justice system, and sentenced to a long prison term. How should this be treated in a CBA framework? The literature would suggest putting a cost of several hundred thousand dollars on this one incident, which could be larger than the total costs of the mentoring program. If this one rare event were included, the analysis could suggest that mentoring programs yield benefits ten times or 100 times their cost. If the event were excluded, the program might not pass a cost-benefit test at all. Econometric solutions to this problem could be developed, and such an inquiry would be worthwhile for future studies. At the very least, research results should be presented transparently, with complete explanations of the role played by rare events and other concerns. Finally, it is important to present costs and benefits in sufficient detail so results can be presented not only as point estimates, but with appropriate confidence intervals as well.

CONCLUSION

Research that examines juvenile justice programs from an economic or CBA perspective is a necessary and positive element of policy formation. The economic approach allows researchers to standardize the outcomes of diverse juvenile justice initiatives implemented in differing contexts and at highly varying scales. Without these methods, it would be difficult if not impossible to compare the relative value of programs and strategies for juvenile crime reduction. CBA, however, is not flawless. The methods of CBA should never be exempt from close and critical scrutiny. The assumptions used to construct CBA should always be examined for their accuracy and relevance by policymakers, practitioners, and other researchers interested in juvenile justice reform. CBA yields simple, easily digestible bottom lines that are welcomed by policymakers. It is precisely because CBA is so influential that its methods should be as transparent and accessible as possible.

ACKNOWLEDGMENT AND DISCLAIMER

Any opinions or points of view in this chapter are those of the authors alone and do not necessarily represent the official position or policies of Chapin Hall at the University of Chicago or the Urban Institute. Portions of the discussion about juvenile mentoring programs were prepared in collaboration with Thomas Keller of Portland State University.

REFERENCES

Anspach, Donald F., Andew S. Ferguson, and Laura L. Phillips. 2003. *Evaluation of Maine's State-wide Juvenile Drug Treatment Court Program: Fourth Year Outcome Evaluation Report*. Portland: University of Southern Maine, Department of Sociology.

Aos, Steve, Polly Phipps, Robert Barnoski, and Roxanne Lieb. 2001. *The Comparative Costs and Benefits of Programs to Reduce Crime, v 4.0*. Olympia, WA: Washington State Institute for Public Policy.

Aspy, Cheryl B., Roy F. Oman, Sara K. Vesely, Kenneth McLeroy, Sharon Rodine, and LaDonna Marshall. 2004. "Adolescent Violence: The Protective Effects of Youth Assets." *Journal of Counseling and Development* 82(3): 268–76.

Bazemore, Gordon. 2006). *Performance Measures: Measuring What Really Matters in Juvenile Justice*. Alexandria, VA: American Prosecutors Research Institute.

Becker, Gary S. 1968. "Crime and Punishment: An Economic Approach." *Journal of Political Economy* 76(2): 169–217.

Bouffard, Jeffrey A., and Faye S. Taxman. 2004. "Looking Inside the 'Black Box' of Drug Court Treatment Services Using Direct Observations." *Journal of Drug Issues* 34(1): 195–218.

Butler-Mejia, Kris. 1998. *Seen But Not Heard: The Role of Voice in Juvenile Justice*. Unpublished master's thesis. Fairfax, VA: George Mason University.

Butts, Jeffrey A., and Janeen Buck. 2000. "Teen Courts: A Focus on Research." *OJJDP Juvenile Justice Bulletin* 3.

Butts, Jeffrey A, Janeen Buck, and Mark Coggeshall. 2002. *The Impact of Teen Court on Youth Offenders*. Washington, DC: The Urban Institute.

Butts, Jeffrey A., and John Roman, editors. 2004. *Juvenile Drug Courts and Teen Substance Abuse*. Washington, DC: Urban Institute Press.

Butts, Jeffrey A., and Howard N. Snyder. 2006. *Too Soon to Tell: Deciphering Recent Trends in Youth Violence*. Chicago: Chapin Hall Center for Children at the University of Chicago.

Campbell, Donald T., and Julian Stanley. 1963. *Experimental and Quasi-Experimental Designs for Research*. Chicago: Rand-McNally.

Cartwright, William S. 2000. "Cost-Benefit Analysis of Drug Treatment Services: Review of the Literature." *Journal of Mental Health Policy and Economics* 3(1): 11–26.

Caulkins, Jonathan P., Susan S. Everingham, C. Peter Rydell, James Chiesa, and Shawn Bushway. 1999. *An Ounce of Prevention, A Pound of Uncertainty: The Cost-Effectiveness of School-Based Drug Prevention Programs*. Santa Monica, CA: RAND.

Clark, David E., and James C. Cosgrove. 1990. "Hedonic Prices, Identification, and the Demand for Public Safety." *Journal of Regional Science* 30(1): 105–22.

Cohen, Mark A. 1988. "Pain, Suffering, and Jury Awards: A Study of the Cost of Crime to Victims." *Law and Society Review* 22(3): 53–56.

———. 1998. "The Monetary Value of Saving a High Risk Youth." *Journal of Quantitative Criminology* 14(1): 5–33.

———. 2000. "Measuring the Costs and Benefits of Crime and Justice." In *Criminal Justice 2000*, vol. 4. Washington, DC: National Institute of Justice, U.S. Department of Justice.

Cohen, Mark A., and Ted R. Miller. 2003. "'Willingness to Award' Nonmonetary Damages and the Implied Value of Life from Jury Awards." *International Review of Law and Economics* 23(2): 165–81.

Cohen, Mark A., Roland T. Rust, Sara Steen, and Simon T. Tidd. 2004. "Willingness-to-Pay for Crime Control Programs." *Criminology* 42(1): 89–109.

Colydas, Violet, and Maureen McLeod. 1997. "Colonie NY Youth Court Evaluation." Unpublished manuscript. Troy, NY: Russell Sage College.

Cook, T. D., and Donald T. Campbell. 1979. *Quasi-experimentation: Design and Analysis Issues for Field Settings.* Boston, MA: Houghton Mifflin.

Cornish, Derek B., and Ronald V. Clarke. 1986. *The Reasoning Criminal.* New York: Springer-Verlag.

Darling, Nancy, Stephen F. Hamilton, and Starr Niego. 1994. "Adolescents' Relations with Adults Outside the Family." In *Personal Relationships during Adolescence,* vol. 6, eds. Raymond Montemayor, Gerald R. Adams, and Thomas P. Gullotta. Thousand Oaks, CA: Sage Publications.

Dickie, Jill L. 2002. *Summit County Juvenile Drug Court Evaluation Report.* Akron, OH: University of Akron, Institute for Health and Social Policy.

Downey, Geraldine, Amy Lebolt, Claudia Rincon, and Antonio L. Freitas. 1998. "Rejection Sensitivity and Children's Interpersonal Difficulties." *Child Development* 69(4): 1074–91.

DuBois, David L., Bruce E. Holloway, Jeffrey C. Valentine, and Harris Cooper. 2002. "Effectiveness of Mentoring Programs for Youth: A Meta-analytic Review." *American Journal of Community Psychology* 30(2): 157–97.

Ehrlich, Isaac. 1973. "Participation in Illegitimate Activities: A Theoretical and Empirical Investigation." *Journal of Political Economy* 81(3): 521–65.

———. 1981. "On the Usefulness of Controlling Individuals: An Economic Analysis of Rehabilitation, Incapacitation, and Deterrence." *American Economic Review* 71(3): 307–22.

———. 1996. "Crime, Punishment, and the Market for Offenses." *Journal of Economic Perspectives* 10(1): 43–67.

Federal Bureau of Investigation. 2007. *Crime in the United States 2006.* Preliminary Report, table 4. Washington, DC: U.S. Department of Justice. www.fbi.gov/ucr/06prelim/index.html.

Ferguson, Andrew, Birch McCole, and Jody Raio. 2006. *A Process and Site-Specific Outcome Evaluation of Maine's Juvenile Drug Treatment Court.* Portland: University of Southern Maine, Department of Sociology.

Fo, Walter S.O., and Clifford R. O'Donnell. 1975. "The Buddy System: Effect of Community Intervention on Delinquent Offenses." *Behavior Therapy* 6(4): 522–24.

Garrison, Arthur H. 2001. "An Evaluation of a Delaware Teen Court." *Juvenile and Family Court Journal* 52(3): 11–21.

Gramlich, Edward M. 1986. "Evaluation of Education Projects: The Case of the Perry Preschool Program." *Economics of Education Review* 5(1): 17–24.

Greenwood, Peter W. 2005. *Changing Lives: Delinquency Prevention as Crime-Control Policy.* Chicago: University of Chicago Press.

Greenwood, Peter W., Karyn Model, C. Peter Rydell, and James Chiesa. 1998. *Diverting Children from a Life of Crime: Measuring Costs and Benefits.* Santa Monica, CA: RAND.

Grossman, Jean B., and Jean E. Rhodes. 2002. "The Test of Time: Predictors and Effects of Duration in Youth Mentoring Relationships." *American Journal of Community Psychology* 30(2): 199–219.

Grossman, Jean B., and Joseph P. Tierney. 1998. "Does Mentoring Work? An Impact Study of the Big Brothers Big Sisters Program." *Evaluation Review* 22(3): 403–26.

Harrison, Paige, James R. Maupin, and G. Larry Mays. 2001. "Teen Court: An Examination of Processes and Outcomes." *Crime and Delinquency* 47(2): 243–64.

Henggeler, Scott W., W. Glenn Clingempeel, Michael J. Brondino, and Susan G. Pickrel. 2002. "Four-Year Follow-up of Multisystemic Therapy with Substance-Abusing and Substance-Dependent Juvenile Offenders." *Journal of the American Academy of Child and Adolescent Psychiatry* 41(7): 868–74.

Henggeler, Scott, Colleen A. Halliday-Boykins, Phillippe B. Cunningham, Jeff Randall, Steven B. Shapiro, and Jason E. Chapman. 2006. "Juvenile Drug Court: Enhancing Outcomes by

Integrating Evidence-based Treatments." *Journal of Consulting and Clinical Psychology* 74(1): 42–54.

Hissong, Rod. 1991. "Teen Court—Is it an Effective Alternative to Traditional Sanctions?" *Journal for Juvenile Justice and Detention Services* 6(2): 14–23.

Jackson, Yo. 2002. "Mentoring for Delinquent Children: An Outcome Study with Young Adolescent Children." *Journal of Youth and Adolescence* 31(2): 115–22.

JDAI News. 2006. *Newsletter of the Juvenile Detention Alternatives Initiative* (July): 1–11. www.aecf .org/upload/publicationfiles/july2006.pdf.

———. 2007. *Newsletter of the Juvenile Detention Alternatives Initiative* (March): 1–12. www.aecf .org/upload/publicationfiles/march2006.pdf.

Keating, Lisa M., Michelle A. Tomishima, Sharon Foster, and Michael Alessandri. 2002. "The Effects of a Mentoring Program on At-Risk Youth." *Adolescence* 37(148): 717–34.

Lally, J. Ronald, Peter L. Mangione, and Alice S. Honig. 1987. *The Syracuse University Family Development Research Program, Long-Range Impact of an Early Intervention with Low-Income Children and Their Families.* San Francisco: Far West Laboratory for Educational Research and Development.

Levitt, Steven D. 1996. "The Effect of Prison Population Size on Crime Rates: Evidence from Prison Overcrowding Litigation." *Quarterly Journal of Economics* 111(2): 319–51.

———. 1998. "Juvenile Crime and Punishment." *Journal of Political Economy* 106(6): 1156–85.

LoGalbo, Anthony P., and Charlene M. Callahan. 2001. "An Evaluation of Teen Court as a Juvenile Crime Diversion Program." *Juvenile and Family Court Journal* 52(2): 1–11.

LoSciuto, Leonard, Amy K. Rajala, Tara N. Townsend, and Andrea S. Taylor. 1996. "An Outcome Evaluation of Across Ages: An Intergenerational Mentoring Approach to Drug Prevention." *Journal of Adolescent Research* 11(1): 116–29.

Maltz, Michael D., and Richard McCleary. 1977. "The Mathematics of Behavioral Change: Recidivism and Construct Validity." *Evaluation Review* 1(3): 421–38.

Marlowe, Douglas B. 2004. "Drug Court Efficacy vs. Effectiveness." In *Join Together* (September 29, 2004). www.jointogether.org.

McNeece, Aaron, Mary Kay Falconer, Chalandra M. Bryant, and Michael Shader. 1996. *Hernando County Teen Court: Evaluation of 1996 Continuation Grant Activity.* Tallahassee: Florida State University, Institute for Health and Human Services Research.

Miller, Ted R., Mark A. Cohen, and Brian Wiersma. 1996. "Victim Costs and Consequences: A New Look." *National Institute of Justice Research Report.* Washington, DC: U.S. Department of Justice.

Miller, Ted R., Mark A. Cohen, and Shelli B. Rossman. 1993. "Victim Costs of Violent Crime and Resulting Injuries." *Health Affairs* 12(4): 186–97.

Miller, Ted R., Deborah A. Fisher, and Mark A. Cohen. 2001. "Costs of Juvenile Violence: Policy Implications." *Pediatrics* 107(1): 1–7.

Minor, Kevin I., James B. Wells, Irina R. Soderstrom, Rachel Bingham, and Deborah Williamson. 1999. "Sentence Completion and Recidivism among Juveniles Referred to Teen Courts." *Crime and Delinquency* 45(4): 467–80.

Mohr, Lawrence. 1995. *Impact Analysis for Program Evaluation,* 2nd ed. Thousand Oaks, CA: Sage Publications.

Moore, Elizabeth, Gay Armsden, and Patrick L. Gogerty. 1998. "A Twelve-Year Follow-up Study of Maltreated and At-Risk Children Who Received Early Therapeutic Child Care." *Child Maltreatment* 3(1): 3–16.

National Drug Court Institute and National Council of Juvenile and Family Court Judges. 2003.

Juvenile Drug Courts: Strategies in Practice. Washington, DC: U.S. Department of Justice, Bureau of Justice Assistance.

Nissen, Laura B., Jeffrey A. Butts, David M. Merrigan, and M. Katherine Kraft. 2006. "The RWJF Reclaiming Futures Initiative: Improving Substance Abuse Interventions for Justice-Involved Youth." *Juvenile and Family Court Journal* 57(4): 39–51.

O'Donnell, Clifford R., T. Lydgate, and Walter S. O. Fo. 1979. "The Buddy System: Review and Follow-Up." *Child Behavior Therapy* 1(2): 161–69.

Olds, David, Peggy Hill, Sharon F. Mihalic, and Ruth O'Brien. 1998. *Nurse-Family Partnership: Blueprints for Violence Prevention, Book 7.* Blueprints for Violence Prevention Series, ed. D. S. Elliott. Boulder: Center for the Study and Prevention of Violence, Institute of Behavioral Science, University of Colorado.

Oman, Roy F., Sara K. Vesely, Cheryl B. Aspy, Kenneth McLeroy, Sharon Rodine, and Ladonna Marshall. 2004. "The Potential Protective Effect of Youth Assets on Adolescent Alcohol and Drug Use." *American Journal of Public Health* 94(8): 1425–30.

Pagani, Linda, Richard E. Tremblay, Frank Vitaro, and Sophie Parent. 1998. "Does Preschool Help Prevent Delinquency in Boys with a History of Perinatal Complications?" *Criminology* 36(2): 245–67.

Parsons, Bruce V., and Edward C. Byrnes. 1998. *Utah Byrne Partnership Evaluation Project: Recidivism Data Synopsis for the Utah Juvenile Drug Court.* Salt Lake City: University of Utah Social Research Institute, Graduate School of Social Work.

Piehl, Anne M., and John J. DiIulio Jr. 1995. "Does Prison Pay? Revisited." *Brookings Review* 13(1): 20–25.

Piper, Elizabeth S. 1985. "Violent Recidivism and Chronicity in the 1958 Philadelphia Cohort." *Journal of Quantitative Criminology* 1(4): 319–44.

Pires, Sheila. 2002. *Building Systems of Care: A Primer.* Washington, DC: National Technical Assistance Center for Children's Mental Health.

Rajkumar, Andrew S., and Michael T. French. 1997. "Drug Abuse, Crime Costs, and the Economic Benefits of Treatment." *Journal of Quantitative Criminology* 13(3): 291–323.

Reichel, Phillip, and Carole Seyfrit. 1984. "A Peer Jury in the Juvenile Court." *Crime and Delinquency* 30(3): 423–38.

Reynolds, Arthur J., Judy A. Temple, Dylan L. Robertson, and Emily A. Mann. 2000. *Long Term Benefits of Participation in the Title 1 Chicago Child-Parent Centers.* Paper presented at the Biennial Meeting of the Society for Research on Adolescence. Chicago (March 30 to April 2, 2000).

Rhodes, Jean E. 2002. *Stand by Me: The Risks and Rewards of Mentoring Today's Youth.* Cambridge, MA: Harvard University Press.

Robertson, Angela A., Paul W. Grimes, and Kevin E. Rogers. 2001. "A Short-Run Cost-Benefit Analysis of Community-Based Interventions for Juvenile Offenders." *Crime and Delinquency* 47(2): 265–85.

Rodriguez, Nancy, and Vincent J. Webb. 2004. "Multiple Measures of Juvenile Drug Court Effectiveness: Results of a Quasi-experimental Design." *Crime and Delinquency* 50(2): 292–314.

Rosen, Sherwin, and Richard H. Thaler. 1975. "The Value of Saving a Life: Evidence from the Labor Market." In *Household Production and Consumption*, ed. N. Terleckyj. Boston, MA: National Bureau of Economic Research.

Royse, David. 1998. "Mentoring High-Risk Minority Youth: Evaluation of the Brothers Project." *Adolescence* 33(129): 145–58.

Sanford, J. Scott, and Bruce A. Arrigo. 2005. "Lifting the Cover on Drug Courts: Evaluation Findings and Policy Concerns." *International Journal of Offender Therapy and Comparative Criminology* 49(3): 239–59.

Schweinhart, Lawrence J., Helen V. Barnes, and David P. Weikart. 1993. *Significant Benefits: The High-Scope Perry Preschool Study through Age 27*. Monograph of the High/Scope Educational Research Foundation, No. 10. Ypsilanti, MI: High/Scope Press.

Sipe, Cynthia L. 2002. "Mentoring Programs for Adolescents: A Research Summary." *Journal of Adolescent Health* 31(6): 251–60.

Slicker, Ellen K., and Douglas J. Palmer. 1993. "Mentoring At-Risk High School Students: Evaluation of a School-based Program." *School Counselor* 40(5): 327–34.

Snyder, Howard N., and Melissa Sickmund. 2006. *Juvenile Offenders and Victims: 2006 National Report*. Washington, DC: U.S. Department of Justice Programs, Office of Justice Programs, Office of Juvenile Justice and Delinquency Prevention.

SRA Associates. 1995. *Teen Court Evaluation of 1994 Activities and Goals: Characteristics, Backgrounds, and Outcomes of Program Referrals*. Santa Rosa, CA: SRA Associates.

Swink, Morgan I. 1998. *Onondaga County Youth Court Recidivism Rates*. Unpublished manuscript. Syracuse, NY: Syracuse University, Maxwell School of Citizenship and Public Affairs.

Thaler, Richard H. 1978. "A Note on the Value of Crime Control: Evidence from the Property Market." *Journal of Urban Economics* 5(1): 137–45.

The White House. 2004. *National Drug Control Strategy (March 2004)*. Washington, DC: Office of National Drug Control Policy.

Thompson, Kevin M. 2004. *An Adult Recidivism Outcome Evaluation of North Dakota's Juvenile Drug Court*. Fargo: North Dakota State University, Department of Criminal Justice and Political Science.

Wells, James B., Kevin I. Minor, and James W. Fox. 1998. *An Evaluation of Kentucky's 1997–98 Teen Court Program*. Richmond: Eastern Kentucky University, Center for Criminal Justice Education and Research.

Chapter 8

Prisoner Reentry Programming

John K. Roman and Christy Visher

In 2006, about 700,000 prisoners were released from state and federal prisons across the country, more than four times as many as were released in 1980. With the exception of those who die while in prison, all prisoners will eventually reenter the community. Prisoner reentry has sweeping consequences for the individual prisoners, their families, and the communities to which they return (Petersilia 2003; Travis 2005). Advocates for expanded prisoner reentry programs argue that prison is expensive and that providing community-based supervision, treatment, and service provision is a more effective, and less expensive, approach. Critics point to the risk to public safety from community-based supervision in lieu of incarceration, and the limited impact of many extant programs on desistance. Although a substantial theoretical and applied literature explores the causes and correlates of desistance, few economic studies have been conducted to test the core hypothesis of prisoner reentry—that these programs are more economically efficient than business as usual. Here, we identify programs, strategies, and policies that have evidence supporting their efficacy, including some that are relatively untested, and propose approaches for economic tests of their effectiveness.

In recent years, significant attention has been focused on the impact of persistent increases in rates of incarceration and rates of return from jail or prison (Clear, Rose, and Ryder 2001; Hagan and Coleman 2001; Travis 2005; Mauer 2000; Bonczar and Beck 1997). Geographic clustering by socioeconomic characteristics has led to disproportionate rates of removal from, and return to, already distressed communities (Lynch and Sabol 2001, 2000; Clear, Rose, and Ryder 2001). As a result, current research on the social and economic impacts of incarceration is increasingly focused on place-based effects of incarceration and prisoner reintegration, and the concurrent effects on family structure, intergenerational offending, and general community well-being (Clear, Rose, and Ryder 2001; Hagan and Dinovitzer 1999). Emerging reentry programs, such as public-private reentry partnerships, seek to address the effects of incarceration by more successfully reintegrating former prisoners and by reducing subsequent offending, thereby insulating communities from the harmful effects of both transitions, the transition from prison to communities, and from communities back to prison.

Reentry programming is designed to break the cycle between offending (which harms victims) and incarceration (which reduces the offenders'—and the communities'—ability to repair those harms). By committing crimes, offenders directly harm a victim or victims, and indirectly harm the community by increasing fear and reducing perceived safety. However, if imprisonment is focused solely on incapacitation rather than on rehabilitation that leads to desistance, offenders' ability to repair these harms is likely reduced. Imprisonment without rehabilitation may reduce human capital levels and impede the acquisition of new pro-social skills, which ultimately reduces the probability the offender will successfully reintegrate into the community of return. As a result, current and former prisoners may disrupt the social structure of their community by reducing their connections to the community and thereby reducing the community's social capital (Clear, Rose, and Ryder 2001; Hagan and Dinovitzer 1999; Sabol and Lynch 1997). Reentry proponents argue that unless each of these issues is addressed—harm to the community caused by criminal acts, and subsequent loss of human and social capital by both the community and the offender—one effect of the return of former prisoners will be to increase, not decrease, the burden on the community.

Incarcerating offenders generally has two purposes: incapacitation and deterrence. Incapacitation leads to temporary instrumental desistance, and specific deterrence may lead to future deterrence. However, desistance is mainly achieved through rehabilitative programming. Predictors of desistance generally do not vary by the pattern of past criminal behavior or by the antecedent characteristics of the offender (Laub and Sampson 2001). Processes that are consistently identified as leading to desistance include marriage and stable families, aging, stable employment and reduced exposure to antisocial peers (stable families, Sampson and Laub 1993; aging, Laub and Sampson 2006; Glueck and Glueck 1974; Gottfredson and Hirschi 1990; Laub and Sampson 2006; employment, Sampson and Laub 1993; exposure, Warr 1998; Laub and Sampson 2006). In addition, all of these outcomes may depend on cognitive changes in identity that are the precursor to changes in behavior (Maruna 2001).

Of the predictors of desistance, only stable employment and cognitive change, and possibly family stability, can be directly addressed through policy or programming. As a result, reentry initiatives have typically focused on preparing returning prisoners to reenter the job market. Reentry services often include interventions directly related to skill acquisition, such as job readiness, training, and placement programs designed to improve labor market prospects. Programming also focuses on reducing human capital deficits, including linkages to substance abuse, and physical and mental health services; improving educational attainment through GED or high school programming; and other initiatives from the small (access to official identification and transfer of prescriptions) to the large (assistance in securing transitional and long-term housing). Reentry initiatives may assist in the cognitive development of participants to promote behavioral change through faith-based or classroom-based programming (anger management, parenting skills, life skills).

EVALUATION OF REENTRY PROGRAMS

The challenge to researchers investigating reentry policies and programs is that the term *reentry* does not refer to a bounded, defined mission, but rather to the time when issues related to desistance may be addressed, specifically in the period surrounding release from jail or prison. A cost-benefit analysis (CBA) of reentry is therefore a CBA of all the social service programming associated with reentry, where the only commonality is the ultimate outcome of interest, desistance. Reentry programming as it is currently understood is nascent—the first broad federal funding of reentry programming began in 2003, and many, if not most, local reentry efforts began concurrently.

As a result, the research literature is sparse, and CBAs are rare. That said, a broad extant literature describes the potential efficacy or effectiveness of various components of reentry. For example, several high-quality studies have been conducted on the efficacy of job training for low-skilled workers. Although the integration of various rehabilitative programs into a unified reentry framework may improve associated outcomes, it is fair to assess these programs by reviewing the literature on the results of their single components.

ECONOMIC ANALYSIS IN REENTRY RESEARCH

A number of challenges exist to conducting useful economic impact analyses over and above those of identifying the average treatment effect of the component programs. These include costs that are often spread across numerous service providers, organizing entities that coordinate or facilitate linkages to extant services—but do not directly provide—services, limited data measuring the amount (dosage) of services (inputs), and benefits that are diffuse and that may accrue to many parties not directly affected by the intervention.

The preferred strategy for measuring the total costs of an intervention based on the criminal justice system is a bottom-up approach that sums the product of the price and the quantity of each good or service provided over all participants. In practice, few evaluations follow this procedure because the CBA is an add-on to an impact evaluation. Data critical to estimating economic impacts (such as the quantity of services consumed by the comparison group) are often not collected because they are not relevant to the impact evaluation. Most existing CBAs rely instead on top-down estimates of average cost using an accounting approach. As a result, cost estimates may include fixed (and sunk) costs not associated with the intervention under study, may exclude opportunity costs, and may not account for economies of scale.

Another limitation of the extant studies is that many cost-benefit approaches do not adopt a social welfare perspective, but instead some sort of "public payer" scheme that counts only the costs and benefits borne by public agencies. Often the perspective is even narrower, counting costs and benefits for only some public agencies. Critical benefits, such as savings to the community from reduced harms resulting from a reduction in victimization are thus excluded, and benefits to public agencies resulting from private efforts are counted though the private costs are excluded. Finally, relatively high-cost (or high-benefit) but rare events (such as an escape or a murder) cannot be modeled using traditional statistical or econometric approaches. For example, a recent evaluation using a randomized control trial of a reentry court in Indiana found about $3 in benefits for every dollar in costs. However, most of the benefit to the community ($1.3 million of the $1.7 million total) was due to a reduction in homicides from an expected 0.42 homicides to zero. Excluding these savings reduces the benefit-cost ratio to less than 2.

Two other important and closely related limitations of the usual cost-benefit approach to reentry evaluation are worth considering—the effect of researching stovepipe programs, and the effects of programs on communities. As noted, many reentry programs are designed to bundle services, and we believe that this holistic approach will ultimately become best practice. That is, programs that attempt to address the whole range of offender deficits are more likely to increase desistance than programs that focus on a single issue. However, data limitations often require evaluators to focus only on the costs and benefits of a single service or a few services in the bundle, because primary data collection in the evaluation of a program providing a dozen or more services is often impractical. The net result is that both costs and benefits are systematically undercounted. As the extent of this cannot be observed with a limited sampling frame, it is difficult to know what to make of the estimates that result.

Current approaches also tend to be offender-centric. That is, cost estimates focus on costs associated with treating and processing offenders, and benefits estimates focus on avoided costs from crime prevention, including benefits to victims who are not victimized and benefits to public agencies that do not need to expend resources to investigate, prosecute, and incarcerate offenders for those prevented crimes. This approach excludes important economic consequences, especially on the benefits side, from effective reentry programs. As Bruce Western noted, "An expanded commitment to prisoner reentry policy has collateral benefits that are also somewhat invisible. Children and spouses will benefit from the improved literacy and subsidized employment of their fathers and partners even if they have trouble finding work" (2007, 355). We believe there are other collateral consequences beyond the offenders' immediate family, including their neighbors and other residents of their communities, all of whom can benefit from the successful reintegration of former prisoners. In economic parlance, CBA of reentry should consider externalities from these programs, and sum the costs and benefits to those who are not party to the reentry exchange of services, but nevertheless experience the consequences.

The challenges to CBAs of reentry programming, though serious, are not intractable. Other disciplines, including environmental economics and health economics, have faced similar issues and developed methods in response. Health economists have developed and widely accepted a set of measures known as quality-adjusted life years (QALYs) that allow for standardized comparisons of outcomes from medical treatment where there is substantial variation in pain and suffering. Environmental economists have used contingent valuation techniques to measure the externalities from investment in public goods, such as clean air or the presence of national parks. Adapting these approaches to public goods related to reentry, such as public safety, seems relatively straightforward. Until those efforts become more routinely used in crime control research, the primary recommendation for cost-benefit analysts interested in studying reentry is to proceed cautiously and comprehensively.

PRE-RELEASE (IN-PRISON) PROGRAMS

Various types of rehabilitative programs for offenders are delivered in correctional settings, including skills training, job readiness, GED and college-level degree programs, drug treatment, individual and group counseling, and cognitive-behavioral therapy. The consensus among researchers is that to be most effective, inmate screening, needs assessment, and the provision of services needs to be integrated into the prevailing correctional philosophy (Mears and Moore 2003; Lawrence et al. 2002). In many, if not most, correctional systems security classification takes precedence over service provision. For example, if the highest-need offenders are also high risk, programming resources may have to be shifted to higher-security institutions (Logan 1993) though there have not been any evaluations testing this hypothesis. There is also general agreement that promising correctional programs should be timed to be close to a prisoner's release date, focus on skills applicable to the local job market, reflect current market demands, and be provided for an extended period of time, generally three to six months (Cullen and Gendreau 2000). However, the duration of in-prison programming is somewhat arbitrary—one possible research area that remains unexplored is whether reentry programs would be more effective if the length of reentry programs varied according to the magnitude of the individual prisoner's deficits.

In many correctional systems, the incentives to participate in programming may run counter to the program's objectives. For instance, if prisoners receive credit toward early release or other in-prison rewards, they are likely to enroll regardless of their need for its specific content. In an analysis that examined the extent to which correctional treatment is matched to individual need, a recent study compared prisoners' need for drug treatment with reported treatment received and found that only 58 percent of prisoners who either had objective indicators of serious drug use or indicated a need for drug treatment received in-prison drug treatment, including Alcoholics Anonymous and Narcotics Anonymous (Winterfield and Castro 2005). Another study of prisoners in Tennessee, who were required to secure either employment or enroll in a training program as a condition of release, found that those who graduated had marginally better outcomes than a matched comparison, and that those who failed had significantly worse outcomes, leading to an overall finding that the costs of the programs were significantly larger than the benefits (Chalfin et al. 2007). Few reentry programs take seriously the issue of incentives to participate and complete programs and real opportunities exist to test strategies to better align program enrollment with incentives.

Education

In the United States, adult corrections have a long history of providing education and employment training (Piehl 1998; Gaes et al. 1999). Comprehensive reviews of dozens of individual program evaluations generally conclude that adult academic and vocational programs lead to modest reductions in recidivism and increases in employment (Gerber and Fritsch 1994; Gaes et al. 1999; Cullen and Gendreau 2000; Wilson, Gallagher, and MacKenzie 2000; Aos, Miller, and Drake 2006). The majority of the evaluations, however, have one or more methodological problems (Wilson, Gallagher, and MacKenzie 2000).

Numerous studies show that recidivism rates are significantly reduced for those with more education; however, just getting a GED--the most prevalent in-prison educational programming—generally does not show impacts on reentry outcomes (Adams et al. 1994; Boudin 1993; Harer 1995; Stillman 1999). Research suggests that correctional education programming is most successful as part of a systematic approach, integrating employability, social skills training, and other specialized programming. Best-practice correctional education programs have carefully tailored programming to the needs of individuals and to related vocational and job skills training. Education and job training for low earners are most successful when they provide workers with credentials that meet private sector demands. Comprehensive programs that provide training, a range of services and supports, job retention incentives, and access to employers are promising, especially when there are strong pressures on ex-offenders to gain employment (Holzer and Martinson 2005; Visher and Courtney 2006), but rigorous evaluations are lacking.

POSTRELEASE PROGRAMS

In the immediate period after release from prison, access to supportive reentry (or transitional) services are critical in those first few days, weeks, and months for men and women as they readjust to life in the community. Among the most important are obtaining photo identification, getting appropriate clothes, securing stable housing, having reliable transportation, and signing up for public assistance, if eligible. Unfortunately, often such needs are not addressed before release and it falls to family and friends to help arrange these for the former prisoner. There are no evaluations of programs that focus exclusively on the immediate post-release period, but one program in Maryland that generally focused on this period was found to reduce recidivism—particularly the most serious and violent offenses—and was cost-effective (Roman et al. 2007).

Developing tailored reentry plans to guide postrelease services begins with an assessment and classification of reoffending risk, needs, and strengths leading to individualized and unified case planning and management that addresses individual variation in likelihood to re-offend (Andrews and Bonta 1998; Weibush, McNulty, and Le 2000; Weibush et al. 2005). These assessments differ from the initial screens conducted at prison entry and are the foundation for an individualized reentry plan. Such targeted assessments not only determine the specific kinds of services and supervision level that individuals need to succeed, but also determine who requires documents, medications, or other immediate transition preparation. The ideal case management approach incorporates a family and social network perspective, a mix of surveillance and services focused on risk and protective factors, realistic and enforceable release conditions, and graduated incentives and sanctions. It also uses service brokering to community service providers and resources and other supportive community organizations (Petersilia 2003; Healy, Foley, and Walsh 1999).

Research suggests that an integrated, multimodal intervention strategy—often referred to as wraparound service delivery— can be effective in meeting the multiple needs of this population. This strategy involves wrapping a comprehensive array of individualized services and support networks around clients, rather than forcing them to enroll in predetermined, inflexible treatment programs (Carney and Buttell 2003). Treatment services are usually provided by multiple agencies working as part of a collaborative interagency agreement, and each individual's treatment plan is determined and managed by an interdisciplinary team of a caseworker, family and community members, and several social services and mental health professionals. These approaches also emphasize the importance of recruiting committed staff and creating programs that focus on the strengths of the client and are culturally appropriate (Bruns et al. 2004). Such approaches capitalize on individual strengths, motivation, and desire for change to address daily problems of living (Clark 2006; De Jong and Berg 2002; Maruna 2001), and have been found to work with families, substance abusers, and persons with mental health issues (Early and GlenMaye 2000), but have not been evaluated specifically with returning prisoners.

Housing

Securing housing is perhaps the most immediate challenge facing prisoners on their release, and the options are limited (Roman and Travis 2006). The majority turn to family or friends. Research has found that released prisoners who do not have stable housing arrangements are more likely to return to prison (Metraux and Culhane 2004). Supportive housing programs could be an option but they have not been implemented on a wide scale (Jason et al. 2006; Roman and Travis 2006). Mutual-help models such as Oxford House are particularly effective at providing positive peer networks and may be an appropriate model for postrelease housing for former prisoners (Jason et al. 2006). Greater peer support from other formerly incarcerated people has been shown to be associated with reduced criminal recidivism (Broome et al. 1996; Wexler 1995). The most rigorous of this work was a random assignment evaluation of an Oxford House program that followed 90 percent of participants for two years. The study reported 50 percent less recidivism among Oxford House residents than among controls. Employment at the two-year follow-up was also significantly higher among Oxford House participants and the number of criminal charges was significantly lower (Olson et al. 2005).

Cognitive-Behavioral Approaches

Cognitive-behavioral approaches include contingency management (relapse prevention), social learning, and moral reasoning techniques. The most widely recognized behavior management approach to change is cognitive-behavioral therapy, or treatment (CBT).

CBT is a problem-focused method designed to help people identify the dysfunctional beliefs, thoughts, and patterns of behavior that contribute to their problems and provide them with the skills they need to modify and improve these behaviors, prevent relapse, and maintain successful behavior (Taxman 2006).

CBT approaches combine two kinds of psychotherapy—cognitive and behavioral. Cognitive therapy concentrates on thoughts, assumptions, and beliefs and individuals are encouraged to change maladaptive thinking that leads to negative behavior (Beck 1995). Behavioral therapy addresses the specific actions and environments that either change or maintain behaviors (Skinner 1974; Bandura 1977). Replacing negative behaviors with reinforced positive behaviors is a well-known strategy to help change behaviors. Cognitive-behavioral therapy strategies have been successfully used to forestall the onset, ameliorate the severity, and change behaviors associated with delinquency and criminal behavior. CBT has been successfully applied across settings (schools, support groups, prisons, treatment agencies, community-based organizations, and churches) and across ages and roles (students, parents, and teachers) (Landenberger and Lipsey 2006; Waldron and Kaminer 2004).

Meta-analyses of evaluations testing CBT's effectiveness among offenders have shown CBT programs to be particularly effective in reducing recidivism rates, most notably among higher risk, hard-to-reach offenders (Little 2005; Lipsey, Chapman, and Landenberger 2001). A comprehensive meta-analysis of the effects of cognitive-behavioral programs that included only randomized control designs shows that, on average, CBT reduced the recidivism rates of a general offender population by 27 percent (Landenberger and Lipsey 2006). Offenders receiving treatment through participation in programs with high quality implementation experienced higher reductions in recidivism rates (49 percent on average) compared to those receiving CBT as part of routine correctional practice (11 percent on average). The largest effects on recidivism were seen for higher risk offenders receiving treatment from providers with at least moderate CBT training and as part of research and demonstration projects; for this group, recidivism rates were reduced by nearly 60 percent. Landenberger and Lipsey found no difference in the effectiveness of various brand name CBT programs (such as Moral Reconation Therapy, Reasoning and Rehabilitation) or generic forms of CBT.

In a review of evidence-based adult corrections programs, Steve Aos and his colleagues found that cognitive behavioral treatment for the general offender population significantly reduces recidivism by an average of 8.2 percent (2006). Prison-based drug treatment programs that employ CBT approaches have also been found to reduce recidivism by an average of about 7 percent. CBT programs for sex offenders that focus on reducing deviant arousal and increasing skills necessary for appropriate social interaction have been shown to result in reduced recidivism rates of 15 percent if received in prison and more than twice the reduction in recidivism rates if the treatment is community based (31 percent). CBT programs have been shown to be cost-effective, yielding $2.54 to $11.48 for every program dollar invested—a substantially better result than punishment-oriented interventions that have yielded returns of only 50 to 75 cents for every program dollar spent (Aos et al. 2001).

Substance Abuse Treatment

Previous problems with substance use—that is, illegal drug use and alcohol abuse—among individuals released from prison pose significant challenges to their successful reintegration into the community. Data from the Arrestee Drug Abuse Monitoring (ADAM) project find that about three-fourths of state prisoners have had some type of involvement with alcohol or drug use in the time leading up to their offense, and almost 40 percent meet clinical measures of being at risk for drug dependence. However, only 15 percent of this group receives drug treatment while incarcerated (Karberg and James 2005).

The three primary treatment approaches for drug-abusing offenders are therapeutic communities (intensive programs that typically have stand-alone custodial units), outpatient treatment (counseling done by a certified drug treatment specialist), and 12-step programs, such as Alcoholics Anonymous and Narcotics Anonymous. It is widely believed that correctional drug treatment programs for offenders lead to postrelease reductions in drug use, criminal behavior, and better outcomes in other areas such as employment. To this end, the federal government has invested more than $450 million in the last decade for states to establish residential substance abuse treatment (RSAT) programs in correctional institutions.

Rigorous evaluations of in-prison drug treatment programs, however, are few and evaluations of the three most well-known model programs—Key/Crest (Delaware), the Amity therapeutic prison (California), and Kyle New Vision (Texas)—suffer from several methodological shortcomings including control groups that cannot be compared, inadequate controls for selection bias, and poor outcome measures (Pearson and Lipton 1999; Gaes et al. 1999). Meta-analysis of these (and other) evaluations finds that treatment programs for drug-involved offenders reduce recidivism by 5 percent, in-prison program without community treatment, to 12 percent, treatment in the community (Aos et al. 2006). Some offenders may benefit from diversion into treatment, but others may only require intensive monitoring through frequent drug testing with threat of criminal justice sanctions (Marlowe 2003). Individuals with dual and triple diagnoses—such as substance abuse, mental illness, and HIV infection—face acute difficulties after release from prison, and the associated service needs are even more challenging.

Continuing drug abuse treatment in the community is believed to be necessary to help the recently released individual deal with problems that only become salient at reentry, such as learning to handle situations that could lead to relapse, learning how to live drug free, and developing a drug-free peer support network. Unfortunately, for the small group of individuals who have access to and take advantage of treatment programs in prison, even fewer continue to receive appropriate treatment once they return to the community (Winterfield and Castro 2005).

A number of strategies that have proven effective in pretrial and diversionary programs have been applied to postrelease supervision of drug offenders, with some success. Postrelease monitoring of drug use through urinalysis or other objective methods, as part of criminal justice supervision and especially in conjunction with a graduated sanctions protocol, has been found to reduce relapse and criminal behavior (Taxman 2006). Increasingly, medications are an important part of treatment for serious drug abusers with long histories, including methadone, buprenorphine, topiramate, and naltrexone. Although these medications may not be appropriate for all drug-using offenders, the criminal justice system has been slow to embrace these approaches and most individuals under supervision in the community are not offered this type of treatment. Enhancing the ongoing coordination between treatment providers and courts or supervision officers is important to address the complex needs of drug-abusing former prisoners, though outpatient addiction treatment and community criminal justice supervision systems historically have limited collaboration (Marlowe 2003).

Sustained abstinence may well be associated with substantial reductions in crime (50 percent or more), but only a small percentage of drug-abusing offenders receive appropriate treatment for the length of time necessary to achieve these outcomes (Harrell and Roman 2001; Marlowe 2003). Best practice would call for intensive treatment for prisoners with histories of serious substance abuse, better coordination between in-prison and postrelease treatment providers, and joint case management between criminal justice and community treatment providers. A broader application of best practices adapted from the specialized courts model might also enhance effectiveness. These programs accept relapse as part of recovery, and focus on creating incentives (both positive and negative) for abstinence and treatment engagement under the intense scrutiny of a legitimate authority (such as a judge). The change in focus from detection of technical violations to a therapeutic orientation has proved effective for those on probation, and could reasonably be expected to yield benefits in outcomes for those released from prison to community supervision.

Gaps in the evaluation literature with respect to the efficacy of in-prison and community-based drug treatment are substantial. First, many of the evaluations of drug treatment fail to control for motivation at the time of program entry, and use matching strategies based on antecedent characteristics (such as criminal history and primary drug) that have not been empirically demonstrated to be associated with motivation. What is needed to move the field of drug treatment research along are studies that use a strong inference design and studies that provide for a comparative examination of various treatment modalities among groups of offenders with equivalent levels of risk and need. By strong inference, design can be defined as those that measure not only the outcome of interest but the intervening factors, such as changes in motivation or self esteem. With respect to CBA, there have been few cost-benefit studies of in-prison treatment programs, and important technical issues in the estimation of prison costs remain unresolved.

From a programmatic perspective, several models offer encouraging results. Long-term (ninety days of treatment or more) treatment has been demonstrated as efficacious, though it is worth noting that many in-prison programs are a month or less. Applying therapeutic principles from specialized courts may yield more effective programming for treatment and supervision. In particular, evidence suggests that using graduated sanctions in responding to technical violations, a magistrate or other authority to monitor progress, consistent mechanisms to encourage treatment engagement, and establishing incentives to complete programs successfully may all yield better outcomes for drug-involved offenders than current strategies. These strategies may also be effective in dealing with prisoners with mental health problems, though the research in this area is more ambiguous.

Finally, community-justice partnerships may be effective in delivering scarce health resources to this population. The challenge for establishing these partnerships, however, is to determine the circumstances in which the lack of a formal, integrated response to infractions might reduce program effectiveness. Many reentry programs use a community-justice partnership model in which the justice system monitors behavior and the community provides the services for a range of interventions, from job training to drug treatment. In these cases, the incentives of the justice system (detection of new offending or violations) may be at odds with the therapeutic orientation of the program, limiting the effectiveness of both. In programs that are mainly community-based, participants may not have incentives to comply, because there are no real consequences for failure. Because programs that coerce abstinence through graduated sanctions have been shown to be at least as effective as voluntary programs, an opportunity to intervene more effectively may be missed in these instances.

Faith-Based Programs

Thousands of faith-based organizations (FBOs) provide services to individuals in prison and to former prisoners in the community. FBOs focus on promoting pro-social values and morals, imparting accountability and responsibility, and providing social support networks and skills, all of which can affect behavioral and social change (Roman et al. 2007). Services include emergency and long-term shelter, job training, mentoring of young adults and children of former prisoners, and treatment for addiction (Hercik et al. 2004; Wilcox 1998). However, there is ambiguity about what constitutes a faith-based program and the current faith-based reentry programs appear to be an extremely diverse set of programs and volunteer-centered efforts that may provide no obvious faith-oriented or faith-specific services (Mears et al. 2006).

Only a few research studies have been conducted to assess the effectiveness of faith-based programs, and even fewer examine the characteristics of the services that exemplify effective programming. Although there is a theoretical link in the criminological literature between religiosity, faith, and spirituality, and crime, there are virtually no rigorous empirical studies and the results from the few existing studies are ambiguous (for examples of linkages, see Clear et al. 1992; Clear et al. 2000; Roman et al. 2004; Evans et al. 1995). Byron Johnson, David Larson, and Timothy Pitts, using a matched comparison group of men participating in the Prison Fellowship programs in four prisons in New York State, found that participants had similar rates of recidivism as prisoners who did not participate in the program, though more active participants had lower rates of re-arrest (1997). Other evaluations of in-prison, faith-based programs report some reductions in recidivism or time to re-arrest but methodological problems such as unclear causal models and self-selection bias limit confidence in the results (Johnson and Larson 2003; Hercik et al. 2004; Mears et al. 2006).

More recently, faith-based organizations have experimented with church members mentoring former prisoners. Mentoring programs have a long history in delinquency prevention and evaluation results show that mentoring has positive impacts for at-risk and delinquent youth (Branch and Tierney 2000). The goal of mentoring is to support the development of healthy individuals by addressing the need for pro-social contact, thereby reducing risk factors and enhancing protective factors for problem behavior. Certain features are essential in implementing mentoring programs, including frequent contact between mentor and mentee and identification of the mentor as a friend rather than as an authoritative figure. Adult mentoring programs for former prisoners are being studied in the context of the Department of Labor's program, Ready4Work (R4W) and Prisoner Reentry Initiative (PRI), both of which have a strong faith-based component. The mentors and coaches are drawn from the community, especially faith-based organizations. A preliminary report provides examples of mentoring in the R4W sites that appear promising (Jucovy 2006). An evaluation of the program will examine the frequency and duration of participation in the mentoring aspects of R4W as it relates to an individual's successful reintegration.

Systematic research and assessment is necessary to build a body of evaluative research that articulates and operationalizes the diverse elements of faith across faith-based social service programs, regardless of service domain (corrections, health, public health, for example), and how these elements make a difference in comparison to other reentry programs. At this point, research is lacking not only on how faith-based programs fare compare to secular programs, but also on whether there are differences between monotheistic and overtly religious programs and nondenominational and implicitly spiritual programs.

Employment Services and Job Counseling

Finding sustained employment is widely considered a key issue for returning prisoners. Although about two-thirds of prisoners were working before they were incarcerated, their education level, work experience, and skills are well below national averages for the general population, and the stigma associated with incarceration often makes it difficult for them to secure jobs (Andrews and Bonta 1998; Holzer and Martinson 2005; Bushway and Reuter 2001). When returning prisoners do find jobs, they tend to earn less than individuals with similar background characteristics who have not been incarcerated (Bushway and Reuter 2001). Research indicates that work is a primary feature of successful reintegration as connections made at work may serve as informal social controls that help prevent criminal behavior (Sampson and Laub 1990, 1993; Laub, Nagin, and Sampson 1998). For former prisoners, employment is correlated with lower recidivism and rates of return to prison are significantly reduced by participation in work readiness programs (Rossman and Roman 2003; Buck 2000; Finn 1998; Sung 2001).

Research thus supports a strong programmatic emphasis on increasing individual employability, both during incarceration through skills training, job readiness, and work release programs, and after release. Although recent studies have indicated that work programs can have a significant impact on the employment and recidivism rates of men, vocational programs often are unavailable in prisons, and their availability has declined over the last decade (Bushway and Reuter 2001; Lynch and Sabol 2001).

The evaluation of the Opportunity to Succeed program, which delivered employment services within a set of comprehensive services for drug-using former prisoners, found that participants were more likely to be employed full time in the year after release, and reported less drug use. Self-reported arrests and official record measures of recidivism showed no differences between participants and controls (Rossman and Roman 2003). Employed participants, however, reported fewer arrests and less drug use. In a meta-analysis examining the impact of employment training and job assistance in the community for persons with a criminal record, Aos et al. conclude that these programs have a modest, but significant, 5 percent impact on recidivism (2006). In another meta-analysis, however, using a very similar set of studies and methods, Christy Visher, Laura Winterfield, and Mark Coggeshall concluded that community-based employment programs do not significantly reduce recidivism for ex-offenders (2005).

Contemporary job assistance and training programs for former prisoners such as the Center for Employment Opportunities (New York), Safer Foundation (Chicago), and Project Rio (Texas) are more holistic in their approach and incorporate other transitional services and reentry support into their programs while maintaining a primary focus on job placement (Buck 2000). Although several rigorous evaluations are under way, the impact of these newer types of comprehensive, employment-focused programs on former prisoners' employment and recidivism rates is not yet known.

Marriage and Family Support Programs

In the general population, research has documented a variety of benefits of marriage for adults and their children (Waite and Gallagher 2000; Lerman 2002). And recently, John Laub and Robert Sampson concluded that marriage is a "potentially transformative institution that may assist in promoting desistance from criminal behavior" (2006, 500). Most incarcerated men are fathers and a majority of state and federal male prisoners have at least one child under eighteen, on average eight years old (Mumola 2000). About one-third of the fathers lived with their children just before arrest, and most also lived with the child's mother (Hairston 2002). Over half of incarcerated parents have been married, and about 23 percent were married at the time they were incarcerated (Mumola 2000).

Family support is related to a variety of outcomes for former prisoners. Greater contact with family during incarceration—whether by mail, phone, or in-person visits—is associated with lower recidivism rates (Adams and Fischer 1976; Glaser 1969; Hairston 2002). Prisoners with close family ties have lower recidivism than those without such attachments (La Vigne, Visher, and Castro 2004; Sullivan et al. 2002). Strong family attachments may keep former prisoners away from peers who encourage criminal behavior (Warr 1998). Emotional and financial family support is associated with better employment and substance use avoidance (La Vigne, Visher, and Castro 2004; Visher, La Vigne, and Farrell 2003; Sullivan et al. 2002). Fathers reporting strong attachment to their children have higher employment and lower depression rates after release (Visher, Naser, and Courtney 2007). Family support is associated with better results concerning depression and pro-social identity (Ekland-Olson, Kelly, and Supancic 1983; Uggen, Manza, and Behrens 2004; Sampson and Laub 1993).

Prison-based programs generally offer parenting education, counseling and support groups, and services to facilitate visitation by family members. Community-based programs usually include counseling, mentoring, assistance with family reunification and rebuilding, continuing parenting education, and family support groups. Marriage and family support services for prisoners and former prisoners are limited, however, and generally have not directly addressed couple relationships. One well-known family-focused reentry program for former prisoners is La Bodega de Familia, developed in New York City. The program uses comprehensive family case management as a mechanism for government and others to work with the returning individual, his or her family, and the community to create a web of support for former prisoners or individuals on probation. Comprehensive family case management uses a strengths-based, client-driven approach to help clients and family members navigate service delivery systems and institutions to access services, maintain employment, tap existing networks for support, and create long-term family well-being. An evaluation demonstrated that focusing on former prisoners together with their families, and emphasizing existing strengths in addition to addressing deficits, successfully decreased illegal drug use without additional treatment, reduced new arrests, and increased overall physical and mental health (Sullivan et al. 2002). The clients (former prisoners and their families) reported more familial conflict in their family relationships, however.

LIMITATIONS OF CURRENT RESEARCH AND EVALUATION

Several reviews of reentry program evaluations have examined the available research on what works with regard to reentry and/or rehabilitative programming (Aos et al. 2006; Lipsey and Cullen 2007; MacKenzie 2006; Petersilia 2004; Seiter and Kadela 2003). Among the conclusions of these reviews are that intensive supervision programs with a clear treatment component show a sizeable impact on recidivism, and that programs focusing on individual-level change, including cognitive change, education, and drug treatment are more effective than those based on a control or deterrent philosophy (Aos et al. 2006; MacKenzie 2006; Lipsey and Cullen 2007).

Few programs have been studied using a random assignment research design. One exception is the evaluation of the Opportunity to Succeed (OPTS) program. OPTS was designed to reduce substance abuse relapse and criminal recidivism by providing comprehensive, case-managed reentry services to felony offenders who had drug offense histories. The evaluation found that OPTS clients had significantly higher levels of full-time employment during the first year after prison release. In turn, high levels of employment were associated with reductions in self-reported commission of person and property crimes, as well as reductions in drug dealing during a one-year follow-up period (Rossman et al. 1999).

Another exception, Project Greenlight, was developed from research and best practice models to create an evidence-based reentry program (Wilson and Davis 2006). An evaluation of the model and its implementation in 2004 in New York, however, revealed that the program did not replicate past best practice but instead modified past practice to fit institutional requirements, was delivered ineffectively, did not match individual needs to services, and failed to implement any postrelease continuation of services and support (Wilson and Davis 2006; see also Visher 2006; Marlowe 2006). The evaluation found that the program participants performed significantly worse than a control group on multiple measures of recidivism after one year. The evaluators attributed these findings to a combination of implementation difficulties, program design, and a mismatch between participant needs and program content. In response to the evaluation report, Douglas Marlowe argued that the evidence base for the program was flawed from the beginning (2006). Edward Rhine and colleagues were more optimistic about reentry programming in general, but remarked that Project Greenlight was not sufficiently different from other failed reentry programs nor was the treatment delivered appropriately (2006). In summary, a critical problem for community-based reentry programs is that they are often are not integrated into an overall continuum of care strategy that links prison and community-based treatment, and are not managed or monitored according to procedures designed to help guide or maximize their effectiveness (Andrews and Bonta 1998).

Many, if not most reentry programs are relatively new, having begun as a result of federal funding in 2003 and 2004. As a result, there are few impact evaluations of programs focused specifically on reentry. Numerous challenges encumber the extant research assessing the effectiveness of programs for formerly incarcerated individuals, whether focused on reentry or general rehabilitation. Foremost among the challenges is the lack of theoretical models that articulate behavior change among former prisoners. Within any particular substantive area, there are also problems of fidelity in that a particular service approach may manifest itself in different ways under different programs and circumstances. As a result, it is often difficult to generalize research findings from one program to others, and variability among the outcome variables examined—employment, homelessness, health, and so on—is substantial. Finally, the research itself is problematic, because rigorous experimental designs—including the use of comparison groups (randomly assigned or otherwise)—are rare in this research literature. Time constraints are also a factor in this research, in that few studies examine outcomes beyond one year.

In summary, limitations on current reentry research and evaluation, and in expanding knowledge on this topic, are numerous. However, current trends in research and practice provide optimism that, in time, access to data and improved coordination across government agencies and systems will lead to more rigorous research that will provide a sound basis for answering important policy questions.

AREAS FOR FURTHER INVESTIGATION

We believe that answering certain questions is important to developing more effective reentry programs.

Are reentry initiatives more effective if implemented as discrete programs or as a change in policy?

The overwhelming majority of evaluations have focused on programs designed to address specific prisoner needs, or a suite of needs. However, many policy issues affect outcomes for returning prisoners, including housing, physical and mental health, and community supervision to name the most important. With respect to housing, it is clear that efforts to increase the public safety of those in public housing by excluding those with felony convictions has had the unintended consequence of increasing instability among that population, likely leading to more rather than less crime. Community supervision strategies have not yet begun to incorporate principles of therapeutic jurisprudence, and therefore policy changes in the length or intensity of community supervision have increased the likelihood that a technical violation or new offense will be detected without implementing programs that could be expected to increase desistance. Assuming diminishing marginal harms from detected crimes, additional resources are being used to detect and punish less serious crime. Finally, little scholarly work exists on the effect of crime on prison populations. A substantial body of work in criminology, sociology, and economics examines whether incarceration reduces crime through incapacitation and deterrence, but little attention is paid to whether changes in the rate of offending have an effect on the number of people incarcerated. Unless those policies are in some equilibrium, it is unclear whether even successful reentry programs can have an effect on recidivism.

Can innovations from other parts of the criminal justice system, such as therapeutic jurisprudence, and from other social service programming, such as permanent supportive housing, be integrated into reentry programs?

One significant criticism of current reentry programs is that the incentives for treatment providers and supervision agencies are often in conflict. The providers are likely to place a premium on therapeutic needs, and the agencies may value adherence to terms of supervision. Incorporating principles of therapeutic jurisprudence may help resolve this tension by creating incentives for participants to comply both with treatment protocols and with the terms of community supervision.

Is the most effective reentry design one that seamlessly delivers services both inside prisons and in the community through a community justice collaborative?

The goal of most reentry programs is to develop a seamless transition from prison to the community. The challenges are enormous, however. Corrections departments and community supervision agencies often have conflicting incentives, and community-justice partnerships linking those two organizations and community groups face even larger hurdles. It may therefore be prudent to consider the effectiveness of programs that independently assist returning prisoners within one system or the other.

Can individuals within the criminal justice system reward behaviors that lead to desistance if those behaviors are not related to security and public safety concerns?

Current reentry programs often have one set of actors bearing the costs of programming (usually, corrections) and another that receives the benefits (usually, private citizens whose risk of harm is reduced). This tension often leads those bearing the costs to conduct decision analyses about implementing reentry on the basis of whether their organization will benefit, which leads to underinvestment in reentry. Passing along some of the benefit (in terms of reallocating resources) to those actors that bear the cost would make reentry allocations more efficient.

Are the most effective reentry programs ones that link public and community agencies rather than directly providing reentry services?

Current reentry strategies are dominated by service providers who represent a single domain from among the possible correlates of desistance. Many programs, for instance, are centered on one-stop workforce centers whose principle function is to prepare individuals for and place them in jobs. However, the needs of returning prisoners often span domains, and these service providers are unlikely to be as effective at providing or facilitating other services as they are in their primary area of expertise. By contrast, a lead entity that has a primary role as a facilitator of services is more likely to identify and direct participants to high quality services across a range of domains.

Is the primary barrier to effective reentry a lack of detailed, coordinated information gathering and sharing or is it a lack of access or availability of service?

The lack of information sharing within the criminal justice system is staggering, and limits information sharing between community and justice agencies. For instance, in many systems, the courts and corrections have limited communication, which means that corrections often cannot anticipate the release of a prisoner. This means that corrections cannot fully prepare prisoners for release, and cannot provide timely information to community supervision organizations. In addition, institutional barriers to sharing this information with community partners are substantial. Individuals are thus often released without a postrelease service plan, without important documentation (such as identification or prescriptions), and limited ability to contact either community service providers or community supervision agents. All of these factors can hasten their quick return to prison. Simply sorting this information morass out could facilitate lower rates of violations and recidivism.

CONCLUSION

The main challenge for reentry programs is that the deficits returning prisoners face are so substantial and the patterns of behavior are so ingrained that anything short of long-term, high-dosage interventions cannot reasonably be expected to alter their course. One of the authors of this chapter recently completed an evaluation of the Maryland Reentry Partnership initiative (REP), a reentry program serving three targeted communities in Baltimore. During the period when the program was under study, it was widely acclaimed as a model reentry program, and indeed, it adhered to many of the best practices described herein. Compared to a well-matched counterfactual, our CBA found substantial positive effects from the program, in particular, large benefits from reductions in the number of high-cost violent victimizations. Yet, almost 73 percent of program participants were arrested for a new crime within thirty-eight months of release. This statistic is similar to findings from other research on recidivism of returning prisoners. Such is the measure of success in prisoner reentry.

Despite this sobering conclusion, a consensus has emerged about the features of reentry programs that are associated with better outcomes for participants. First, fidelity to essential principles of effective correctional treatment—articulated at least a decade ago—must be the cornerstone of successful reentry programs for former prisoners (Andrews et al. 1990). If an intervention is poorly conceived or poorly implemented, the program is unlikely to be successful. Second, programs must identify participant needs through early and ongoing assessments, and link participants to appropriate services. Third, active case management that responds to changes in the needs of participants is needed. Fourth, integrated performance management approaches that define success, measure the correlates of success on an ongoing basis, and adjust accordingly are important. Fifth, supervision strategies that integrate therapeutic responses to relapse—rather than simply using reentry programs as a means of more closely supervising participants and detecting more violations. Sixth, more rigorous evaluation to test both general and specific hypotheses about the correlates of desistance is needed.

Nothing structural about reentry programs would prevent rigorous CBA. The data needed, however, are different from those to detect an average treatment effect in a standard program evaluation. Future work in this area should be designed not merely as a complement to existing evaluation approaches but also as an independent test of reentry hypotheses. Significant scholarly attention would ideally be devoted to adapting methods used in other disciplines, such as standard outcome measures like QALYs in health research and contingent valuation techniques to value externalities, to allow a more complete accounting of the costs and benefits of reentry programs.

REFERENCES

Adams, Don, and Joel Fischer. 1976. "The Effects of Prison Residents' Community Contacts on Recidivism Rates." *Corrective and Social Psychiatry* 22(1): 21–27.

Adams, K., K. J. Bennett, T. J. Flanagan, J. W. Marquart, S. J. Cuvelier, E. Fritsch, J. Gerber, D. R. Longmire, and V. S. Burton, Jr. 1994. "A Large-Scale Multidimensional Test of the Effect of Prison Education Programs on Offenders' Behavior." *The Prison Journal* 74(4): 443–49.

Andrews, D. A., and James Bonta. 1998. *The Psychology of Criminal Conduct*, 2nd ed. Cincinnati: Anderson Publishing.

Andrews, Don A., Ivan Zinger, Robert D. Hoge, James Bonta, Paul Gendreau, and Francis T. Cullen. 1990. "Does Correctional Treatment Work: A Clinically Relevant and Psychologically Informed Meta-Analysis." *Criminology* 28(3): 369–404.

Aos, Steve, Marna Miller, and Elizabeth Drake. 2006. *Evidence-Based Adult Corrections Programs: What Works and What Does Not.* Olympia: Washington State Institute for Public Policy.

Aos, Steve, Polly Phipps, Robert Barnoski, and Roxanne Lieb. 2001. *The Comparative Costs and Benefits of Programs to Reduce Crime.* Olympia: Washington State Institute for Public Policy.

Bandura, Albert. 1977. *Social Learning Theory.* Englewood Cliffs, NJ: Prentice-Hall.

Beck, Judith S. 1995. *Cognitive Therapy: Basics and Beyond.* New York: Guilford.

Bonczar, Thomas P., and Allen J. Beck. 1997. "Lifetime Likelihood of Going to State or Federal Prison." *Bureau of Justice Statistics Bulletin, NCJ 160092.* Washington, DC: U. S. Department of Justice.

Boudin, Kathy. 1993. "Participatory Literacy Education Behind Bars." *Harvard Educational Review* 63(2): 207–32.

Branch, Albia, and Joe Tierney. 2000. *Big Brother Big Sister Impact Study.* Philadelphia: Public/Private Ventures.

Broome, K. M., K. Knight, M. L. Hiller, and D. D. Simpson. 1996. "Drug Treatment Process Indicators for Probationers and Prediction of Recidivism." *Journal of Substance Abuse Treatment* 13(6): 487–91.

Bruns, Eric J., Christine Walrath, Marcia Glass-Siegel, and Marl D. Weist. 2004. "School-Based Mental Health Services in Baltimore: Association with School Climate and Special Education Referrals." *Behavior Modification* 28(4): 491–512.

Buck, Maria L. 2000. "Getting Back to Work: Employment Programs for Ex-Offenders." Field Report Series. Philadelphia, PA: Public/Private Ventures.

Bushway, Shawn, and Peter Reuter. 2001. "Labor Markets and Crime." In *Crime*, eds. James Q. Wilson and Joan Petersilia. Oakland: ICS Press.

Carney, Michelle M., and Frederick Buttell. 2003. "Reducing Juvenile Recidivism: Evaluating the Wraparound Services Model." *Research on Social Work Practice* 13(5): 551–68.

Chalfin, Aaron, Bogdan Tereshchenko, John Roman, Caterina Roman, and Christine Arriola. 2007. *Cost-Benefit Analysis of Building Bridges.* Washington, DC: Urban Institute Press.

Clark, Michael D. 2006. "Motivational Interviewing and the Probation Executive: Moving into the Business of Behavior Change." *Executive Exchange* (Spring): 17–21.

Clear, T. R., P. L. Hardyman, B. D. Stout, K. Lucken, and H. R. Dammer. 2000. "The Value of Religion in Prison: An Inmate Perspective." *Journal of Contemporary Criminal Justice* 16(1): 53–74.

Clear, Todd R., Dina R. Rose, and Judith A. Ryder. 2001. "Incarceration and the Community: The Problem of Removing and Returning Offenders." *Crime & Delinquency* 47(3): 334–51.

Clear, T. R., B. D. Stout, H. R. Dammer, L. Kelly, P. L. Hardyman, and E. Shapiro. 1992. "Does Involvement in Religion Help Prisoners Adjust to Prison?" *National Council on Crime and Detention, Focus* (November):1–7.

Cullen, F. T., and P. L. Gendreau. 2000. "Assessing Correctional Rehabilitation: Policy, Practice, and Prospects." In *Criminal Justice 2000: Policies, Processes, and Decisions of the Criminal Justice System*, vol. 3. Washington, DC: U.S. Department of Justice.

De Jong, P., and I. K. Berg. 2002. *Interviewing for Solutions*, 2nd ed. Australia: Wadsworth.

Early, Teresa J., and Linnea F. GlenMaye. 2000. "Valuing Families: Social Work Practice with Families from a Strengths Perspective." *Social Work* 45(2): 118–30.

Ekland-Olson, Sheldon, William R. Kelly, and Michael Supancic. 1983. "Sanction Severity, Feedback and Deterrence." In *Evaluating Performance of Criminal Justice Agencies, Sage Research Progress Series in Criminology*, eds. Gordon Whitaker and Charles Phillips. Beverly Hills, CA: Sage Publications.

Evans, T. David, Francis T. Cullen, R. Gregory Dunaway, and Velmer S. Burton. 1995. "Religion and Crime Re-examined: The Impact of Religion, Secular Controls, and Social Ecology on Adult Criminality." *Criminology* 33(2): 195–224.

Finn, Peter. 1998. "Successful Job Placement for Ex-Offenders: The Center for Employment Opportunities and Texas' Project RIO. Re-Integration of Offenders, Program Focus." Washington, DC: National Institute of Justice, National Institute of Corrections and the Office of Correctional Education.

Gaes, Gerald G., Timothy J. Flanagan, Laurence L. Motiuk, and Lynn Stewart. 1999. "Adult Correctional Treatment." In *Prisons*, eds. Michael Tonry and Joan Petersilia. Chicago: University of Chicago Press.

Gerber, Jerry, and Eric J. Fritsch. 1994. "The Effects of Academic and Vocational Program Participation on Inmate Misconduct and Reincarceration." In *Prison Education Research Project: Final Report*. Huntsville, TX: Sam Houston State University.

Glaser, Daniel. 1969. *The Effectiveness of a Prison and Parole System*, abridged ed. Indianapolis, IN: Bobbs-Merrill.

Glueck, Sheldon, and Eleanor Glueck. 1974. *Of Delinquency and Crime*. Springfield, IL: Charles C. Thomas.

Gottfredson, Michael R., and Travis Hirschi. 1990. *A General Theory of Crime*. Stanford, CA: Stanford University Press.

Hagan, John, and Juleigh Petty Coleman. 2001. "Returning Captives of the American War on Drugs: Issues of Community and Family Reentry." *Crime & Delinquency* 47(3): 352–67.

Hagan, John, and Ronit Dinovitzer. 1999. "Collateral Consequences of Imprisonment for Children, Communities, and Prisoners." In *Prisons*, eds. Joan Petersilia and Michael Tonry. University of Chicago Press.

Hairston, Creasie F. 2002. "The Importance of Families in Prisoners' Community Reentry." *The ICCA Journal on Community Corrections* (April): 11–14.

Harer, M. D. 1995. *Prison Education Program Participation and Recidivism: A Test of the Normalization Hypothesis*. Washington, DC: Federal Bureau of Prisons, Office of Research and Evaluation.

Harrell, A., and J. Roman. 2001. "Reducing Drug Use and Crime among Offenders: The Impact of Graduated Sanctions." *Journal of Drug Issues* 31(1): 207–32.

Healy, K., D. Foley, and K. Walsh. 1999. *Parents in Prison and Their Families*. Queensland, Australia: Catholic Prison Ministry.

Hercik, J., R. Lewis, B. Myles, C. G. Roman, J. Zweig, A. Whitby, G. Rico, and E. C. McBride. 2004. *Development of a Guide to Resources on Faith-based Organizations in Criminal Justice*. Fairfax, VA: Caliber Associates.

Holzer, Harry J., and Karin Martinson. 2005. *Can We Improve Job Retention and Advancement among Low-Income Working Parents?* Washington, DC: Urban Institute Press.

Jason, L. A., B. D. Olson, J. R. Ferrari, and T. LoSasso. 2006. "Communal Housing Settings Enhance Substance Abuse Recovery." *American Journal of Public Health* 96(10): 1727–29.

Johnson, Byron R., and David B. Larson. 2003. "The InnerChange Freedom Initiative: A Preliminary Evaluation of a Faith-based Prison Program." Philadelphia: University of Pennsylvania, Center for Research on Religion and Urban Civil Society Center for Research on Religion and Urban Civil Society.

Johnson, Byron, David Larson, and Timothy Pitts. 1997. "Religious Programs, Institutional Adjustment, and Recidivism among Former Inmates in Prison Fellowship Programs." *Justice Quarterly* 14(1): 145–66.

Jucovy, Linda. 2006. *Just Out: Early Lessons from the Ready4Work Prisoner Reentry Initiative.* Philadelphia: Public/Private Ventures.

Karberg, Jennifer C., and Doris J. James. 2005. *Substance Dependence, Abuse, and Treatment of Jail Inmates 2002.* Washington, DC: U.S. Department of Justice.

Landenberger, Nana A., and Mark Lipsey. 2006. "The Positive Effects of Cognitive-Behavioral Programs for Offenders: A Meta-Analysis of Factors Associated with Effective Treatment." *Journal of Experimental Criminology* 1(4): 435–50.

Laub, John H., and Robert J. Sampson. 2001. "Understanding Desistance from Crime." In *Crime and Justice: A Review of Research*, vol. 28, ed. Michael Tonry. Chicago: University of Chicago Press.

———. 2006. *Shared Beginnings, Divergent Lives: Delinquent Boys to Age 70.* Cambridge, MA: Harvard University Press.

Laub, John H., Daniel S. Nagin, and Robert J. Sampson. 1998. "Trajectories of Change in Criminal Offending: Good Marriages and the Desistance Process." *American Sociological Review* 63(2): 225–38.

La Vigne, Nancy G., Christy Visher, and Jennifer Castro. 2004. *Chicago Prisoners' Experiences Returning Home.* Washington, DC: Urban Institute Press.

Lawrence, Sarah, Daniel P. Mears, Glenn Dubin, and Jeremy Travis. 2002. *The Practice and Promise of Prison Programming.* Washington DC: Urban Institute Press.

Lerman, Robert I. 2002. *How Do Marriage, Cohabitation, and Single Parenthood Affect the Material Hardships of Families with Children?* Washington, DC: Urban Institute Press.

Lipsey, Mark W., Gabrielle L. Chapman, and Nana A. Landenberger. 2001. "Research Findings from Prevention and Intervention Studies: Cognitive-Behavioral Programs for Offenders." *The American Academy of Political and Social Science* 578(November): 144–57.

Lipsey, Mark W., and Francis T. Cullen. 2007. "The Effectiveness of Correctional Rehabilitation: A Review of Systematic Reviews." *Annual Review of Law and Social Science* 3(December): 297–320.

Little, Gregory L. 2005. "Meta-Analysis of Moral Reconation Therapy®: Recidivism Results from Probation and Parole Implementations." *Cognitive-Behavioral Treatment Review* 14(1/2): 14–16.

Logan, Charles. 1993. *Criminal Justice Performance Measures for Prisons.* Washington, DC: Bureau of Justice Statistics.

Lynch, James P., and William J. Sabol. 2000. "Prison Use and Social Control." In *Criminal Justice 2000*, vol. 3., *Policies, Processes, and Decisions of the Criminal Justice System*, ed. Julie Horney. Washington, DC: U.S. Department of Justice.

———. 2001. "Prisoner Reentry in Perspective." *Crime Policy Report* 3 (September). Washington, DC: Urban Institute Press.

MacKenzie, Doris L. 2006. *What Works in Corrections: Reducing the Criminal Activities of Offenders and Delinquents.* New York: Cambridge University Press.

Marlowe, Douglas B. 2003. "Integrating Substance Abuse Treatment and Criminal Justice Supervision." *NIDA Science, and Practice Perspectives* 2(1): 4–14
———. 2006. "When 'What Works' Never Did: Dodging the 'Scarlet M' in Correctional Rehabilitation." *Criminology and Public Policy* 5(2): 339–46.
Maruna, Shadd. 2001. *Making Good: How Ex-Offenders Reform and Reclaim Their Lives.* Washington, DC: American Psychological Association Books.
Mauer, Marc. 2000. *Race to Incarcerate.* Washington, DC: The Prison Project.
Mears, Daniel P., and Gretchen E. Moore. 2003. "Voices from the Field: Practitioners Identify Key Issues in Correctional-Based Drug Treatment." Research Report (January). Washington, DC: Urban Institute Press. www.urban.org/UploadedPDF/410617_NIDA2_IntRpt.pdf.
Mears, Daniel P., Caterina G. Roman, Ashley Wolff, and Janeen Buck. 2006. "Faith-based Efforts to Improve Prisoner Reentry: Assessing the Logic and Evidence." *Journal of Criminal Justice* 34(4): 351–67.
Metraux, Stephen, and Dennis P. Culhane. 2004. "Homeless Shelter Use and Reincarceration Following Prison Release: Assessing the Risk." *Criminology and Public Policy* 3(2): 201–22.
Mumola, Christopher. 2000. "Incarcerated Parents and Their Children." *Bureau of Justice Statistics Special Report* NCJ 182335. Washington, DC: U.S. Department of Justice.
Olson, Bradley D., Leonard.A. Jason, Jospeh R. Ferrari, and Tresza D. Hutcheson. 2005. "Bridging Professional- and Mutual-Help through a Unifying Theory of Change: An Application of the Transtheoretical Model to the Mutual-help Organization." *Journal of Applied and Preventive Psychology* 11(3): 168–78.
Pearson, Frank, and Douglas S. Lipton. 1999. "A Meta-analytic Review of the Effectiveness of Corrections-based Treatments for Drug Abuse." *The Prison Journal* 79(4): 384–410.
Petersilia, Joan. 2003. *When Prisoners Come Home: Parole and Prisoner Reentry.* New York: Oxford University Press.
———. 2004. "What Works in Prisoner Reentry? Reviewing and Questioning the Evidence." *Federal Probation* 68(2): 4–8.
Piehl, Anne Morrison. 1998. "Economic Conditions, Work, and Crime." In *Handbook on Crime and Punishment,* ed. Michael Tonry. New York: Oxford University Press.
Rhine, Edward, Tina Mawhorr, and Evalyn C. Parks. 2006. "Implementation: The Bane of Effective Correctional Programs." *Criminology and Public Policy* 5(2): 347–58.
Roman, Caterina Gouvis, and Jeremy Travis. 2006. "Where Will I Sleep Tomorrow: Housing, Homelessness and the Returning Prisoner." *Housing Policy Debate* 17(2): 389–418.
Roman, Caterina Gouvis, Alyssa Whitby, Janine Zweig, and Gabrielle Rico. 2004. *Religion, Crime, and Delinquent Behavior: A Synthesis of the Empirical Research on Theory and Practice.* Washington, DC: Urban Institute Press.
Roman, Caterina Gouvis, Ashley Wolff, Vanessa Correa, and Janeen Buck. 2007. "Assessing Intermediate Outcomes of a Faith-Based Residential Prisoner Reentry Program." *Research on Social Work Practice* 17(2): 199–215.
Roman, John, Lisa Brooks, Erica Lagerson, Aaron Chalfin, and Bogdan Tereshchenko. 2007. *Impact and Cost-Benefit Analysis of the Maryland Reentry Partnership Initiative.* Washington, DC: Urban Institute Press.
Rossman, Shelli B., and Caterina Gouvis Roman. 2003. "Case Managed Reentry and Employment: Lessons from the Opportunity to Succeed Program." *Justice Research and Policy* 5(2): 75–100.
Rossman, Shelli B., Sanjeev Sridharan, Caterina Gouvis, Janeen Buck, and Elaine Morley. 1999. *Impact of the Opportunity to Succeed. OPTS Aftercare Program for Substance-Abusing Felons: Comprehensive Final Report.* Washington, DC: Urban Institute Press.

Sabol, William J., and James P. Lynch. 1997. *Crime Policy Report: Did Getting Tough on Crime Pay?* Washington, DC: U.S. Justice Department.

Sampson, Robert J., and John H. Laub. 1990. "Crime and Deviance over the Life Course: The Salience of Adult Social Bonds." *American Sociological Review* 55:609–27.

———. 1993. *Crime in the Making: Pathways and Turning Points through Life.* Cambridge, MA: Harvard University Press.

Seiter, Richard P., and Karen R. Kadela. 2003. "Prisoner Reentry: What Works, What Doesn't, and What's Promising." *Crime & Delinquency* 49(3): 360–88.

Skinner, B. F. 1974. *About Behaviorism.* New York: Random House.

Stillman, Joseph. 1999. *Working to Learn: Skills Development under Work First.* Philadelphia, PA: Public/Private Ventures.

Sullivan, Eileen, Milton Mino, Katherine Nelson, and Jill Pope. 2002. *Families as a Resource in Recovery from Drug Abuse: An Evaluation of La Bodega de la Familia.* New York: Vera Institute of Justice.

Sung, H. 2001. "Rehabilitation Felony Drug Offenders through Job Development: A Look into a Prosecutor-led Diversion Program." *The Prison Journal* 81(2): 271–86.

Taxman, Faye. 2006. "A Behavioral Management Approach to Supervision: Preliminary Findings from Maryland's Proactive Community Supervision." Paper prepared for the National Research Council's semi-annual meeting of the Committee on Law and Justice and Workshop on Community Supervision and Desistance from Crime. Irvine, CA (January 18, 2006).

Travis, Jeremy. 2005. *But They All Come Back: Facing the Challenges of Prisoner Reentry.* Washington, DC: Urban Institute Press.

Uggen, Christopher, Jeff Manza, and Angela Behrens. 2004. "Less Than the Average Citizen: Stigma, Role Transition and the Civic Reintegration of Convicted Felons." In *After Crime and Punishment: Ex-Offender Reintegration and Desistance from Crime*, eds. Shadd Maruna and Russ Immarigeon. Cullompton, Devon: Willan Publishing.

Visher, Christy. 2006. "Editorial Introduction: Effective Reentry Programs." *Criminology and Public Policy* 5(2): 299–302.

Visher, Christy, and Shannon Courtney. 2006. *Cleveland Prisoners' Experiences Returning Home.* Washington, DC: Urban Institute Press.

Visher, Christy A., Nancy La Vigne, and Jill Farrell. 2003. *Illinois Prisoners' Reflections on Returning Home.* Washington, DC: Urban Institute Press.

Visher, Christy A., Rebecca Naser, and Shannon Courtney. 2007. "Incarcerated Fathers: Pathways from Prison to Home." In *Incarcerated Parents, Their Children, and Their Families*, eds. Vivian L. Gadsen and Philip Genty. Florence, KY: Lawrence Erlbaum Associates.

Visher, Christy A., Laura Winterfield, and Mark B. Coggeshall. 2005. "Ex-Offender Employment Programs and Recidivism: A Meta-analysis." *Journal of Experimental Criminology* 1(3): 295–316.

Waite, L. J., and M. Gallagher. 2000. *The Case for Marriage: Why Married People Are Happier, Healthier, and Better Off Financially.* New York: Random House.

Waldron, Holly Barrett, and Yifrah Kaminer. 2004. "On the Learning Curve: The Emerging Evidence Supporting Cognitive-Behavioral Therapies for Adolescent Substance Abuse." *Addiction* 99(2): 93–105.

Warr, Mark. 1998. "Life-Course Transitions and Desistance from Crime." *Criminology* 36(2): 183–216.

Weibush, R. G., B. McNulty, and T. Le. 2000. *Implementation of the Intensive Community-Based Aftercare Program.* Washington, DC: U. S. Department of Justice, Office of Justice Programs, Office of Juvenile Justice and Delinquency Prevention.

Weibush, R. G., S. Wagner, B. McNulty, Y. Wang, and T. N. Le. 2005. *Implementation and Outcome Evaluation of the Intensive Aftercare Program: Final Report*. Washington, DC: U. S. Department of Justice, Office of Justice Programs, Office of Juvenile Justice and Delinquency Prevention.

Western, Bruce. 2007. "The Penal System and the Labor Market." In *Barriers to Re-Entry? The Labor Market for Released Prisoners in Postindustrial America*, ed. by Shawn Bushway, Michael A. Stoll, and David F. Weiman. New York: Russell Sage Foundation.

Wexler, Harry K. 1995. "The Success of Therapeutic Communities for Substance Abusers in American Prisons." *Journal of Psychoactive Drugs* 27(1): 57–66.

Wilcox, S. 1998. "Release Is Just the Beginning: Aftercare Programs." *Christian Social Action* (June): 27–29.

Wilson, David B., Catherine A. Gallagher, and Doris L. MacKenzie. 2000. "A Meta-Analysis of Corrections-Based Education, Vocation, and Work Programs for Adult Offenders." *Journal of Research in Crime and Delinquency* 37(4): 347–68.

Wilson, James A., and Robert C. Davis. 2006. "Good Intentions Meet Hard Realities: An Evaluation of the Project Greenlight Reentry Program." *Criminology and Public Policy* 5(2): 303–38.

Winterfield, Laura, and Jennifer Castro. 2005. "Matching Drug Treatment to Those in Need: An Analysis of Correctional Service Delivery in Illinois and Ohio." *Justice Research and Policy* 7(2): 30–55.

Chapter 9

Housing Assistance to Promote Human Capital

Lance Freeman

Human capital—the skills, habits, and knowledge that allow one to command remuneration in a market economy—is increasingly recognized as critical in determining an individual's life chances. For that reason, investing in human capital has come to be recognized as one of the best ways for individuals and societies alike to achieve upward mobility and economic prosperity. When policymakers, social scientists, and other informed observers think of mechanisms for boosting human capital, however, housing is typically not at the top of lists of instruments for intervention. Here I show how housing that is decent, affordable, and proximate to economic opportunities is critical to successful development of human capital.

WHY DOES AFFORDABLE HOUSING MATTER?

After food, housing might be considered the most important material item in a person's life. It is a place of shelter and, for most people, the single place they spend the most time. Housing is also the single largest item in most household budgets. For these reasons, housing has the potential to affect human capital development in innumerable ways. I outline three mechanisms—physical conditions, cost burdens, and location—through which housing might positively impact human capital development. I also consider the possibility that housing assistance programs that aim to assist households with housing problems could in fact have a detrimental impact on human capital development.

The physical condition of a unit is significant in this regard for several reasons. Housing that is not safe or sanitary poses serious health risks and at the most extreme can be life threatening. Indeed, during the early years of the industrial revolution life expectancies declined among those migrating from the countryside to the cities in part because of the unhealthful housing conditions in the cities (Preston and Haines 1991). Housing that is overcrowded can also increase the spread of infectious diseases and contributes to stressors that affect mental health. It is hard to imagine someone with no access to decent and safe housing being able to develop his or her human capital to its full potential.

Rising living standards in the United States have rendered substandard housing to the dustbin of history for all but a small slice of the populace (Schwartz 2006). The vast majority of Americans, including the very poor, live in housing that in a physical sense at least does not pose a significant threat to their health and therefore does not interfere with this element of human capital development. Yet, because housing remains the most expensive item in most household budgets, it still affects the development of human capital significantly. On the one hand, funds devoted to housing cannot be used for anything else related to the development of human capital (Mayer 1997). On the other, the stresses associated with excessive house burdens stunt the development of that capital (Conger et al. 1994). Money spent on housing, for example, cannot be spent on private school education for children. It is easy to imagine a household that, when confronted with the choice between keeping a roof overhead or paying for SAT preparation courses, opts for the roof. The consequences of this choice might be admission to a less selective college and lower lifetime earnings for the household's children. In addition, the stress associated with not being able to pay for one's home could contribute to depression, high blood pressure, or other potentially debilitating diseases.

Because housing is immobile, location emerges as a third determining factor. Goods and services are not randomly distributed across space, and therefore where one lives has a profound effect on access to schools, jobs, and social networks—all important inputs into the development of human capital. Furthermore, not only is the distribution of goods and services not randomly distributed across space, it is also stratified in such a way that often leaves the poor in the least desirable neighborhoods, more particularly, those least amenable to developing human capital.

Stratification of space manifests itself a number of ways. It is well known that the quality of local schools is a significant factor in determining the selling prices of houses. Families must pay significantly more for an otherwise similar house that is nearer to better schools. More affluent households tend therefore to live in areas with better schools. Households also tend to sort themselves by socioeconomic status. The more affluent, who are socially connected to opportunities and resources, tend to live near others who share these traits. Likewise, people with little in the way of connections to opportunities and resources tend to share locales with others who are similarly disadvantaged.

Job opportunities, too, tend not to be randomly distributed. Although the relationship between housing cost and job opportunities is not linear—many people do not want to live in the middle of the central business district, for example—accessibility to job opportunities is also an important determinant of housing prices. Where job opportunities are abundant, housing prices tend to rise and, conversely, where job opportunities are scarce, prices tend to stagnate and even fall. When access to places rich in inputs for human capital development are allocated to the highest bidder, those with limited means tend to live in neighborhoods that are poor in such inputs.

To address the problems associated with inadequate means, numerous types of housing assistance has been made available to many needy families. Although housing assistance likely improves the recipients' living conditions and thereby augments their potential for developing human capital, it can also reduce that development. Consider that with housing assistance an individual may decide to substitute leisure, defined here as nonpaid activities, for work. A mother with small children, for example, might decide to use housing assistance so that she can spend more time with her children. In addition, because most housing assistance programs are means tested there is an implicit tax on earnings. If a household's income increases, then it may have to either pay a larger of share of its housing costs or lose eligibility for that assistance altogether. Both forces act as a work disincentive for housing assistance recipients. Because work experience is an important component of human capital, these forces could also reduce human capital.

In sum, the affordability of housing and programs to increase affordability intersect with the development of human capital in at least four ways: adequacy of physical conditions, magnitude of cost burdens, locational attributes, and possible substitutions of leisure for work and disincentives to work. To what extent does empirical evidence support this conceptualization of how affordable housing is important to human capital development?

THE LITERATURE

The notion that decent and safe housing is necessary for people to realize fully their human capital potential has strong common sense appeal. A substantial body of research has documented links between the physical quality of a dwelling and outcomes related to human capital. Health outcomes in particular indicate housing to be a determinant. Research has linked substandard housing to the spread of infectious diseases and childhood mortality (Hardy 1993; Dedman et al. 2001; Marsh, Gordon, and Pantazis 1999). The lead paint found in some older buildings has been definitely linked to neurodevelopmental abnormalities (Needleman and Gatsonis 1990). In sum, significant empirical evidence documents the link that poor housing quality can have to adverse physical and mental health outcomes.

The notion that costs that are too high for a household's budget might negatively affect the development of human capital also has strong intuitive appeal. Most housing analysts argue that no more than 30 percent of a household's income should be spent for housing expenses, and most housing assistance programs stipulate that no more than 30 percent of a household's income be spent on rent. Despite this, empirical evidence on how the lack of affordable housing affects individuals, including their human capital development, is relatively scarce (Harkness and Newman 2006). Several studies, however, have attempted to document this link. Janet Currie and Aaron Yellowitz found that children living in public housing do better than their otherwise similar counterparts, presumably because of the subsidy provided by public housing (2000). Sandra Newman and Joseph Harkness estimated that every year of public housing residence between the ages of ten and sixteen increases a youth's probability of working between age twenty-five and twenty-seven by 7 percentage points, raises annual earnings by $1,860, and reduces welfare use between age twenty and twenty-seven by 0.70 of a year (2002, 34). Again, this pattern would presumably be attributable to the more affordable public housing. Finally, Joseph Harkness and Sandra Newman found that children living in areas where housing is more affordable have better health and educational outcomes and fewer behavioral problems (2006). Taken together, these results provide consistent, albeit limited, evidence that excessive cost burdens can be detrimental to the development of human capital.

The relationship between location and human capital development has been studied extensively. Numerous quasi-experimental and even experimental studies have attempted to document the role one's immediate environs play in determining life chances. Quasi-experimental studies have generally found individuals living in poorer neighborhoods have lower levels of cognitive development and educational attainment, fewer ties to employed persons, are more likely to be unemployed, and have lower earnings (Ellen and Turner 2003). This pattern is consistent with the notion that location matters for the development of human capital.

Perhaps the most compelling of these studies are those associated with the Moving to Opportunity (MTO) experimental program. MTO randomly assigned public housing residents to three groups: those remaining in public housing, those moving to a high poverty neighborhood outside of public housing, and those moving to a low poverty neighborhood outside of public housing. As a true experiment, with households randomly assigned to treatment and control groups, confounding factors like self-selection can be ruled out with confidence. In the quasi-experimental studies cited, the threat of self-selection to the internal validity of inferences looms large. That is, individuals with lower earnings and educational attainment may be choosing to live in poorer yet cheaper neighborhoods. It could also be that individuals who attach little importance to their children's education may choose, or be only able to afford, to live in poorer neighborhoods. Because households are not randomly assigned to neighborhoods, it is extremely difficult to rule out these alternative explanations for the pattern of results just described.

The results of the MTO experiment are more mixed than those found using quasi-experimental methods. A review of the available evidence finds the strongest impacts among younger children. Children of elementary school age whose families moved to low poverty neighborhoods had better physical and mental health, fewer injuries, fewer behavioral problems, and better scholastic achievement. The findings for teens were more mixed, with those who moved to low poverty neighborhoods faring worse in school and more likely to be arrested for property crimes, but less likely to be arrested for violent crimes. For adults, impacts thus far appear to be limited to improvements in mental and self-reported health (Ellen and Turner 2003).

The MTO results suggest that, to the extent that neighborhoods matter, they are most important for young children and less so for teens and adults. This makes intuitive sense. Infants and preschoolers presumably have only limited contact with their neighborhood outside of their parents. Adult patterns of behavior are likely to be relatively fixed and to change only slowly if at all. Teens appear to be both harmed and helped by moving to low poverty neighborhoods. Poorer school outcomes could be the result of higher standards in the teens' new schools. If we are looking to make an impact on the development of human capital through the location of affordable housing, the evidence provided by the MTO experiment suggests young children will be the most affected.

Programs that disperse the poor from concentrated poverty neighborhoods would therefore seem likely to raise the stock of human capital among those who move. Living near better-off neighbors will improve their life chances for the reasons described. As George Galster pointed out, however, it is possible that dispersing the poor also disperses their social problems with them (2003). If this were the case, residents of neighborhoods where the poor resettled would be made worse off. The extent to which society as a whole were made better or worse off by poverty deconcentration programs would depend on the relationship between poverty concentration and human capital. For example, if adding poor people to a neighborhood increases social problems in a proportional fashion, society as a whole would not benefit from the deconcentration of poverty. Those moving into the nonpoor neighborhood might see their human capital increase, as would the residents of the neighborhood the poor were leaving, but this would be counterbalanced by the losses in human capital by residents of the receiving neighborhoods. If the residents of poor neighborhoods are among the most motivated the residents of the origin neighborhoods could actually be made worse off as well. Theories on neighborhood effects are virtually silent on the precise nature of the relationship between neighborhood poverty and social problems, and consequently on implications for human capital. Similarly, the empirical evidence on this question is too thin to draw any firm conclusions (Galster 2003). Thus, though we have reason and empirical evidence to support the notion that living in a poor neighborhood is bad for an individual's human capital, we have no a priori reason to believe that policies that deconcentrate poverty would increase human capital in the aggregate.

Concerned citizens, policymakers, and researchers have all linked human capital to the accessibility of affordable, decent, and safe housing. Typically this link has been made implicitly, by stressing the importance of housing for health or access to good schools. But health and education are surely important components of human capital. Thus, the evidence that has linked housing—including its cost, quality, and location—to health and educational outcomes has important implications for thinking about investments in human capital. Based on both theory and the empirical evidence, there appears to be near consensus that both housing quality and location are important for human capital development, especially for children. Evidence linking housing affordability to human capital development is relatively scarce, but the evidence that does exist is consistent with the notion that reducing the amount poor families expend on housing can positively augment development of human capital.

Just as a lack of adequate housing can be an obstacle, so can programs to assist needy families with housing problems. As noted, housing assistance might cause recipients to work less, thereby decreasing their work experience and the contribution that work experience makes to human capital development.

The evidence on whether housing assistance actually dampens work effort is mixed. Studies addressing the question have been bedeviled by a lack of both accurate data and experiments that allow researchers to rule out selection bias. Many secondary data sets, such as the Panel Study of Income Dynamics or the Survey of Income and Program Participation, that have been used to study the impacts of welfare receipt are known to have serious problems in measuring the receipt of housing assistance because of respondent confusion over the meaning of the term *public housing*. This renders studies that rely on this type of data suspect (Shroder 2002). Because receipt of housing assistance is voluntary, quasi-experimental studies are confronted with the threat that those who sign up for housing assistance are different in unobserved ways from those who chose not to. This is especially problematic in studies that attempt to link work effort to housing assistance. Low-income households that anticipate substantial increases in their income in the near future are probably less likely to sign up for housing assistance. To the extent this group is included among the controls in a quasi-experimental design, any finding of an impact of housing assistance on work effort is likely to be biased.

In view of these challenges, it is perhaps not surprising that the evidence on the impacts of housing assistance on work effort is decidedly mixed. After an exhaustive review, Mark Shroder concluded that "the distribution of results from these [eighteen] empirical studies is consistent with a true housing assistance/short-term employment effect of zero" (2002, 394). In a more recent study using administrative data, Edgar Olsen and his colleagues did find that housing assistance depresses earnings (2005). Although the researchers' use of administrative data addresses the problem of data inaccuracy, their results are bedeviled by the self-selection problem. They used very low income households as a control group, reasoning that everyone in this group would try to obtain housing assistance. Nevertheless, they cannot rule out the possibility that those not receiving housing assistance are different from housing assistance recipients.

Research on welfare reform also provides evidence relevant to whether the disincentive effects of housing assistance are real. Some research has shown that in some instances housing assistance helps welfare recipients keep jobs and leave welfare (Sard and Waller 2002; Verma, Riccio, and Azurdia 2003). Other studies have found that housing assistance recipients have similar employment experiences as nonrecipients under welfare reform (Harkness and Newman 2006; Lee, Beecroft, and Shroder 2005). This pattern of results is inconsistent with the notion that housing assistance negatively affects work effort. In view of the inconclusiveness of the empirical work on housing assistance and work effort, one can only conclude that the notion that housing assistance reduces work effort, and subsequently reduces human capital, is an intriguing yet unproven idea.

COST-BENEFIT ANALYSES

The discussion makes clear the strong theoretical and empirical arguments for linking investments in affordable housing to human capital development. By enabling poor families to live in affordable, decent, and favorably located housing, affordable housing increases the stock of human capital. Depending on how this assistance is delivered, however, improving the housing of the poor could decrease human capital among recipients. Before advocating a policy of promoting affordable housing, then, one would want to know if the costs of making housing affordable exceeded the benefits coming, in part, from improved human capital. Such a cost-benefit calculus should consider all the benefits accruing from providing affordable housing.

An obvious benefit is the increased housing consumption by housing assistance recipients, which could be estimated as the difference between what the assisted household pays for their unit and the market price for the unit. Another benefit would stem from positive externalities associated with the improved housing conditions of the assisted housing unit. For example, if housing assistance enabled a household occupying substandard housing to upgrade the conditions of their unit, the improvement could benefit neighbors as well. Indeed, empirical research has shown that subsidized housing can improve surrounding property values (Freeman and Botein 2002). Moreover, the CBA would have to consider the increases in human capital associated with households receiving housing assistance, as described. Finally, to the extent that housing assistance contributes to the deconcentration of poverty any benefits associated with fewer pockets of concentrated poverty would have to be weighed as well.

A CBA would also have to consider the cost of providing housing assistance—its opportunity cost, any negative externalities associated with the provision of subsidized housing, and the possible detrimental impacts to human capital associated with housing assistance. Subsidized housing may have a positive effect on surrounding housing, but it may also have negative impacts as well, particularly if the subsidized housing is of substantially lower quality. Evidence here too is mixed (Freeman and Botein 2002; Nguyen 2005).

Table 9.1 summarizes the costs and benefits of policies to address housing problems. The first column lists the categories of costs and benefits and the second indicates our certainty of their magnitudes based on the extant empirical evidence. A question mark indicates a great deal of uncertainty about this specific cost or benefit. One plus indicates a modest degree and two plusses indicate near consensus in literature on the putative cost or benefit. Table 9.1 suggests that, though confidence about most of the benefits associated with housing programs that might raise human capital is considerable, for some benefits and most costs there is a great deal of uncertainty.

Table 9.1   Costs and Benefits of Housing Assistance Programs

	Certainty of Empirical Benefits and Costs
Benefits	
Improved housing	++
Improved health	++
Additional resources to invest in human capital	+
Better employment opportunities	+
Improvements to surrounding neighborhoods	?
Costs	
Costs of subsidizing housing	++
Disincentives to work	?
Detrimental impacts on surrounding neighborhoods	?

Source: Author.
++ very certain, + certain, ? uncertain.

In view of what we do and do not know, then, conducting a valid CBA of housing mobility programs to promote human capital development would be a daunting task indeed. Some of the most convincing evidence on the benefits of housing mobility programs, for example, is being compiled through the MTO experiment. Using a rigorous experimental design allows impacts to be estimated with a great deal of confidence. Yet MTO's experimental design cannot discern what impact, if any, the program participants are having on the receiving neighborhoods, or if there was any impact on the neighborhoods they left. Moreover, evidence to help answer this question is not to be found in the extant literature. Without knowledge of such impacts, a complete CBA cannot be conducted.

A similar problem arises with CBAs of programs that make housing more affordable. Virtually all the evidence suggests that these programs can augment the development of human capital by improving health, allowing more consumption of nonhousing items that help development, or facilitating living in better neighborhoods. But because such programs are means tested, the possibility that they also diminish work effort and consequently work experience and its contribution to human capital also needs to be considered. Those looking to the extant empirical literature for an estimate of the work disincentive effects of housing assistance, however, will be disappointed. Disagreement about whether one should expect housing assistance to have a disincentive effect is considerable. Furthermore, to the extent these disincentives do reduce work effort, whether this subsequently affects development of human capital is unknown. Without more certainty about this potential cost of housing assistance, it is hard to imagine a very convincing CBA being conducted.

In view of our ignorance about many of the costs and some of the benefits associated with housing assistance programs, it is perhaps not surprising that very little in the way of CBAs of housing assistance and human capital development has been done. Most CBAs regarding housing assistance have focused on the differences in costs and benefits between different types of housing assistance such as vouchers versus project-based assistance (Deng 2005). Although such analyses are informative for determining which type of housing assistance is most efficient, they shed little light on the costs and benefits of these approaches with regard to human capital development. Robert Simons and David Sharkey measured the costs and benefits of a new construction program that subsidizes homeownership in Cleveland (1997). Their focus, however, was fiscal only. They considered whether the government expenditures for an affordable housing program are recouped from increased property values, increased sales tax revenue from residents of the newly constructed housing, and sales tax revenues from workers who construct the housing. Again, such an analysis is useful but does not take into consideration the costs and benefits associated with human capital as a result of this initiative.

FUTURE DIRECTIONS

Policymakers, researchers, and housing advocates have made implicit and explicit links between human capital and access to affordable and decent housing for decades. In recent years, compelling empirical evidence has been compiled that documents the relationship between housing and different facets of human capital, confirming the intuition of those who have argued about the importance of such links. Although this research is beginning to paint a complete picture of how housing can influence human capital development, important gaps in our knowledge remain. In terms of developing human capital, there are several possible benefits and costs associated with housing assistance programs about which we know very little. Specifically, the extent to which housing affordability improves human capital or housing assistance impedes work effort and the development of human capital is uncertain. We also have little knowledge of how housing mobility programs affect residents of receiving or origin neighborhoods. Because of these gaping holes in the literature, CBAs of how housing assistance could be used to promote human capital development would be premature.

Future research should focus on the following: the extent to which affordable housing allows families to make other investments that improve human capital; the degree to which, if any, housing assistance discourages work effort and, if so, how this subsequently hinders human capital development; and the impacts housing mobility programs have on origin and receiving neighborhoods. With more certainty about these issues, CBAs could be useful tools for assessing the desirability of the use of housing assistance programs to promote human capital development.

REFERENCES

Conger, Rand D., Xiaojia Ge, Glen H. Elder, Jr., Frederick O. Lorenz , and Ronald L. Simons. 1994. "Economic Stress, Coercive Family Process, and Developmental Problems of Adolescents." *Child Development* 65(2): 541–61.

Currie, Janet, and Aaron Yellowitz. 2000. "Are Public Housing Projects Good for Kids?" *Journal of Public Economics* 75(1): 99–124.

Dedman, D.J., D. Gunnell, G. Davey Smith, and S. Frankel. 2001. "Childhood Housing Conditions and Later Mortality in the Boyd Orr Cohort." *Journal of Epidemiology and Community Health* 55(1): 10–15.

Deng, Lan. 2005. "The Cost-Effectiveness of the Low-Income Housing Tax Credit Relative to Vouchers: Evidence from Six Metropolitan Areas." *Housing Policy Debate* 16(3/4): 469–511.

Ellen, Ingrid Gould, and Margery Turner. 2003. "Do Neighborhoods Matter and Why?" In *Choosing a Better Life? Evaluating the Moving to Opportunity Social Experiment*, eds. John Goering and Judith D. Feins. Washington, DC: Urban Institute Press.

Freeman, Lance, and Hilary Botein. 2002. "Subsidized Housing and Neighborhood Impacts: A Theoretical Discussion and Review of the Evidence." *Journal of Planning Literature* 16(3): 359–78.

Galster, George. 2003. "Investigating Behavioral Impacts of Poor Neighborhoods: Towards New Data and Analytic Strategies." *Housing Studies* 18(6): 893–914.

Hardy, Anne. 1993. *The Epidemic Streets: Infectious Diseases and the Rise of Preventive Medicine, 1856–1900.* New York: Oxford University Press.

Harkness, Joseph M., and Sandra J. Newman. 2006. "Recipients of Housing Assistance under Welfare Reform: Trends in Employment and Welfare Participation." *Housing Policy Debate* 17(1): 81–108.

Lee, Wang S., Erik Beecroft, and Mark Shroder. 2005. "The Impacts of Welfare Reform on Recipients of Housing Assistance." *Housing Policy Debate* 16(3/4): 433–68.

Marsh, A., D. Gordon, and C. Pantazis. 1999. *Home Sweet Home? The Impact of Poor Housing on Health.* Bristol, UK: The Policy Press.

Mayer, Susan E. 1997. *What Money Can't Buy: Family Income and Children's Life Chances.* Cambridge, MA: Harvard University Press.

Needleman, H. L., and C. A. Gatsonis. 1990. "Low-Level Lead Exposure and the IQ of Children: A Meta-Analysis of Modern Studies." *Journal of the American Medical Association* 263(5): 673–78.

Newman, Sandra J., and Joseph M. Harkness. 2002. "The Long-Term Effects of Public Housing on Self-Sufficiency." *Journal of Policy Analysis and Management* 21(1): 21–43.

Nguyen, Mai Thi. 2005. "Does Affordable Housing Detrimentally Affect Property Values? A Review of the Literature." *Journal of Planning Literature* 20(1): 15–26.

Olsen, Edgar O., Catherine A. Tyler, Jonathan W. King, and Paul E. Carrillo. 2005. "The Effects of Different Types of Housing Assistance on Earnings and Employment." *Cityscape: A Journal of Policy Development and Research* 8(2): 163–87.

Preston, Samuel H., and Michael R. Haines. 1991. *Fatal Years: Child Mortality in Late Nineteenth Century America.* Princeton, NJ: Princeton University Press.

Sard, Barbara, and Margery Waller. 2002. "Housing Strategies to Strengthen Welfare Policy and Support Working Families." Washington, DC: Brookings Institution Press.

Schwartz, Alex. 2006. *Housing Policy in the United States.* New York: Routledge.

Shroder, Mark D. 2002. "Does Housing Assistance Perversely Affect Self-Sufficiency? A Review Essay." *Journal of Housing Economics* 11(4): 381–417.

Simons, Robert A., and David S. Sharkey. 1997. "Jump-Starting Cleveland's New Urban Housing Markets: Do the Potential Fiscal Benefits Justify the Public Subsidy Costs?" *Housing Policy Debate* 8(1): 143–71.

Verma, Nandita, James Riccio, and Guilda Azurdia. 2003. *Housing Assistance and the Effects of Welfare Reform: Evidence from Connecticut and Minnesota.* Washington, DC: U.S. Department of Housing and Urban Development, Office of Policy Development and Research.

Encouraging Work

Robert Lerman

Work plays a central role in achieving a healthy standard of living and in making use of one's abilities (Sen 1992). In the United States, by the standards of other developed countries, the overall employed share of the adult population is high and the aggregate unemployment rate is low. In 2007, the unemployment rate averaged 4.6 percent, well below the 7.1 percent rate for OECD Europe. Of the largest European countries, only the UK rate was near the U.S. level (5.3 percent), with France at 8.3 percent, and Germany at 8.4 percent (www.oecd.org).

Nonetheless, some critical groups have long faced serious problems finding jobs, especially jobs with enough pay to allow people to support a decent living standard. Young people, minority workers, noncustodial fathers, ex-offenders, and displaced workers experience a range of barriers to getting and keeping good jobs. Many lack the incentives, others lack the skills and information, and still others lack the credibility among employers to perform well in the job market (Holzer 1996). As a result, unemployment rates are still about 11 percent for all sixteen- to twenty-four-year-olds and more than 20 percent for black youth. Particularly troubling is the declining job market position of young black men (Edelman, Holzer, and Offner 2006; Raphael 2008).

In attempting to deal with the job market problems facing selected groups of workers, policymakers usually focus on expanding jobs and lowering unemployment. Yet the goal of helping people obtain work at adequate wages is equally important. A major complication is that jobs and wages depend on productivity and market demand, and adequacy of wages relates to the size of the individual's family and the availability of income from other family members. What is an adequate wage for a teenager in a middle-income family differs from an adequate wage for an adult responsible for an entire family with children. Government policies recognize this distinction. For young workers who can afford to forego current income, the emphasis is on schooling, training, and work experience even at low wages. For low-wage workers who must support a family, the goal is to achieve income adequacy, either by helping workers increase their skills quickly to earn high wages or by promoting a combination of earned income through work and income from public supplementary benefits.

One long-term and ubiquitous problem with the income supplement strategy is the work disincentive the policy creates. The very effort to supplement earnings so that families can achieve income adequacy can discourage work and add to the already difficult barriers workers face. A low-wage worker able to earn no more than $7.50 per hour may well find his or her net wage falls to between $2.50 and $3.75 per hour after taking account of the reductions in benefits induced by the worker's own earnings. In extreme cases, workers have found themselves in welfare traps, situations in which welfare benefits strongly discourage low-wage work, but not working at low wages limits work experience and erodes skills, leading to even lower wages and even weaker incentives to work (Coe et al. 1998). The result is bad for the government and taxpayers, as they must bear nearly the entire burden of insuring income adequacy. Such a result is unfortunate for workers as well, because they will be unlikely to make progress in reaching middle-class incomes and they will not be using their capacities and might experience a sense of exclusion from the broader society.

Under the current structure of benefits and taxes, financial incentives to work are highly variable, depending on the state of residence, family circumstances, and on the specific changes in hours worked. The marriage calculator developed for the Administration for Children and Families (ACF) (see http://marriagecalculator.acf.hhs.gov/marriage/index.php) allows one to show that, in the average state, a mother heading a family with two children would increase her monthly family income by $1,000 to 1,200 by entering the labor force and working forty hours per week at $10 per hour assuming that the family is receiving food stamps, a housing subsidy, Medicaid or state child health insurance (SCHIP), and a child care subsidy if the mother works. This gain represents about 57 to 70 percent of the $1,732 gross earnings per month. In the case of low-income married couples with children, the interaction of tax and transfer systems can impose significant disincentives to work added hours. Suppose a mother with two children is working half-time (at $9 per hour) and receiving a housing subsidy, food stamps, and Medicaid. If her unemployed husband starts working at a full-time job (at $10 per hour), then the gain in family income would be less than 40 percent of his increased earnings and the family is likely to lose some health insurance coverage under Medicaid or child health insurance.

Governments have tried several strategies to overcome the adverse incentives resulting from income transfer programs. They have developed alternative supplement strategies that encourage, or at least do not discourage, work by low-wage workers. They have put strict requirements in place for those receiving income-related cash and in-kind benefits, limiting benefits to workers who work or at least make active efforts to find a job. They have also limited the time nonworking recipients can obtain assistance. Unemployment insurance has always provided only temporary benefits (usually no more than twenty-six weeks in the United States), but recently the cash welfare assistance programs (under Temporary Assistance to Needy Families) have limited benefits to no more than five years. Activation strategies, or policies in which social benefit programs require or strongly encourage work or job-related training, are increasingly common in Europe as well as in the United States (Roed and Westlie 2007).

Active labor market programs generally emphasize raising the earnings capacities of workers and expanding social supports for work, such as subsidized child care. Job search, job placement, education and training, and subsidized job programs are all aimed at improving employment opportunities. A variety of trade-offs—costs and benefits—arise in implementing all of these policies. Improving the work incentive features of supplementary benefits often means doing less to target benefits on the neediest families or increases in program costs. Rigorous work requirements on beneficiaries of transfer programs can create heavy administrative burdens for the government and recipients alike and risk leaving some families without basic resources. The job search, training, and job subsidies may cost taxpayers more than the income they ultimately generate for participants.

In recent years, concerns over work disincentives and other barriers to work induced by government programs have extended to the child support enforcement and the criminal justice arenas. The public effort to ensure noncustodial parents financially support their children can both stimulate and reduce work effort. For noncustodial parents who face high current or past obligations, about 25 to 50 percent of earned income is commonly withheld by employers. The reduction in the return from work may increase work effort as a way of raising spendable income or may decrease work effort, especially in the mainstream economy, because of the fall in the worker's net wage after taxes and support payments (Holzer, Offner, and Sorensen 2005). Ex-offenders face serious barriers to employment because many of them lack academic, technical, and communication skills, because some occupations are barred to ex-offenders or require high bonds to prevent damages, and because employers fear the former offenders will commit new crimes. Programs for these workers have used remedial skills training, job placement, postemployment services in cooperation with employers, subsidized jobs, and efforts to improve financial incentives to work.

Dislocated workers are another target group for programs trying to increase employment. Although millions of workers part ways with their employers every month and millions enter jobs with new employers as well, workers displaced from jobs they have held for more than two years are a special concern. Often, they have worked for a firm for decades, acquiring specific skills and high wage rates that cannot be easily replicated in new jobs. In some cases, the dislocation arises from the negative effects of international trade on businesses. Because these workers experience serious problems trying to find jobs that pay comparable wages, many stay unemployed for long periods. The Congress has sponsored special Department of Labor programs for this group—combining weekly unemployment payments (for extended periods if the employment problems stem from the impacts of international trade) and long-term retraining opportunities.

Other groups that have been the subject of government programs to increase employment include residents of public housing projects, the homeless, those suffering from mental or physical impairments, poor youth in specific neighborhoods, unemployed in tribal communities, and even college students. For most groups, job search, job placement, remedial education, classroom training, and on-the-job training are the primary tools for increasing employment.

Most policies have followed a supply-side strategy—increasing the productive capacity of workers and their willingness to work at available jobs. Some have attempted to improve the connections between supply of workers and demand by employers. Still others have emphasized a demand-side strategy, through subsidized job creation, subsidies to employers, and living wage and minimum wage laws. Recently, foundations and governments have turned to sectoral strategies in which local nonprofits and government agencies develop close relationships on workforce issues with businesses in specific industries within a geographic area. The joint effort allows for improved communication concerning specific skill requirements, approaches for upgrading workers, and the development of job ladders.

At this point, the United States has amassed extensive experience with government-sponsored policies and programs to increase employment and earnings, especially for workers at risk of joblessness or very low wages. Researchers and evaluators have conducted studies of an extensive number of programs, assessing their impacts on employment, earnings, and often other outcomes such as family income, criminal activity, and child well-being. However, only a few studies have performed cost-benefit analyses. This chapter attempts to extract important lessons from the record of past programs by answering three questions: What existing programs and policies are generally believed by experts in the field to be socially desirable and why? What are the key program evaluations that have included high quality cost-benefit analyses? What programs and policies are promising enough to merit additional emphasis and analysis? To avoid excessive overlap with another chapter in this volume, this review focuses on programs operating outside welfare-to-work initiatives and others linked to the income-targeted cash assistance system.

EXISTING PROGRAMS AND POLICIES

Close observers of the many efforts to encourage employment have come to recognize the complexities of the task. Many programs have achieved at most modest success and others have not been able to document substantial gains in jobholding or earnings over what would have taken place without an intervention. Still, some efforts to subsidize, educate, and train workers have attracted the support of experts. Others have shown promise but have not documented sufficient benefits to gain wide support among experts and policymakers.

Work-Conditioned Benefits and Work-Related Subsidies
Work-conditioned income transfers and wage subsidies to workers have often been proposed as ways of increasing the incomes of low-wage individuals without reducing their incentive to work. One approach is to impose work requirements within welfare or income-tested benefit programs (Besley and Coate 1992). To offset the work disincentives that arise when providing income support and phasing out benefits as people raise their earnings, the program uses a second policy instrument—the requirement that

beneficiaries prove their willingness to work by taking an existing job or working at a subsidized job.

Work requirements have long been a staple of income-conditioned benefit programs and unemployment insurance in the United States. The Aid to Families with Dependent Children (AFDC) and food stamp programs have mandated that individuals deemed "expected to work" must take any available job and engage in an active job search. With the passage of the 1996 Personal Responsibility and Work Opportunity Reconciliation Act (PRWORA), Congress expanded coverage of work requirements and limited how long benefits could be received. Although employment of single mothers increased and poverty declined significantly after PRWORA, the contribution of stricter work requirements and time limits to these developments is in dispute (Swann 2005; Hofferth, Stanhope, and Harris 2002; Pingle 2003; Cadena, Danziger, and Seefeldt 2006). Moreover, some argue that the job gains induced by work requirements impose unintended costs on single mothers facing severe employment barriers (Meara and Frank 2006). In the context of unemployment insurance, the consensus is that work requirements and time limits are critical tools for maintaining work incentives not only in the United States but in Europe as well (Roed and Westlie 2007; Boone et al. 2007).

A second way to encourage work is to provide benefits that increase with the work effort of recipients, at least over some range of hours worked. Since the 1960s, economists have proposed a wage rate subsidy for this purpose (Kesselman 1969). The subsidy would raise the effective wage, thereby increasing the return for each added hour of work. For example, a wage rate subsidy might equal half the difference between some threshold hourly wage (say, $12 per hour) and the worker's actual wage. A worker paid $6 per hour by an employer would qualify for a $3 per hour subsidy, raising the gross return to an hour of work to $9 per hour and thus improving work incentives. This approach was not implemented, partly because of concerns about potential fraud that might result from underreporting wage rates and overreporting hours work.

Instead, beginning in 1975, the United States adopted the Earned Income Tax Credit (EITC), a subsidy to the earnings of families with children. The program pays a subsidy equal to a share of earnings up to some threshold level and then at some range of earnings begins to phase out. Over the initial range of earnings, each $1 of earnings increases the subsidy payment, thereby raising the worker's return to work. The opposite happens in the phase-out range in that each added $1 of earnings lowers the subsidy and thus lowers the gain from an extra hour of paid work. Initially, the subsidy began at only 10 percent up to $5,000 of earnings and was aimed partly at offsetting the social security taxes for low-wage workers in families with children. Over time, the EITC has expanded through increases in subsidy rates, increases in the share of earnings subsidized, and increases in the range of earnings over which the subsidy is phased out. In 2006, the EITC subsidy rate amounted to 40 percent for families with two or more children (up to a maximum of $4,536 per year) and 36 percent for families with one child (up to a maximum payment of $2,747 per year). Tax filers with two or more children reach the maximum credit at an income of $11,300 per year; married filers continue to receive the maximum as their income rises to $16,850; beyond this point, the credit phases out at a 21 percent rate, falling to zero at about $38,000. Thus, though the EITC raises the return to work up to some income range, EITC lowers the incentive to work over the phase-out range.

Outlays on the EITC in 2006 amounted to about $35 billion, far exceeding other benefit programs for low income nonelderly families. In addition, EITC cost about $5 billion in tax reductions. States have adopted add-ons to the federal EITC, nearly always raising the subsidy rate and increasing work incentives but raising the phase-out as well, lowering work incentives beyond some threshold level.

The EITC substantially increases the incentive for low-wage workers to participate in the work force, but not necessarily to work full time. The gain to taking a part-time job over not working at all is most dramatically affected. For example, a single parent with two children and working half time (1,000 hours per year) at $10 per hour receives about $4,000 in EITC payments, a jump of 40 percent or $4 in the effective hourly wage. However, as Nada Eissa and Hillary Hoynes showed, moving from part-time to full-time work yields a smaller increase in earnings under the EITC than in the absence of the EITC (2005). In addition, the EITC lowers the incentive to work among some married women with a working husband because of the phase-out of the EITC benefit. For example, a married woman who can earn $10 per hour and whose husband is already working full time at the same wage will gain less from working than she would in the absence of the EITC.

At this point, there is an extensive body of research on the EITC dealing with a wide range of outcomes (for reviews, see Eissa and Hoynes 2005; Hotz and Scholz 2003). Although the evidence comes from econometric estimates and not random assignment research, the consensus is that the subsidy has contributed significantly to increasing the employment rates of single mothers. The subsidies are a critical component of the make-work-pay agenda for low-income families with children. Indeed, the improved work incentives for single mothers may have contributed to welfare reforms that impose strong work requirements. The presence of the EITC allows caseworkers to implement the mandates knowing that recipients who go to work will achieve substantially higher total incomes than they would without working. According to Bruce Meyer and Dan Rosenbaum, employment of single parents is approximately 6 percentage points higher as a result of the EITC (2001). In addition, the EITC has lowered poverty rates. At the same time, the phase-out aspect of the EITC has decreased hours of work among wives. Few experts, however, have viewed this decrease as a major concern.

Income transfers generally induce economic distortions, because resources leak out in the process of moving resources from one group to another (Okun 1975). Both Jeffrey Liebman and Edgar Browning have undertaken assessments of the resource costs and benefits of the EITC (Liebman 2001; Browning 1995). Even using Liebman's low cost estimates, providing an EITC benefit worth $1 to recipients costs taxpayers about $2 in lost economic welfare. This calculation assumes, however, that taxpayers place no value on raising the incomes of low-income families. Compared with conventional income-tested programs, the EITC has clear efficiency advantages that are empirically important. As EITC stimulates entry into the labor market rather than simply raising hours of work, the EITC benefit structure begins to resemble the optimal tax plan (Eissa and Hoynes 2005).

Another potential impact of the EITC is to lower wage rates. As EITC increases labor force participation, the increases in labor supplied, holding constant the overall demand, would lead to a decline in wage rates. If so, some of the beneficial impact of EITC on incomes would be offset by lost pre-EITC wage rates. In fact, there is no clear evidence that this is the case (Eissa and Hoynes 2005).

Wage subsidies tried in an experimental context have generated positive outcomes as well. Canada's Self-Sufficiency Project (SSP), which operated in British Columbia and New Brunswick, offered generous but temporary wage subsidies to single parents who moved from income assistance to working at least thirty hours per week and leaving welfare (Michalopoulos et al. 2002). The experimental evaluation of SSP found substantial increases in employment and earnings. The gains peaked in the second year of the program, with earnings jumping by 23 percent among new recipients. Although gains in earnings moderated in subsequent years, they stood at 12 percent in the first quarter of the fifth year after random assignment. The increases in income for the SSP experimental group were substantial enough to exceed the incremental costs to the government of paying for earnings supplements instead of welfare payments.

The New Hope project in Milwaukee, Wisconsin, reached out to all low-income families in two Milwaukee neighborhoods, making a special effort to enroll two-parent families and to avoid financial penalties to marriage. Participants who worked a minimum of thirty hours a week were provided an earnings supplement or subsidized job to bring their income to 200 percent of poverty. Participants received subsidized child care and health care, in addition to job placement assistance (Huston et al. 2003). Employment increased by 9 and 10 percent in follow-up years 1 and 2, and earnings jumped by 23, 11, and 13 percent in follow-up years 1 through 3 (Huston et al. 2003). In none of the subsequent years did New Hope generate statistically significant increases in employment and earnings. Still, the average increase in earnings over five years was a 7 percent gain for low-income families.

The specifics of the New Hope subsidies were complicated by their interaction with the EITC, the effort to avoid benefit reduction rates over 70 percent, the establishment of a maximum income by which benefits had to phase out, and Wisconsin's expansion of community service jobs and provision of health insurance and child care to all eligible low-income residents. This lessened the difference between the benefit packages available to the treatment and control groups.

Still, several benefits materialized from the program. During the first three years after random assignment (the period of program participation), the demonstration generated gains in earnings of about $700 per year during the eligibility period, increases in family income by over $1,000 per year, declines in poverty rates by about 30 percent (from about 70 to about 50 percent), reduced reports of symptoms of depression, improvements in several dimensions of family functioning, and better outcomes for children. Marriage rates increased as well (Gassman-Pines and Yoshikawa 2006). At the five-year follow-up, marriage rates of never-married mothers in the New Hope treatment group were almost double those of their counterparts in the control group (21 percent to 12 percent).

In today's context—with increases in child-care funding, in the child tax credit, and in the EITC—the most distinctive features would be the availability of community service jobs and the coverage of single individuals and childless couples, especially for the earnings subsidies and health insurance. The availability of jobs and earnings subsidies for single men and women might be of special importance to helping couples gain economic security and to ensuring both men and women can contribute economically. The benefit structure did have some questionable aspects. First, it imposed high marginal tax rates on earnings, commonly at about 60 percent for an individual with a child. Second, it ignored food stamp benefits, a program that provides a basic guarantee to all households and, over some income ranges, would add to the phase-out rate. Third, it provided very modest earnings subsidies, beyond the existing EITC, to many low-wage couples with children.

Although New Hope covered all types of households, the highest cost group and the group for which cost data are readily available is the Child and Family Study sample, those with at least one child between the ages of one and eleven. For this group, nearly 40 percent of New Hope's gross costs spent went for child care, and only about 18 percent went for earnings subsidies and the community service jobs. Although the gross cost of New Hope was approximately $6,600 per participating household per year (2006 dollars), the expansion of government child-care and health-care coverage would substantially lower today's costs. One estimate for the current Wisconsin policy environment is about $3,300. Neither estimate accounts for offsetting savings in other programs nor for the value of the output generated in community service jobs.

Another wage subsidy experimental project operated in Canada. The Earnings Supplement Project (ESP) offered wage supplements to displaced workers who took full-time jobs (at least thirty hours per week) within twenty-six weeks that paid less than their prior job (Bloom et al. 1999). Those in the treatment group qualified for supplements equal to 75 percent of the difference between the worker's current wage and previous wage. The project was intended to speed the return to work and to compensate displaced workers for some of their wage losses. Ideally, the offer would stimulate increased employment and earnings, reduce the costs of unemployment insurance, and raise the incomes of displaced workers. Results were mixed. Although the supplement offer increased the share of displaced workers holding a full-time job within twenty-six weeks, the gains were small. Earnings over the fifteen-month follow-up were slightly lower for the treatment group than for the control group. Although the program did not generate any added social benefits, the supplement did compensate for lost wages without significantly lowering earnings. The average supplement for fifteen months spread over the entire treatment group (including those who did not claim a supplement) was CN$1,161, but the amount paid to those receiving a supplement averaged about CN$8,700. Thus, though the treatment group experienced only a CN$570 mean gain in income (supplements minus slight earnings losses), supplementary payments played a much larger role in limiting income losses for the 20 percent who actually used the program.

Sometimes, improving work incentives involves reducing significant disincentives. For noncustodial fathers, the requirement to make high child support payments and re-pay arrearages can substantially reduce the incentive to work in formal jobs. The Parents' Fair Share demonstration tested whether mitigating these disincentives in the context of programs that provide training, peer support, and mediation with the custodial parent might affect outcomes (Miller and Knox 2001). The demonstration randomly assigned noncustodial fathers behind in their support payments to services or to control status. The goals were to help low-income noncustodial fathers attain more stable, higher-paying jobs, to pay their child support, and to become more involved with children and more responsible parents. Although average impacts were limited, the treatment induced sub-stantial gains in employment and earnings for the most disadvantaged fathers (those without high school degrees or those without recent work experience). Among the high school dropouts, experimentals earned $7,431, compared to the $4,924 earned by the controls, nearly a 50 percent gain. Because the demonstration explicitly provided on-the-job training, some of the employment gains took place directly as a result of in-program activity. Because Parents' Fair Share did not have a long-term follow-up study, the poten-tial for sustained impacts on employment and earnings is unclear.

Some incentive schemes involve significant service and information components, and others alter financial incentives and expect affected individuals to understand the implications of the incentives for their incomes. The demonstration projects generally explain the options workers face in much greater detail than in a broad-based program, such as EITC. On the other hand, the broader access and long duration of programs may help workers learn at least as much about incentives and disincentives as they would in a demonstration context.

Overall, the evidence for the effectiveness of subsidizing work is mixed. Wage sub-sidies and subsidized employment sometimes exert positive impacts on employment, hours worked, and total income, especially for single parents and where the subsidy increases the returns to workers above their wage rate (EITC, SSP, and New Hope). For displaced workers, the incentives did not stimulate additional work output. Still, even when the stimulus to added work is temporary, work subsidy programs are generally able to raise incomes of low-income individuals and families without generating reductions in work effort. In addition, indirect gains from New Hope indicate that work-related subsidies can improve child outcomes and possibly encourage marriage. Despite their demonstrated positive impacts, few formal cost-benefit analyses have been performed on work-related subsidy programs.

Job Training Programs to Promote Employment
Education and training programs play a central role in encouraging positive employment outcomes. The United States spends more than $900 billion dollars on the education and training of future workers, with more than $500 billion going to the K–12 school system. On the other hand, investments in training programs for low-income, displaced, and

disadvantaged workers are modest, under $10 billion per year. Despite the small scale of these programs, researchers have learned much about their impact on employment and earnings of participants.

Overall, the evidence from evaluations of programs targeted at low-income workers typically show limited gains. A meta-analysis of thirty-one evaluations of government-funded training programs for the disadvantaged found that annual earnings gains were about $1,400 (1999 dollars) for adult women, $300 for adult men, and zero or negative for youth (Greenberg, Michalopoulos, and Robins 2003). The review highlights several differences in impacts by type of program for each subgroup. For adult men, classroom skills training and on-the-job training showed positive effects in some specifications but not others. The additional earnings gains in random assignment experiments were about $1,200, nearly four times the average $300 effect. In addition, programs covering adult men did better in areas with high manufacturing employment. For adult women, several program types achieved consistently positive and significant impacts, with the mix of classroom and workplace training generating the highest earnings gains. Oddly, the cost of the program did not appear to affect the impacts on men or women. For youth, programs with classroom skills training generated earnings gains of nearly $2,000, but when combined with basic education, the increases declined by $1,000. One interesting interaction is that training programs worked far better when youth unemployment rates were low. This interaction did not show up in results for adults. The level of program costs was positively associated with earnings gains for youth, but surprisingly not for adults.

Although the review article did not provide benefit-cost estimates, several training evaluations have calculated whether the benefits (mainly from added earnings) are enough to offset program costs. The two largest experimentally based evaluations, both with benefit-cost studies, are the National Job Training Partnership Act (JTPA) evaluation and the National Job Corps evaluation. The JTPA evaluation involved sixteen independent and diverse sites drawn from hundreds of locally managed programs. JTPA participants typically obtain some classroom training in basic and occupation-specific skills, on-the-job training, and job search assistance. The Job Corps provides longer and more intensive education and occupational skills training, usually in a residential environment where participants have access to health and other services.

Under JTPA's operational programs, earnings increased about 15 percent for adult women and 8 percent among adult men, enough to justify the program's costs (Orr et al. 1996). Especially effective were the gains to those expected to use on-the-job and job search training. Unfortunately, the programs did nothing to raise the earnings of young men and women. Although gains from training programs are uneven, nonexperimental evidence shows substantial increases in earnings associated with years of general and vocational education. In addition, intensive job search programs, especially teaching people how to find their own jobs, have shown positive impacts. Like the JTPA effects on adults, the gains are small but enough to offset the modest costs of the intervention. Subsidized jobs and work experience programs, often involving jobs that gradually increase in difficulty and stress, raise earnings, especially during the period when these jobs are available. The gains beyond the subsidized job period have varied, depending on the target group and combination of activities.

Many training programs for low-income individuals begin with life skills training aimed at changing attitudes about the importance of work and about the habits necessary to succeed in the workplace. Although we should attach some weight to the consensus of practitioners about the importance of these aspects of preemployment training, we know of no studies that have documented the impact of this program component. Job Corps attempts to alter the context of at-risk youth. Individuals receive housing, education, training, health care, and other services mostly at residential Job Corps centers. Although the targeting of the program puts at-risk youth into an environment populated mainly by other economically disadvantaged youth, the centers try to change the context within which participants learn, work, and interact in positive ways. In view of the high cost per participant in Job Corps, the program must raise earnings substantially to achieve an adequate rate of return. Initially, the evaluation found sizable earnings increases, which, when projected forward, indicated that the program's social benefits exceeded its costs. However, further analysis based on administrative data through 2001 (almost three years beyond the earlier follow-up) documented a rapid erosion of Job Corps earnings gains after the four-year follow-up and a likely overstatement of earlier earnings gains because of differential attrition (Schochet, McConnell, and Burghardt 2003). For the full sample, earnings gains from Job Corps had eroded completely soon after the forty-eight month follow-up. The sharp reduction in medium-term and long-term earnings gains meant that projected social benefits per participant were over $10,000 (in 1995 prices) below social costs. Some groups of participants, such as youth entering in their early twenties, sustained their earnings gains, but others (Hispanics and those with a serious arrest record) did worse than their counterparts in the control group. The disappointing results are in some ways surprising, because Job Corps did stimulate participants to achieve a GED or vocational certificate. Moreover, though there is some indication that the Job Corps context matters, differences in impacts between those in a residential center (away from neighborhood peers) and those in a nonresidential setting were not statistically significant.

The industry context for employment interventions is the emphasis of sectoral strategies. Under this approach, workforce programs target an industry (or subset of an industry), become a strategic partner of the industry by learning about the factors shaping the industry's workforce policies, reach out to low-income job seekers, and work with other labor market groups, such as community colleges, community nonprofits, employer groups, and policymakers. The Aspen Institute and the Urban Institute have conducted studies of the operations of sectoral projects along with some analysis of data on the earnings of workers before and two years after participating (Blair 2002). The goal is to link the training and career strategies for low-income job seekers to the industry needs. By design, the programs deal with a particular industry and thus generalizations are hazardous. Nonetheless, the nonexperimental evidence indicates that the six sectoral programs taking part in the Sectoral Employment Development Learning Project (SEDLP) have yielded impressive results (Blair 2002). Earnings jumped by 73 percent in two years for the 95 percent of participants employed two years. Although most of the gains came from higher work levels, wage rates increased by 23 percent. Moreover, two years after training, 69 percent of participants were employed in occupations related to their training. The focused nature of the training, the linkages with employers, the development of pathways for entry level workers, and the expertise gained by the training organizations probably all have contributed to the apparent success of the sectoral strategy approach.

The most elaborate training takes place through apprenticeships, which usually involve three to four years of learning on the job together with course work. Nearly always, employer-led training takes place in the context of a work environment; indeed, one reason for its greater effectiveness is contextualized learning—examples include teaching basic skills using materials that working students use on a daily basis (Resnick 1989). Employers are central to the process, setting up the programs and paying the apprentices during their work-based learning. Although formal, registered apprenticeships are most common in the construction and manufacturing industries, the role of apprenticeship is expanding in other occupations and industries, including metalworking, nursing, information technology, and geospatial occupations. The evidence indicates significant gains for participants in apprenticeship training (Cook 1989). Researchers from the Upjohn Institute found that the gains associated with apprenticeship training in Washington were substantial two to three years after leaving the program (Washington State Workforce Training 2004). Those completing apprenticeships earned nearly $4,300 more a quarter than the primary comparison group. These earnings gains are nearly three times the comparably estimated gains for those graduating with a vocational degree from community colleges.

Broader studies indicate private sector training yields modest gains in wage rates but very high rates of return on typical training. One recent study (Frazis and Loewenstein 2005) found that sixty hours of training increased wage rates by about 5 percent, indicating rates of return on an annualized basis of at least 40 to 50 percent. Employers finance 96 percent of formal company training, but also 42 percent of training in the category involving business school, apprenticeship, vocational or technical institute and correspondence course (Loewenstein and Spletzer 1998). Firms certainly gain some of the benefit from training, but how much is not well understood.

A great deal of skill development takes place informally on the job as workers gain expertise in their occupations and industries. The wage gains from occupation-specific experience are especially high in craft occupations, and managers see especially high returns to industry-specific experience. Professionals gain significantly from both types of experience. These gains provide confirming evidence of the importance of skill development through contextualized learning and communities of practice so that workers in the same field can share their understanding of how to be effective.

Another program linked to specific industry sectors is the Career Academy. Although operating within schools and as part of a local school system, such as finance (22 percent), information technology (14 percent) and hospitality and tourism (12 percent), these programs try to weave related occupational or industrial themes into a college preparatory curriculum. The more than 1,588 academies try to weave related occupational or industrial themes into a college preparatory curriculum. Students take two to four classes per year taught by a common team of teachers and at least one course is industry-focused or occupation-focused. Academies attempt to use applied learning in academic courses as well as career-focused courses. They try to form partnerships with employers and local colleges. An experimental evaluation using random assignment has documented some striking gains (Kemple 2008). The test involved a social experiment in eight cities, with random assignment of applicants to the program or to the regular school. The results showed that the academies generated a striking 16 percent earnings gain for young men that persisted through a follow-up period of eight years after high school. Moreover, the earnings gains were concentrated among students with a high or medium risk of dropping out of high school. Their returns were as much as two to three years of additional education. The improved outcomes may be due to the small and closely linked learning community or the occupational-industry focus of the education. It is still too early to determine the sustainability of the Career Academy model, especially its ability to develop and maintain close links with businesses and other employers.

Community colleges are important institutions providing skills training for a variety of occupations and subgroups of workers. One recent analysis examined the impact of community college training in Washington State on displaced workers—workers who have lost their jobs, are unlikely to return, and have a strong attachment to their former employer and industry (Jacobson, LaLonde, and Sullivan 2005). The article not only shows the earnings gains from community college courses, but also presents a cost-benefit analysis (CBA) that considers the forgone earnings of students and other costs of education and training. The benefits were particularly high for technically oriented courses, including health-related courses, technical trade courses, and science and math courses. The internal rates of return to these types of courses were about 10 percent among males and 17 percent among females.

Several lessons emerge from this review. Education and training programs appear to work best in having students learn and retain skills when the instruction uses hands-on or project-based learning, often in a work context. Integrating training with employers or employer organizations is typically beneficial as well. Unfortunately, the modest outlays on public job training programs for the disadvantaged yield varying returns but rarely achieve significant earnings gains. Employer-sponsored training generates high rates of return, but the dollar amount of increased earnings is often low because employer training is usually short term. The most successful programs, or at least among them, are those that build occupation-specific skills in collaboration with employers, unions, or other organizations and that involve considerable learning at the workplace.

Subsidizing Firms to Hire Workers

Another approach for stimulating employment and raising wage rates is to subsidize the wage employers pay, which lowers the cost of hiring workers without lowering wages, thereby encouraging employers to increase their demand for workers. The United States has implemented several employer wage subsidy schemes, including the New Jobs Tax Credit (NJTC), the Targeted Jobs Tax Credit (TJTC), the Work Opportunity Tax Credit, and the Welfare-to-Work Tax Credit. Enacted in 1977, the NJTC provided an incremental subsidy to firms that increased hiring by more than 2 percent (Bishop and Haveman 1979). Although the credit did appear to speed up hiring, it was phased out and replaced by the TJTC when the perceived policy problem shifted from aggregate employment to the joblessness of selected disadvantaged subgroups. Since then, a variety of employer subsidies targeted at specific groups of workers have been tried at the federal and state levels (Dickert-Conlin and Holtz-Eakin 2000). Edmund Phelps, a Nobel prize-winning economist, has called for a graduated employer-based, wage rate subsidy in which the government provides half the difference between a target wage—say $12 per hour—and the actual wage—say, $6 per hour (1997). Thus, employers willing to pay $6 per hour to hire a worker would receive $3 per hour from the government, allowing the worker to receive $9 per hour.

Who benefits from wage subsidies? If wages are subsidized, will employers gain a windfall and be compensated for what they would have done anyway? The theory and evidence are mixed on these points, but employer wage subsidies face special problems. First, untargeted wage subsidies—those available to any low-wage worker—are unlikely to be effective in reaching needy groups. Only about 15 to 20 percent of low wage workers are in poor families. Second, targeted wage subsidies—those available to disadvantaged workers—face other problems. They are costly to administer (someone has to certify or audit eligibility). Firms receive subsidies for some of their workers but not others doing the same job. Members of subsidized target group may be stigmatized, making firms wary of hiring people that the government sees as requiring compensatory payments. For this reason, employer participation has been extremely low in the TJTC and in a variety of state grant diversion programs in which welfare offices pay employers who hire welfare recipients. Employer wage subsidies as part of an overall training, counseling, and support service strategy may be more successful.

Limiting employer subsidies to low-wage workers who are at risk of long-term unemployment does allow the benefits to flow to those most in need. And, despite the low employer participation in TJTC, the subsidy appears to have generated some increase in employment among disadvantaged youth (Katz 1998). I know of no good CBAs of employer wage subsidy programs.

CBA IN A WORK-INCENTIVE, EMPLOYMENT CONTEXT

Studies of interventions to enhance work incentives, employment, and earnings only occasionally incorporate CBA, though evaluations of job training programs do sometimes use it. Assessments of transfer and work incentive programs, however, typically focus on the costs, reductions in poverty, and increases in employment—examining efficiency considerations only theoretically. Usually only theoretical arguments or simulations provide serious analyses of the economic efficiency aspects of programs linked to work incentives. Perhaps this is because most work incentive issues arise in the context of redistribution programs that will involve efficiency losses alongside distributional gains.

Without a good metric to quantify the value of redistribution and the utility gains associated with self-support, even the most efficient programs to help low-income families, such as EITC, will show a cost to society that is higher than the benefits. Another obstacle is with the treatment of leisure, or time spent not working. From an economic efficiency viewpoint, leisure and housework have real value, for low-income welfare recipients as well as anyone else. Policymakers typically give little weight to this potential benefit. On the other hand, economists generally ignore the value people and policymakers place on self-sufficiency. To most political leaders and often to low-income people themselves, $1 of earned income has a higher value than $1 of income received through income transfers.

Training is an important exception. Training is an investment particularly well-suited to standard CBA. The most recent, comprehensive CBA dealt with Job Corps (Schochet, McConnell, and Burghardt 2003). Using an experimental design, evaluators estimated the benefits as the present value of the gains in earnings, of savings from reductions in criminal activity, and of reductions in the resource costs of other education and training programs. In addition, evaluators measured the resource costs of Job Corps (mainly education, training, health care, residential, and administrative costs), appropriately not including the transfers from taxpayers to participants. Comparing the resource benefits with the resource costs, the evaluators concluded that the net benefit was a negative $9,200 for all Corps members but a positive $17,200 for Job Corps members who entered at ages twenty to twenty-four. The evaluators recognized the sensitivity of their results to projections of future earnings.

Even this most careful and well-done CBA did little to address a few issues. One is the resource costs involved in taxing individuals to finance the program. A second is the distribution of the gains—did some benefit a great deal and others see little benefit? Were those who gained most otherwise destined for adequate earnings or for very poor earnings levels? Third, as with transfer programs, the standard analyses take no explicit account of distributional benefits of the program. Examining these magnitudes and variations is difficult, but not impossible.

Notwithstanding these qualifications, high-quality CBA can be a valuable tool and should be employed more frequently to evaluate the effectiveness of alternative programs and demonstration projects. However, because research and CBAs of programs require considerable time and money, it is critical to study those interventions that are most promising carefully. Ideally, the proposed demonstrations should have a solid theoretical rationale, build on successful elements of past programs or demonstrations, be designed to significantly improve work-related outcomes, deal with key problems, and be easily replicated and implemented on a large scale, if successful. Several employment-oriented strategies meet these criteria, but differ in approach, intensity, duration, scale, delivery mechanisms, involvement of partners, target groups, and the relative emphasis placed on current employment versus long-term careers. Some emphasize incentives (wage subsidies), others focus on skills (classroom and on-the-job training, job search skills), on attitudes (work experience and work readiness programs), or on the individual's context (programs that try to alter the participant's peer group or change the hiring and training practices of a local industry sector). I now present specific work-enhancing strategies to test.

PROMISING STRATEGIES FOR CBA

In considering the programmatic options to test, a good starting point is to ask whose work incentives, employment, and earnings outcomes we wish to promote. A natural priority group is adults in low-income families with children, especially single mothers. This group has experienced rising employment and wage rates through a combination of more favorable financial incentives and a healthy economy. Over the last eleven years, the employed share of single mothers rose from about 61 to 72 percent, their unemployment dropped from 10 to 7.5 percent, and their real wage rates increased by 11 percent. On the other hand, young black men have faced stagnant or worsening employment options. Of twenty-five- to twenty-nine-year-old black men in the noninstitutionalized population, more than one in four were not employed and their spring 2008 unemployment rate was 40 percent higher than among single parents. When one accounts for the rising number of black men in jail or prison, the number of their employed counterparts shows a sharp decline (Raphael 2008). Declining real wages for less skilled workers account for only a modest part of this reduction. But other disincentives, including deductions from earnings for child support obligations, apparently weakened black male participation in the formal labor market (Holzer, Offner, and Sorensen 2005).

Marriage and family status interact with work incentives in complex ways. The presence of tax and transfer programs may lower the net gain from working or working more hours, especially for spouses. The EITC encourages work effort over a specific range, but raises the implicit tax rate on earnings beyond the range of $14,000 to16,000 of family earnings. Together with benefit programs that phase out benefits with earnings, the tax system ends up causing workers to face marginal tax rates well over 50 percent. For a man with a child support order, the net gain from working may fall well below 50 percent of his earnings.

Unfortunately, it would take a major budget increase to lower the marriage and work disincentives built into existing income transfers without reducing benefits to current recipients. Some new financial incentives have been suggested that might mitigate these disincentive problems, but cost constraints and other considerations suggest the use of other policy instruments as well. Programs aimed at enhancing the skills required for employment and for marriage, parenting, and other relationships are examples of non-financial policies that attempt to affect work and family stability.

A Comprehensive Model

Ensuring access to a job as a way of helping individuals and families attain a reasonable living standard is an idea that goes back centuries. In the 1970s, proposals for job guarantees in combination with wage subsidies in the private sector led to President Jimmy Carter's welfare reform proposals (Lerman 1974; Lynn and Whitman 1981). The New

Hope demonstration represented a generally successful implementation of this work-based, antipoverty strategy. In a recent assessment of New Hope, Greg Duncan and his colleagues recommend replicating the program at the state level, with administration taking place through one-stop job centers (2007). However, before a full program becomes operational, some fine tuning, replication, and CBA will have to take place.

The plan would offer all adults a chance to escape poverty through work effort. The test would be to determine whether the approach is a cost-effective way to reduce poverty, increase employment and earnings, and achieve other positive social outcomes, such as less crime, better child adjustment and achievement, and increased marital and family stability. Like New Hope, the plan would supplement earnings of adults (say, age twenty-one and over) working at low-wage jobs, provide low-wage, subsidized employment, and help workers obtain subsidized health insurance. Subsidizing wage rates of individuals might weaken the targeting of benefits to low-income families, but strict income-targeting could also weaken the positive incentives that are built into wage subsidies. The 2007 poverty thresholds for a single individual and couple are $10,210 and $13,690. In principle, earnings can allow individuals to reach these levels with full-time, year-round work for individuals at about $5 per hour and for couples at about $7 per hour. A head of a family of four would have to earn over $10 per hour for about 2,000 hours per year. With the minimum wage rising to over $7, assured job access even at minimum wages would allow all single individuals and couples to reach the poverty threshold, even without a subsidy. However, to secure a net income above poverty while paying a fee toward subsidized health insurance, individuals and couples would have to earn more, possibly through a program that would subsidize wage rates.

The demonstration and evaluation would operate as follows. One-stop centers in selected inner cities would be solicited to operate a program to fund subsidies and services to potential clients. Individuals who enter the center would not only have access to the standard job search services, but would also be asked if they wished to participate in a self-support demonstration. If so, they would be randomly assigned to two possible treatments or to control status. The first treatment would provide enough wage subsidies and employment to ensure a stable, adequate income (125 percent of the poverty line) if they were willing to work full time. The wage subsidy would equal half the difference between some target wage rate (say $10 per hour) and the worker's actual wage (say $6 per hour). Although economic needs increase with family size, the EITC and food stamp benefits are both higher for married couples than singles, for one child than no children, and for two or more children than one child. As a result, the program can use the same wage subsidy formula for all workers and still achieve similar antipoverty impacts across families of different sizes as long as workers take up the benefits for which they qualify. An additional task of program staff would be to help participants use available work supports and supplements. For those unable to find a job, the program would offer transitional employment at the minimum wage. To ensure greater financial security, the program would offer a contributory health insurance program to all families.

The second treatment group would combine the subsidy components with classes that teach relationship skills with partners, children, and employers. Including a relationship skills component recognizes the critical importance of marital and family stability for limiting economic hardship and income poverty. Until now, programs aimed at strengthening relationships and marriage have operated in isolation from employment and subsidy programs. This demonstration would add assured economic support alongside the teaching of relationship and healthy marriage skills.

Mitigating Work Disincentives of Noncustodial Parents

Low-income, noncustodial parents (NCPs), usually fathers, are a critical group of workers often susceptible to work disincentives. After paying 20 to 25 percent of their low wages on child support, 7.65 percent on social security taxes, and 10 to15 percent on income taxes, these men often find that they can keep only a modest share of their formal wages. A few state programs offer low-income NCPs a special Earned Income Tax Credit (EITC) to offset these disincentives to work and to encourage the payment of child support obligations. The credits are available only to NCPs who are current with their child support payments.

A CBA of a similar credit could value the impacts of the approach on formal employment, work effort, child support payments, and father involvement. To the extent that the availability of credits made formal work pay, the credits could end up yielding significant social benefits. Income transfers to custodial parents—through TANF, food stamps, or public housing—would decline with added child support payments, as would the resource costs involved in the transfers.

The form of the existing and proposed credits currently mirrors the structure of the EITC, rising with initial earnings, hitting a plateau, and then phasing out with additional earnings. This approach would improve the incentives for the lowest income NCPs to work in the formal market and pay child support.

Expanding Apprenticeships in Low-Income Communities

A major incentive to work is that the on-the-job learning and work experience enhance occupational skills and career prospects. Improving access to rewarding careers could serve as a very important incentive for low-income workers, especially inner-city men. Making the future value of today's work more transparent can be important in encouraging workers to learn and to maintain steady work habits. One mechanism is to use work-based learning in an occupational field. Sectoral initiatives are one approach to working with groups of sectors, creating coalitions, assessing the skill requirements for existing positions, projecting skills required to upgrade jobs, recruiting and targeting potential trainees, developing training modules, and obtaining a mix of public and private funding. Often the workers who receive training come from groups targeted under DOL-sponsored training programs, such as disadvantaged youth, dislocated workers, veterans, and individuals with basic skills deficiencies. Participating firms often include some of their current (incumbent) workers. The focus on industry needs and close links with employers, however, are sound principles that have led to some effective programs that train workers to improve their jobs and earnings. So far, the programs are ad hoc arrangements and not a systemic part of the landscape. The training is usually short term and only occasionally leads to a recognized qualification. The programs should be encouraged, but the long-term goal should be to develop a large-scale, more intense, sustainable skill-building system using the same principles.

The current apprenticeship system already provides demand-driven, long-term training to potential workers. The programs generate high skills for participants, involve extensive work-based learning, require little or no forgone earnings on the part of participants, and fill positions that are in demand and have both job ladders and long-term options. They promote productivity of firms and the life chances of workers (Steedman, Gospel, and Ryan 1998; Steedman 2005). Unfortunately, the current federal budget for the Office of Apprenticeship (OA) is very small; the government provides no direct funds to help finance the training and conducts virtually no research and little monitoring of many aspects of the program.

A well-structured CBA of existing and new apprenticeships could help determine the potential gains for workers and for firms. Relative to other training programs and even college programs, apprenticeships involve very little forgone earnings by workers and offer a range of benefits to firms. Expanding apprenticeships could be highly cost-effective in skill-building for high-demand occupations and in raising productivity and earnings at intermediate levels. Although no definitive analysis has estimated the returns to apprentices (over, say, high school graduates with no other certification), the evidence from the state of Washington indicates earnings gains in the range of $15,000 to $17,000 per year. If confirmed, expanding apprenticeships would almost certainly yield high rates of social returns, especially compared to existing public training programs.

CONCLUSION

The role of work and work incentives in promoting desirable social outcomes is a complex subject. Even when employment opportunities are widespread, low wages and high tax rates can cause many to reduce their productive activity. Sometimes, the reduced work effort not only reduces current capacity but also lowers future productivity. Other secondary losses in real resources are the administrative and economic costs of collecting taxes and making income transfers to those who do not maximize their earnings.

Decades of research and policy have yielded a consensus on the value of work-related subsidies, such as the Earned Income Tax Credit, and work-conditioned benefits, such as work requirements in welfare programs. Although high benefit reduction rates persist, especially when tax rates on earnings interact with disincentives to marry, some promising demonstrations have pointed the way toward renewed efforts to eliminate poverty through work.

Work incentives are often defined in terms of how much added effort and earnings translate into added income, but decisions about how hard to work and what jobs to take are often influenced by long-term considerations. Will the job lead to higher earnings or higher status in the future? I believe it is important to consider this perspective when assessing future demonstrations aimed at improving work outcomes.

New CBAs can play a critical role in informing policymakers about the potential effectiveness of wage subsidies, subsidized jobs, and reducing work penalties on selected groups. In addition, cost-benefit research can determine the potential effectiveness of apprenticeships, which remains a highly promising approach for improving work and career outcomes as well as the economic performance of firms. Broadening the notion of work incentives to incorporate long-term career goals is appropriate not only for generating good jobs but also for attracting and increasing the commitment of many in the at-risk population.

REFERENCES

Besley, Timothy, and Stephen Coate. 1992. "Workfare versus Welfare: Incentive Arguments for Work Requirements in Poverty Alleviation Programs." *American Economic Review* 82(1): 249–61.

Bishop, John, and Robert Haveman. 1979. "Selective Employment Subsidies: Can Okun's Law Be Repealed?" *American Economic Review* 69(2): 124–30.

Blair, Amy J. 2002. *Measuring Up, and Weighing In: Industry-Based Workforce Development Training Results in Strong Employment Outcomes*, Sector Policy Project Series Report No. 3. Washington, DC: The Aspen Institute.

Bloom, Howard, Saul Schwartz, Susanna Lui-Gurr, and Suk-Won Lee. 1999. *Testing a Reemployment Incentive for Displaced Workers: The Earnings Supplement Project*. Ottawa, Canada: Social Research, and Demonstration Corporation.

Boone, Jan, Peter Fredriksson, Bertil Holmlund, and Jan C. van Ours. 2007. "Optimal Unemployment Insurance with Monitoring and Sanctions." *Economic Journal* 117(518): 399–421.

Browning, Edgar. 1995. "Effects of the Earned Income Tax Credit on Income, and Welfare." *National Tax Journal* 48(1): 23–43.

Cadena, Brian, Danziger, Sheldon, and Seefeldt, Kristin. 2006. "Measuring State Welfare Policy Changes: Why Don't They Explain Caseload and Employment Outcomes?" *Social Science Quarterly* 87(4): 808–17.

Coe, Norma, Gregory Acs, Robert Lerman, and Keith Watson. 1998. "Does Work Pay? An Analysis of Work Incentives under TANF." *Assessing the New Federalism*, Occasional Paper No. 9. Washington, DC: Urban Institute Press.

Cook, Robert. 1989. *Analysis of Apprenticeship Training from the National Longitudinal Study of the Class of 1972*. Rockville, MD: Westat.

Dickert-Conlin, Stacy, and Douglas Holtz-Eakin. 2000. "Employee-Based Versus Employer-Based Subsidies to Low-Wage Workers: A Public Finance Perspective." In *Finding Jobs*, eds. David Card and Rebecca Blank. New York: The Russell Sage Foundation.

Duncan, Greg, Aletha Huston, and Thomas Weisner. 2007. *Higher Ground*. New York: Russell Sage Foundation.

Edelman, Peter, Harry Holzer, and Paul Offner. 2006. *Reconnecting Disadvantaged Young Men* Washington, DC: Urban Institute Press.

Eissa, Nada, and Hillary Hoynes. 2005. "Behavioral Responses to Taxes: Lessons from the EITC, and Labor Supply." *NBER* Working Paper 11729. Cambridge, MA: National Bureau of Economic Research.

Frazis, Harley, and Mark Loewenstein. 2005. "Reexamining the Returns to Training: Functional Form, Magnitude, and Interpretation." *Journal of Human Resources* 40(2): 453–76.

Gassman-Pines, Anna, and Hirokazu Yoshikawa. 2006. "Five-Year Effects of an Anti-Poverty Program on Marriage among Never-Married Mothers." *Journal of Public Policy Analysis, and Management* 25(1): 11–31.

Greenberg, David, Charles Michalopoulos, and Philip Robins. 2003. "A Meta-Analysis of Government-Sponsored Training Programs." *Industrial and Labor Relations Review* 57(1): 31–53.

Hofferth, Sandra L., Stephen Stanhope, and Kathleen Mullan Harris. 2002. "Exiting Welfare in the 1990s: Did Public Policy Influence Recipients' Behavior?" *Population Research and Policy Review* 21(5): 433–72.

Holzer, Harry J. 1996. *What Employers Want: Job Prospects for Less-Educated Workers*. New York: Russell Sage Foundation.

Holzer, Harry J., Paul Offner, and Elaine Sorensen. 2005. "Declining Employment among Young Black Less-Educated Men: The Role of Incarceration and Child Support." *Journal of Policy Analysis, and Management* 24(2): 329–50.

Hotz, Joseph, and John Karl Scholz. 2003. "The Earned Income Tax Credit." In *Means-Tested Transfer Programs in the United States,* ed. Robert Moffitt. Chicago: University of Chicago Press.

Huston, Aletha C., Cynthia Miller, Lashawn Richburg-Hayes, Greg J. Duncan, Carolyn A. Eldred, Thomas S. Weisner, Edward Lowe, Vonnie C. McLoyd, Danielle A. Crosby, Marika N. Ripke, and Cindy Redcross. 2003. *New Hope for Families, and Children: Five-Year Results of a Program to Reduce Poverty, and Reform Welfare.* New York: MDRC.

Jacobson, Louis, Robert LaLonde, and Daniel Sullivan. 2005. "Estimating the Returns to Community College Schooling for Displaced Workers." *Journal of Econometrics* 125(1-2): 271–304.

Katz, Lawrence. 1998. "Wage Subsidies for the Disadvantaged." In *Generating Jobs: How to Increase Demand for Less-Skilled Workers,* eds. Richard Freeman and Peter Gottschalk. New York: Russell Sage Foundation.

Kemple, James. 2008. *Career Academies: Long-Run Impacts on Labor Market Outcomes, Educational Attainment, and Transitions to Adulthood.* New York: MDRC.

Kesselman, Jonathan. 1969. "Labor Supply Effects of Income, Income-Work, and Wage Subsidies." *Journal of Human Resources* 4(3): 275–92.

Lerman, Robert I. 1974. "JOIN: A Jobs and Income Program for American Families." In *Studies in Public Welfare, Paper No. 19.* Subcommittee on Fiscal Policy, Joint Economic Committee, U.S. Congress. Washington, DC: U.S. Government Printing Office.

Liebman, Jeffrey. 2001. "The Optimal Design of the Earned Income Tax Credit." *NBER* Working Paper 7363. Cambridge, MA: National Bureau of Economic Research.

Loewenstein, Mark, and James Spletzer. 1998. "Dividing the Costs and Returns to General Training." *Journal of Labor Economics* 16(1): 142–71.

Lynn, Lawrence, and David Whitman. 1981. *The President as Policymaker: Jimmy Carter and Welfare Reform.* Philadelphia, PA: Temple University Press.

Meara, Ellen, and Richard Frank. 2006. "Welfare Reform, Work Requirements,, and Employment Barriers." *NBER* Working Paper 12480. Cambridge, MA: National Bureau of Economic Research.

Meyer, Bruce, and Dan Rosenbaum. 2001. "Welfare, the Earned Income Tax Credit, and the Labor Supply of Single Mothers." *Quarterly Journal of Economics* 116(3): 1063–114.

Michalopoulos, Charles, Doug Tattrie, Cynthia Miller, Philip K. Robins, Pamela Morris, David Gyarmati, Cindy Redcross, Kelly Foley, and Reuben Ford. 2002. *Making Work Pay. Final Report on the Self-Sufficiency Project for Long-Term Welfare Recipients.* New York: MDRC.

Miller, Cynthia, and Virginia Knox. 2001. *The Challenge of Helping Low-Income Fathers Support Their Children: Final Lessons from Parents' Fair Share.* New York: MDRC.

Okun, Arthur. 1975. *Equality and Efficiency: The Big Tradeoff.* Washington, DC: Brookings Institution Press.

Orr, Larry, Howard S. Bloom, Stephen H. Bell, Fred Doolittle, and Winston Lin. 1996. *Does Training for the Disadvantaged Work? Evidence from the National JTPA Study.* Washington, DC: Urban Institute Press.

Pingle, Jonathan F. 2003. "What If Welfare Had No Work Requirements? The Age of Youngest Child Exemption, and the Rise in Employment of Single Mothers." *Finance and Economics Discussion Series* Working Paper 2003–57. Washington, DC: Board of Governors of the Federal Reserve.

Phelps, Edmund. 1997. *Rewarding Work.* Cambridge, MA: Harvard University Press.

Raphael, Stephen. 2008. "Boosting the Employment and Earnings of Low-Skill Workers in the

United States: Making Work Pay and Removing Barriers to Employment and Social Mobility." In *A Future of Good Jobs?* eds. Timothy J. Bartek and Susan N. Houseman. Kalamazoo, MI: W. E. Upjohn Institute for Employment Research.

Resnick, Lauren. 1987. "Learning In School and Out." *Educational Researcher* 16(9): 13–20.

Roed, Knut, and Lars Westlie. 2007. "Unemployment Insurance in Welfare States: Soft Constraints, and Mild Sanctions." *IZA* Discussion Paper 2877. Bonn: Institute for the Study of Labor.

Schochet, Peter, Shenna McConnell, and John Burghardt. 2003. *National Job Corps Study: Findings Using Administrative Earnings Data.* Princeton, NJ: Mathematica Policy Research.

Sen, Amartya. 1992. *Inequality Reexamined.* Cambridge, MA: Harvard University Press.

Steedman, Hilary. 2005. "Apprenticeship in Europe: 'Fading' or Flourishing?" *Centre for Economic Performance* Discussion Paper 710. London: London School of Economics.

Steedman, Hilary, Howard Gospel, and Paul Ryan. 1998. "Apprenticeship: A Strategy for Growth." *Centre for Economic Performance* Paper CEPSP11. London: London School of Economics.

Swann, Christopher. 2005. "Welfare Reform When Recipients Are Forward-Looking." *Journal of Human Resources* 40(1): 31–56.

Washington State Workforce Training and Education Coordinating Board. 2004. *Workforce Training Results: 2004.* Olympia: State of Washington.

Next Steps in Welfare-to-Work

Michael Wiseman

Welfare-to-work policies seek to build human capital by encouraging and facilitating participation in labor markets. Effective policies not only increase income but also generally raise the return to additional human capital investment. What are possibly effective policies? How can we know if they would be effective? How do we know if they are desirable?

I answer the first two questions by proposing several policy demonstrations. Each is motivated to some extent by existing research and executing it would generate enough information to enable researchers to determine its effectiveness. I answer the third question by reviewing the application of cost-benefit analysis (CBA) to the Minnesota Family Investment Program, one of the most important state initiatives in the welfare policy area in terms of breadth of assessment and contribution to policy development.

I propose three demonstrations: first, an experiment with subsidized third-party provision of strategic financial advice and support for working low-income families; second, coordinated state experimentation with a transitional incentive package for recipients of Temporary Assistance for Needy Families (TANF); and, third, an employment intervention for TANF applicants and recipients with substantial disabilities. A common theme runs through these proposals. Each involves changes in factors that influence what is gained both from existing human capital and from additional investment in skills and reputation for targeted families. For working families, the third-party advisor demonstration targets access to benefits, information, and sense of personal control. The transitional incentive intends to rekindle state interest in active efforts to improve TANF policies that influence incentives to work. The employment intervention creates an incentive for refocusing the attention of TANF applicants and recipients with substantial disabilities on habilitation and skill development rather than benefits acquisition. All three involve uncertain benefits or costs about which a well-designed experiment should produce considerable information.

FINANCIAL INTERMEDIATION AND STRATEGIC SUPPORT

The first proposal is to subsidize a financial planning and services firm to act as an agent for working low-income families. The effort includes using such firms to administer certain publicly financed work and income supports, most notably food stamps. The motivating hypothesis is that a third party, behaving as an agent for working families, would help increase their savings and improve their labor market outcomes. These good things would come about because such firms would provide better integration of support services, better explication of strategy, and more consistent and income-focused family support through time. The same firms, acting as agents of government, would be able to improve accuracy in both determining eligibilty and providing benefits. The value added in this function, plus benefits to target families, have the potential to justify the subsidy. The idea of the proposal germinated during discussions of the behavioral effects on households of the Earned Income Tax Credit (EITC) and my observation of certain developments in the private tax-preparation market the EITC has generated, specifically, the activities of H&R Block, Inc., with which I consulted briefly in 2005. For shorthand, I refer to this financial intermediation and strategic support demonstration as the FISS proposal.

There is widespread agreement that the Earned Income Tax Credit played a central role in the increase in employment rates among single parents in the 1990s (Eissa and Hoynes 2006). The contribution of the EITC to the dramatic declines in TANF receipt that occurred over the same period is more controversial. Scholars such as Jeffrey Grogger have attributed much of the caseload decline to the combination of EITC benefits and a very strong economy (2004). Others, most notably Lawrence Mead, have argued that though the EITC played an important role in making work pay, the principal factor behind decline in welfare receipt was terminations generated by aggressively applied work requirements (Mead 2006). This controversy may in part be resolved by appreciating that caseloads can decline both because exit rates rise and because accession rates fall. It is possible that EITC has had little direct effect on job-taking by TANF recipients (as Mead claimed), but has had substantial consequences for the likelihood that families at risk of welfare dependence are in fact forced to apply for TANF. Studies of working poor life and interaction with welfare—notably Jason DeParle's *American Dream*—often provide anecdotal information on the importance of EITC-based tax refunds in preserving the financial viability of self-support for families at risk of TANF accession (2004).

The average beneficiary of an EITC refund receives a substantial amount of money—$1,815 per tax return in 2004. This creates what some analysts call a moment of opportunity for savings and has spurred an effort to offer recipients the opportunity to divert part of the refund to some sort of saving instrument. Several changes in tax policy have been introduced to encourage saving part or all of tax refunds, including an option allowing taxpayers to designate that part of their refund be deposited in up to three separate accounts (including IRAs). Those contributing to an IRA or other employer-sponsored savings plan can also benefit from the Saver's Credit. One suspects that these initiatives would be more effective if delivered in the context of more general and trusted advice on financial strategy, but giving such advice is not an Internal Revenue Service responsibility.

A substantial portion of EITC returns are received by filers who use tax preparation services, most notably H&R Block. The EITC is arguably the single most important factor contributing to recent growth of Block and its aggressive expansion in recent years into areas with substantial numbers of low-wage workers. Block and its competitors have suffered considerable bad publicity for provision of short-term refund anticipation loans (RALs) that provide its clients with an instant EITC for a charge that is probably in line with costs but, when converted into an annual interest equivalent, appears usurious (Berube et al. 2002). In addition, in 2006, in his former capacity as New York State attorney general, Elliott Spitzer sued Block for promoting investment of EITC refunds in individual retirement accounts (IRAs) managed by the firm. Like many others, between 2001 and 2003, these investments yielded very low and sometimes negative returns, and Spitzer has attempted to hold the firm liable. Block has responded aggressively, both directly and indirectly. The direct response was to argue that over the longer run the firm's mutual funds are good investments and that such accounts offer low-income workers a useful opportunity. While asserting that the RALs provide a useful service sought after by consumers, for a time Block reduced its marketing of RALs and instead promoted savings. Much of the lawsuit was dismissed in 2007.

The indirect Block response has been both political and strategic. The firm has formed alliances with significant left-of-center interest groups in Washington, including the Center for Budget and Policy Priorities and the New America Foundation. At the same time, it has begun actively participating in experimental work on savings incentives, presumably in part because a national policy of subsidizing saving by its clients would redound to the firm's benefit. A signal example of this effort was the funding and conduct in 2004 of an evaluation of the effect of financial incentives on the willingness of its clients in the St. Louis area to invest EITC refunds. The evaluation was done by random assignment, with oversight and results analysis by a group of researchers affiliated with the Brookings Institution (Duflo et al. 2005). The mixed results of this investigation prompted an expanded research effort with a greater variety of treatments and at more sites in 2005.

Congressional testimony by its officers and other firm activities seem to indicate that Block sees the public support system for working low-income families to be an important source of opportunities for the future. The firm has begun to offer state and local governments support in program outreach for the State Children's Health Insurance Program (SCHIP) and for the Food Stamp Program. One of Block's subcontractors, Onesta, Inc. (now cleverly renamed Nets to Ladders), has developed an artful software system to support integrated social assistance intake that has attracted widespread interest in both the government and the philanthropic community.

All this serves to reassure us that H&R Block has turned from the Dark Side, even if we trust that the apparent reorientation is in part propelled by profit. Moving beyond cynicism, it is important to consider the general issue. What in abstract does H&R Block appear to be doing? The firm is developing a strategic financial management service for families that potentially provides something quite similar to the advice financial counselors provide to middle-income families. The difference, however, is that financial assistance services for middle-income families are typically almost entirely focused on portfolio management and tax avoidance, whereas the emphasis of the Block effort is on gaining benefits as an initial step in developing savings—getting that portfolio in the first place. From the client's perspective, Block potentially offers both agency and integration. Clients see the firm, unlike social assistance agencies, as their employee. Block wants the client's business, and Block is willing to open thousands of storefronts and to stay open at odd hours to get it. Block is adopting a more comprehensive approach to assisting its clients in marshaling all available resources for increasing income and, in consequence, increasing both work and tax refunds as well as savings deposited in Block-related financial instruments. What the firm's critics seem to miss is that Block's clients appreciate the services they receive, and they are loyal. This is the foundation for productive agency.

Block has made overtures to a number of states to become involved in Food Stamp program (FSP) outreach. At the simplest level, the firm would like to do what many non-profit organizations do now, namely, assist clients in filling out FSP applications that are then forwarded to the local FSP office. But more substantial connections are possible. One model is for Block to establish direct data exchange relationships with local FSP offices and to transmit the required information directly to the FSP agency's system. Food Stamp regulations require a direct interview with a government agency employee, which could be accomplished from the Block office. The benefits of such a system for the firm's clients is clear. As to Block, conceivably states could pay Block for administering the program and for guaranteeing payment accuracy.

In recent years, and especially since passage of the Personal Responsibility and Work Opportunity Reconciliation Act, much attention has been paid to finding ways to support working low-income households. For a variety of reasons, benefits and support programs have multiplied, creating a difficult maze of rules and regulations for households that by definition are short on time. Time lost in consequence of financial mismanagement is time not available for developing human capital, and obtaining and enjoying the gains from such development may require financial expertise that households lack. I suggest that the agenda include an experiment in which some population of working low-income households is offered an opportunity for comprehensive assistance with financial management, to cover not only tax filing and saving but access to some subset of basic social services, including food stamps, as well. I suggest the service be offered at minimal cost, subject only to compliance with reporting requirements, but think that to retain the sense of agency it is important that the service not be free. The service provider would be challenged to both develop individualized strategy for clients and to find ways to maximize participation.

Development of the FISS experiment would be complex. Public agencies would need to agree to employ the financial service provider to administer the public benefits included in the basic services package. (To my knowledge all of the statutory and regulatory restrictions can be waived in experimental contexts.) If Block were the agent, then the political issue that both privatization and the residual RAL stigma raise must be addressed. One way to do so would be to emphasize that should the project prove successful, licensing of organizations for provision of these services could be made competitive and open to a variety of nonprofit and for-profit organizations, as well as partnerships cutting across groups.

To repeat, the motivating hypothesis of the demonstration is that a third party, behaving as an agent of working families, would—by better integrating support services, explaining strategy, and consistent support through time—increase saving and improve labor market outcomes. The consequence for public costs is uncertain, because part of the strategy is to increase, rather than reduce, access to services and benefits supported from public funds. This uncertainty—combined with a plausible model that identifies a role for intermediation, the corporate H&R Block enthusiasm, and the experimental evidence to date—justifies planning a more widespread demonstration supported by an evaluation partner experienced in labor force and assistance issues, the operation of relevant government agencies, and philanthropic underwriting.

TRANSITIONAL INCENTIVES PACKAGE

The second experiment I propose has objectives on two levels. The immediate focus is a structural choice states must make in designing their TANF programs. I want to embed this experiment, however, within an effort to improve methods for collective learning by states and the federal government about TANF policy choices. This is the Transitional Incentives Package (TIP) demonstration.

As with the other proposals, some background is useful. The first major social policy experiment, the New Jersey Negative Income Tax, focused on studying the effect on labor supply of variations in basic assistance benefits and the rate at which benefits were taxed as income increased. This tax rate is commonly called the benefit reduction rate. Forty years have now passed since the New Jersey experiment was fielded, and the financial work incentives created by means-tested benefits programs continue to be a matter of major concern. One design objective for benefit systems is commonly cast as making work pay, taken to mean ensuring a benefit reduction rate of less than one. As is well understood, providing an adequate minimum income guarantee while preserving financial incentives to work, and restraining costs, is difficult given the distribution of earnings and income in the American economy. The problem is compounded when public assistance is delivered through multiple programs, each with its own benefit reduction rate.

TANF provides states great leeway in designing the interaction between a recipient's earnings and benefits. This latitude results in great diversity and great confusion. In a recent paper, Linda Giannarelli and I counted forty-three procedures for varying benefits with TANF recipient earnings across the fifty states and the District of Columbia (Giannarelli and Wiseman 2006). Moreover, despite frequent references to the states as laboratories of democracy, in the ten years since TANF was established, there has been no appreciable convergence of work incentive policy. Arguably, such convergence has failed because no institutions to organize learning from this diversity or to share lessons gained across states exist.

The design of TANF benefits policies for working families differs from the classical negative income tax because most TANF programs are time limited. Moreover, negative income tax systems are basically static; they take income as given and augment it as appropriate given the benefits schedule. In contrast, TANF programs are typically intended as transitional—as temporary assistance for those needy families. This dynamic character is underscored in twelve states in which TANF policy is to disregard a substantial amount of earnings in benefit calculation for the first few months following employment initiation, and then to reduce TANF benefits, presumably as the family stabilizes in its new situation and in coordination with food stamp adjustments. Some states disregard essentially all earnings for a time. Other states treat earnings in standard negative tax fashion. Maryland, for example, has a flat benefit reduction rate of 60 percent. California uses 50 percent.

If TANF were the only income support system available, a system that limited the duration of benefits for working families would hardly be appropriate. In the United States, however, every dollar reduction in TANF benefits is offset by an increase of $0.30 in food stamps, and working households eventually receive the EITC. Thus, one choice states face might be cast as between, on the one hand, a regime in which a constant benefit reduction rate is applied to earnings for as long as permitted by the state's time limit and, on the other, a regime in which the benefit reduction rate starts very low—perhaps at zero—and then rises with time on the job. Obviously some condition would be required to prevent people from cycling on and off TANF to obtain the zero disregard repeatedly. With such a restriction, it is not clear at all which of the two regimes would have the more favorable effect on employment and welfare utilization at, say, a year past employment initiation. Available experimental evidence provides little information pertinent to such a prediction or for choosing the best length for the high disregard interval (see Michalopoulos 2005).

A demonstration of this sort is hardly glamorous. However, what is important about it is that it addresses a policy choice that lies wholly within the sphere of state discretion, and one could imagine hammering out details as a collaborative exercise among states. Because it is difficult to see in advance which system provides the greater advantage for unemployed TANF recipients, setting up a randomized experiment would probably meet less line worker resistance than many other possible innovations. Thus, regardless of glamour, the choice is real and possibly significant in view of TANF objectives. The fiscal risks are minimal, as are the potential costs for recipients.

This brings us back to the larger objective. This overview provides few details; actual implementation would require much more design work. The issues that have to be addressed—how much is disregarded in the first months of job taking, how long first months should be, under what circumstances families should get a second chance, how to conduct the randomized trials, the penalties for states that fail to deliver—are generally easy to understand and usefully discussed directly with and among policymakers. But there are no procedures for bringing states together with federal officials to discuss options, secure commitment, and plan distribution of evaluation resources. I see picking up on an issue like this and using it as a means for developing better institutions for making state (including the District of Columbia) social policy laboratories work as a common discipline. The experience of collaborative execution of a simple experiment with transitional work incentives might lay the foundation for other, more ambitious interstate collaboration. The architects of such a project would benefit from careful study of the evolution of the European Union's Open Method of Coordination in social policy (Walker and Wiseman 2006).

EMPLOYMENT INTERVENTION FOR THE DISABLED DEPENDENT

All available evidence indicates that disabilities are common among both adults and children in families applying for, and receiving, TANF benefits (Nadel, Wamhoff, and Wiseman 2003/2004). Those with substantial disabilities are candidates for Supplemental Security Income (SSI). It is possible that the SSI eligibility determination process retards rehabilitation or employability development and movement to self-support for some persons. The third demonstration proposal involves early work-oriented intervention for TANF applicants and recipients who are potential candidates for SSI. SSI is the responsibility of the Social Security Administration, but TANF is the responsibility of the Department of Health and Human Services and state social assistance agencies. As a result, any such intervention in the TANF-SSI interface is complicated by problems of interagency collaboration. External financial support might encourage such collaboration, improve design, and ensure rigorous evaluation of effects. As with the other proposals, I begin with background and then outline the idea, which I call the Employment Intervention for the Dependent with Disabilities (EIDD) demonstration.

Disabilities vary in both character and severity. A disability severe enough to preclude substantial gainful activity (SGA) combined with little income and few assets in principle qualifies working-age adults for supplemental security income (SSI). Moving people from TANF to SSI is attractive both to recipients and to states. For recipients, the result is typically a substantial income gain. In 2005, moving the adult in a three-person TANF recipient family would have on average more than doubled family income and removed the time limit on TANF assistance for children in the family. For states, such a transfer at least initially offers a financial windfall. States pay all TANF benefits on the margin, and the federal government pays all SSI. Twenty-three states supplement the federal SSI benefit out of state funds. For these states, the transfer from TANF to SSI offers less net financial reward but is generally still desirable.

The interaction between TANF and SSI is substantial. By FY2003, 11 percent of all SSI awards to adults age eighteen to sixty-four and 35 percent of awards to children were to TANF-SSP recipients. (SSP refers to separate state programs.) About 16 percent of families receiving TANF-SSP in 2003 included an adult or child SSI recipient (Wamhoff and Wiseman 2005/2006). State efforts to qualify persons with disabilities for SSI assistance are increasing as a result of changes in TANF brought about by the Deficit Reduction Act of 2005 (DEFRA). Before DEFRA, states could circumvent TANF work activity requirements for adults with disabilities or who were caring for children with disabilities by placing them in what was called a separate state program. DEFRA changed the treatment of SSPs in assessing states' TANF-related fiscal effort so that the SSP option has become much more costly. This has increased the incentive to move recipients from TANF to SSI for all states.

Moving eligible persons from TANF to SSI is a good thing, because by definition Congress intended SSI for those entitled and their income increases, at least in the short term, as a result. However, over the long term, the process appears to have perverse consequences for the employability of some adults. Establishing absence of capability for substantial gainful activity is a time-consuming process, often requiring as much as two years. During the application period, SSI applicants are disinclined even to explore opportunities for employment or skill acquisition because it is commonly believed that such efforts may be taken as evidence of capacity for SGA. Oddly, once an applicant is awarded SSI, the Social Security Administration offers him or her a Ticket to Work—that is, access to a voucher system for obtaining work-related rehabilitation and training. Those who fail to gain SSI awards have used up TANF eligibility time and possibly are even less employable after having spent time outside the workforce striving to demonstrate absence of employment capacity. That such a system may be counterproductive for rehabilitation and movement to self-support is widely recognized (U.S. Government Accountability Office 2004).

The SSI application process is similar to that used for making awards in the much larger Social Security Disability Insurance (SSDI) program. SSDI differs from SSI in that it is not means tested. All that counts is entitlement (established by work history) and, again, loss of capacity for SGA. Far more policy attention has been directed at SSDI than at SSI because the numbers are greater, the caseload trend is more dramatic, and SSDI claims are charged against the beleaguered Social Security Trust fund, whereas SSI payments come from general revenues (Autor and Duggan 2006). Like SSI, SSDI is seen as being too focused on establishing eligibility and too little concerned with restoring employability. In its September 2006 report the Social Security Advisory Board stated:

> We [the Social Security Advisory Board] are convinced that the primary issue with our national disability system is not to be found in how the current Social Security disability programs are designed and operated but rather in the absence of an adequate culture and methodology to guide and support impaired individuals into a more work-oriented path that could avoid or delay their need to depend on those Social Security Programs. (22)

The Social Security Administration did considerable development work in 2006 on an Early Intervention Initiative (EII) for SSDI applicants. In broad outline, the EII process would have been as follows. Applicants for SSDI in demonstration locations would be prescreened for eligibility using an assessment tool developed by IBM. A triage would take place that was intended to separate applicants into three groups: those unlikely to receive SSDI awards, those likely to receive awards but judged capable of rehabilitation and job entry within some horizon (probably two to three years), and those not considered candidates for near-term rehabilitation. A randomly selected subset of the second group were to be offered a cash stipend, immediate access to Medicare, and opportunity to participate in a rehabilitation program intended to achieve employment if they suspended their SSDI applications. This intervention would apparently have offered the work-oriented path to which the Social Security Advisory Board refers. It would have been attractive to SSDI applicants because of both the Medicare component and the immediate stipend. Otherwise SSDI awardees must wait two years to become Medicare eligible and be subject to the uncertainty of the disability adjudication process. One of the planned objectives of the EII evaluation was to do a cost-benefit analysis of the results. Clearly there would be more up-front costs to this system than are incurred under current procedures, but if the work-oriented path reduced the likelihood of long-term dependence on SSDI, the savings might justify the investment on even narrow benefits-to-government grounds. Whatever the project's merits, the EII project was terminated without field trial in early 2007, apparently because of projected cost.

Despite this setback, I think it important to consider something akin to the EII for adult SSI applicants, and it may be useful to focus on those connected to TANF. Administrative barriers, however, are significant. There is little communication between local TANF agencies and local offices of the Social Security Administration on matters other than the incidence of SSI awards. There are also incentive problems. States gain from moving people from TANF to SSI. TANF recipients are categorically eligible for Medicaid, so the health insurance incentive is missing for these individuals. Assessment triage would likely be much more difficult, because features of work history are important factors in assessing probability of rehabilitation, and TANF recipients typically have much weaker ties to the labor force than applicants for SSDI do. On the other hand, for the states that supplement the federal SSI payments, SSI take-up is not without cost, and in any event the children in such families typically stay on TANF, without time limit. Involvement of SSI applicants who are TANF recipients in work training or rehabilitation programs will serve to help states reach TANF participation goals.

I propose an early intervention initiative for adult TANF recipients who are potential or actual applicants for Supplemental Security Income. In it, TANF applicants and recipients would be reviewed for disabilities and some subset would be identified as candidates for SSI. This at-risk group would be triaged into the three groups identified for the SSDI Early Intervention Initiative. Again, the target is the group that appears likely to be successful in applying for SSI but also capable of employment or rehabilitation and, eventually, some contribution to self-support. In return for deferring application for SSI, the selected group would be offered a stipend that approximates the SSI benefit for a horizon to be determined coupled with ongoing TANF eligibility for their children.

There are basically four hypotheses to be investigated in the context of design and implementation of the EIDD. One is that persons in the second group, that is, promising candidates for such an intervention, can be reliably identified. The second is that there are enough of them within any administrative catchment to justify focus of a serious innovation effort. The third is that such persons will respond to such an offer. Last but hardly least comes the motivating hypothesis that such an innovation would lead over time to increased employment and reduced at-cost dependence on assistance commensurate with the benefits.

THE MINNESOTA FAMILY INVESTMENT PROGRAM

Over the thirty years leading up to the reforms instituted by the Personal Responsibility and Work Opportunity Reconciliation Act of 1996 (PRWORA), the evolution of welfare and work policy in the United States was closely intertwined with social experimentation. The experimental side of this policy double helix began in 1967 with planning for the New Jersey negative income tax experiment and continued in the 1970s with the Seattle-Denver income maintenance experiment and other related initiatives (Munnell 1986). In response to the welfare reforms introduced by the Reagan administration and the entrepreneurship of the Manpower Demonstration Research Corporation (now MDRC), in the 1980s initiative for welfare experimentation partially devolved to states. The result was a series of work-related state initiatives that produced evidence on the effects of work requirements that observers credited with influencing the content of the major welfare reform initiative of the 1980s, the Family Support Act of 1988 (Wiseman 1991). The Family Support Act in turn produced a set of initiatives collectively termed the National Evaluation of Welfare-to-Work Strategies (NEWWS), experiments that focused on strategic choices for the Job Opportunities and Basic Skills program (JOBS) established by the act (Hamilton 2002). At the same time, state experiments multiplied, creating a national perception of innovation and competence at the state level that contributed to passage of PRWORA, the law that famously replaced Aid to Families with Dependent Children (AFDC) with Temporary Assistance for Needy Families (TANF). Since 1996 neither the federal government nor states have initiated any significant welfare demonstrations, though some experimentation continues with welfare-related policies such as marriage promotion and efforts to support job retention and advancement among low-skilled workers. The reasons for this retreat are complex, reflecting both the ideology of PRWORA and the second Bush administration and the change in financial incentives for research and evaluation brought about by PRWORA and subsequent budget developments.

A central feature of this age of experimentation was the widespread use of random assignment and growing acceptance, at least within the policy analysis community, of classical experimental design as the gold standard for assessment of innovation effects. Judged in terms of refinement of methodology, breadth of assessment, and contribution to policy development, the Minnesota Family Investment Program (MFIP) is among the most important of the last generation of the state initiatives. MFIP outcomes are both fascinating and troublesome; the MFIP evaluation illustrates problems with achieving both internal validity and external utility of welfare and work research. To get to the problems, it is necessary to briefly explain the experiment and the cost-benefit analysis applied. It is impossible in a short overview to do justice either to MFIP or the literature to which the experiment's results have contributed; interested readers are encouraged to read more generally, beginning with the source for the present summary, the two volumes of the MFIP *Final Report*. Volume 1 covers effects on adults and volume 2 covers effects on children (Miller et al. 2000; Gennetian and Miller 2000). This commentary focuses exclusively on effects on adults. Follow-up studies continue to be released by the evaluation contractor and posted on the firm's website (www.MDRC.org).

The Experiment
MFIP began in 1994. The program was an experimental change from public assistance as delivered in Minnesota's AFDC program.

As in most other states, Minnesota's AFDC program differentiated between policy for single- and two-parent families. To obtain assistance, single parents and two-parent families with a disabled adult were required to meet a standard of need based on income and assets. Able-bodied two-parent families were required in addition to satisfy the unemployed parent rule that the family's primary earner was involuntarily working fewer than 100 hours per month and in general were expected to engage more intensively in employment-related activities. Single parents were required to attend an orientation for the JOBS program (called STRIDE in Minnesota). The primary earner in a two-parent family was required to participate in job search and, in some instances, a Community Work Experience Program (CWEP) job in return for benefits.

Minnesota was exceptional in that the Food Stamp benefit was cashed out and included in recipient families' cash payment. For families with other income, however, the benefit reduction was calculated separately for the AFDC and the Food Stamp components of the grant. The larger AFDC grant calculation followed national AFDC regulations in excluding $120 and one-third of any monthly earnings in excess of $90 during the first four months of work, $120 during the next eight months, and $90 per month thereafter. Thus AFDC incorporated a transitional inventive of the type targeted for experiment earlier in this discussion. For single-parent families, eligibility for AFDC was lost once earnings reached the point that the AFDC component of the benefit fell to zero; the cutoff point for Food Stamp receipt was somewhat higher. In addition, two-parent families were subject to the 100 hours restriction: No matter how large the family or how low the primary earner's earnings, once he (or, in rare instances, she) began working more than 100 hours a month, in principle eligibility for AFDC was lost.

MFIP was a state initiative that addressed four common concerns about AFDC: long-term welfare dependency, lack of work incentives, the effects of the two-parent 100-hour rule, and administrative complexity. The initiative altered treatment of families in several important ways. Food Stamp and AFDC benefits were integrated to produce a single eligibility standard with for some families an increased maximum benefit. The AFDC variable financial work incentive was replaced with a single more generous schedule that did not vary with time on the job. Work history requirements and the 100-hour test were eliminated as eligibility tests for two-parent households. Participation in employment and training programs was made mandatory for certain recipients. These included single parents with no child under one who had received AFDC payments for more than two years and one parent in two-parent families that had received assistance for more than six months.

The Evaluation

Changing AFDC and Food Stamp rules in this way required a waiver of federal regulations. To obtain a waiver, the state had to assume fiscal responsibility for costs above what would have been incurred in the absence of the intervention. That is, from the federal government perspective the intervention needed to be cost neutral. Assessing fiscal effects is difficult, but by the time of MFIP initiation, it was common to construct estimates of cost impact by comparing costs for cases subject to the innovation to costs for a control group subject to AFDC rules. In general, the administering agency, the Office of Policy Research and Evaluation in the Department of Health and Human Services Administration for Children and Families, required that controls be established by random assignment and that project evaluation include assessment of differences between costs for cases subject to MFIP rules and cases subject to AFDC. Minnesota agreed to this condition and contracted with the Manpower Demonstration Research Corporation (MDRC), a nonprofit organization with substantial support from the Ford Foundation and other philanthropic organizations, to conduct the evaluation. In this and many other projects, MDRC's exceptional third-party resources were used to expand substantially the purview of evaluation activity.

The field evaluation of MFIP was conducted in four rural and three urban Minnesota counties. Random assignment began in April 1994 and continued for twenty-four months. At the end of March 1996, more than 14,600 families had been added to the research (control and treatment) sample. Random assignment was applied to both new applicants and those whose assistance was ongoing. Outcomes were then followed, using a variety of instruments, for up to four years. Differences between the treatment and control groups are the foundation for a cost-benefit analysis.

As is often the case with social policy experiments, various external developments complicated matters. In the Minnesota experiment, such changes included first general increases in AFDC work requirements for single parents and, in 1997, replacement of AFDC with a statewide TANF program, called MFIP-S (for statewide), that included time limits, more aggressive work requirements, and a reduction in financial work incentives. The 100-hour rule was eliminated for ongoing eligibility for all two-parent families, including those involved in the MFIP control group, but otherwise most rules were retained for control and experimental families until mid-1998. The MFIP experiment was conducted in the context of a very tight job market, an environment likely to affect the productivity of the initiative's components.

Outcomes

The MFIP demonstration yielded a wide range of outcomes. The final report differentiates between those for single- and two-parent families and, within each of these groups, between applicants and recipients. Applicants and recipients are defined differently for the two family types. Effects were measured over the first twenty-eight months following random assignment. Other parts of the evaluation incorporate longer windows. Lisa Gennetian, Cynthia Miller, and Jared Smith, for example, report six-year impacts (2005).

For single parents, the MDRC analysis defines a recent applicant group that includes, in addition to actual applicants, those who at the point of random assignment had received benefits for less than two years. Long-term recipients were those who had received benefits for twenty-four months at the point of random assignment. Families in MFIP stayed on welfare longer than their counterparts in the control group but tended to be more likely to combine work with welfare. In general, most positive effects were found for long-term recipients. Some important benefits were not financial. For example, three years after random assignment, women from the MFIP long-term recipient group were more likely to be married than their AFDC counterparts. These outcomes came at a price: MFIP cost more per case per year than comparable cases in the control did.

For two-parent families, MDRC differentiates between persons randomly assigned at application (applicants) and those randomly assigned while receiving assistance (recipients). By design, applicants received the experiment's financial incentives immediately, but work requirements were deferred for the first six months. For both applicants and recipients, family labor supply fell in the experimental group relative to the control, generally as a result of lower employment rates and hours of work among women. Both applicants and recipients in the experimental group were more likely to receive some welfare benefits subsequent to assignment than controls were. For recipients (but not applicants), the higher benefits offset the loss of earnings so that experimental households had greater income. Survey evidence and administrative data indicate that couples in the two-parent recipient experimental group were more likely to stay married over the three years following assignment than the controls were; the survey sample size for applicants was not enough to support analysis of marital stability for that group.

The CBA

Like virtually every other MDRC program evaluation, the MFIP study includes a cost-benefit analysis. The summary results are reproduced in table 11.1. In addition to the distinction already drawn between applicants and recipients (defined, it should be recalled, differently for single- and two-parent families), the final analysis differentiates between single-parent families living in urban and rural counties. Costs of service delivery were greater for rural families.

The template analysis distinguishes four perspectives on the experimental outcomes and recognizes a variety of effects, not all commensurable. The first is that of families receiving the experimental treatment—the welfare sample. For them, the gains, compared to controls, are positive. Gains are measured over five years, discounted to year one. Thus, at the end of the first year, the sum of income gains in the first year of random assignment plus discounted (at 5 percent) income gains in years two to four is $10,222 in 1996 dollars for urban single parent long-term recipients, $521 for two-parent applicant families. The second perspective is that of the combined federal and state government budget, basically the combination of incremental transfer and services costs attributable to the intervention minus net additional taxes paid by treatment group families. Taxpayers in the analysis is everyone except those in the experimental group; taxpayers differ from government only in that government counts net change in business payroll tax contribution as a benefit, which does not apply to taxpayers. The social perspective is the sum of net gains of the welfare sample and taxpayers. It is only for the long-term urban recipients sample that benefits exceed costs; for families in the two-parent applicant sample, MFIP cost taxpayers a great deal ($12,173 per treatment group member) for insignificant financial gain ($512). Both financial benefits and costs are measured comprehensively.

Total financial gains and losses are just that—financial. The MFIP analysis recognizes that public support for transfer programs involves numerous qualitative considerations.

Table 11.1 Financial and Nonfinancial Gains and Losses (in 1996 Dollars)

Perspective	Single-Parent Long-Term Recipients			Single-Parent Recent Applicants			Two-Parent Families	
	Urban	Rural	Total[a]	Urban	Rural	Total[a]	Recipients	Applicants
Total financial gains and losses over five years								
Welfare sample	$10,222	$9,301	$9,891	$5,967	$10,477	$7,762	$6,855	$521
Government budget	($8,465)	($12,068)	($9,762)	($8,122)	($11,912)	($9,630)	($19,147)	($12,762)
Taxpayers	($8,678)	($12,113)	($9,915)	($8,111)	($12,008)	($9,662)	($18,669)	($12,173)
Society	$1,545	($2,812)	($24)	($2,144)	($1,531)	($1,900)	($11,814)	($11,652)
Nonfinancial effects over observation period[b]								
Work, welfare, and income per quarter[b]								
Percentage with income below poverty	↓	↓	↓	↓	↓	↓	↓	0
Percentage working	↑	↑	↑	↑	↑	↑	0	0
Welfare use								
Percentage receiving welfare	↑	↑	↑	↑	↑	↑	↑	↑
Percentage relying solely on welfare	↓	↓	↓	↓	0	↓	0	0
Other family outcomes								
Continuous health coverage[c] (%)	↑	0	↑	↑	↑	0	0	n/a
Homeownership[d] (%)	0	0	0	0	↓	0	↑	n/a
Mother married and living with spouse[e] (%)	0	0	↓	0	0	0	↓	n/a
Time spent out of the home[f]	↑	0	↑	↓	0	↓	0	n/a
Child environment and child well-being[g]	↑	n/a	n/a	0	n/a	n/a	n/a	n/a

Sources: Reproduced from Miller et al. 2000, table 7.1. MDRC calculations using data from Minnesota's Unemployment Insurance (UI) and public assistance benefit records, the thirty-six-month client survey, state and federal tax codes, aggregate fiscal data, and county child care payment records (see Gennetian and Miller 2000; Miller et al. 2000).

Notes: The arrows on this table reflect positive and negative statistically significant effects. Outcomes indicated as n/a are not measured. A more in-depth explanation of these impacts can be found in Miller et al. (2000) and Gennetian and Miller (2000).

a Total gains and losses were estimated as a weighted average of urban and rural results, based on urban and rural proportions and losses were estimated as a weighted average of urban and rural results, based on urban and rural proportions in total caseloads of the seven field trial counties.

b From welfare sample perspective. Average quarterly during the follow-up period.

c Percentage who had continuous health insurance coverage from random assignment through time of the thirty-six-month survey.

d Percentage who owned their home at the time of the thirty-six-month survey.

e Percentage married and living with spouse at the time of the thirty-six-month survey.

f Measured on thirty-six-month survey as average hours worked per week in current or most recent job. For two-parent families, measured only for the survey respondent (usually the mother).

g Measured for families with children age two to nine. Summary of full MFIP impacts on domestic abuse and on behavior and school outcomes for children age two to nine at random assignment. For urban long-term recipients, MFIP produced statistically significant impacts on domestic abuse and on children's behavior and school performance. For urban recent applicants, MFIP produced few statistically significant impacts on child well-being. For single-parent families in rural counties and for two-parent families, results are not reported due to small sample sizes.

The bottom section of the table identifies qualitative outcomes produced by the MFIP treatment. Thus, if taxpayers define dependency as degree of reliance on welfare payments for family needs, MFIP may have increased the percentage of time families received welfare, but the program reduced the proportion of families that rely solely on welfare for support.

Why the MFIP Contribution Is Important

The MFIP analysis reflects a template developed over two decades of welfare initiative analysis, a template with many desirable attributes, including random assignment design.

It is nevertheless important to recognize the limitations of the MFIP. First, the more comprehensive the reform effort, the greater the difficulty is in implementing both the policy change and the evaluation in a way that produces well-defined treatment and control groups. In the MFIP case, general policy developments and a changing public perception of welfare trends over time shifted the difference between treatment and control.

Second, the experiment cannot capture all the consequences of general implementation. Changes in the character of assistance systems are likely to alter the number and characteristics of people seeking help and given assistance. Eligibility for MFIP was determined by AFDC standards for both the treatment and control groups; any general implementation would presumably affect both initial and ongoing eligibility. This problem is particularly important for the two-parent group, where the 100-hour rule was applied in determining initial eligibility for the treatment group but not thereafter. This made the treatment an exceptional prize. This attractiveness is possibly reflected in the substantial difference (72.1 percent for MFIP, 59.7 percent for AFDC two-parent controls) in welfare take-up rates following random assignment (Miller et al. 1997, 154). Those informed of the special opportunity may have been uncertain about whether the offer would have still be available should they have returned. In any general implementation, elimination of the 100-hour rule only after entry would over time create a growing inequity between those families with employed principal earners fortunate enough to have gained access to the special work incentive and families in similar current circumstances but ineligible. This is the inequity that creates interest in the sorts of time-limited support policies that are proposed for testing in the Transitional Incentives Package Demonstration described earlier.

Third, though the cost-benefit analysis has internal validity provided by random assignment, the external relevance of analysis is problematic. In any full-scale implementation of a program like MFIP, the mix of applicant and ongoing and long-term cases would change. It might be tempting, for example, to argue that because the efficiency of the program seems greatest for long-term single-parent cases, one has no guarantee that implementing the program only for such cases would not change the incentives for those in newly opened cases to continue receiving benefits until they qualify for the advantages of long-term status. This would raise costs.

Finally, in constructing MFIP, an important objective of Minnesota's policymakers was to simplify and better integrate support provided for working low-income households.

Within the project, this was accomplished by making the benefit disregard within the program more generous, eliminating the short time horizon for work incentives in AFDC, and cashing out food stamps. Although the period of implementing MFIP coincided with a substantial increase in the Earned Income Tax credit, the EITC was not part of the program and, like other taxes, EITC receipt was imputed for the MFIP cost-benefit analysis. An alternative strategy would have been to experiment with better integration of the EITC and food stamps and treating MFIP as a transitional program designed to move people out of welfare and into employed status. The result of the treatment as implemented was, not surprisingly, a tendency for those who received the MFIP prize to stay within the welfare system. The choice of strategy was largely dictated by what was under the state's control: Federal EITC policy definitely was not, and the cash-out of the Food Stamp benefit came about only by congressional authorization achieved by the state's adroit legislators. Grassroots welfare reform efforts produced important innovations in the 1990s, but states faced then, and continue to face, important constraints in choosing alternatives.

In sum, the past quarter-century has seen remarkable development in procedures for evaluating welfare initiatives. The central achievement is more procedural than methodological, a common template for such evaluations that is founded on random assignment and incorporates cost-benefit analysis as an accounting framework. The evaluation of the Minnesota Family Investment is exemplary of this template and state welfare reform initiatives. The MFIP experience provides many insights pertinent to welfare strategy, but significant questions remain concerning the external utility of the cost-benefit analysis.

CONCLUSION: WELFARE AND WORK

This chapter has explored various possibilities for additional experimentation in matters related to the intersection of welfare and work. Although the initial charge referred to welfare to work initiatives, I have argued that there are important aspects of the interplay between public assistance and work that call for thinking more generally.

Before moving on to new demonstrations, it might be useful to develop a template for reviewing the benefits and costs of new evaluations. Benefits are hard to predict. I doubt that many people expected to learn much about the consequences of expanded work support for marriage when the MFIP experiment was initiated. Well-run evaluations have important spillover effects. To improve the efficiency of the national system of evaluation, it is important to find ways to identify these effects and to create incentives and procedures to ensure that the public interest generally is reflected in the choice of the next steps to be taken.

REFERENCES

Autor, David, and Mark Duggan. 2006. "The Growth in the Social Security Disability Rolls: A Fiscal Crisis Unfolding." *NBER* Working Paper 12436. Cambridge, MA: National Bureau of Economic Research.

Berube, Alan, Anne Kim, Benjamin Forman, and Megan Burns. 2002. *The Price of Paying Taxes: How Tax Preparation and Refund Loan Fees Erode the Benefits of the EITC*. Washington, DC: Brookings Institution Press.

DeParle, Jason. 2004. *American Dream: Three Women, Ten Kids, and a Nation's Drive to End Welfare*. New York: Viking.

Duflo, Esther, William Gale, Jeffrey Liebman, Peter Orszag, and Emmanuel Saez. 2005. "Saving Incentives for Low- and Middle-Income Families: Evidence from a Field Experiment with HandR Block." *Retirement Security Project* Working Paper 2005–5. Washington, DC: Brookings Institution Press.

Eissa, Nada, and Hilary Williamson Hoynes. 2006. "Behavioral Responses to Taxes: Lessons from the EITC and Labor Supply." In *Tax Policy and the Economy*, ed. James M. Poterba. Cambridge, MA: MIT Press.

Gennetian, Lisa, and Cynthia Miller. 2000. *Reforming Welfare and Rewarding Work: Final Report on the Minnesota Family Investment Program*, vol. 2, *Effects on Children*. New York: MDRC.

Gennetian, Lisa, Cynthia Miller, and Jared Smith. 2005. *Turning Welfare into a Work Support: Six-Year Impacts on Parents and Children from the Minnesota Family Investment Program*. New York: MDRC.

Giannarelli, Linda, and Michael Wiseman. 2006. "The Working Poor and the Benefit Doors: Entrance, Exit, and Employment Incentive Policy in TANF." Paper presented at the 46th Annual Workshop, National Association for Welfare Research and Statistics, Jackson, WY (August 21–23, 2006).

Grogger, Jeffrey. 2004. "Welfare Transitions in the 1990s: The Economy, Welfare Policy, and the EITC." *Journal of Policy Analysis and Management* 23(4): 671–95.

Hamilton, Gayle. 2002. *Moving People from Welfare to Work: Lessons from the National Evaluation of Welfare-to-Work Strategies*. New York: MDRC.

Mead, Lawrence. 2006. "Did EITC Raise Work Levels? If So, How?" Paper presented at the Annual Research Conference of the Association for Public Policy Analysis and Management. Madison, WI (November 3, 2006).

Michalopoulos, Charles. 2005. *Does Making Work Still Pay? An Update on the Effects of Four Earnings Supplement Programs on Employment, Earnings, and Income*. New York: MDRC.

Miller, Cynthia, Virginia Knox, Patricia Auspos, Jo Anna Hunter-Manns, and Alan Orenstein. 1997. *Making Welfare Work and Work Pay: Implementation and 18-Month Impacts of the Minnesota Family Investment Program*. New York: MDRC.

Miller, Cynthia, Virginia Knox, Lisa A. Gennetian, Martey Dodoo, Jo Anna Hunter, and Cindy Redcross. 2000. *Reforming Welfare and Rewarding Work: Final Report on the Minnesota Family Investment Program*, vol. 1, *Effects on Adults*. New York: MDRC.

Munnell, Alice, ed. 1986. *Lessons from the Income Maintenance Experiments*. Boston, MA: Federal Reserve Bank of Boston.

Nadel, Mark, Steve Wamhoff, and Michael Wiseman. 2003/2004. "Disability, Welfare Reform, and Supplemental Security Income." *Social Security Bulletin* 65(3): 14–30.

Social Security Advisory Board. 2006. *A Disability System for the 21st Century*. Washington, DC: SSAB.

U.S. Government Accountability Office (GAO). 2004. *TANF and SSI: Opportunities Exist to Help*

People with Impairments Become More Self-Sufficient. Report GAO-04–878. Washington, DC: U.S. Government Printing Office.

Walker, Robert, and Michael Wiseman. 2006. "Opening Up American Federalism: Improving Welfare the European Way." Unpublished manuscript.

Wamhoff, Stephen, and Michael Wiseman. 2005/2006. "The TANF-SSI Connection." *Social Security Bulletin* 66(4): 21–36.

Wiseman, Michael. 1991. "Research and Policy: A Symposium on the Family Support Act of 1988." *Journal of Policy Analysis and Management* 10(4): 588–666.

Chapter | 2

Welfare-to-Work and Work-Incentive Programs

David Greenberg

Numerous welfare-to-work programs—that is, programs that use some combination of structured job search, education, vocational training, work experience, and financial work incentives to increase employment among welfare recipients—have been subjected to cost-benefit analysis (CBA). Government-funded training programs for disadvantaged workers (both welfare recipients and nonrecipients) have also often been the subject of CBAs. One possible reason for frequently subjecting such programs to CBA, at least in the United States, is that most of the target groups of the programs are drawn from the low-income population and expenditures of public funds on this population seems to draw greater scrutiny than expenditures on those further up the income distribution. Another reason is that key benefits, such as those programs produce through earnings increases and reductions in transfer payment receipts, can usually be measured with administrative data, greatly reducing the costs of conducting CBAs. In addition, welfare-to-work, financial work incentive, and training programs have often been evaluated using random assignment experiments, which result in more accurate estimates of program effects on both costs and benefits and thereby encourage application of CBA.

PROGRAM ACTIVITIES

Two key goals of welfare-to-work programs are reducing government welfare expenditures and increasing the time that program participants spend working. To achieve these objectives, increasingly stringent requirements to participate in welfare-to-work programs have been imposed on welfare recipients in recent years. Specifically, under these so-called mandatory programs, welfare recipients are required to participate in program activities or risk losing some or all of their benefits through sanctions. The rationale for participation requirements is obvious: to secure cooperation by welfare recipients who may not see program participation or employment as being in their immediate best interests.

Although the mix of activities in welfare-to-work and government training programs changes over time and differs from one program to the next, all such programs include one or more of the following: remedial education in reading and math, vocational training in specific occupational skills, subsidies paid to private sector employers to hire program participants for a specified period to provide them with on-the-job training, and short-term subsidized work experience positions (paid or unpaid) at government or nonprofit agencies to give participants an opportunity to build an employment record and acquire general work skills. Some welfare-to-work programs have also provided financial incentives, which usually reduce the amount by which welfare benefits fall as earnings rise, thereby increasing the amount of transfer payments that recipients who take jobs can keep. Nearly all welfare-to-work and training programs also provide job search assistance (including training in resume preparation and interviewing, help in job finding, and direct job placement). In addition, financial support, child care, personal and career counseling, and expense reimbursements during training are sometimes provided.

A META-ANALYSIS OF CBAs OF WELFARE-TO-WORK PROGRAMS

Of all the CBAs of welfare-to-work and government training programs, most are probably of mandatory welfare-to-work programs targeted on recipients of either Aid to Families with Dependent Children (AFDC) or Temporary Assistance for Needy Families (TANF). One reason for this is that such programs are so numerous; they are found in every state, and they often change over time. Most CBAs of these programs have been based on random assignment.

Findings from these studies appear to have had some influence on policy. For example, based on formal CBAs of some of the earlier welfare-to-work programs, Peter Szanton wrote that they "were cost-effective. In most cases, they benefited both participants and tax-payers" (1991, 596). Participating in the same symposium as Szanton and also focusing on CBA findings, two congressional staffers, Ron Haskins and Erica Baum, who helped draft legislation, the Family Assistance Act, which promoted the use of welfare-to-work programs by state and county welfare agencies, reached similar conclusions (Haskins 1991, 609; Baum 1991, 620).

David Greenberg and Andreas Cebulla recently examined seventy-one welfare-to-work programs that were targeted at the AFDC population and evaluated using random assignment (2008; for a list, see table 12.1). They found that CBAs had been conducted of fifty of these programs, and that the twenty-one others had had much smaller effects on earnings and AFDC benefit payment amounts than these fifty.

Greenberg and Cebulla concluded that the costs of a typical evaluated welfare-to-work program probably exceeded its benefits from the perspective of the government and society, but those assigned to the program may reap small positive net benefits on average (2008). This said, certain individual programs were found to be very cost-beneficial. The findings for the programs that included financial work incentives differed considerably from those that did not. Programs with the incentives provided considerably larger net benefits to welfare recipients, but the benefits were more or less offset by the cost to government, suggesting that the incentives are a nearly cost-neutral method of transferring income to low-wage workers. Their findings, the researchers suggest, imply that

Table 12.1   U.S. AFDC Random Assignment Welfare-to-Work Evaluations

Program Title	Short Program Name	Evaluator/Author	Mid-Point	CBA	Financial Incentive Scheme
Greater Avenues for Independence Program	GAIN (California)	MDRC	1989	✓	
Job Search and Work Experience in Cook County	Cook County	MDRC	1985	✓	
Community Work Experience Demonstrations	West Virginia	MDRC	1983	✓	
WORK Program	Arkansas	MDRC	1983	✓	
Employment Initiatives	Baltimore	MDRC	1983	✓	
Saturation Work Initiative Model	SWIM (San Diego)	MDRC	1985	✓	
Employment Services Program	Virginia	MDRC	1984	✓	
Project Independence (Florida's JOBS Program)	Florida	MDRC	1991	✓	
Jobs First	Connecticut	MDRC	1996	✓	✓
Family Transition Program	FTP (Florida)	MDRC	1994	✓	
Los Angeles Jobs-First GAIN Evaluation	Los Angeles	MDRC	1996	✓	
San Diego Job Search and Work Experience Demonstration	San Diego	MDRC	1983	✓	
National Evaluation of Welfare-to-Work Strategies	NEWWS	MDRC	1993	✓	
Minnesota Family Investment Program	MFIP	MDRC	1994	✓	✓
Vermont's Welfare Restructuring Project.	Vermont	MDRC	1995	✓	✓
Teenage Parent Demonstration	Teenage Parents	MPR	1988		
Wisconsin Welfare Employment Experiment	Wisconsin	Wisconsin	1988		
Ohio Transitions to Independence Demonstration	Ohio	Abt Associates	1990	✓	
Indiana Welfare Reform Program	Indiana	Abt Associates	1995	✓	
Saturation Work Program	Philadelphia	Pennsylvania	1986		
To Strengthen Michigan Families	TSMF (Michigan)	Abt Associates	1993	✓	
A Better Chance	ABC (Delaware)	Abt Associates	1996		
Virginia Independence Program	VIEW	MPR	1996		
Family Investment Program	FIP(Iowa)	MPR	1994	✓	
Personal Responsibility and Employment Program	PREP (Colorado)	Colorado	1995		✓
California Work Pays Demonstration Program	CWPDP	UCLA	1993		✓
Child Assistance Program	CAP (New York)	Abt Associates	1989	✓	

Source: Author with the assistance of Andreas Cebulla.

Notes: MPR (Mathematica Policy Research); Abt Associates; UCLA (UCLA School of Public Policy and Social Research); Pennsylvania (Pennsylvania Department of Public Welfare); Colorado (The Centers of the University of Colorado); Wisconsin (University of Wisconsin)

less successful welfare-to-work programs might be made more cost-beneficial by dropping vocational training and basic education as program components, leaving mainly lower-cost components, such as mandated job search and sanctions, but also, perhaps, the more costly financial work incentives.

Greenberg and Cebulla also attempted to assess potential biases to the CBA findings they examined (2008). They concluded that of the substantial number of biases they examined, three are most likely to be important. First, CBAs of welfare-to-work programs exclude the value of the nonmarket time that members of the program group lose. Second, they exclude losses to nonassignees that result from displacement effects. Third, they typically assume that program effects on earnings and welfare benefits continue for only a limited time (most often, five years). To the extent they exist, the first of these biases would cause social net benefits and the net benefits of program participants to be overstated; the second would cause social net benefits to be overstated; and the third would cause the net benefits received by the government and society to be understated.

SAMPLE CBAs

We next present brief descriptions of four cost-benefit studies. The first was conducted as part of the random assignment evaluation of California's Greater Avenues for Independence (GAIN) program and is arguably the best known CBA of a welfare-to-work program ever undertaken (Riccio, Friedlander, and Freeman 1994). The second covered Canada's Self-Sufficiency Project (SSP), a randomized test of a generous financial work incentive program (Michalopoulos et al. 2002). The programs examined in the first two CBAs targeted lone parents who received welfare. The program assessed in the third analysis, by contrast, Britain's New Deal for Disabled Persons (NDDP), attempts to increase employment among disabled welfare recipients (Greenberg and Davis 2007). To close the synopses of these studies, we discuss an ambitious attempt to use a uniform CBA framework to compare the cost-effectiveness of nearly all the employment and welfare-to-work programs in the United Kingdom (Department for Work and Pensions 2007).

California GAIN

GAIN, a mandatory job search and job training program for AFDC recipients in California, was initiated statewide in 1986, with random-assignment evaluations conducted in six counties. This evaluation has been highly influential.

The CBA of GAIN is a good illustration of those conducted by MDRC, a research firm based in New York that has done more random assignment evaluations of welfare-to-work programs than any other organization (see table 12.1). MDRC's CBAs all use a similar framework, one that focuses almost entirely on program monetary effects.

Because California provided substantial latitude to its counties in how they implemented GAIN, the programs that developed varied considerably from one another. One of them, Riverside, placed strong emphasis on placing welfare recipients into jobs—any job—as quickly as possible and used the threat of reductions in AFDC benefits to help ensure that recipients sought and accepted available jobs. Only participants who were initially unable to find a job could receive training. To varying degrees, the remaining five counties placed greater emphasis on providing training for program participants before they found jobs, though, like Riverside, AFDC recipients in these five counties could also be sanctioned for failure to take part in program activities. GAIN was thus widely perceived as a test of two competing approaches for moving public assistance recipients from welfare to work: a human capital approach in which recipients first receive training and then (it was hoped) obtain a stable, well-paying job, and a job attachment approach stressing immediate job placement, reserving training as a last resort. Under the job attachment approach, it was hoped that, regardless of the quality of the initial job, work experience would eventually allow welfare recipients to advance to a good job.

As it turned out, the evaluation findings for Riverside's version of GAIN were much more positive than those of the other five counties (Riccio, Friedlander, and Freedman 1994). Indeed, the findings for Riverside were more positive than for virtually all previous evaluations of welfare-to-work programs, regardless of where these programs were implemented. For example, single-parent AFDC recipients in the program group enjoyed increases in net income (measured as increases in net earnings less increases in tax payments and decreases in transfer benefits) in five of the six evaluation sites as a result of GAIN, with the net income for the Riverside group increasing the most. (At the time of the evaluation, single-parent AFDC recipients constituted more than 80 percent of California's AFDC caseload. Therefore, in reporting findings from GAIN, the focus is on this group.) In addition, the Riverside program resulted in substantial government budgetary savings for single-parent AFDC recipients during the first three years of the evaluation. The GAIN programs in two of the remaining five evaluation counties were also associated with net savings for the government, but much less than in Riverside. The programs in the remaining three counties led to increases in government budgetary costs.

The strong positive findings for Riverside have often been attributed to Riverside's strong emphasis on sanctioning and placing GAIN participants into jobs as quickly as possible, program features that have been widely adopted throughout the United States. However, Riverside differed from the other five evaluation sides in numerous other respects—including especially strong leadership—making the source of Riverside's success not entirely clear.

Canada SSP

SSP was an experimental welfare-to-work program that offered a generous monthly earnings supplement for up to three years to single-parent families who had been on Income Assistance (welfare) in British Columbia and New Brunswick for at least a year and who were randomly assigned to a program group. To qualify for the earnings supplement, the parent had to leave the Income Assistance program (IA), work full time (an average at least thirty hours a week), and take up the supplement within a year of when it was first offered. The supplement was equal to one-half the difference between a target earnings level (initially CN$37,000 in British Columbia and CN$30,000 in New Brunswick) and an individual's earnings. Because the income individuals could receive if they worked full time was much larger under SSP than under IA, the program provided a strong monetary incentive to leave welfare and work full time.

According to MDRC's evaluation of SSP, which was based on random assignment, one-third of those offered the earnings supplement worked full time and took up the supplement offer (Michalopoulos et al. 2002). It was estimated that close to three-fifths of these recipients worked full time because of the incentives, and that the remainder took advantage of the offer even though they would have worked full time without it. The CBA of the program found that even though government agencies spent more than CN$4,700 on administering the program and distributing transfer payments, various benefits to both the government (increases in tax payments, for example) and program participants (increases in earnings and receipt of the bonuses) were far larger. As a result, society gained nearly CN$2,600 per program group member, making the program extremely cost-effective (Michalopoulos et al. 2002). Most of this additional net social benefit resulted from increases in participant hours at work and hence earnings.

Like most CBAs of welfare-to-work programs, including the GAIN analysis, the one of SSP has several potential weaknesses, some of which the evaluators noted. For example, Charles Michalopoulos and his colleagues observed that improvement or deterioration in child and parent well-being and community effects, such as reduced or increased crime and drug use, should be considered in a full assessment of the net social benefits of the SSP program (2002). In addition, general equilibrium effects that result from SSP—such as persons who are not eligible for the SSP earnings supplement facing greater job competition, effects on the wages of IA recipients and other workers, and exit and entry effects—may be important, but are ignored in the SSP CBA (see Lise, Seitz, and Smith 2004). Costs associated with becoming employed were also ignored, such as the value of relinquished nonwork time, and the cost of child care, transportation, and clothing. The analysis also ignores both any value that taxpayers may place on reductions in the income assistance rolls and the increase in work effort on the part of participants that result from SSP. Moreover, the SSP earnings supplement meant that income was transferred from taxpayers to program participants. Because participants had much lower incomes than taxpayers, on average, their marginal utility of income is likely to be higher. It can thus be argued that a dollar gained by participants should be valued more highly than a dollar lost by taxpayers. However, as with most CBAs of programs that have distributional implications, dollars gained by SSP participants are not treated as having more value than dollars lost by taxpayers.

Some of these limitations have recently been examined. For example, David Greenberg and Philip Robins found that if the value of losses in nonmarket time that resulted from SSP are taken into account, the net societal benefits of the program decrease significantly, even becoming negative under certain assumptions; and Jeremy Lise and colleagues found that SSP was no longer cost-beneficial once general equilibrium effects were incorporated into the analysis (Greenberg and Robins 2007; Lise, Seitz, and Smith 2004).

UK New Deal for Disabled People

Until recently, the national New Deal for Disabled People (NDDP) was the major British employment program for people claiming incapacity benefits. The program still exists but in only about 40 percent of the United Kingdom. As such, it continues to play an important role in the government's welfare-to-work strategy. The program is voluntary and is delivered locally by job brokers, which are a mixture of voluntary, public, and private sector organizations. Although job brokers vary enormously in size and in how they operate, most help clients with their job search, engage in job development, and attempt to increase clients' confidence in their ability to work. Many also attempt to develop clients' work-related skills and monitor clients' progress in jobs after they are placed, sometimes intervening when the client encounters problems on the job. At the time the CBA of the NDDP was conducted, job brokers received a payment from the government for each client they registered, for each client they placed in a job, and for each placed client who remained in a job for at least six months.

The NDDP CBA (Greenberg and Davis 2007) relies heavily on estimates from the NDDP impact analysis (see Orr, Bell, and Lam 2007), as well as on the cost estimates obtained from the job brokers. The impact analysis provided estimates of program effects on the cash benefit payments that registrants receive and on their employment. These estimates were adopted for use in the CBA. For example, monthly impact estimates, which were provided for three years after registration, were used to estimate regressions drawn on to predict future impacts. In addition, estimates of impacts on employment were converted to earnings effect estimates by multiplying them by the average monthly earnings of employed disabled persons, a value that was obtained from a survey of NDDP registrants.

The cost and impact estimates used in the CBA, which have all been converted to 2005 prices, pertain to a typical NDDP registrant. Separate analyses were conducted for continuing claimants of incapacity benefits and new (or returning) claimants. CBA analysts made a special effort to assess the extent to which their central findings were biased by a number of different factors (Greenberg and Davis 2007). These included the value NDDP registrants placed on the time they gave up to go to work, increases in the hours of working registrants attributable to NDDP (data were not available to estimate this effect), displacement effects, reductions in economic distortions because NDDP allowed taxes to be lower than otherwise, and possible reporting errors in the data used to obtain NDDP's impacts on employment.

Taking account of reductions in benefit payments received by NDDP registrants, reductions in the cost of administering benefits, and increases in tax payments, the analysis indicates that NDDP reduced the government's budgetary requirements by more than £2,500 for a typical continuing claimant who registered and by more than £750 for an average new claimant who registered (during the period covered by the evaluation, £1 was worth a little less than US$2). For each pound expended on NDDP, the government saved between £3.41 and £4.50 for continuing claimants and between £1.71 and £2.26 for new claimants in benefit payments and administrative expenditures. Based on various sensitivity tests, Greenberg and Davis concluded that NDDP is cost-beneficial for both groups of program registrants from the government's perspective and that this conclusion is highly robust to the assumptions that underlie it (2007).

On the other hand, they also found considerable uncertainty as the extent to which NDDP improved the welfare of those who registered in the program. Much of this uncertainty results from shortcomings in the administrative data used to estimate the effects of NDDP on incapacity benefit amounts and employment and from program benefits and costs that could not be estimated. Overall, Greenberg and Davis' estimates suggest that the income of a typical NDDP registrant was probably increased by the program, but not by a large amount. The incomes of NDDP registrants would have been found to have increased somewhat more than the estimates suggest if, as is likely, NDDP increased the hours of work of employed registrants, as well as the proportion of registrants who were employed, but this could not be determined. However, to have had much effect, the increase in hours would have had to be fairly large.

Whether NDDP improved the well-being of its registrants is not determined only by its effects on their incomes. For example, those who go to work as a result of NDDP may face increased child-care and commuter costs and, in addition, will have to give up time during which they might do other things of value to themselves or their families. On the other hand, their health and quality of life may improve. Unfortunately, information about all these factors is limited. Taking the scant available information into account, Greenberg and Davis concluded that it is likely that a typical NDDP registrant benefited as a result of having participated in the program but only to a modest degree (2007).

The CBA determined that net benefits of NDDP to society as a whole are very likely positive but considerably larger for continuing claimants than for new claimants. Specifically, the reported estimates were £2,915 to £3,163 for a typical continuing claimant and £613 to £861 for an average new claimant or about £4 or £5 for each pound the government expended on NDDP in serving continuing claimants and around £2 for each pound expended on the new claimant group. After assessing a large number of potential biases to these estimates, Greenberg and Davis concluded that, although actual net benefits received by society could be somewhat smaller or larger than estimated, it was highly probable that the net social benefits of NDDP were positive (2007).

UK Department for Work and Pensions

The British Department for Work and Pensions (DWP) has primary responsibility for most welfare-to-work and employment programs in the United Kingdom. These include programs that feature mandatory work focused interviews, counseling, financial work incentives, job search, work experience, training, and funds to cover work-related expenditures. DWP has developed a cost-benefit framework (CBF) to conduct CBAs of these programs and rank them in terms of their relative cost-effectiveness systematically and consistently (Department for Work and Pensions 2007). The goal is to help ensure that public funds are spent efficiently so as to generate the greatest net benefits to society. The CBF was developed in consultation with analysts from across DWP, as well as representatives from other government departments, academia, and evaluation firms.

The CBF guidance focuses on the net impact of programs—for example, it is concerned only with the benefits arising from job entries that would not have happened in the absence of the program. The framework thus uses two main measures of cost-effectiveness: net benefits to the government that result from additional jobs and net benefits to the economy that result from additional jobs. Both these measures are intended to be indicative and are not meant to be considered in isolation but interpreted alongside other evidence. In general, net benefits to the government are easier and more straightforward to estimate than the broader net benefits to the economy.

During 2006, DWP applied the CBF across all its welfare-to-work and employment programs for the first time. In doing this, it attempted to determine the comparative cost-effectiveness of the programs it operated, using data on costs and performance in 2004 and 2005. This rather heroic effort is, perhaps, the first and only time this has been done by a government department in any country. Because of the limited time and resources available, however, this work was done quickly and therefore had to rely on readily available data and evidence to produce the estimates. This was an acknowledged limitation of the work, given that the available evidence varies considerably among DWP's programs. For example, estimates of program effects were available for some programs but not others. Thus, in the latter cases, informed guesses were sometimes necessary. This is not to suggest that the cost-benefit analyses were unsophisticated. For instance, unlike most CBAs of welfare-to-work and employment programs, there were attempts to take account of deadweight losses resulting from taxes and of monopoly power in product and labor markets. In light of the limitations, analysts in the department did not stress the detailed findings but instead emphasized the broader messages emerging from the results and how these might be used in connection with other evidence.

Because of resource and time constraints in applying the CBF, important potential benefits from DWP programs (such as improved health, changes in self-esteem and life satisfaction, reduced crime, and child-care costs) were necessarily excluded from the analyses. It was also assumed that program benefits persist for only a year or two. As a result, program benefits were perhaps systematically understated relative to program costs.

The emphasis in applying the CBF was on comparing programs, rather than on the estimates of the net benefits of individual programs. Consequently, cost-effectiveness ratios for each of the studied programs were reported in league tables. With this in mind, considerable effort was made to maintain consistency in conducting the CBAs of different programs, though these efforts were only partially successful in practice. The league tables and the underlying analyses have not been published externally.

Following the experience of applying the cost-benefit framework for the first time, DWP internally reviewed how effective the exercise had been and made several revisions to the CBF to improve its CBAs. For example, to increase uniformity across future CBAs, more of the work will be performed by a small group of DWP economists in the same office. DWP also recently commissioned an external review to examine their cost-benefit efforts so far and to suggest possible ways improvements might be made in the future (Greenberg and Knight 2007).

CONCLUSION

CBAs of welfare-to-work programs such as those discussed are highly useful, if only because they formalize assessments of programs that policymakers tend to make in any event. Moreover, the better ones make the limitations of the analysis explicit so that readers can decide for themselves whether a program is or is not cost beneficial (or, alternatively, decide that the information that is available does not allow a reasonable conclusion to be drawn). There is considerable room for improvement, however. I now review five areas, which were touched on earlier, where additional research might improve future CBAs of welfare-to-work programs.

First, dollars gained or lost by participants in welfare-to-work programs are usually valued the same as dollars gained or lost by nonparticipants. Participants, however, have much lower incomes, on average, than do nonparticipants. The marginal utility of income may therefore differ between the two groups. This issue is relevant whenever a welfare-to-work program makes participants better off and nonparticipants worse off, or vice versa. A considerable literature exists concerning the possibility of treating this issue by giving each dollar of the gains and losses of relatively low-income persons greater weight in cost-benefit analyses than each dollar of the gains and losses of higher-income persons (see Boardman et al. 2006). Unfortunately, the weights needed to do this are unknown. Research that can help determine these weights would therefore be highly useful.

Second, assessing whether welfare-to-work programs are cost-beneficial depends on how long effects on earnings and transfer benefits last. Unfortunately, with some exceptions, data on program effects are usually limited to three years or less. One obvious approach to determining how long program impacts persist is to follow program participants for a longer period, but this delays the availability of cost-benefit findings. The issue can also be addressed by examining evidence from previous evaluations. Although some research that used this approach has already been done, more would be potentially useful (see Greenberg et al. 2004; Greenberg, Michalopoulous, and Robins 2004).

Third, because intangible effects (such as the value of nonmarket time that program participants forgo when their employment increases and the value of satisfaction both participants and taxpayers gain from the substitution of earnings for welfare payments) are difficult to measure, they are rarely assigned a value in evaluations of welfare-to-work programs. The few attempts that have been made to impute the value of nonmarket time relinquished as employment increases imply that it is a potentially important program cost (Bell and Orr 1994; Greenberg 1997; and Greenberg and Robins 2007). No attempt has ever been made to elicit taxpayers' willingness to pay for the substitution of work for transfer payments that result from welfare-to-work programs. One approach that could be used for this purpose is contingent valuation, which uses surveys to attempt to measure willingness-to-pay for changes in the quantity and quality of goods not exchanged in markets (for an overview, see Boardman et al. 2006).

Fourth, if training program services or program-provided financial incentive payments are perceived as beneficial, then some who are initially ineligible to participate in a program may leave their jobs in order to qualify (an entry effect). On the other hand, in the case of mandatory welfare-to-work programs for welfare recipients, some people who might otherwise have entered the welfare rolls may decide not to do so to avoid the hassle of participating (a deterrent effect). Several somewhat old studies that relied on aggregate-level time series data to examine entry and deterrent effects show contradictory findings, but a recent study that relied on simulation techniques suggest that they could be important (for a summary of the older contradictory studies, see Friedlander, Greenberg, and Robins 1997; for the simulation techniques, see Lise, Seitz, and Smith 2004). A direct random assignment test of entry effects found that they were fairly small in SSP (Berlin et al. 1998). Given the lack of conclusive information about entry and deterrent effects, additional research could make an important contribution to cost-benefit analyses of welfare-to-work programs.

Fifth, the graduates of welfare-to-work programs and training programs may end up in jobs that otherwise would have been held by individuals not in the program. If these displaced individuals become unemployed or accept lower-wage jobs, their earnings will fall, reducing program net benefits. Some theoretical arguments suggest that displacement effects may be small. Macroeconomic policy, for example, might effectively expand employment enough to absorb program graduates and thereby prevent displacement. If training programs can improve skills that allow trainees to leave slack occupational labor markets for tight ones, then they can decrease the competition for job vacancies in the slack markets, making it easier for those who remain in these markets to find jobs. No conclusive empirical evidence concerning the actual size of displacement effects, however, exists—though there have been a few recent efforts to measure their magnitude (see, for example, Blundell et al. 2002; Adam et al. 2008; and Lise, Seitz, and Smith 2004).

ACKNOWLEDGMENT

Parts of this chapter appeared in Friedlander, Greenberg, and Robins 1997; Greenberg, Mandell, and Onstott 2000; and Greenberg and Cebulla 2008.

REFERENCES

Adam, Stuart, Antoine Bozio, Carl Emmerson, David Greenberg, and Genevieve Knight. 2008. *The Costs and Benefits of Pathways to Work and the Generalisability of the Findings.* DWP Research Report 498. London: Department for Work and Pensions.

Baum, Erica. 1991. "When the Witch Doctors Agree: The Family Support Act and Social Science Research." *Journal of Policy Analysis and Management* 10(4): 603–15.

Bell, Stephen H., and Larry L. Orr. 1994. "Is Subsidized Employment Cost Effective for Welfare Recipients? Experimental Evidence from Seven State Demonstrations." *Journal of Human Resources* 19(1): 42–61.

Berlin, Gordon, Wendy Bancroft, David Card, Winston Lin, and Philip Robins. 1998. *Do Work Incentives Have Unintended Consequences? Measuring Entry Effects in the Self-Sufficiency Project.* Ottawa: Social Research and Demonstration Corporation.

Blundell, Richard, Monica Costa Dias, Costas Meghir, and John Van Reenen. 2002. "Evaluating the Employment Impact of a Mandatory Job Search Program: The New Deal for Young People in the UK." Unpublished manuscript. London: University College London and Institute for Fiscal Studies.

Boardman, Anthony, David Greenberg, Aidan Vining, and David Weimer. 2006. *Cost-benefit Analysis: Concepts and Practice*, 3rd ed. Upper Saddle River, NJ: Prentice Hall.

Department for Work and Pensions. 2007. *The DWP ALMP Cost Benefit Framework. CBF: Guidance and Technical Methodology.* Unpublished manuscript. London.

Friedlander, Daniel, David Greenberg, and Philip Robins. 1997. "Evaluating Government Training Programs for the Economically Disadvantaged." *Journal of Economic Literature* 35(4): 1809–55.

Greenberg, David. 1997. "The Leisure Bias in Cost-Benefit Analyses of Employment and Training Programs." *Journal of Human Resources* 32(2): 413–39.

Greenberg, David, Karl Ashworth, Andreas Cebulla, and Robert Walker. 2004. "Do Welfare-to-Work Programmes Work for Long?" *Fiscal Studies* 25(1): 27–53.

Greenberg, David, and Andreas Cebulla. 2008. "The Cost-Effectiveness of Welfare-to-Work Programs: A Meta-Analysis." *Public Budgeting and Finance* 28(2): 1212–45.

Greenberg, David, and Abigail Davis. 2007. *Evaluation of the New Deal for Disabled People: The Cost and Cost-Benefit Analyses.* DWP Research Report 431. London: Department for Work and Pensions.

Greenberg, David, and Genevieve Knight. 2007. "Review of the DWP Cost Benefit Framework and How It Has Been Applied." DWP Working Paper 40. London: Department for Work and Pensions.

Greenberg, David, Marvin Mandell, and Mathew Onstott. 2000. "The Dissemination and Utilization of Welfare-to-Work Experiments in State Policymaking." *Journal of Policy Analysis and Management* 19(3): 367–82.

Greenberg, David, Charles Michalopoulous, and Philip Robins. 2004. "What Happens to the Effects of Government-Funded Training Programs over Time?" *Journal of Human Resources* 39(1): 277–93.

Greenberg, David, and Philip Robins. 2007. "Incorporating Nonmarket Time into Benefit-Cost Analyses of Social Programs: An Application to the Self-Sufficiency Project." *Journal of Public Economics* 92(3): 766–94.

Haskins, Ronald. 1991. "Congress Writes a Law: Research and Welfare Reform." *Journal of Policy Analysis and Management* 10(4): 614–32.

Lise, Jeremy, Shannon Seitz, and Jeffrey Smith. 2004. "Equilibrium Policy Experiments and the

Evaluation of Social Programs." *NBER* Working Paper 10283. Cambridge, MA: National Bureau of Economic Research.

Michalopoulos, Charles, Doug Tattrie, Cynthia Miller, Philip K. Robins, David Gyarmati, Cindy Redcross, Kelly Foley, and Reuben Ford. 2002. *Making Work Pay: Final Report on the Self-Sufficiency Project for Long-Term Welfare Recipients.* Ottawa: Social Research and Demonstration Corporation.

Orr, Larry L., Stephen H. Bell, and Kenneth Lam. 2007. *Long-term Impacts of the New Deal for Disabled People: Final Report.* DWP Research Report 432. London: Department for Work and Pensions.

Riccio, James, Daniel Friedlander, and Stephen Freedman. 1994. *GAIN: Benefits, Costs, and Three-Year Impacts of a Welfare-to-Work Program.* New York: Manpower Demonstration Research Corporation.

Szanton, Peter. 1991. "The Remarkable 'Quango': Knowledge, Politics, and Welfare Reform." *Journal of Policy Analysis and Management* 10(4): 590–602.

Chapter 3

Overview of the State-of-the-Art of CBA in Social Policy

Aidan R. Vining and David L. Weimer

How frequently and how well is cost-benefit analysis (CBA) used to assess the desirability of social policy interventions? In the foregoing chapters, the substantive experts contributing to this volume have identified many of the important CBAs in their fields. To provide a comprehensive assessment, we supplemented their reviews by searching for additional reasonably available CBAs in the ten policy areas. Based on our own reviews of representative, and sometimes all the available CBAs in these areas, we provide here an overall assessment of the state-of-the-art of CBA in social policy. Specifically, we consider the quantity and quality of available CBAs.

Assessing the quantity of CBAs in each of the ten areas is relatively straightforward. We first consider whether multiple CBAs are available. Next, we consider whether there are enough CBAs that those working in the policy area have found it useful to review these analyses.

Assessing quality is, for a number of reasons, much more challenging. Quality has two distinct but equally important dimensions: the plausibility of the prediction of major impacts (broadly defined to include both the resources used and the effects they produce) and the credibility of the valuation of those impacts. We discussed both these issues at some length in chapter 1. Unfortunately, however, published studies often do not provide enough detail to allow readers to understand fully either the basis of the predicted impacts or the methods used. Further, those not familiar with the area have difficulty assessing whether possible, but excluded, impacts are likely to be small enough to justify their being excluded. In our view, perhaps the most important problem is, metaphorically, identifying the dog that did not bark. In other words, are there (potentially) important impact categories that the analyst missed? If so, then they could substantially change the magnitude, or even the sign, of net benefits. Many CBAs do a good job monetizing one or a few social impacts, but totally ignore, or fail to monetize, other impacts that may also be important. Even a well-informed reader on social policy in general may be unable to sense the relevance or importance of these unstudied impacts. As a consequence, our assessment of quality puts the most weight on the extent to which the analysis comprehensively considers impacts and estimates their costs and benefits. We put less weight on the credibility of predictions within a given impact category. Although a few exemplary CBAs do discuss the basis for their predictions of important impacts, most do not. This remains an important topic for further research that is just beginning to be addressed for more traditional applications of CBA in areas like infrastructure investment (Boardman, Mallery, and Vining 1994; Anguera 2006).

Another important criterion of quality in our view is the extent to which analyses actually assess, or attempt to assess, social costs and benefits rather than simply the fiscal impact on a single government agency or on some larger collection of government agencies. These kinds of analyses come under a wide variety of labels, such as budgetary costs and benefits, government expenditures perspective, and fiscal analysis. It is quite common to find authors who either choose to perform some form of fiscal analysis, or to confuse and conflate such analyses with CBA. Indeed, they often describe their work as being CBA. We believe that *choose* is usually a more appropriate verb to describe what they are doing, rather than *confuse* or *conflate*. This mislabeling is understandable in view of political realities, but it does present a number of problems. Most obviously, net government expenditures usually do not correlate closely with net social benefits, though they may occasionally do so. Nonetheless, government employees often cannot clearly distinguish between costs and benefits, on the one hand, and expenditures, on the other, so there can be considerable confusion (Boardman, Vining, and Waters 1993). Additionally, even the most dedicated cost-benefit analysts may be tempted to focus more on interventions that hold constant or reduce government expenditures, because such interventions are the most politically attractive and therefore more likely to attract the interest of pragmatic policy entrepreneurs. The benign fiscal impact of welfare-to-work is certainly one of the major reasons that it has attracted so much policy attention and support. As a result, a degree of selection bias tends to be introduced into the discussion and appraisal of alternative social policy interventions.

Any overall assessment of quality also depends on how well impacts are monetized. This is related to how comprehensively impacts are assessed, as discussed, because impacts vary enormously in how easily they can be monetized and therefore how likely it is that analysts include them. As we discussed in chapter 1, some major impacts can be monetized using market prices or relatively good shadow prices. Others, however, cannot because plausible shadow prices are not readily available. This is a common problem with impacts that represent important benefits of social programs, such as cognitive gains from early childhood programs. In practice, most analysts attempt monetization only when a plausible and readily available plug-in shadow price is available (Boardman et al. 1997). One cannot necessarily blame analysts for this hesitancy, but it does introduce another selection bias: Interventions with costs and benefits (but especially benefits) that do not have market-based proxies or well-established shadow prices are less likely to be published as CBAs. Works that do offer new shadow prices may be published as original contributions, but usually not in the format of a complete CBA.

We also tried to assess the quality of CBAs in terms of the ability to avoid double-counting of either costs or benefits. For example, one would not want to treat both the market value of goods and services produced and the wages of participants as benefits; the wages are an often-used proxy for the market value. To count both would be double-counting benefits. In general, CBAs that are published in peer-reviewed journals do not appear problematic in terms of double-counting.

Finally, we primarily report on CBAs and avoid discussion of cost-effectiveness analyses (CEAs). However, had we consistently applied this rule, we would have had little to discuss in several of the areas. So, instead, we occasionally turned to CEAs to round out the discussion.

WHAT DID WE FIND?

We found a very mixed picture. CBAs of generally good quality have become fairly common in several social policy areas: mental health, substance abuse treatment, and welfare-to-work. Interventions in these areas involve clients in settings where either experiments with random assignment or reasonably strong quasi-experiments are possible. Early childhood development also has some very strong CBAs, particularly those based on longitudinal data from the Perry Preschool. Caution is warranted, however, in placing too much weight for public policy purposes on a single experiment with a relatively small number of subjects. There have also been some strong CBAs of health interventions for disadvantaged populations, including for prenatal care (overlapping with early childhood development) and mammography.

The preponderance of CEAs in the health area suggests that many more CBAs could be produced if decision makers and analysts were willing to monetize key outcomes like quality-adjusted life years. However, the CEAs often take the narrow view of benefits as avoided medical system costs only and therefore may be less of a CBA than one might expect. For example, Peter Neumann found that only about 30 percent of CEAs of health-care interventions published between 1998 and 2001 took a societal perspective (2005, figure 10.2). More generally, looking across social policy areas, we found that many did not include relevant impacts. Sometimes they are missing because they could not be estimated with available data, but also because appropriate, or at least plausible, shadow prices were not readily available.

The mixed picture we find can be viewed as being a glass either half empty or half full. The reason for the half empty is clear: We can say little about the efficacy and efficiency in major areas of social policy involving interventions requiring large expenditures of resources and potentially important social consequences. This is the case even in those areas we see as having made the most progress in applying CBA. The reasons for the half full, or even more than half full, are not quite as apparent. Nonetheless, there are two. First is increasing acceptance that rigorous evaluations generally, and CBAs specifically, are legitimate and central to social policy. This was much less true even a decade ago. Second, many of the exemplary CBAs we discuss have been published in peer-reviewed journals during the last five years—though some of the earliest studies we consider were also exemplary. We hope the more recent studies represent the leading edge of a growing market (both incremental supply and demand are necessary for this growth) for CBAs of social policy interventions. We fear that the major risk to continued growth is that even specialist journals will quickly move to a mantra of: "yes, this is valuable to the public policy community, but where is the methodological uniqueness?" This would be unfortunate, even tragic, because we hope to demonstrate that a wide variety of interventions have not been assessed with CBA and even those that have often involved small samples of participants and therefore require replication to increase confidence in their findings. It usually takes a number of studies—perhaps even three, four, or five—to demonstrate some degree of robustness and really get the attention of policymakers.

We now briefly review the conclusions that the experts reached concerning the actual and potential use of CBA in each social policy area in light of our review of relevant CBAs. We begin by reviewing the current supply of CBAs in each policy area, whether identified by the policy expert or ourselves (some CBAs have been published since the chapters were written). We also summarize the interventions the experts identify in each policy area as good candidates for CBAs (see table 13.1). The first column after the policy area in table 13.1 notes representative CBAs and reviews of CBAs. Among the representative CBAs, those we consider exemplary are in bold. Reviews are shown in italics. The second column identifies those interventions for which we found either exemplary or multiple CBAs. The third column lists types of interventions the policy experts identified as good candidates for CBA.

We then consider the issue of monetization of relevant costs and benefits for each of the policy areas. Ideally, we would prefer to monetize all the impacts because a number of relatively small impacts might, in total, determine the net benefits of an intervention. We identify the extent to which any particular impact in an area can be monetized using either market prices or relatively good shadow prices. Obviously, if all major impacts can be credibly based on market prices and standard shadow prices, the valuation aspect of future CBAs becomes much easier. The prediction aspect, of course, is unaffected. We also try to identify the important shadow prices still needed in each area to do truly comprehensive CBAs. Table 13.2 summarizes this information. Although it is useful for our purposes to divide impacts into either costs or benefits, this division is somewhat arbitrary. For example, avoided victimization costs from a prisoner reentry program would be a positive impact and a benefit if the program had a rehabilitative effect, but a negative impact and a cost if the program effectively gave offenders who were not rehabilitated greater opportunity to commit crime.

Table 13.2 identifies a number of areas for further research that basically speak for themselves. A few points are worth a brief mention, however. A quick review of table 13.2 suggests that most future research should focus primarily on impacts that will normally be benefits. This is not surprising. Most costs in these areas require relatively conventional inputs that are regularly purchased in relatively well-functioning markets. Many interventions, for example, require at least some highly skilled professional staff. Although one might quibble about the monopolistic power of certain professions—and a consequent ability to price their labor above its social opportunity cost—in general, analysts can treat pretax earnings as the social opportunity cost of the resource. The same rule of thumb can be applied to labor inputs in general, though there is some evidence that public sector employees can extract wages above their social opportunity cost

(Bender 2003; Belman and Heywood 2004). A number of impacts, however, normally show up as costs and warrant further research, essentially all related to the opportunity cost of time (such as patients in some health interventions, parents in some educational interventions, and volunteers in some juvenile justice interventions).

As table 13.2 shows, the range of benefit categories that require further research is extensive. We do nothing more here than note this need. Setting the agenda for this research is the central task of the next chapter. We now turn to the specific policy areas.

Early Childhood

In chapter 2, Barbara Wolfe and Norman Tefft conclude that early childhood education is the most studied and widely recognized early childhood intervention category. They note its robust correlation with many indicators of success, including higher wages and reduced crime rates. In contrast to many other social policy contexts, experiments have been numerous and some programs have diffused widely enough to be beyond the experimental stage. In contrast to early childhood education, Wolfe and Tefft suggest that the largest social returns may come from various health interventions. They emphasize, however, that hard evidence to back this claim up is scant and that designing convincing experiments that are ethically and politically acceptable is a big challenge. They do note an extensive analysis of the nutritional effects of the School Breakfast Program (Bhattacharya et al. 2006). This study found that the program led to better dietary outcomes including reductions in the percentage of calories from fat, reduced vitamin and mineral deficiencies, improved intakes of high fiber, iron and potassium, and better scores on the healthy eating index. Wolfe and Tefft conclude that most other areas relating to early childhood development require much more extensive evidence.

In terms of CBA, in the last few years a number of studies have appeared, mainly relating to early childhood education, including some on child care. Notable studies have examined Perry Preschool, the Abecedarian Early Childhood Intervention, and Chicago Child-Parent Centers. Clive Belfield and his colleagues provided a comprehensive analysis of the High/Scope Perry Preschool program in 2006. They estimated monetary values for program costs, child care provided by the program, elementary and secondary education, adult secondary education, postsecondary education, employment-related compensation, delinquency and crime, and public welfare assistance. The study tracked participants through age forty, which is highly unusual in a social policy CBA context, and is exemplary in a number of other respects. It reported distributions of the costs and benefits as well as aggregate social costs and benefits, carries out sensitivity analysis, and uses theoretically grounded discount rates. The authors found benefits in terms of gains in earnings, reductions in crime, and changes in welfare receipts. In aggregate, they found social net benefits of over $229 thousand (year 2000 dollars, 3 percent real discount rate) per enrolled child of which participants receive approximately $50 thousand. As with other programs that reduce crime and generate employment earnings for those that might otherwise receive welfare payments (such as welfare-to-work programs), the great majority of benefits accrue to nonparticipants. The size of the aggregate estimated net benefits is impressive, as is the quality of this CBA.

Table 13.1 Overview of CBA in Social Policy Areas

Policy Area	Representative CBAs	Interventions with Exemplary or Multiple CBAs	Other Interventions
Early childhood development	*Karoly, Kilburn, and Cannon* (2005) Aos et al. (2004) **Belfield et al.** (2006) **Temple and Reynolds** (2007) Barnett and Masse (2007) Reynolds et al. (2002)	preschool programs	child care; nutrition; prenatal, infant, childhood health
Elementary and secondary education	Levin et al. (2007) Aos et al. (2007) Stern et al. (1989)		teacher quality; class size; school size; summer school; grade retention; peer tutoring; school choice and competition; accountability standards; whole-school reform
Health for disadvantaged populations	*Diener, O'Brien, and Gafni* (1998) [contingent valuation] Hahn et al. (2006) [CEA] Lu et al. (2000) Devaney, Bilheimer, and Score (1992) Lai and Sorkin (1998) **Clarke** (1998)	mammography prenatal care	chlamydia screening; childhood vaccination; screening/intervention for problem drinking and tobacco use; cervical cancer screening; colorectal cancer screening; breast cancer screening
Mental health	*Roberts, Cumming, and Nelson* (2005) Barrett, Byford, and Knapp (2005) [CEA] **Weisbrod** (1981) Gourney and Brooking (1995) Culhane, Metraux, and Hadley (2002) Lo Sasso, Rost, and Beck (2006)	community treatment	medication management; cognitive-behavioral psychotherapy; psycho-education for patients and families; supported housing; supported employment; involuntary outpatient commitment; advanced directives; crisis intervention and criminal diversion; peer support clubhouses; supported education
Substance abuse	*French* (2000) *Cartwright* (2000) *McCollister and French* (2003) *Harwood et al.* (2002) *Blenko, Patapsis, and French* (2005) French et al. (2002) Daley et al. (2000) Fleming et al. (2002) Logan et al. (2004)	treatment; drug courts	supply control; prevention; harm reduction; legalization; coerced abstinence

Table 13.1 Overview of CBA in Social Policy Areas (*continued*)

Policy Area	Representative CBAs	Interventions with Exemplary or Multiple CBAs	Other Interventions
Juvenile justice	*Greenwood (2005)* *McDougall et al. (2003)* Aos et al. (2004) [review/new] Robertson, Grimes, and Rogers (2001) Fass and Pi (2002) Caldwell, Vitacco, and Van Rybroek (2006)		cognitive-behavioral interventions; mentoring programs; teen courts; juvenile drug courts; juvenile detention alternatives
Prisoner reentry	*Welsh and Farrington (2000)* Welsh (2004) **Aos et al. (2006)** [review/new] **Friedman (1977)** **Roman et al. (2007)**	supported work	cognitive-behavioral: drug abuse, health, and mental health; faith-based; employment and job counseling; marriage and family
Affordable housing	*Turner and Malpezzi (2003)* Simons and Sharkey (1997) Johnson, Ladd, and Ludwig (2002) Deng (2005)	rent control	public housing; tax expenditures; vouchers; supply subsidies; deconcentration of poor families
Work incentives	*Greenberg, Michalopoulos, and Robbins (2003)* **Long, Mallar, and Thornton (1981)** **Schochet, McConnell, and Burghardt (2003)**	Job Corps	earned income tax credits; wage subsidies; job training; apprenticeships; reducing work-disincentives; community colleges
Welfare-to-work	*Greenberg and Cebulla (2007)* Riccio, Friedlander, and Freedman (1994) Michalopoulos et al. (2002) Greenberg and Davis (2007) Department for Work and Pensions (2007)	job placement/work requirements	transitional incentives; financial intermediation; integration of disabled

Source: Author

Note: Reviews in italics; exemplary studies in bold.

Table 13.2 Overview of Monetization of Impacts in Social Policy CBAs

	Costs			Benefits		
	Market-Based Prices	Good Shadow Prices	Shadow Prices Needed	Market-Based Prices	Good Shadow Prices	Shadow Prices Needed
Early childhood development	Program resources (PR) especially staff time and space	Parent time		Market productivity Avoided medical care	Avoided tangible crime victimization Avoided criminal justice system Quality of life	Nonmarket productivity IQ gains Avoided intangible crime victimization
Elementary and secondary education	PR especially teacher time	Parent time	Student time	Market productivity	Avoided tangible crime victimization Avoided criminal justice system	Non-market productivity Avoided intangible crime victimization Direct utility of education
Health for disadvantaged populations	PR especially physician and medical staff time	Patient time		Market productivity Avoided medical care	Quality of life Avoided mortality	Nonmarket productivity Option value of access Public health externalities
Mental health	PR especially mental health professional time Therapeutic drugs	Patient time	Family time	Market productivity Avoided hospital care	Quality of life Avoided tangible crime victimization Avoided criminal justice system	Nonmarket productivity Option value of labor participation Avoided intangible crime victimization Utility to family
Substance abuse	PR especially counselor time	Patient time	Family time	Market productivity	Avoided tangible crime victimization Avoided criminal justice system Avoided drug expenditures	Nonmarket productivity Avoided intangible crime victimization Avoided crime victimization Avoided victimless crime

Table 13.2 Overview of Monetization of Impacts in Social Policy CBAs (*continued*)

	Costs			Benefits		
	Market-Based Prices	Good Shadow Prices	Shadow Prices Needed	Market-Based Prices	Good Shadow Prices	Shadow Prices Needed
Juvenile justice	PR especially police, prosecutor, and correctional staff time		Volunteer time	Market productivity	Avoided tangible crime victimization; Avoided criminal justice system	Nonmarket productivity; Avoided intangible crime victimization
Prisoner reentry	PR especially police, prosecutor, parole and correctional staff time			Market productivity	Avoided tangible crime victimization; Avoided criminal justice system	Nonmarket productivity; Family preservation; Indirect intangible victimization
Affordable housing	Land and construction for direct supply; Subsidy expenditure		Network externalities to origin and destination communities	Housing consumption; Market productivity	Educational gains; Health improvement; Avoided tangible crime victimization; Avoided criminal justice system	Nonmarket productivity; Labor market access; Social capital access; Avoided intangible crime victimization
Work incentives		Leisure time	Household production; Tax expenditures	Market productivity	Avoided tangible crime victimization; Avoided criminal justice system	Nonmarket productivity; Avoided intangible crime victimization; Nonparticipant value of labor; Value of labor market participation
Welfare-to-work	PR especially training, monitoring, and enforcement time	Leisure time	Household production	Market productivity	Avoided tangible crime victimization; Avoided criminal justice system	Nonmarket productivity; Avoided intangible crime victimization; Nonparticipant value of labor

Source: Authors.

Steven Barnett and Leonard Masse recently conducted a CBA of the Abecedarian Early Childhood Intervention (AECI), which provides intensive pre-school education and daycare services to children in low-income families from infancy to the age of five (2007). The center is open five days a week for fifty weeks of the year, with a curriculum that emphasizes language and other development through learning games. The CBA followed 104 economically disadvantaged children and their families who were randomly assigned to the program through age twenty-one. The benefits of the program include increased maternal earnings, decreased K-12 schooling costs, increased lifetime earnings, and decreased costs related to smoking. They found, in contrast to the Perry Preschool Program, no reduced criminal justice costs. Using a 3 percent real discount rate, they reported a net present value of almost $95 thousand per student (2002 dollars).

Judy Temple and Arthur Reynolds studied the federally funded Child-Parent Centers (CPC) and produced an exemplary CBA (2007). These centers provide educational interventions to children from preschool through grades two or three in high-poverty neighborhoods in Chicago. Temple and Reynolds reported net present values for CPC in 2002 dollars and compared them to Perry and AECI net present values. They estimated the net present value (per participant) for each of the three programs at about $68 thousand for the CPC for a large urban school district (the authors noted that the net present values for the model programs were larger), about $123 thousand for Perry, and about $100 thousand for AECI. The two major sources of CPC benefits were reduced crime costs and increased earnings, primarily by participants (table 4). In aggregate, the researchers found that CPC generates approximately between $6 and $10 in benefits for every dollar invested.

Elementary and Secondary Education

In chapter 3, Clive Belfield divides elementary and secondary interventions into three categories: general policies, programs, and reforms. After extensively reviewing the literature relating to each of these types of intervention, he concludes that we only can be certain about a few stylized facts. First, although the quantity of elementary and secondary education matters, we can be much less certain about the social value of almost any quality increment. Second, the private returns to elementary and secondary education are substantial. Third, the public (external) benefits are almost certainly substantial, but they have multiple dimensions, they are complex, and their magnitudes are uncertain. Fourth, targeting interventions to disadvantaged groups will almost certainly raise social returns, whether because this targeting results in greater quantity of schooling (additional high school years, for example) or because social benefits are likely to be higher. Belfield concludes that the extant CBAs and research on the economic value of specific educational investments are far from compelling and that the available evidence does not give much guidance on what investments are optimal under any particular set of circumstances.

In view of the paucity of relevant CBAs, Belfield makes several rough estimates from the candidate categories as to where positive net benefits may be found. He first considers teacher quality. Making what we believe a questionable assumption, at least in terms of short-term impacts, he argues that raising salaries would raise quality. He further argues that increasing teacher salaries across the K–12 years would raise the high school graduation rate and, as the economic benefits of graduating from high school are large, this investment would probably produce net benefits. Belfield next considers the potential social benefits of reduced class sizes. He is not able to make a confident statement about the likely net benefits, however, though he does note it is a costly intervention. Third, he concludes there is essentially no CBA evidence on reducing school size, but suggests that any net social benefits would be dependent on whether there are economies, or diseconomies, of scale to school (as opposed to class) size. Fourth, he suggests that summer school is probably cost-effective. Finally, he is more optimistic on peer tutoring and concludes that it scores well in terms of cost-effectiveness. Belfield is most pessimistic when it comes to major reforms; his conclusion is that many of these reforms have small impacts, except when targeted on well-defined disadvantaged groups.

In our search for CBA results, we considered Henry Levin's attempt to extract both cost-effectiveness and CBA estimates from three education interventions: the Tennessee STAR program (class size reduction, or CSR), teacher salary increases (or TSI, used as a proxy for teacher quality) and the First Things First (FTF) program in Kansas City, Kansas (2007). Levin and colleagues considered these three interventions in terms of their beneficial impact on male African American student high school completion rates. Apart from the (estimated) direct incremental costs of the interventions, they included in their estimate of the social costs only the educational costs related to additional high school grades (no estimate of the opportunity costs of time, for example), but did include expected increased future tertiary education costs. Somewhere between 25 percent and 50 percent of the total costs are expected to flow from these additional years of schooling. All costs were converted to 2004 dollars and estimated as present values at age twenty using a 3.5 real discount rate. They considered three benefit categories: earning and tax increases, reductions in public health costs and crime reduction benefits. Their counterfactual for estimation purposes was the high school graduation rate of white males (for a single age cohort, twenty years old). The net present value of TSI is, Levin and colleagues estimated, approximately $136,000, the net present value of CSR approximately $169,500, and the net present value of FTF approximately $198,000. They concluded that all the three programs would provide net benefits for African American males if targeted at them.

We also considered an older CBA that evaluated the California Peninsula Academies (CPAs), which are schools within schools, mostly in the Bay Area in northern California (Stern et al. 1989). The CPAs combine academic education and vocational training for students identified as at high risk of dropping out. Costs included additional teacher time, additional aide and administrator time, additional facility and equipment costs, but no student time. Stern and his colleagues used the difference in average lifetime earnings between graduates and dropouts as the benefit measure. They found that the present value at age eighteen was $77,500 (5 percent discount rate) for the 1984 year. Because this evaluation has a number of weaknesses, it cannot be considered exemplary, though it is informative.

Finally, we reviewed a recent Washington State Institute for Public Policy (WSIPP) study of the costs and benefits of K–12 educational policies that was published after chapter 3 was written (Aos, Miller, and Mayfield 2007). The WSIPP analysts reported cost-benefit findings relating to class size reductions and on the incremental value of full-day versus half-day kindergarten. They focused only on academic performance and did not consider other potential benefits, such as reduced criminal activity or alcohol and drug use. In assessing the value of class size reductions, they analyzed thirty-eight previous evaluations. Consistent with the evidence presented in chapter 2 of this volume, they found that reducing class size during kindergarten and through second grade increases test scores. They also found, however, that between third and sixth grades gains are much smaller, though still significant. The real average return on investment for a one-unit drop in class size they estimated at about 6 percent, or $1.38 in benefits per dollar cost. For middle school and high school, however, they found no statistically significant test score gains and therefore did not compute a social return on investment for middle school or high school.

In assessing the social value of full-day kindergarten, the authors reviewed twenty-three evaluations. They concluded that, relative to half-day counterpart, it produced a statistically significant boost to test scores either during, or shortly after, kindergarten. These test score gains, however, eroded almost completely during grades one through three. They concluded that if this erosion cannot be reduced or eliminated full-day kindergarten offers no net benefits, and in fact results in a net cost of $2,611 per student.

Health for Disadvantaged Populations

In his chapter 4, David Vanness posits eight categories of health-care interventions for disadvantaged populations that he considers to be most promising based on extant research: chlamydia screening, prenatal care for the prevention of low birth weight, childhood vaccination, screening and brief clinical intervention for problem drinking, screening and brief intervention for tobacco use, cervical cancer screening using pap smears, colorectal cancer screening, and breast cancer screening using mammography. He argues, however, that these interventions cannot be considered in isolation from health insurance for the disadvantaged, even though the pathways from lack of insurance to poor health care are complex and not well understood.

Vanness emphasizes that though CEAs relating to clinical practice are common in the health policy and medical care areas, only a few CBAs address policies aimed at improving the health of disadvantaged populations. An important reason for the dominance of CEAs is an unwillingness to monetize the value of life (at least explicitly). Another fundamental weakness is that CEAs consider only changes in costs to the health-care system and ignore costs to patients or other program participants, especially the opportunity cost of their time. Furthermore, they typically assume that the quantified outcome, such as change in the number of quality-adjusted life years (QALYs), is the only benefit of the intervention. They do not address other benefits to patients as well as any costs or benefits external to them and the health-care system.

Confirming Vanness, we found in our review of the CBA literature only a few health policy CBAs. In fact, only one focused somewhat on what might be described as a disadvantaged population, though it was not in the United States but in rural Australia (Clarke 1998). This lack of studies is surprising. Because of it, we assessed three additional studies that focus almost exclusively on changes in taxpayer and health-care system costs: prenatal care for undocumented immigrants, prenatal participation in the Special Supplemental Food Program for Women, Infants, and Children, and pharmaceutical coverage for Medicaid enrollees (Lu et al. 2000; Devaney, Bilheimer, and Score 1992; Lai and Sorkin 1998).

In view of this paucity, we summarize only Clarke's assessment of mobile mammography units in rural Australia (1998). It is exemplary for several reasons. It analyzed costs and benefits from a social perspective using the travel cost method, a technique commonly used by environmental and recreational economists to value goods with administered prices, demonstrating how the method could be used more generally in the health policy context. Clarke also used a somewhat more sophisticated sensitivity analysis than the other studies reviewed. He identified two categories of benefits: reduced costs for women who have been getting recommended mammograms, and mammograms for women who do not get them but would if the mobile units were available. Clarke used a survey of women in rural areas as the basis for assessing their willingness to pay for the greater access. The sensitivity analysis calculated net benefits of the mobile unit as a function of the distance women lived from the currently available mammography site, the shadow price of their time, and the fraction of women who would be able to engage in joint consumption when they traveled to receive mammograms.

Mental Health

In his chapter 5, Mark Salzer identified two broad categories of intervention in the mental health field. The first includes various kinds of pharmacological interventions and medication management for psychiatric symptoms. The second includes various forms of case management that emerge from evidenced-based practices. Regarding the first, he concludes that newer medications have generally been found to have a greater impact on symptoms than the older medications, and appear to have fewer side effects, though concerns are growing about some of the side-effects of newer medications. Regarding the second, Salzer notes that recent research has reasserted the value of psychotherapy as a socially desirable intervention for the treatment of serious mental illnesses. Both categories of intervention focus on symptom management and reducing the need for institutional or hospital-based care.

Salzer argues that the impacts that currently motivate policy interest in mental health have broadened considerably over time. Historically, the major justification for mental health interventions focused primarily on their ability to reduce the costs of institutionalization in hospitals, jails, and prisons. Over the last twenty years, there has been an increasing emphasis on productivity. This has generated the development of interventions primarily relating to employment, as it has become increasingly recognized that individuals with serious mental illnesses can and should work. Finally, in the last decade, there has been a growing interest in enhancing the well-being, recovery, and community integration of those suffering from mental illness.

Dennis Culhane and colleagues assessed the fiscal implications of a supported housing program in New York City and made a truly impressive effort to develop the data base of public service use for participants and controls across eight administrative data sets (2002). These included NY/NY participants, New York City Department of Homeless Services, New York State Office of Mental Health, New York State Department of Health (Office of Medicaid Management), New York City Health and Hospitals Corporation, U.S. Department of Veterans Affairs, New York State Department of Correctional Services, and the New York City Department of Corrections. The researchers found small negative fiscal effects that would most likely be offset by nonfiscal benefits to participants and society, had they been included.

In terms of comprehensiveness of the identified categories of costs and benefits and sensitivity to the conceptual bases for valuation, Burton Weisbrod set a high standard in his early CBA of a community mental health care program (1981). Because such programs have fairly large per client costs, they would be excellent candidates for additional CBAs with more recent data and larger sample sizes. In terms of the state-of-the-art, Weisbrod raises some issues about the measurement of productivity gains that remain unresolved. Most important is the lack of consensus about how to value the opportunity cost of labor for those who would otherwise be prevented from entering the labor market.

Substance Abuse

In his chapter 6, Jonathan Caulkins identifies six broad types of drug programs: supply control, prevention, treatment, harm reduction, integrative interventions that transcend these boundaries, and legalization. He concludes, for a number of reasons, that it is impossible to judge the social value of supply control programs even though these programs are extremely popular with U.S. policymakers and enormous resources are devoted to them. Turning to prevention, Caulkins argues that many scholars are increasingly skeptical that supply control programs have any material effect on drug use, though some researchers believe that in certain contexts and for certain behaviors certain prevention interventions may be cost-effective. The most common prevention programs are school based. Caulkins does find some evidence that they produce positive effects. Some of his important observations about them include the fact that any favorable benefit-cost ratios come mostly from prevention being relatively cheap, that the absolute reduction of lifetime substance use is small (in the single digit percentage range), that social benefits mostly stem from reduced alcohol and tobacco use, that spillover effects on people not in the programs may be quite large, and that social costs are dominated by the opportunity cost of classroom time. Caulkins concludes that the evidence on the efficacy of nonschool based programs is even weaker. He suggests, however, that three types of interventions are worthy of further study: media campaigns, community-level efforts, and those that are not drug-specific. He notes that that media campaigns harness the same social marketing talents that drive consumer trends, but in reverse, to discourage rather than encourage consumption.

Caulkins notes the conventional mantra that treatment works. This is true both for clients, in the sense of improving their life outcomes, and for society, in the sense of being a good societal investment (Cartwright 2000; Harwood et al. 2002; Belenko, Patapsis, and French 2005). Nevertheless, he concludes that the picture is not totally optimistic because treatment success is very uneven across drugs. The strongest evidence for cost-effectiveness is for opiates, such as heroin. There is also reasonably good evidence that treatment works with marijuana and cannabis. In contrast, the evidence on the efficacy of treating stimulants (cocaine, including crack, and various amphetamines including methamphetamine) is far less developed, though these drugs are estimated to account for three-quarters of drug-related social costs in the United States. Indeed, the National Research Council concluded that there is no solid evidence on which to estimate effectiveness, let alone the cost-effectiveness, of cocaine treatment (Manski, Pepper, and Petrie 2001). A possible exception to this general pattern of failure is immunotherapies against cocaine and methamphetamine, as well as some other substances, including nicotine. Caulkins argues that the early research with humans is intriguing (Harwood 2002). He points out that Mark Kleiman's 2004 study offers a preliminary cost-benefit projection and suggests that updating that work based on recently completed Phase II clinical trials would be valuable.

Caulkins cautions that if harm reduction is viewed as an overall philosophy of drug control policy, rigorous data concerning effectiveness is scant because it tends to be implemented at a national level, and there is no relevant comparison group. Cross-national comparisons rarely provide a solid basis for quantitative estimation of social returns on investment. The potential for quantitative evaluation is therefore greater for specific harm reduction interventions. With respect to specific programs, Caulkins argues for a distinction between needle and syringe exchange programs (NSP) and everything else. Although NSPs are controversial in the United States, the consensus in the academic literature is that they are an effective way to reduce the spread of HIV/AIDS and are cost-effective (see Ritter and Cameron 2005). Caulkins concludes that the evidence on all other harm reduction interventions is much weaker.

Integrative interventions do not fall neatly into the supply-control, prevention, treatment, or harm reduction categories. Employee, athlete, and student drug testing programs are examples of these types of programs. Testing is common, with about half of full-time employees working for firms that drug test. Despite a modestly large literature on drug testing, few return-on-investment studies at the societal or even organizational level have been undertaken.

Caulkins argues that, except for marijuana, there is no empirical basis on which to build a CBA of legalization because no developed nation today has legalized substances such as cocaine or heroin. Several have decriminalized some of these substances and most have far less stringent forms of prohibition than the United States, but none have made production, distribution, possession, and use legal for recreational purposes. There is evidence concerning marijuana regime changes, such as decriminalization or depenalization, because various jurisdictions have experimented with alternate regimes. In 2003,

Wayne Hall and Rosalie Pacula offer one point-in-time state of the art in the analysis of the social costs and benefits of marijuana regime change.

Our review of the CBA literature confirms that there is an extensive literature on economic analyses of substance abuse treatment programs. Many of these studies, however, attempt to measure only the resource costs of treatment programs, often from a purely fiscal perspective or to assess the impact of treatment on some category of costs. Quite a few CEAs attempt to determine the incremental opportunity cost required to produce some incremental change in an outcome of interest. Most important for our purposes, a fair number of CBAs are available. Michael French identified five CBAs of alcohol treatment programs since 1986 (2000). William Cartwright identified eighteen of drug treatment programs since 1970 (2000). Kathryn McCollister and Michael French reviewed eleven economic studies and found that avoided crime was the most important contributor to benefits (2003). Henrick Harwood and colleagues reviewed fifty-eight studies, including a number of CBAs, though it is not clear exactly how many actually are CBAs (2002). Steven Belenko and colleagues identified ten recent CBAs of treatment programs as well as four of drug courts (2005).

These reviews show consistent positive net benefits for treatment programs though the estimation of outcomes usually comes from quasi-experimental comparisons of pre- and posttreatment outcomes for participants, and therefore risks incorrect inferences because of nonrandom selection into participation and regression toward the mean. These studies usually have relatively short follow-up periods, which leads to an underestimation of benefits when effects persist. As even small reductions in abuse can greatly reduce social costs (especially negative externalities), it is very likely that most types of treatment yield positive net benefits.

In addition to these reviews, we consider four recent studies: residential treatment, treatment for pregnant women, brief physician advising of problem drinkers, and drug courts (French et al. 2002; Daley et al. 2000; Fleming et al. 2002; Logan et al. 2004).

Michael French and his colleagues assessed residential treatment in Washington State for a sample of 222 participants (2002). Total estimated costs included not only program costs but as well the opportunity cost of participants. The CBA assessed the sensitivity of results to uncertainties in the shadow prices employed to calculate upper- and lower-bound estimates of net benefits, which ranged from about $4.7 thousand per patient to about $91 thousand with a mid-range estimate of about $16 thousand.

Marilyn Daley and her colleagues studied a sample of pregnant women who entered one of five Massachusetts substance abuse treatment programs: detoxification only, methadone maintenance only, residential treatment only, outpatient treatment only, and residential followed by outpatient treatment (2000). The study was innovative in that it focused on crime reduction benefits for pregnant women, who have generally been viewed as less criminally active than men or nonpregnant women. The study has several major flaws, however. Most important, it excluded several potentially large benefits: health improvements for mothers and children, reductions in foster-care costs resulting from fewer incarcerations, and reductions in the risks posed to the rest of society through sexually transmitted diseases.

The CBA by Michael Fleming and his colleagues is based on approximately 400 patients randomly assigned to an intervention to determine the effectiveness of two visits to physicians and follow-up calls from nurses (2002). The visits included a brief assessment, providing patients with personalized feedback, dealing with resistance and ambivalence, establishing a goal of abstinence or reduced alcohol use, reviewing a patient-centered workbook, and conducting reinforcement visits. Patients receiving care at seventeen clinics in southern Wisconsin participated in the experiment if they had high consumption levels of alcohol. Three benefit categories were estimated: medical use, motor vehicle events, and legal events. Most benefits were realized in the form of costs of avoided motor vehicle events. Costs were estimated in terms of program resources and the opportunity costs of patients' time. The authors reported social net benefits of approximately $7,800, though these benefits were not discounted for time.

T. K. Logan and colleagues estimated the net benefits if three drug courts that operate in Kentucky (2004), comparing 222 defendants who completed participation to 371 defendants who did not during the year following graduation or termination. The effort was innovative in using statistical techniques to address the problems associated with using those assessed for participation but either not accepted or declining to participate (152 defendants). They did so by estimating a selection equation for the probability of participating based on those who did and did not participate and using these probabilities (through an inverse Mills ratio) as a control in the outcome equations. The benefit categories were the avoided costs from reduced criminal justice system involvement, reduced number of crimes, reduced inpatient and outpatient mental health service use, reduced deficits in child support payments, and increased annual earnings. The net benefits were estimated to be about $14,500 for graduates and about $230 for terminators, for an overall net benefit of about $5,500 per participant.

In aggregate, drug abuse treatment is one of the few areas of social policy offering a relatively large number of CBAs. Compared to other areas of social policy, the quality of these studies is relatively high.

Juvenile Justice

Jeffrey Butts and John Roman argue in chapter 7 that four types of juvenile justice interventions should be investigated for their potential effectiveness: juvenile mentoring programs, teen courts, juvenile drug courts, and systemic reform strategies. Some evidence, they point out, suggests that each of these types of interventions generate beneficial outcomes, though to date no published CBAs have assessed them.

Butts and Roman point out that the social costs of crime are high and that many community-based interventions for youthful offenders would be cost-effective if they prevented even a few young offenders from becoming career criminals. Overintervening, however, is likely to be socially costly—poorly targeted programs that deliver services to many youth but affect only a few future offenders will generate high costs without producing comparable benefits in reduced crime. Butts and Roman note that reviews by both Steve Aos and his colleagues and Peter Greenwood found several clinically oriented interventions, including multisystemic therapy, functional family therapy, and multidimensional treatment foster care, that appear to be cost-beneficial Aos et al. 2004; Greenwood 2005). They also note, however, that Greenwood concluded that the Drug Abuse Resistance Training program (DARE) appears not to work (consistent with chapter 6). Both reviews agreed that Scared Straight, a program in which prison inmates inform delinquents about the perils of the criminal life style, also does not work. Greenwood further argued that youth boot camps do not work, although Aos and his colleagues concluded that the Washington Basic Training Camp is cost-beneficial.

Focusing specifically on CBA, we conclude after our review that its application to juvenile justice programs has been relatively rare. Cynthia McDougall and her colleagues found only nine CBAs of sentencing, only one of which focused on juvenile offenders (2003). Since that 2003 review, Aos and colleagues at the Washington State Institute for Public Policy (WSIPP) have applied CBA to a wide range of juvenile justice interventions (2004). WSIPP evaluated forty-six programs in the categories of youth development, mentoring, youth substance abuse prevention, teen pregnancy, and juvenile offenders and found thirty-two with positive net benefits per youth participant. In terms of the nineteen juvenile offender programs that WSIPP evaluated, the per-youth net benefits ranged from a high of more than $31,000 for dialectical behavior therapy to about negative $12,400 for regular parole versus no parole and about negative $11,000 for Scared Straight.

We also consider published articles by Simon Fass and Chung-Ron Pi and Michael Caldwell and colleagues on particular interventions (Fass and Pi 2002; Caldwell, Vitacco, and Van Rybroek 2006). Only the first study can be considered a CBA, though the latter has some elements of one. Fass and Pi tracked four years of data from the Dallas County Juvenile Department to assess the net benefits of increases in the severity of disposition: probation instead of deferred prosecution, intensive supervision probation rather than probation, local institutional placement rather than intensive supervision probation, and Texas Youth Commission institutional placement rather than local institutional placement. They concluded that, as might be expected, harsher dispositions do not yield positive net fiscal benefits for the justice system. More surprisingly, however, they also concluded that harsher dispositions do not consistently yield positive net benefits for victims. Only the incremental move from local institutional placement to Texas Youth Commission incarceration came close to offering positive net benefits for a value of life of over $1.9 million.

Caldwell and his colleagues examined a juvenile correction alternative in Wisconsin whereby mental health services were provided to violent youths who had difficulty within the regular secure juvenile detention facilities (2006). The program used decompression treatment and was supervised by clinical staff. Unfortunately, the researchers estimated only the net costs of the program to the state, thus conducting a fiscal analysis rather than a proper CBA. The program appeared to offer positive net benefits of approximately $43 thousand per participant and a benefit-cost ratio of about 7. The analysts argue that the ratio would likely be even higher if costs and benefits beyond those incurred by the state were estimated.

Our overall conclusion is that, in view of the numerous mentoring programs, teen courts, and juvenile drug courts, it is very surprising and somewhat sobering that almost the only available CBAs are through the WSIPP comparisons. Clearly, much more needs to be done. In view of the extensive resources devoted to these interventions and their possibly large social benefits, they, and possibly other programs not considered here, seem to be appropriate candidates for CBAs.

Prisoner Reentry

In chapter 8, John Roman and Christy Visher distinguish between interventions undertaken in prisons, which have traditionally been thought of as rehabilitation, and those undertaken after inmates have been released. Within these two settings, they identify five categories: cognitive-behavioral programs, drug abuse programs, health and mental health programs, faith-based programs, employment and job counseling, and marriage and family support. After reviewing each in some detail, they conclude that research suggests potentially valuable interventions can be found in most of these categories, even though the reductions in recidivism may be modest and baseline recidivism may remain high. They are cautious, however, noting the lack of theoretical models that articulate the behavioral change process. They also argue that cataloguing the benefits of these programs is difficult for three reasons. First, they believe that integrative programs (which, by definition, are complex) offer the best chance of efficacious outcomes. Second, many of the benefits are likely to accrue to spouses, children, and neighbors. Third, many of the programs are relatively new (beginning with greater federal involvement in 2003) and data on any behavioral changes are limited. Although Roman and Visher see no fundamental barriers to the wider application of CBA, they find that currently CBAs of prisoner reentry interventions are rare.

Our own review of the CBA evidence agrees with this assessment, even when defining prisoner-reentry broadly to include all correctional interventions intended to reduce recidivism. Brandon Welsh and David Farrington were able to find only seven published CBAs through 1998 (2000). More recently, Welsh expanded the list to fourteen by finding a few additional studies previously missed and adding several juvenile justice studies (2004). Three studies are exemplary: Lee Friedman (1977), Steve Aos, Marna Miller, and Elizabeth Drake (2006), and John Roman and his colleagues (2007).

Although an early application of CBA to social policy generally, and to prisoner reentry specifically, Lee Friedman's assessment of the New York City Supported Work Experiment remains exemplary (1977). Friedman looked in-depth at a representative set of nine projects ranging from contract painting to staffing off-track betting parlors, assessed the value added for each project, and then estimated an overall value-added per person-year. The estimation included the opportunity costs of participant labor, savings from reduced crime, and health-care costs. The major external benefit (but still less than 10 percent of total benefits) was the savings from avoided crime. Interestingly, participants on average used more medical care than controls did, therefore medical costs fall in the net cost category. This offset program provides benefits equivalent to those accruing from avoided crime. Friedman estimated positive social net benefits for the average participant (and a benefit-cost ratio of 1.64). He also estimated net benefits from the social perspective by including transfers and excluding benefits to participants, finding smaller but still positive net benefits and a benefit-cost ratio of 1.13.

Steve Aos and his colleagues at WSIPP analyzed 571 evaluations of adult corrections, juvenile corrections, and prevention programs (2006; see also our review of the application of CBA to juvenile justice). They used a two-step approach. First, based on a meta-analysis of studies of existing programs, they projected impacts, primarily changes in crime rates. These rates were then applied to the relevant target populations in Washington to make predictions about what would happen if the programs were adopted there. Second, they estimated the social costs, benefits, and net benefits on a per participant basis for the programs. They limited the benefits to those resulting from changes in crime, however, and did not include benefits such as improved mental and physical health, less drug abuse, and increased productivity. It is noteworthy that they used marginal rather than average operating costs for criminal justice system units. They identified ten adult programs that appeared to offer positive net benefits, ranging from vocational education in prison to electronic monitoring as an alternative to jail time; several programs that appeared to generate negative net benefits, including sex offender treatment in prison with aftercare and surveillance-oriented (as opposed to treatment-oriented) intensive supervision; and six programs for youth offenders in the juvenile offender system that they believe offered larger net benefits than the most cost-beneficial adult programs.

John Roman and his colleagues performed a CBA of Maryland's Reentry Partnership Initiative (REP), which targets prisoners returning to specific Baltimore neighborhoods (2007). Public and community organizations coordinate a variety of services, including housing assistance, substance abuse treatment, mental health counseling, education, and vocational training to the prisoners being released. Case managers and community advocates support reentry for up to two years after release. As with the Aos, Miller, and Drake analysis, the only benefit category was avoided crime-related costs (2006). Although REP reduced the total number of arrests by only a small amount, it resulted in many fewer arrests for homicide and attempted homicide. The analysis thus showed fairly large per participant reductions in social costs. The authors assessed the use of real resources by REP in-house, program partners, and subcontractors. Combining the benefit and cost estimates resulted in net benefits of about $21.5 thousand per REP participant, and a cost-benefit ratio of approximately 3.

Affordable Housing

In chapter 9, Lance Freeman eloquently argues that decent and affordable housing proximate to economic opportunities is critical to the successful development of human capital. He points out that the affordability of housing—and therefore interventions to increase affordability—intersects with the development of human capital in four distinct ways, through the adequacy of physical conditions, the magnitude of cost burdens, location attributes, and possible substitutions of leisure for work and disincentives to work.

Freeman reviews the research that has documented links between the physical quality of a dwelling and human capital development and concludes that a substantial body of empirical evidence documents the link between poor housing quality and adverse physical and mental health outcomes. He argues that Janet Currie and Aaron Yellowitz and Sandra Newman and Joseph Harkness have provided consistent, albeit limited, evidence that excessive cost burdens are detrimental to human capital development (Currie and Yellowitz 2000; Newman and Harkness 2002). Freeman finds that both quasi-experimental and experimental studies have attempted to document the role one's immediate environs play in determining life chances. Quasi-experimental studies have generally found people living in poorer neighborhoods have lower levels of cognitive development and educational attainment, have fewer ties to employed persons, are more likely to be unemployed, and have lower earnings. These findings are consistent with the idea that location matters for the development of human capital.

Because housing programs can encourage substitution of leisure for work and consequently discourage work, they also have the potential to reduce human capital development. For example, because housing assistance raises the implicit income of recipients, the recipients may substitute leisure for work. In addition, because most housing assistance programs are means tested, the tax on earnings is implicit. If household income increases, the household may have to pay a larger of share of its housing costs or lose its eligibility for housing assistance. Both forces act as a work disincentive for housing assistance recipients. Because work experience is an important component of human capital formation, the result could be to reduce human capital. Overall, Freeman concludes that the empirical evidence on this question is inconclusive.

The common policy interventions available to make housing more affordable to those with low incomes include public housing, income-based rent subsidies, incentives to induce private supply of low-rent housing (such as tax credits), regulations to induce the supply of low-rent housing in higher-rent locations (inclusive zoning), and supported housing for targeted groups. Subsidies can also be targeted specifically at placing low-income recipients into higher-income neighborhoods. Possibly, rent control could also be considered to be an affordable housing policy, though we consider this to be a stretch in light of its adverse implications for aggregate supply and access to supply by lower-income persons.

In our own review of the CBA literature, we found that CBAs of affordable housing interventions are virtually nonexistent except for those that analyze rent controls. Bengt Turner and Stephen Malpezzi identified numerous rent control CBAs and demonstrated an empirical consensus that these studies show negative net benefits (2003). We note, however, that these studies are usually narrow in impact focus and generally do not incorporate human capital implications. Apart from rent control, a number of analyses have focused on subsidized provision of housing to people with mental illness, including CEA and fiscal analysis, both of which we considered in our review of mental health interventions (Rosenheck et al. 2003; Culhane, Metraux, and Hadley 2002).

Aside from these analyses, CBA has not been widely applied to interventions intended to make housing more affordable for low-income families. Much more needs to be done.

Freeman set out an appropriate conceptual framework for such studies that consider not only the impacts on participants, but also the effects their moves have on origin and destination neighborhoods (see also Johnson, Ladd, and Ludwig 2002).

Work Incentives

In chapter 10, Robert Lerman suggests that policymakers concerned with low levels of family and individual income have usually focused on expanding jobs and lowering unemployment. He makes the case, however, that it is equally important to help disadvantaged people get work at adequate wages. A major complication is that both jobs and wages depend on productivity and market demand, whereas wage adequacy relates more to family size and total family income. Government policies do recognize this distinction. Emphasis is typically on schooling, training, and low-wage work experience for young workers who can forgo current income. For low-wage workers who must support a family, the policy emphasis is either on helping workers to increase their skills and raise their wages or on combining earned income with income from public supplementary benefits. The former programs—generically known as welfare-to-work programs—are also the focus of the chapters by Michael Wiseman and David Greenberg discussed earlier.

Interventions that focus on supplementing income, however, face the problem that income supplements almost always result in work disincentives. In extreme cases, workers can be locked into welfare traps, where benefits strongly discourage low-wage work, but not working limits work experience and erodes skills. This can result in a vicious circle of even lower wages and even weaker incentives to work (Coe et al. 1998). Because of state variations in tax rates and policies, it is extremely difficult to generalize about the aggregate impact of these disincentives except to say that they are highly variable, depending on the state of residence, family circumstances, and on the specific changes in hours worked.

Apart from training, Lerman considers two major categories of interventions, work-conditioned income transfers and wage subsidies, and employer wage subsidies. Work-conditioned income subsidies to workers have been proposed as a way to increase the incomes of low-wage individuals without reducing their incentive to work. One approach is to impose work requirements within welfare or income-tested benefit programs. To offset the work disincentives that arise when providing income support and phasing out benefits as people raise their earnings, the program requires that beneficiaries prove their willingness to work by taking an existing job or working at a subsidized job.

Another approach is to provide benefits that increase with the work effort of recipients over some range of worked hours. Lerman believes that this approach was not implemented directly partly because of concerns about potential fraud. Instead, the United States has adopted the Earned Income Tax Credit (EITC). The EITC boosts the earnings of families with children by paying a subsidy equal to a share of earnings up to some threshold level that then phases out over some range of earnings. Over the initial range, each \$1 of earnings increases the subsidy payment, thereby raising the worker's return to work. In 2006, the EITC subsidy rate amounted to 40 percent for families with two or more children up to a maximum of approximately \$4,500 per year. Lerman concludes that there is a research consensus that the subsidy contributes significantly to increasing the employment of single mothers and is a critical component of a making-work-pay agenda for low-income families with children.

Yet another approach to raising wage rates is to subsidize the wage employers pay. The United States has implemented several employer wage subsidy schemes, including the New Jobs Tax Credit (NJTC), the Targeted Jobs Tax Credit (TJTC), the Work Opportunity Tax Credit, and the Welfare-to-Work Tax Credit. These subsidies lower the cost of hiring workers without lowering wages, thereby encouraging employers to increase their demand for workers. Subsequently, a variety of employer subsidies targeted at specific groups of workers have been tried at the federal and state levels. Lerman argues that the employer wage subsidies face special problems for three reasons. First, untargeted wage subsidies are unlikely to be effective in reaching needy groups. Second, targeted wage subsidies are costly to administer and firms receive subsidies for some of their workers but not others doing the same job. Third, target group members may be stigmatized, making firms wary of hiring people that the government sees as requiring compensatory payments. Lerman concludes that employer participation has been extremely low in the TJTC and in state grant diversion programs where employers are paid to hire welfare recipients, but he believes that wage subsidies as part of an overall training, counseling, and support service strategy may be more successful.

Few CBAs have been undertaken on work incentive interventions. The major exception is Job Corps, which targets disadvantaged youths, providing them with a package of services, including vocational skills, classroom training, and health care. Typically, the services are provided at approximately 120 residential centers nationwide. Two CBAs of the Job Corps conducted more than twenty years apart are exemplary. Using data from a Mathematica Policy Research evaluation of the Job Corps, David Long and his colleagues conducted a CBA that is commendable in its comprehensive approach to benefits and costs, its creative piecing together of needed shadow prices, its care in handling transfers, and its disaggregation of net benefits to society into those accruing to program participants and those accruing to the rest of society (Long, Mallar, and Thornton 1981). They found positive net social benefits, but slightly negative net benefits to the rest of society.

Peter Schochet and his colleagues have also provided a commendable CBA of Job Corps (Schochet, McConnell, and Burghardt 2003). They took, like Long and his colleagues, a comprehensive approach to benefits and costs. Perhaps reflecting a change in the times, they even expanded the benefit categories to include avoided crime against program participants. Their follow-up period was up to four years after random assignment of study participants into Job Corps participation and control groups.

The initial analysis relied on responses to surveys administered to participants. The researchers observed that productivity gains did not appear to decline between years three and four of the follow-up. Based on this observation and several other pieces of supporting evidence, they assumed that the fourth-year gains would persist each year for the rest of the Job Corps participants' working lives. With this assumption, the Job Corps offered net benefits of approximately $17 thousand per participant and a benefit-cost ratio greater than 2.

The researchers also assembled administrative data on earnings of study participants from annual Social Security earnings reported by employers to the Internal Revenue Service and the Social Security Administration and quarterly wage reports by employers to state unemployment insurance agencies. Analyses of these data questioned the persistence of productivity gains. Rather than full persistence, the analysis suggested that gains decayed at a rate of approximately 68 percent per year. Because productivity gains projected over the working lives of participants accounted for the bulk of program benefits, applying this decay rate resulted in net benefits of approximately negative $10,000 per participant.

Welfare-to-Work

In chapter 11, Michael Wiseman considers several integrated interventions for increasing the movement of people from welfare to work: financial intermediation provided by third-parties to low-income families, transitional incentives to reduce benefit reductions from entry into employment, and interventions aimed at those who are dependent because of disabilities. For each of these, he proposes a demonstration that would provide the empirical bases for CBA.

The motivation behind providing financial intermediation through third parties is that the parties would serve as agents for low-income families, helping them qualify for public benefits such as food stamps and encouraging them to build savings, especially those receiving the earned income tax credit. Wiseman envisions the services being provided by firms such as H&R Block. The third party would play a role similar to financial advisors to middle-income families, except that their primary focus would be on helping families build rather than on helping allocate a portfolio.

It has long been recognized that the many government programs for low-income families, each with its own income eligibility requirements, can result in substantial benefit reductions as earnings increase. Indeed, the reductions may more than offset the income gains, leaving families financially worse off, creating a disincentive to work. Wiseman believes that the best way to reduce these disincentives, such as phasing out benefits as a function of job tenure rather than as a function of income, would be best determined by state-level experimentation. An explicit federal program to encourage such experimentation might have the added benefit of contributing to greater policy experimentation capacity within the welfare system.

Many low-income people have disabilities that may eventually qualify them for the federal Supplemental Security Income (SSI). Wiseman argues that the SSI eligibility determination process may discourage rehabilitation and either slow or stop movement to self-support for some people. He proposes a demonstration, similar to that being undertaken as an alternative to the Supplemental Security Disability Income (SSDI) program the federal government offers, that provides support to the disabled without means testing. Those seeking to qualify for SSI must stay out of the labor force to establish that their disability is severe enough to preclude substantial gainful employment. Those who fail to establish eligibility often find their welfare benefits exhausted and their labor market potential reduced. Wiseman proposes identifying welfare recipients who are potential candidates for SSI and providing them with early work-oriented support to encourage those who are employable to not stay out of the labor force to establish eligibility.

In his chapter 12 review of CBAs in the welfare-to-work area, David Greenberg considers additional interventions. All these are multidimensional and often include work incentives. Typically they include one or more of the following elements: work requirements, remedial education, vocational training in occupational skills, subsidies to private sector employers to hire program participants and provide them with on-the-job training, and subsidized work-experience positions at government or nonprofit agencies to give participants an opportunity to build an employment record and acquire work skills. Some welfare-to-work programs also provide financial incentives, which usually reduce the amount by which welfare benefits fall as earnings rise, thereby increasing the amount of transfer payments that recipients can keep. Nearly all welfare-to-work and training programs also provide job search assistance and placement. Financial support, child care, personal and career counseling, and expense reimbursements during training are sometimes provided.

In contrast to most other areas considered in this volume, Greenberg finds that CBAs of training programs for disadvantaged workers are numerous and that most have been performed on mandatory welfare-to-work programs targeted at welfare recipients, probably because most of the target groups of these programs are low income and because the two key benefits of these programs—earnings increases and reductions in transfer payments—can be measured with administrative data, greatly reducing the costs of conducting CBAs. He also points out that the evidence from these CBAs is relatively convincing because many build on random assignment experiments, which result in more accurate estimates of program costs and benefits. However, variations in the components of programs means that this large number of CBAs is slightly deceptive in that findings do not have quite the robustness one might expect.

Greenberg reprises a review he completed with Andreas Cebulla that examined seventy-one welfare-to-work programs targeted at the Aid to Families with Dependent Children (AFDC) population and evaluated using random assignment (2007). Using meta-analysis, they assessed the forty-nine sets of available CBA findings and concluded that the costs of a typical program probably exceeded its benefits from the perspective of the government, but those assigned to the programs and society as a whole appeared to have reaped modest positive net benefits. They did find individual programs that were very cost-beneficial. They also found that programs with financial work incentives provided considerably larger net benefits to welfare recipients than those without such incentives. The benefits were offset by the cost to government, however, suggesting that these incentives provide a nearly cost-neutral method of transferring income to low-wage workers. They also concluded that their findings imply that less successful welfare-to-work programs might be made more cost-beneficial by dropping vocational training and basic education as program components, leaving mainly lower cost components, such as mandated job search and sanctions along with (more costly) financial work incentives.

CONCLUSION

The authors of these chapters have identified a number of promising interventions. With only a few exceptions, such as substance abuse treatment, these interventions have only occasionally been subjected to CBA to assess their efficiency. We therefore do not have a sound basis for offering advice about how to choose among the many possible ways to invest in human capital. In the next (and final) chapter, we propose an agenda for broadening and improving the application of CBA to social policy interventions.

REFERENCES

Aos, Steve, Roxanne Lieb, Jim Mayfield, Marna Miller, and Annie Penucci. 2004. *Benefits and Costs of Prevention and Early Intervention Programs for Youth.* Olympia: Washington State Institute for Public Policy.

Aos, Steve, Marna Miller, and Elizabeth Drake. 2006. *Evidence-Based Public Policy Options to Reduce Future Prison Construction, Criminal Justice Costs, and Crime Rates.* Olympia: Washington State Institute for Public Policy.

Aos, Steve, Marna Miller, and Jim Mayfield. 2007. *Benefits and Costs of K-12 Educational Policies: Evidence-Based Effects of Class Size Reductions and Full-Day Kindergarten.* Document 07-03-2201. Olympia: Washington State Institute for Public Policy.

Anguera, Ricard. 2006. "The Channel Tunnel—An Ex Post Evaluation." *Transportation Research Record Part A* 40, 291-315.

Barnett, W. Steven, and Leonard N. Masse. 2007. "Comparative Benefit-Cost Analysis of the Abecedarian Program and Its Policy Implications." *Economics of Education Review* 26(1): 113-25.

Barrett, Barbara, Sarah Byford, and Martin Knapp. 2005. "Evidence on the Cost-Effectiveness of Treatments for Depression: A Systematic Review." *Journal of Affective Disorders* 84(1): 1-13.

Belfield, Clive, Milagros Nores, Steven Barnett, and Lawrence Schweinhart. 2006. "The High/Perry Preschool Program: Cost-Benefit Analysis Using Data from the Age-40 Follow-up." *Journal of Human Resources* 41(1): 162-90.

Belenko, Steven, Nicholas Patapsis, and Michael T. French. 2005. "Economic Benefits of Drug Treatment: A Critical Review of the Evidence for Policy Makers." http://www.nsula.edu/laattc/documents/EconomicBenefits_2005Feb.pdf.

Belman, Dale, and John S. Heywood. 2004. "Public-Sector Wage Comparability: The Role of Earnings Dispersion." *Public Finance Review* 32(6): 567-87.

Bender, Keith. 2003. "Testing Equality between the Public and Private Sector Earnings Distribution." *Economic Inquiry* 41(1): 62-79.

Bhattacharya, Jayanta, Janet Currie, and Steven J. Haider. 2006. "Breakfast of Champions? The School Breakfast Program and the Nutrition of Children and Families." *Journal of Human Resources* 41(3): 445-66.

Boardman, Anthony E., David Greenberg, Aidan R. Vining, and David Weimer. 1997. "Plug-in Shadow Price Estimates for Policy Analysis." *Annals of Regional Science* 31(4): 299-324.

Boardman, Anthony E., Wendy L. Mallery, and Aidan R. Vining. 1994. "Learning from *Ex Ante/Ex Post* Cost-Benefit Comparisons: The Coquihalla Highway Example." *Socio-Economic Planning Sciences* 28(2): 65-84.

Boardman, Anthony E., Aidan R. Vining, and W. W. Waters. 1993. "Costs and Benefits through Bureaucratic Lenses: Example of a Highway Project." *Journal of Policy Analysis and Management* 12(3): 532-55.

Caldwell, Michael F., Michael Vitacco, and Gregory J. Van Rybroek. 2006. "Are Violent Delinquents Worth Treating? A Cost-Benefit Analysis." *Journal of Research in Crime and Delinquency* 43(2): 148-68.

Cartwright, William S. 2000. "Cost-Benefit Analysis of Drug Treatment Services: Review of the Literature." *The Journal of Mental Health Policy and Economics* 3(1): 11-26.

Clarke, Philip M. 1998. "Cost-Benefit Analysis and Mammographic Screening: A Travel Cost Approach." *Journal of Health Economics* 17(6): 767-87.

Coe, Norma, Gregory Acs, Robert Lerman, and Keith Watson. 1998. "Does Work Pay? An Analysis of Work Incentives under TANF." *Assessing the New Federalism* Occasional Paper 9. Washington, DC: The Urban Institute.

Culhane, Dennis P., Stephen Metraux, and Trevor Hadley. 2002. "Public Service Reductions Associated with Placement of Homeless Persons with Severe Mental Illness in Supportive Housing." *Housing Policy Debate* 13(1): 107–63.

Currie, Janet, and Aaron Yelowitz. 2000. "Are Public Housing Projects Good for Kids?" *Journal of Public Economics* 75(1): 99–124.

Daley, Marilyn, Milton Argeriou, Dennis McCarty, James J. Callahan, Jr., Donald S. Shepard, and Carol N. Williams. 2000. "The Costs of Crime and the Benefits of Substance Abuse Treatment for Pregnant Women." *Journal of Substance Abuse Treatment* 19(4): 445–58.

Deng, Lan. 2005. "The Cost-Effectiveness of the Low-Income Housing Tax Credit Relative to Vouchers: Evidence from Six Metropolitan Areas." *Housing Policy Debate* 16(3/4): 469–511.

Department for Work and Pensions. 2007. "The DWP ALMP Cost Benefit Framework. CBF: Guidance and Technical Methodology." Unpublished manuscript. London.

Devaney, Barbara, Linda Bilheimer, and Jennifer Score. 1992. "Medicaid Costs and Birth Outcomes: The Effects of Prenatal WIC Participation and the Use of Prenatal Care." *Journal of Policy Analysis and Management* 11(4): 573–92.

Diener, Alan, Bernie O'Brien, and Amiram Gafni. 1998. "Health Care Contingent Valuation Studies: A Review and Classification of the Literature." *Health Economics* 7(4): 313–26.

Fass, Simon M., and Chung-Ron Pi. 2002. "Getting Tough on Juvenile Crime: An Analysis of Costs and Benefits." *Journal of Research in Crime and Delinquency* 39(4): 363–99.

Fleming, Michael F., Marlon P. Mundt, Michael T. French, Linda Baier Manwell, Ellyn A. Stauffacher, and Kristen Lawton Barry. 2002. "Brief Physician Advice for Problem Drinkers: Long-Term Efficacy and Benefit-Cost Analysis." *Alcoholism: Clinical and Experimental Research* 26(1): 36–43.

French, Michael T. 2000. "Economic Evaluation of Alcohol Treatment Services." *Evaluation and Program Planning* 23(1): 27–39.

French, Michael T., Kathryn E. McCollister, Stanley Sacks, Karen McKendrick, and George De Leon. 2002. "Benefit Cost Analysis of a Modified Therapeutic Community for Mentally Ill Chemical Abusers." *Evaluation and Program Planning* 25(2): 137–48.

Friedman, Lee S. 1977. "An Interim Evaluation of the Supported Work Experiment." *Policy Analysis* 3(2): 147–70.

Gourney, Kevin, and Julia Brooking. 1995. "The Community Psychiatric Nurse in Primary Care: An Economic Analysis." *Journal of Advanced Nursing* 22(4): 769–78.

Greenberg, David, and Andreas Cebulla. 2007. "The Cost-Effectiveness of Welfare-to-Work Programs: A Meta-Analysis." Unpublished manuscript.

Greenberg, David, and Abigail Davis. 2007. "Evaluation of the New Deal for Disabled People: The Cost and Cost-Benefit Analyses." *DWP* Research Report 431. London: Department for Work and Pensions.

Greenberg, David H., Charles Michalopoulos, and Philip K. Robbins. 2003. "A Meta-Analysis of Government-Sponsored Training Programs." *Industrial and Labor Relations Review* 57(1): 31–53.

Greenwood, Peter W. 2005. *Changing Lives: Delinquency Prevention as Crime Control Policy.* Chicago: University of Chicago Press.

Hahn, Robert W., Katrina Kosec, Peter J. Neumann, and Scott Wallsten. 2006. "What Affects the Quality of Economic Analysis for Life-Saving Investments?" *Risk Analysis* 26(3): 641–55.

Hall, Wayne, and Rosalie L. Pacula. 2003. *Cannabis Use and Dependence: Public Health and Public Policy.* Melbourne, AU: Cambridge University Press.

Harwood, Henrick J., Deepti Malhotra, Christel Villarivera, Connie Liu, Umi Chong, and Jawaria Gilani. 2002. *Cost Effectiveness and Cost Benefit Analysis of Substance Abuse Treatment: A Literature Review.* Falls Church, VA: The Lewin Group.

Johnson, Michael P., Helen F. Ladd, and Jens Ludwig. 2002. "The Benefits and Costs of Residential Mobility Programmes for the Poor." *Housing Studies* 17(1): 125–38.

Karoly, Lynn A., M. Rebecca Kilburn, and Jill S. Cannon. 2005. *Early Childhood Interventions: Proven Results, Future Promise.* Santa Monica, CA: RAND Corporation.

Kleiman, Mark A. R. 2004. "Costs and Benefits of Immunotherapies or Depot Medications for the Treatment of Drug Abuse." In *"Behavioral, Ethical, Legal, and Social Implications of Immunotherapies and Depot Medications for Treating Drug Addiction,* ed. Henrick Harwood. Washington, DC: National Academy Press.

Lai, L. Leanne, and Alan L. Sorkin. 1998. "Cost Benefit Analysis of Pharmaceutical Care in a Medicaid Population—from a Budgetary Perspective." *Journal of Managed Care Pharmacy* 4(3): 303–8.

Levin, Henry M., Clive Belfield, Peter Muennig, and Cecillia Rouse. 2007. "The Public Returns to Public Educational Investments in African-American Males." *Economics and Education Review* 26(6): 699–708.

Logan, T. K., William H. Hoyt, Kathryn E. McCollister, Michael T. French, Carl Leukefeld, and Lisa Minton. 2004. "Economic Evaluation of Drug Court: Methodology, Results, and Policy Implications." *Evaluation and Program Planning* 27(4): 381–96.

Long, David A., Charles D. Mallar, and Craig V. D. Thornton. 1981. "Evaluating the Benefits and Costs of the Job Corps." *Journal of Policy Analysis and Management* 1(1): 55–76.

Lo Sasso, A. T., K. Rost, and A. Beck. 2006. "Modeling the Impact of Enhanced Depression Treatment on Workplace Functioning and Costs: A Cost-Benefit Approach." *Medical Care* 44(4): 352–58.

Lu, Michael C., Yvonne G. Lin, Noelani M. Prietto, and Thomas J. Garite. 2000. "Elimination of Public Funding of Prenatal Care for Undocumented Immigrants in California: A Cost/Benefit Analysis." *Journal of Obstetrics and Gynecology* 182(1): 233–39.

Manski, Charles F., John V. Pepper, and Carol V. Petrie. 2001. *Informing America's Policy on Illegal Drugs: What We Don't Know Keeps Hurting Us.* Washington, DC: National Academy Press.

McCollister, Kathryn E., and Michael T. French. 2003. "The Relative Contribution of Outcome Domains in the Total Economic Benefit of Addiction Interventions: A Review of First Findings." *Addiction* 98(12): 1647–59.

McDougall, Cynthia, Mark A. Cohen, Raymond Swaray, and Amanda Perry. 2003. "The Costs and Benefits of Sentencing: A Systematic Review." *Annals of the American Academy of Political and Social Science* 587(1): 160–77.

Michalopoulos, Charles, Doug Tattrie, Cynthia Miller, Philip K. Robins, David Gyarmati, Cindy Redcross, Kelly Foley, and Reuben Ford. 2002. *Making Work Pay: Final Report on the Self-Sufficiency Project for Long-Term Welfare Recipients.* Ottawa: Social Research and Demonstration Corporation.

Neumann, Peter J. 2005. *Using Cost-Effectiveness Analysis to Improve Health Care: Opportunities and Barriers.* New York: Oxford University Press.

Newman, Sandra J., and Joseph M. Harkness. 2002. "The Long-Term Effects of Public Housing on Self-Sufficiency." *Journal of Policy Analysis and Management* 21(1): 21–43.

Reynolds, Arthur J., Judy A. Temple, Dylan L. Robertson, and Emily A. Mann. 2002. "Age 21 Cost-Benefit Analysis of the Title I Chicago Child-Parent Centers." *Educational Evaluation and Policy Analysis* 24(4): 267–303.

Riccio, James, Daniel Friedlander, and Stephen Freedman. 1994. *GAIN: Benefits, Costs, and Three-Year Impacts of a Welfare-To-Work Program.* New York: MDRC.

Ritter, Alison, and Jacqui Cameron. 2005. "A Systematic Review of Harm Reduction." *DPMP* Monograph Series. Fitzroy, VIC: Turning Point Alcohol and Drug Centre.

Roberts, Evan, Jacqueline Cumming, and Katherine Nelson. 2005. "A Review of Economic Evaluations of Community Mental Health Care." *Medical Care and Research Review* 62(5): 503–43.

Robertson, Angela A., Paul W. Grimes, and Kevin E. Rogers. 2001. "A Short-Run Cost-Benefit Analysis of Community-Based Interventions for Juvenile Offenders." *Crime & Delinquency* 47(2): 265–84.

Roman, John, Lisa Brooks, Erica Lagerson, Aaron Chalfin, and Bogdan Tereshchenko. 2007. *Impact and Cost-Benefit Analysis of the Maryland Reentry Partnership Initiative*. Washington, DC: Urban Institute Press.

Rosenheck, Robert, Wesley Kasprow, Linda Frisman, and Wen Liu-Maries. 2003. "Cost-Effectiveness of Supported Housing for Homeless Persons with Mental Illness." *Archive of General Psychiatry* 60(9): 940–51.

Schochet, Peter Z., Sheena McConnell, and John Burghardt. 2003. *National Job Corps Study: Findings Using Administrative Earnings Records Data*. Report 8140-840. Princeton, NJ: Mathematica Policy Research.

Simons, Robert A., and David S. Sharkey. 1997. "Jump-Starting Cleveland's New Urban Housing Markets: Do the Potential Fiscal Benefits Justify the Public Subsidy Costs?" *Housing Policy Debate* 8(1): 143–71.

Stern, David, Charles Dayton, Il-Woo Paik, and Alan Weisberg. 1989. "Benefit and Costs of Dropout Prevention in a High School Program Combining Academic and Vocational Education: Third Year Results from Replications of the California Peninsula Academies." *Educational Evaluation and Policy Analysis* 11(4): 405–16.

Temple, Judy A., and Arthur J. Reynolds. 2007. "Benefits and Costs of Investments in Preschool Education: Evidence from the Child-Parent Centers and Related Programs." *Economics of Education Review* 26(1): 126–44.

Turner, Bengt, and Stephen Malpezzi. 2003. "A Review of the Empirical Evidence of the Costs and Benefits of Rent Control." *Swedish Economic Policy Review* 10(2003): 11–56.

Weisbrod, Burton A. 1981. "Benefit-Cost Analysis of a Controlled Experiment: Treating the Mentally Ill." *Journal of Human Resources* 16(4): 523–48.

Welsh, Brandon C. 2004. "Monetary Costs and Benefits of Correctional Treatment Programs: Implications for Offender Reentry." *Federal Probation* 68(2): 9–13.

Welsh, Brandon C., and David P. Farrington. 2000. "Correctional Intervention Programs and Cost Benefit Analysis." *Criminal Justice and Behavior* 27(1): 115–33.

Chapter 4

An Agenda for Promoting and Improving
the Use of CBA in Social Policy

David L. Weimer and Aidan R. Vining

A variety of limitations—institutional, conceptual, and practical—hinder the wide-spread application of CBA to social policy. Promoting wider use means finding ways of loosening these constraints. Here we set out a research agenda for this project. It is both a general call to researchers and a suggestion to foundations, like the MacArthur Foundation, which sponsored their research, of how to invest their resources if they wish to contribute to the project.

We emphasize issues of valuation rather than prediction. Clearly, the validity of CBA depends on both accurately predicting the effects society values and imputing those values. We share the almost universal preference among researchers for more inferences from true experiments with random assignment of subjects into treatment and control groups. However, as policy analysts, we also recognize the disadvantages of true experiments: They are costly, require patience (and forethought), and are difficult to implement. High costs limit the number of interventions that can be assessed—basing CBAs only on true experiments would mean having fewer of them. The need for patience to plan, implement, and bring experiments to term introduces long delays between the decision to conduct the experiment and the results. Without foresight about what findings will have policy relevance in the future, the experiment may deliver fairly confident estimates of effects that have little potential for policy impact.

Of course, there is also the question of whether the integrity of the experiment can be maintained during implementation in light of administrative problems in carrying out random assignment and following subjects, the ethical problem of denying equal treatment to subjects, and the problem of a small number of experimental units when treatments are delivered at the level of the state, community, or organization rather than the individual.

CBA certainly has the strongest empirical base when its predictions come from valid experiments. Limited resources and opportunities restrict the number of experiments that can be done—David Greenberg and Mark Shroder were able to identify only 240 completed social experiments conducted in the United States through 2004 (2004). Consequently, we believe that CBA cannot realize its potential for usefully informing public policy if its practitioners shun nonexperimental evidence. CBA is most useful when it allows comparison of the full range of alternative policies for addressing some public policy problem—very accurate CBAs of only a small set of alternatives may not be as valuable as somewhat less accurate CBAs of the full set of plausible alternatives.

Most of the thrust of modern econometrics has been toward making more confident inferences from nonexperimental data, and widespread use of CBA requires that analysts understand and use such inferences. At the margin, the CBA project may be advanced more by what might be called wholesale experiments that help assess nonexperimental methods or provide estimates of important general relationships than by retail experiments that evaluate particular interventions. For example, experiments that help identify when propensity scoring provides valid comparison groups would help guide evaluators in using it as an alternative to random assignment experiments. An experimentally based estimate of an important elasticity could be widely useful. For example, the estimate of the price elasticity of demand for medical care—approximately -0.2 when nonexperimental evidence at the time gave a range of -0.1 to -2.1—from the RAND Health Insurance Experiment has value well beyond the estimated effects for the particular health insurance plans evaluated (Manning et al. 1987). Although the validity of its findings has been challenged, the RAND Health Insurance Experiment is widely viewed as showing the potential value of general findings from well-planned experiments (Nyman 2007).

Our primary focus on valuation assumes already strong academic incentives to improve experimental and nonexperimental empirical methods. Scholarly journals place a high value on methodological innovation, which in turn encourages researchers to seek ever more clever ways of making inferences from available data. It may also encourage innovative methods of valuation, but not necessarily in response to the sorts of issues faced in the routine application of CBA. We see potentially large payoffs to the CBA project from giving explicit attention to the weaknesses in valuation that might be strengthened through research. In particular, we argue for investment in developing plausible ranges for a number of critical shadow prices. Multiple studies, using a variety of approaches, are desirable if confidence is to be built in the estimates and if their plausible ranges are to be narrowed. Sensitivity analyses should routinely take account of these ranges in assessing the certainty of net benefit estimates.

Our agenda for research draws on the expert reports and CBA assessments presented in parts 2 and 3 as well as our own experience in doing, teaching, and researching CBA. The items range from a broad institutional issue to specific shadow prices that, if available to practitioners as plug-ins, would make CBA feasible for more interventions by more practitioners.

INSTITUTIONALIZING CBA AT THE STATE AND LOCAL LEVELS

Government demand for CBA has always played a role in its development and use. Beginning with the U.S. Army Corps of Engineers during the early years of the twentieth century and codified by the U.S. Flood Control Act of 1936, the federal government required that water resource projects be evaluated in terms of the difference between their costs and benefits; the Bureau of the Budget later set out guidelines for conducting CBA of water projects in 1952 (Steiner 1974; Persky 2001). President Reagan in Executive Order 12,291 and President Clinton in Executive Order 12,866 placed demands on federal regulatory agencies to conduct CBA for major regulations that have substantially increased its use (Hahn and Sunstein 2002). The acceptance of contingent valuation surveys as evidence by federal courts in environmental damage cases has been a major impetus to the development of stated preference methods, which have made the application of CBA to environmental and other policy areas involving nonuse values feasible (Kopp, Portney, and Smith 1990). In social policy areas, especially welfare-to-work, federal agencies sometimes require evaluations to include a CBA component (Harvey, Camasso, and Jagannathan 2000, 171).

Decisions about the allocation of resources in most social policy areas, however, are made primarily by state and local governments. Were these governments to demand more CBA and invested resources to facilitate its supply, use of CBA in social policy would get a huge boost. The demand would signal opportunities for conducting CBAs with policy relevance. Currently, CBAs tend to be produced by academics for idiosyncratic reasons, typically opportunities presented in connection with research or consulting. Doing routine, but nonetheless useful, CBAs is unlikely to be consistent with their professional goals to innovatively produce general knowledge. Some institutional capacity, either within or tied closely to government, is needed to provide readily available capacity for responding to demands for CBA.

The Washington State Institute for Public Policy (WSIPP) appears to be the only example of a state investing in substantial CBA capacity and placing regular demands on that capacity. WSIPP was established in 1983 to provide objective and nonpartisan research on topics of interest to the legislature. Governed by a board of directors representing the legislature, governor, and public universities, in recent years it has produced a large number of CBAs, especially in the criminal justice and childhood development areas (Aos et al. 2001, 2004; Aos, Miller, and Drake 2006). These analyses are evidence-based in that they typically use predictions of impacts for programs from sophisticated meta-analyses of existing research. They usually compare large numbers of programs, including not only those that have been implemented in Washington but also those that could be. Thus, unlike most published CBAs that take an evaluative ex post perspective on a particular implementation of a program, the WSIPP reports take an explicit ex ante perspective on the costs and benefits that would occur if a program were implemented. Although the CBAs are not always comprehensive in terms of program benefits, they otherwise show sound application of CBA principles.

The WSIPP CBAs have been widely and favorably cited in the academic literature, especially by criminal justice scholars, indicating that they have considerable value nationally. The more interesting question is the extent to which they meet a demand by the legislature and have impact on policy. It appears that demand from the legislature for CBA, or at least broad fiscal analysis, from WSIPP continues. For example, in 2005 the legislature appropriated $50,000 to WSIPP to undertake a study of intervention, prevention, and sentencing policies that reduce the future need for prison beds, reduce costs for state and local governments, and reduce crime. The legislature recognized previous CBA studies: "The institute shall use the results of its 2004 report on cost-beneficial prevention and early intervention programs and its work on effective adult corrections programs to project total fiscal impacts under alternative implementation scenarios" (Aos, Miller, and Drake 2006, 2). In allocating $125,000 to WSIPP to develop CBAs on programs to improve K–12 schooling, the state budget notes stated: "The goal of the effort is to allow policy makers to have additional information to aid in decision making" (State of Washington 2006, 245).

There would be much more CBA of social policy if more states had organizations like WSIPP. Whether this would be socially beneficial would depend on the extent to which the WSIPP CBAs have actually influenced policy and therefore might be expected to influence policy if produced in other states. (If it were practical, one would ideally want a CBA on CBA use.) Research on WSIPP would provide a basis for predicting the impact similar organizations would have in other states. It should also determine the factors that contributed to legislative demand and organizational supply to help identify circumstances favorable to replication.

In summary, WSIPP is exceptional in terms of the quantity and quality of CBA relevant to social policy it produces. Determining the impacts of its CBAs and the reasons for those impacts would be an important step in determining the feasibility and desirability of replication in other states. How important is the nonpartisan governance structure? How important was establishing a track record? Careful research that answered these sorts of questions and demonstrated positive impacts in terms of improved legislation would also provide a resource for encouraging replication.

OPPORTUNITY COST OF PUBLIC EXPENDITURES

The chapters in this volume have identified many potentially beneficial investments in human capital in each of the social policy areas. Despite some possible selection biases—program advocates as analysts, advocacy influence in substantively oriented journals, and reviewing and editorial bias toward statistically significant effects so that the associated CBAs are based on large but not necessarily representative impacts—the preponderance of positive net benefits we found reported in published CBAs suggests that many of the suggested interventions would also show positive net benefits if assessed using common conventions with respect to the opportunity cost of public funds. Because most social policy interventions require net public expenditures, at least in the short term, pursuing all apparently cost-beneficial interventions would require much larger budgets and the greater taxation required to fund them, and consequently would not be politically feasible. However, common practice, which is widespread even beyond social policy applications, distorts net benefits and therefore the assessment of the relative efficiency of alternative policies by not using the proper opportunity cost for government expenditures.

Raising one dollar of revenue from taxes typically costs society more than one dollar of resources, for two reasons. First, with only a few exceptions, such as an excise tax on a good with a negative externality, a tax in effect creates inefficiency, or so-called deadweight loss, from taxpayers' responses to the tax. For example, income taxes may induce taxpayers to work less or take other actions with production or consumption implications to reduce their tax payments. Second, taxes require the use of real resources to collect. Economists refer to the ratio of these additional costs to the amount of revenue collected as the marginal excess tax burden (METB). Each dollar of expenditure funded by tax revenue costs society ($1+$METB) in resources. So, though in common CBA practice, a dollar raised by a government tax and transferred to an individual would involve a $1 cost to government exactly offset by a $1 benefit to the recipient, in the correct opportunity cost perspective the transfer would result in a net cost of $METB.

Economists have generally accepted the concept of METB and attempted to estimate its magnitude for major taxes in the United States and elsewhere (see Boardman et al. 2006, 428–29.) The estimated METBs for sales and property taxes tend to be lower than for the income tax. For example, in one of the first general equilibrium studies of the welfare losses associated with U.S. taxes, Charles Ballard, John Shoven, and John Whalley estimated METBs of $0.11 for excise taxes on goods other than alcohol, tobacco, and gasoline and $0.31 for income taxes (1985).

The METB is rarely used in CBA. Indeed, we found no examples of its use in the published CBAs in the social policy areas we reviewed and we know of only a few examples of its use in government-sponsored reports (see, for example, Greenberg and Davis 2007). The implication of not using the METB is that the conventionally calculated net benefits of interventions involving an excess of government expenditures over revenues will be too large, and those for interventions involving an excess of government revenue over expenditures will be too small.

Why do analysts usually ignore the METB? One possible explanation is that much of the basic practice of CBA evolved before the availability of METB estimates. When estimates became available, those seeing use of the METB as appropriate had to overcome common practice. Another explanation may be that borrowing has typically been considered the marginal source of project revenue, leading analysts to consider the opportunity costs of public investment as forgone returns to displaced private investment. Although this perspective in itself is correct, it ignores the reality that governments must eventually pay off debt through taxes. The most relevant explanations are probably practical. First, we have relatively few estimates of METB. Second, many of the estimates we do have depend on models of the economy and tax system that may be dated, though theoretical contributions to the basic concept of METB continue (Snow and Warren 1996, Dahlby 1998, Slemrod and Yitzhaki 2001). Third, in any particular context, especially at the state and local levels, it is not always clear which tax should be viewed as the marginal source of government revenue.

If shadow pricing of government expenditures using the METB is to become part of conventional practice, then research is needed to address these practical issues.

Continuing advances in computable general equilibrium models give economists better tools with which to make METB estimates. Attention should also be given to developing guidelines for determining the appropriate METB to use under different fiscal arrangements.

PRODUCTIVITY ASSESSMENT

Investments in human capital generally seek to increase productivity. The generally accepted procedure for measuring productivity gains focuses on increases in wages rather than increases in hours worked. The reasoning is that, at the margin, the value of the lost leisure (broadly defined to include household production and other nonlabor market uses of time) from additional hours of work equals the full wage (dollar wage plus the marginal value of benefits) rate. Consequently, the gain to society from the added production is offset by the loss to the worker providing it. Recognizing that the equality is actually between the value of lost leisure and the after-tax wage rate, analysts generally argue that the tax revenue resulting from additional hours worked should be counted as an external benefit—a portion of the additional production gained by others in society that is not offset by the worker's loss of leisure. A slightly more sophisticated treatment recognizes that workers most likely have upward-sloping supply schedules that indicate their marginal opportunity costs at various levels of hours worked (Greenberg and Robbins 2008). Programs that increase hours worked at the same wage rate may yield net productivity gains on the additional inframarginal units.

The simple procedure for measuring productivity gains can be readily implemented: The productivity benefit accruing to the worker is the increase in income attributable to higher wages and the external productivity benefit is the additional wage taxes paid; the more sophisticated treatment requires estimates of the worker's elasticity of supply of labor. However, implicit in either of these approaches is the strong assumption of perfectly competitive labor markets in which all workers are able to adjust the hours they work in response to changes in wage rates. Involuntary unemployment or underemployment, removal from the labor market due to mortality, and work absences due to morbidity all challenge this assumption and therefore raise questions about the proper approach for measuring productivity changes resulting from social policies.

Assuming that the opportunity cost to the worker of the marginal hour of labor equals the after tax (and after work-related expenses) wage rate does not apply to those denied access to the labor market because they cannot find employment at the minimum wage set by fiat or custom, or because they face discrimination related to some characteristic not relevant to their productivity. One could imagine that many in these situations would receive utility from the option of working. This option value would offset, to some extent, the conventionally measured opportunity cost of their labor. Interventions that give those otherwise denied access to the labor market the option of working would be undervalued using the standard approach to productivity measurement.

Labor market access is likely to be particularly important to mental health and prisoner reentry interventions. For instance, the conditions and treatments of people with severe mental illnesses may prevent them from satisfying the many demands of labor market participation (Baron and Salzer 2002). Interventions that accommodate such individuals may offer benefits in excess of those obtained from the difference between the total after tax wages and the total opportunity cost of supply as measured using a typical labor supply schedule. Indeed, Burton Weisbrod reached this conclusion in his CBA of a comprehensive community treatment program, and therefore estimated productivity benefits as total increases in earnings (1981).

The treatment of lost labor attributable to morbidity or mortality has been actively debated in the health policy literature (Olsen 1994; Weinstein et al. 1997; Olsen and Richardson 1999). The standard approach has been to treat absences from work because of illness as costing society an amount equal to the missed hours times the full wage rate. However, work by Sean Nicholson and his colleagues found that, because of team production, absences may involve social losses beyond the value of the lost labor of the ill worker (2006). The authors provided estimates of these external effects for a number of professions. The direct productivity costs of mortality, or other involuntary exit from the labor market, have generally been viewed as included in the value of quality-adjusted life years. Assuming the availability of replacement workers, the external costs of involuntary labor market exit have been assumed to equal the costs firms incur to replace the lost workers.

Beyond these issues, there is also that of the projection of productivity gains into the future. Current gains may persist, contribute to further gains, or decay over time. And, as suggested by a meta-analysis of available evidence for training programs, it may differ by demographic group (Greenberg, Michalopoulos, and Robbins 2004). Gains earned through workers' initiative may have different futures than gains induced through various social policy interventions. The Job Corps CBAs that Peter Schochet and his colleagues conducted illustrate the importance of projected gains: Assuming no decline in productivity gains leads to estimates of large positive net benefits, but assuming declines suggested by analysis of earnings data leads to estimates of large negative net benefits (2003). Administrative data on earnings provided by employer reports to the Internal Revenue Service, the Social Security Administration, and state unemployment agencies may provide an empirical basis for developing rules of thumb about decline rates for productivity gains resulting from various sources. The few long-term longitudinal studies may also provide a basis for such rules of thumb.

In view of the importance of productivity as a benefit category in many areas of social policy, comprehensive guidelines for its measurement would help improve CBAs and contribute to their comparability. More empirical work—to develop rules of thumb for productivity-related parameters such as nonwage benefits and tax rates, the externalities of network production in various categories of employment, the replacement costs of workers, and the decay rate for induced productivity gains—would increase the capability of practitioners for appropriately measuring productivity gains from social policy interventions.

SHADOW PRICE OF SCHOOLING

A variety of social policy interventions affect the level of schooling attained. Most obviously, educational interventions affect years of schooling and completion of degrees. So, too, do interventions in the areas of early childhood development, juvenile justice, mental and physical health, and substance abuse. For example, a preschool program may increase the number of years a child voluntarily stays in school, a first-offender program may require juveniles charged with crimes to complete high school degrees, or a substance abuse treatment may increase the chances a youth will remain in school. Increasing the number of years of schooling or the completion of degrees are thus sources of benefits in several important social policy areas.

Economists have provided estimates of the productivity gains to schooling as reflected in higher earnings and nonwage labor market remuneration (for a review, see Card 2001). Schooling may have other benefits, however. Some of these benefits, such as improved health, accrue directly to the schooled persons. Their families may benefit from improved consumption efficiency and effectiveness in choosing the desired number of children. Children benefit in terms of cognitive development, health, and the effectiveness of schooling, and these benefits may carry over to some extent to successive generations. Communities enjoy some external benefits, such as reductions in crime.

In a seminal article, Robert Haveman and Barbara Wolfe set out a method for valuing many of these effects within the framework of a household utility function in which schooling was one of the inputs (1984). Noting that maximizing utility requires households to purchase schooling and other inputs to produce some output such that the ratios of the marginal products of the inputs to their prices were equal, Haveman and Wolfe were able to extract shadow prices for schooling in the production of outputs as a function of the marginal productivity of some other input, such as family income. The total nonproductivity benefit of schooling could then be estimated by summing across the various outputs other than productivity to which the benefit contributes. Based on available studies, they estimated that the nonproductivity benefits of schooling were comparable to the commonly measured productivity benefits. Their estimates thus suggest that in CBA the appropriate shadow price for a year of schooling is roughly double the estimated productivity benefit.

Wolfe and Haveman not too long ago updated their review of empirical evidence relevant to the nonproductivity benefits of schooling and expanded the categories of benefits (2001). For example, studies indicate that parental education not only affects their fertility choices, but also affects the probability that teenage daughters will give birth out of wedlock (Hayward, Grady, and Billy 1992; Lam and Duryea 1999). Although Wolfe and Haveman did not provide specific monetary estimates, they do conclude that their earlier finding of comparable magnitudes of the labor and nonlabor market benefits of schooling most likely still holds (2001). Jim Davies reviewed the empirical macroeconomic literature and concludes that there are likely additional external benefits of education beyond those considered by Wolfe and Haveman that result from increases in total factor productivity (2003). Thomas Dee found empirical support for the common belief that education contributes to voter participation and support for free speech, suggesting the possibility of eventually monetizing the civic return to education (2004).

A widely accepted range of shadow prices for schooling would be an extremely valuable contribution to improving CBA. Because much of the nonlabor market benefit arises from the increased earnings that result from schooling, a practical rule of thumb for scaling up productivity gains measured in markets to the full social benefits would be also be valuable. Although it would not incorporate all the benefits of schooling, it would also not become obsolete as estimates of the benefits of productivity gains changed over time.

Shadow prices for two types of schooling gains are desirable. First, for various levels of education, the shadow price for an additional year of education would be useful in estimating the benefits of programs that increased school attendance. Analysts, for example, would in many cases find the shadow prices for additional years of schooling for those without a high school diploma and those without a college degree to be useful. Second, shadow prices for the most important educational benchmarks, which may have important signaling roles in terms of employment opportunities, would be useful in estimating the benefits of programs that increased the chances of students reaching these benchmarks. The most obvious benchmarks are high school diplomas, general education degrees, associates' degrees, and college degrees.

SHADOW PRICE OF IQ POINTS

Prenatal, nutritional, and early education interventions all have the potential to improve the cognitive development of children, which is usually measured in terms of IQ. Cognitive development, in turn, contributes to other desirable outcomes. The most obvious contributions are to education: increased school readiness, which reduces grade retention and the need for special education, higher achievement within school, more years of schooling completed, and higher graduation rates. It may also contribute to better social skills that in turn reduce delinquent and criminal behavior, teen pregnancy, and substance abuse. CBA of early childhood development interventions should take account of all these possible impacts.

The rare long-term longitudinal studies, such as those of Perry Preschool or the Carolina Abecedarian Project, measure many of the impacts that may result from improved IQ. In such studies, though there may be a small residual effect of IQ gain that is not captured, it is likely to be relatively small, especially given that IQ gains appear less likely to persist over time than scholastic success (Currie 2001). Many evaluations of early childhood interventions, however, do not follow children for long periods. Rather, the primary outcome measured is IQ gain. If CBA is to be applied to these studies, then it is desirable to have a shadow price of IQ points that captures all likely future effects. This would enable researchers to apply CBA to promising interventions without waiting the ten to twenty years necessary to begin to make assessments about teenage and adult outcomes.

How might this shadow price be developed? The starting point would be analyses of data from the longitudinal studies to relate short-term IQ gains to long-term outcomes.

The shadow prices of schooling discussed earlier could be used to link the IQ gains to monetized outcomes through schooling. That is, IQ gains would be related to schooling gains, which in turn would be shadow priced to take account of their productivity and nonproductivity benefits. There would also be potential gains in terms of fewer grade repeats and less need for special education that would not be captured in the shadow prices for schooling. Any additional impacts of IQ gain that could be identified would also be monetized and included in the IQ shadow price. The long chains of inference might very well yield such a wider range of values for the shadow price that it would be of little value. Nonetheless, having at least some idea of the value of IQ gains would be valuable, if for no other reason than assessing whether such gains could potentially be large enough to affect the sign of net benefit.

SHADOW PRICE OF MOVING A CHILD, ADULT, OR FAMILY OUT OF POVERTY

CBA compares alternative policies in terms of only one social goal: efficiency. It takes the initial distribution of wealth in society as a given and ignores the distributional consequences of the alternatives it compares. The decision rule is to adopt the combination of feasible policies that maximize net benefits without consideration of who receives the benefits and who bears the costs. Yet many social policy interventions explicitly seek to improve the circumstances of disadvantaged people. Is there no social benefit from such improvements that should be counted in CBA?

Economists have indirectly addressed this issue in proposals for distributionally weighted cost-benefit analysis (for a review, see Boardman et al. 2006, chap. 18). The primary rationale for distributional weighting is declining marginal utility of money—an additional dollar of income to a poor person produces greater marginal utility than an additional dollar of income to a rich person. Applying this rationale poses the practical problem of empirically determining the ratios of the marginal utilities of income at various wealth levels to some base level of wealth. Although there have been some clever attempts to develop weights based on politically determined tax rates and expenditure patterns, economists generally see distributionally weighted CBA as a supplement to, rather than replacement for, the standard approach (Eckstein 1961; Haveman 1965; Weisbrod 1968; Harberger 1978). In practice, using average shadow prices for normal goods indirectly introduces some distributional weighting. Economists, for example, tend to use a single shadow price for the value of a statistical life despite the empirical evidence that willingness-to-pay for reductions of mortality risk rise with income. Nonetheless, distributional values are generally considered separately from the efficiency assessment provided by CBA.

An alternative approach to finding the social value of improvements to the circumstances of the least advantaged recognizes that many people are altruistic in an economically meaningful way—that is, they are willing to pay something to help the most disadvantaged. The spontaneous outpouring of charitable giving after major disasters is one indication of such altruism. Experiments that attempt to put subjects behind a veil of ignorance in terms of the consequences of distributive policies for their own circumstances suggest general preferences for providing everyone with at least some minimum level of income (Frohlich, Oppenheimer, and Eavey 1987). To the extent that these preferences translate into willingness to pay, they can be incorporated into standard CBA.

The conceptual starting point for valuing improvements in circumstances for the least advantaged is a hypothetical (or contingent) comparison between two states of the world: the current situation and an alternative to it that differs only in terms of the number of people who are disadvantaged. For example, the alternative state might be described as having one less family with an income below the poverty line. If a person were willing to pay some amount to have the alternative over the current state, then that amount would be interpreted as the person's willingness to pay to have one fewer family in poverty. Adding these willingness-to-pay amounts over the entire population would provide a shadow price for valuing changes in the number of families in poverty resulting from alternative policy interventions.

Contingent valuation (CV) surveys could provide data for estimating such shadow prices. In the 1960s, economists began experimenting with CV surveys to estimate passive use value, the value people place on environmental goods beyond any value they derive from directly observable use value (David 1963; Ridker 1967). For example, someone may value hiking in a wilderness (use value) but also place a value on the very existence of that wilderness (passive use). Despite considerable controversy over its validity, CV developed within environmental economics during the 1980s for three reasons. First, there simply was no alternative means of measuring benefits in many applications where one might expect passive use value to be an important component of value overall. Second, random digit dialing (RDD) techniques and computer-assisted surveying technology (CATI) introduced during the previous decade provided a method for drawing random samples from a population and conducting surveys by telephone at lower cost than could be done in person. Surveying thus became a more viable option for researchers, especially for studies requiring national samples that would too expensive to conduct through in-person surveys. Third, there was an infusion of resources when U.S. federal courts gave surveys of citizen's values "rebuttable presumption" in cases involving the assessment of natural resource damages (Kopp, Portney, and Smith 1990). With potentially large damages at stake, both plaintiffs and defendants hired environmental economists to conduct CV surveys and assess their validity.

In 1993, CV received important acceptance from a blue-ribbon panel assembled by the U.S. National Oceanic and Atmospheric Administration. The panel, which included two Nobel laureates and other distinguished economists, concluded that CV could appropriately be used in natural resource damage assessment cases and provided a set of guidelines for conducting CV surveys that helped establish standards of practice and focused research on important methodological issues (Arrow et al. 1993). Since then, environmental economists have continued to refine the CV methodology (for overviews, see Bateman and Willis 1999; Haab and McConnell 2003). Although critics remain, CV is now widely used and accepted in environmental economics. It has spread to health policy (Diener, O'Brien, and Gafni 1998) and has been used to value goods ranging from sports arenas (Johnson and Whitehead 2000) to the preservation of aboriginal arti-facts (Boxall, Englin, and Adamowicz 2003). CV studies now number in the thousands (Carson 2008).

Mark Dickie and Victoria Messman illustrated how CV can be used to estimate al-truist value (2004). They assessed parents' willingness-to-pay to relieve both their own acute illness and that of their children. They estimate that parents of three-year-olds are willing to pay about three times as much to relieve their children's symptoms as they are to relieve their own. Extrapolating to even younger children suggests that the ratio may be about ten for newborns. Perhaps not surprising to those who have reared children during their teenage years, however, this ratio falls to unity by the time children reach age eighteen. That is, parents value relief of their own symptoms equally to that of their adult children's symptoms.

Using CV to develop shadow prices for the populations' altruistic value of improving the circumstances of the disadvantaged would make an important contribution to the application of CBA to social policy. Because CV requires clear descriptions of the good being valued, a relatively narrow focus on shadow prices for moving a child, an adult, or a family above the poverty line would be a good starting point. In view of the remaining controversy over CV in general, as well as over specific methods of eliciting willingness to pay, it would be unrealistic to think that convincing shadow prices could be developed from a single study. Rather, a series of CV studies using a variety of methods would be necessary and ultimately be useful if they converged on similar values. Fortunately, the fairly large number of environmental economists with advanced CV skills offers a source of appropriate researchers. A substantial commitment of government or philanthropic resources would be needed to recruit them to this task, however.

UPDATED SHADOW PRICES OF CRIMES BASED ON SOCIAL COSTS

Interventions in a number of social policy areas affect the incidence of crime. Indeed, crime reduction is one of the primary policy goals in areas such as juvenile justice, pris-oner reentry, and substance abuse. The incidence of crime may also be affected by inter-ventions in mental health, primary and secondary education, and, taking an appropri-ately long-term perspective, early childhood development. The availability of appropriate shadow prices for crimes that take account of their full social costs are thus extremely important in promoting good social policy CBA.

Analysts generally divide the costs of crime into three categories: tangible costs to victims, intangible costs to victims, and criminal justice system costs. Here we discuss the need for better shadow prices for the victim costs and later the appropriate measurement of criminal justice system costs.

The primary source for estimates of the costs of crime currently used in CBAs was produced by Ted Miller, Mark Cohen, and Brian Wiersema in 1996 for the National Institute of Justice. They estimated the costs of fatal crimes (rape, assault, arson, driving while intoxicated), child abuse (sexual, physical, emotional), nonfatal rape and sexual assault, assault or attempted assault (with and without injury), robbery or attempted robbery (with and without injury), drunk driving (with and without injury), arson (with and without injury), larceny or attempted larceny, burglary or attempted burglary, and motor vehicle or attempted motor vehicle theft. Estimates of tangible costs included property damage and loss, medical care, mental health care, police and fire services, victim services, and productivity losses. Estimates of intangible costs were based on estimates of the average value of life revealed by people's willingness to bear mortality risks and estimates of the costs of pain, suffering, fear, and lost quality of life were based on jury awards (see Cohen 1988). Overall, the effort of Ted Miller, Mark Cohen, and Brian Wiersema is one of the most important contributions to the promotion of the application of CBA to social policy interventions (1996).

Nonetheless, the social costs of crimes should be re-estimated, for three reasons. First, the estimates Miller and colleagues made rely on data from the early 1990s, data that are now more than a decade old. It is possible that the nature of crime has changed somewhat since then. Theft may involve different commodities, for example. Estimates of the statistical value of life have also changed substantially—in the early 1990s the empirical evidence pointed to estimates generally around $2.8 million to $4.2 million in 2002 dollars (Viscusi 1993). More recently they have been estimated to be around $5.5 million to $6.5 million in 2002 dollars (Viscusi and Aldy 2003; for a review that argues for a range of $2 million to $6 million, see Boardman et al. 2006, chap. 15).

Second, the estimates do not cover victimless crimes that nevertheless may be important in some social policy areas such as substance abuse. Drug addicts, for example, sometimes support themselves through prostitution, which involves enforcement costs and public health risks from the spread of sexually transmitted diseases. Andrew Rajkumar and Michael French estimated enforcement, but not external costs, for several victimless crimes, including prostitution (1997). Estimates of the full social costs of victimless crimes are needed.

Third, alternative approaches—CV surveys and housing price capitalization—to measuring intangible victim costs have been demonstrated and suggest social costs quite different from those based on jury award data (Ludwig and Cook 2001; Lynch and Rasmussen 2001). Mark Cohen and his colleagues conducted a CV survey to estimate the willingness of households to pay for reductions of the incidences of specific crimes in their communities by 10 percent (2004). The willingness-to-pay amounts enabled the researchers to estimate the social costs of several major crimes. These ex ante estimates (willingness to pay to avoid crime) were consistently higher than ex post estimates (monetized harms) of Miller, Cohen, and Wiersema, ranging from 1.6 to 2.4 times larger for serious assault to 5.5 to 9.9 times larger for armed robbery. In theory, the ex ante estimate is the correct one. In practice, one must worry about the various concerns raised about the validity of contingent valuation studies (for a review, see Boardman et al. 2006, chap. 14).

Any revisiting of Miller and colleagues should update their ex post social cost estimates and expand their coverage to victimless crimes (1996). The updating would be most useful in terms of flexibility and its legs if it provided underlying formulas in terms of important parameters, such as the value of life, wage rates (for productivity loss measurement), and medical costs, about which there is considerable uncertainty, change over time, or regional variation. More contingent valuation studies of the ex ante social costs of crime should also be undertaken to build confidence in their magnitudes and prepare for their possible use as the primary source of shadow prices for crime victimization.

MARGINAL COSTS OF CRIMINAL JUSTICE RESOURCES

Reductions in crime benefit not only those who would otherwise be victimized, but also society more broadly by reducing the real resources devoted to the criminal justice system. Analysts face the task of estimating these benefits in terms of avoided marginal costs. This task is complicated, especially for correctional resources.

The most common approach to estimating the benefits of an avoided crime is to estimate the time savings to various criminal justice system employees, typically including police, public defenders, prosecutors, judges, court staff, and probation officers, and valuing these time savings at the employees' hourly wages and benefits. A conceptual problem with this approach is that, unlike in the case of firms buying inputs and selling outputs in competitive markets, criminal justice agencies do not necessarily equate marginal cost to marginal benefit in the application of labor and other resources. The expenditure of additional employee hours could produce marginal benefits in terms of crime reduction and justice that were either smaller or larger than the full wage rate. For example, adding the time of another police officer might very well reduce crime costs to victims by more than the wages and benefits of that officer. Further, an exclusive focus on employees may result in underestimated marginal costs because nonemployees, victims, witnesses, jurors, and innocent defendants also bear time costs in the operation of the criminal justice system.

Incarceration—whether in jails, prisons, and other correctional facilities—poses the most serious challenge to measuring the marginal costs of the criminal justice system. These sorts of facilities often require large capital costs that, though sunk for any existing facility, would have to be expended if the inmate population grows to such an extent to require new construction. Average operating costs that include wages and benefits of security personnel, maintenance, and hotel services (food service and laundry), rehabilitation, and medical care may overestimate the marginal cost of adding an additional inmate to the facility in the absence of overcrowding. Adding another inmate to an already overcrowded facility could conceivably result in marginal costs larger than the average operating cost if it increased the risk of violence among prisoners or against prison personnel.

Incarceration within existing arrangements may involve large external costs. Approximately a quarter of people in the United States with HIV, and an even higher fraction with hepatitis C, passed through correctional facilities within a year (Hammett, Harmon, and Rhodes 2002). Because inmates with these infections have the potential to spread them to other inmates while incarcerated and to members of the community after release, the potential external costs are quite large. Incarceration may also impose external costs on the families of inmates, especially if it necessitates foster care of dependent children.

An issue of standing may also arise in assessing the marginal costs of jails or correctional services provided at a fee to local jurisdictions. Often these fees are based on budgetary expenditures and therefore may not correspond closely to marginal costs. For example, the fees for correctional services provided by the state of Wisconsin to counties for juveniles are based on the average costs of operation (Engle and Weimer 2005). Analysts may have difficulty convincing local governments that such fees are not the real costs society bears.

Better estimates of the marginal social costs of the use of criminal justice system resources, especially incarceration, that carefully take account of the difference between the average operating costs and marginal costs of agencies, and include marginal external costs, would increase confidence in CBAs of the many social policy areas that affect crime. Practical guidelines that analysts could apply in moving from available budgetary and average operating cost data in specific states or locales to appropriate shadow prices would also be useful.

SOCIAL COSTS OF ILLICIT DRUG CONSUMPTION

Evaluations of drug prevention or treatment interventions typically have short follow-up periods and often provide limited opportunity to observe socially relevant behaviors. Applying CBA to these interventions by shadow pricing all major effects is therefore often impractical. Most evaluations, however, can provide some estimates of changes in drug consumption at least during program participation and the follow-up. Consequently, most economic analyses are CEAs that estimate cost per unit of substance consumption reduction. Shadow prices for reductions in the consumption of illicit drugs would make it more feasible to assess and compare programs with CBA, most immediately by allowing researchers to monetize drug reduction effects in the numerous CEAs.

A number of researchers have attempted to estimate the social costs of drug use. For example, Henrick Harwood, Douglas Fountain, and Gina Livermore provided estimates of the health, productivity, crime, and other social costs of alcohol and illicit drug abuse (1999). Using these estimates, as well as other sources of information (school-based treatment evaluations, drug use surveys, and various literatures), Jonathan Caulkins and colleagues estimated the average social cost per unit of marijuana consumption, $12 per gram, and cocaine consumption, $215 per gram (2002). More recently, Tim Moore estimated the social costs in terms of health and crime effects in Australia of AU$1.10 per gram for cannabis, AU$360 per gram of cocaine, AU$13,653 per gram of opiates, and AU$6,488 per gram of amphetamines (2007). The annual social costs for dependent and nondependent users of these substances range from AU$192 for a nondependent cannabis user to AU$105,342 for a dependent opiate user.

Some care is needed in taking account of the costs of price rises to consumers of legal substances with addictive characteristics, such as tobacco and perhaps alcohol. In the common CBA approach assuming fully rational consumers, increases in the prices of these goods inflict social surplus losses on consumers (Weimer and Vining 2005, 413–25). Addiction brings into question how to measure this loss (Australian Productivity Commission 1999; Laux 2000). A contingent valuation study of the willingness of smokers to pay to eliminate their addiction suggests that only about 70 percent of the loss in consumer surplus from higher prices should be counted as a social cost (Weimer, Vining, and Thomas 2008).

More research is needed to piece together available information to develop shadow prices for alcohol and illicit drug consumption based on marginal social costs and disaggregated by type of user (nondependent versus dependent and by demographic groups such as age and sex). The process of developing these shadow prices would likely identify critical pieces of missing information that could be addressed through focused research. Narrowing the confidence bounds on these shadow prices would increase confidence in CBA comparisons among treatment and prevention programs as well as with other social policy interventions.

VALUATION OF VOLUNTEER TIME

The proper treatment of the opportunity cost of volunteer time seems conceptually straightforward. In the area of health policy, for example, the two leading sources of economic evaluation guidelines (Gold et al. 1996; Drummond et al. 2005) argue that volunteer time has an opportunity cost that should be included in program cost. That is, time spent volunteering could be used for leisure or labor. A recent review of reviews of costing studies in health policy, however, found that very few studies actually included volunteer time among the relevant program inputs (Adam, Evans, and Koopmanschap 2003). When volunteer time is included, analysts face the practical difficulty of choosing a shadow price based on the value of the services being provided or the value of the time of the donor. For example, consider a corporate executive who volunteers one hour each week washing dishes in a soup kitchen. Is the appropriate shadow price the wages that would have to be paid to a dishwasher or the effective hourly wage of the executive, which is likely many times larger? Many analysts would skirt this issue by shadow pricing as some fraction of the median wage in the local market as is usually done to value changes in commuter time.

Nonetheless, the ambiguity over the proper shadow price suggests more fundamental question: Why would someone who has skills highly valued in the marketplace volunteer to do much lower-skilled labor? The guiding principle of revealed preference requires that volunteers realize utility from the activity at least as large as their opportunity costs of time. The utility may result from being virtuous, from being perceived by others as virtuous, or from the social processes surrounding the volunteering. No matter what the specific source of utility, the act of volunteering indicates that the volunteers have willingness to pay for the volunteering experience at least as large as the opportunity costs of their time. Consequently, from this perspective, the shadow price of volunteer time may reasonably be treated as zero—the opportunity cost of the time is fully offset by the benefit realized by the volunteer. We found at least one article that explicitly considered this argument and therefore shadow priced volunteer time at both the wage rate and zero (Mukamel, Gold, and Bennett 2001). We also found several cases where the shadow pricing of volunteer time was substantively important. For example, a WSIPP study of Big Brother/Big Sister programs reported benefit-cost ratios of greater than 3 when volunteer time was shadow priced at zero but very close to 1 when volunteer time was shadow priced at the wage rate (Aos et al. 2004).

Several considerations make the revealed preference argument less clear-cut. First, one can imagine a world in which, for religious, ethical, or social pressure reasons, people committed themselves to volunteering a certain fixed number of hours per week no matter how their time was put to use. In this world, the total supply of volunteer time would be fixed so that time used for one project would not be available for another. If the total amount of volunteer time offered were less than the total amount demanded, using the time for one project would deny it to some other. It would be reasonable to argue that the proper opportunity cost of volunteer time would be its contribution to value in its next best use.

Second, organizations making use of volunteer time bear the costs of recruiting, training, and monitoring volunteers. These costs should be included in the shadow price of volunteer time. Further, externalities may be involved in these functions. An organization that provides poor experiences for volunteers may depress the total supply of volunteers in the community. Wasting volunteers' time or assigning volunteers tasks that members of the organization see as undesirable or low priority may encourage some volunteers to withdraw their contributions of time.

Third, donated time may differ in the extent to which it provides utility to the donor. In contrast to volunteering to help a community organization, which may involve substantial positive social interaction, easily limited commitments of time, and easy termination, providing unpaid care to a family member with, say, Alzheimer's disease, may offer little positive social interaction, inflexible commitments of time, and difficult termination. Such voluntary caregiving may not provide only minimal psychic benefits that would be readily sacrificed if paid care were economically feasible. In these cases, the wage rate of caregivers would probably be a better estimate of the opportunity cost of time than zero. Similar arguments apply whenever volunteer time is not really voluntary (requirements that parents volunteer a certain number of hours to school activities, for example).

Having a greater consensus on the proper method for valuing volunteer time strikes us as important, especially when comparing faith-based and other privately delivered social services to those delivered by government agencies. More sophisticated guidelines that took account of the nature of the volunteering would be valuable to analysts.

PROPER HANDLING OF UNCERTAINTY WITH MONTE CARLO ANALYSES

Very few of the CBAs we reviewed provided adequate sensitivity analysis for conveying the levels of certainty one should have in the reported net benefits. When sensitivity analyses were provided, they usually focused on the consequences of uncertainty in only one or two important parameters. CBAs in the social policy areas would convey more, and more appropriate, information if they routinely included sensitivity analyses that take account of the multiple sources of uncertainty in the predicted effects of interventions and their shadow prices.

Unlike the other agenda items we discuss, this is a call for better practice rather than more research. CBA analysts already have available a flexible and appropriate tool for running sensitivity analysis and conveying it to readers: Monte Carlo analysis. The logic of Monte Carlo analysis is straightforward and relatively easy to implement with readily available spreadsheet, statistical, or specialized software. Net benefits are calculated for a large number, typically in the thousands, of trials. In each trial, values are randomly drawn from the assumed distributions of the uncertain parameters. The net benefits for the trials can be displayed as a histogram, which can be interpreted as an estimate of the distribution of net benefits. The mean value of the trials is an estimate of the expected net benefits of the intervention. The fraction of the trials with negative net benefits is an estimate of the probability that the intervention would be inefficient.

The expected net benefits from a Monte Carlo analysis can differ substantially from the expected net benefits calculated by the standard procedure of using point estimates at the centers of estimated distributions. CBA calculations often involve multiplying uncertain parameters, typically an estimated effect and a shadow price. Sometimes one estimated parameter is divided by another estimated parameter, making it even more likely that using center points for the parameters will yield expected values far from those that one would estimate from a Monte Carlo analysis that allows the random processes to play out appropriately. The division problem makes Monte Carlo analysis especially valuable for CEA and the calculation of benefit-cost ratios (for an illustration, see Boardman et al. 2006, 470–72).

The low cost and flexibility of computing makes it possible for any analyst to conduct a Monte Carlo analysis. Although specialized software is available, it can be easily implemented using the capabilities of most statistical packages and, with a bit more effort, the commonly available spreadsheets. The standard errors of estimated effects provide a basis for specifying Student's t or normal distributions from which to draw values in the trials. (More sophisticated analyses may even take account of the estimated correlations among estimated parameters.) The same approach can be taken for shadow prices based on statistical estimations. When the statistical distributions of the estimates of shadow prices are not available, their uncertainty can be represented by drawing from a uniform distribution over a plausible range.

A few uncertain parameters may be better handled across several rather than within a single Monte Carlo analysis. For example, because of disagreement over the appropriate social discount rate, analysts may wish to treat it as uncertain. They may find it informative to display different net benefit distributions for different social discount rates. The shape of each distribution would reflect the uncertain effects and shadow prices; the comparison across distributions would show the consequences of different assumed discount rates.

We do not advocate abandoning commonly used forms of sensitivity analysis, such as partial sensitivity analysis focusing on the consequences of different values of important parameters for net benefits or break-even analysis calculating the values of key parameters that make net benefits zero. Nonetheless, the many uncertainties in impacts and their shadow prices involved in CBAs of social programs make Monte Carlo analysis the most appropriate approach. Because modern computing capabilities also make this method feasible for almost anyone who has the skill to conduct a credible CBA, it should be part of every CBA.

CONCLUSION

We have set out an ambitious agenda for promoting more widespread and appropriate use of CBA to assess the efficiency of social policy interventions. The agenda items pose different degrees of difficulty and novelty. At one extreme, routinely employing Monte Carlo analysis to take account and convey levels of uncertainty is neither difficult nor novel and can be implemented by analysts with readily available tools and without any additional research. At the other extreme, developing plausible ranges of shadow prices for moving people out of poverty is both very difficult, at least to do it convincingly, and novel, yet nonetheless of potentially great value to analysts in the assessment of social policy. Developing shadow prices for IQ points is also relatively novel and even more difficult. Actually monetizing the nonmarket benefits of schooling is somewhat less novel, but doing so would also be difficult yet particularly valuable. Because of previous efforts, updating estimates of the crime-related shadow prices and the marginal excess tax burden would be somewhat less difficult, but, though not novel, still important in light of the many social policy interventions that affect crime and net public expenditures.

Two of the agenda items involve conceptual issues that may possibly be informed by empirical research. The treatment of productivity gains that result from the employment of those who would otherwise be excluded from the labor market requires one to make assumptions about the value of the labor market access as an offset to lost leisure. One could imagine research directed at estimating this value for a relevant population. The treatment of volunteer time as a program input hinges on determining the appropriate opportunity cost, which in turn may depend on the nature of the supply of volunteer time. Health economists have taken the lead in addressing these issues, but how they are resolved has much broader implications and therefore deserves more attention from public finance economists working in other fields as well.

All of these agenda items except one operate primarily on the supply side. That is, they are intended to make it easier for analysts to do social policy CBAs and to do them well, or at least better. Research on the role of WSIPP involves the demand side as much as the supply side. Shifting the supply curve for CBA outward will not greatly increase the quantity of CBA if the demand curve for CBA is relatively inelastic. Shifting the demand curve could have even larger effects. A better understanding of the role of WSIPP, especially the extent to which past performance has shifted the demand for CBA by the Washington state legislature outward, would be valuable in informing the desirability and feasibility of replication in other states. We believe that the influence of CBA on social policy will depend substantially on the demand for it expressed by the state and local governments that make the most important decisions concerning social policy interventions.

REFERENCES

Adam, Taghreed, David B. Evans, and Marc A. Koopmanschap. 2003. "Cost-Effectiveness Analysis: Can We Reduce Variability in Costing Methods?" *International Journal of Technology Assessment in Health Care* 19(2): 407–20.

Aos, Steve, Marna Miller, and Elizabeth Drake. 2006. *Evidence-Based Public Policy Options to Reduce Future Prison Construction, Criminal Justice Costs, and Crime Rates.* Olympia: Washington State Institute for Public Policy.

Aos, Steve, Roxanne Lieb, Jim Mayfield, Marna Miller, and Annie Pennucci. 2004. "Benefits and Costs of Prevention and Early Intervention Programs." Olympia: Washington Institute for Public Policy.

Aos, Steve, Polly Phipps, Robert Barnoski, and Roxanne Lieb. 2001. "The Comparative Costs and Benefits of Programs to Reduce Crime." Olympia: Washington State Institute for Public Policy.

Arrow, Kenneth, Robert Solow, Paul Portney, Edward Leamer, Roy Radner, and Howard Schuman. 1993. "Report of the NOAA Panel on Contingent Valuation." *Federal Register* 58(10): 4601–14.

Australian Productivity Commission. 1999. *Australia's Gambling Industries,* 3 vols. Inquiry Report No. 10. Canberra: Productivity Commission. www pc.gov.au/projects/inquiry/gambling/docs/finalreport.

Ballard, Charles L., John B. Shoven, and John Whalley. 1985. "General Equilibrium Computations of the Marginal Welfare Costs of Taxes in the United States." *American Economic Review* 75(1): 128–38.

Baron, Richard C., and Mark S. Salzer. 2002. "Accounting for Unemployment among People with Mental Illness." *Behavioral Sciences and the Law* 20(6): 585–99.

Bateman, Ian J., and Kenneth G. Willis. 1999. *Valuing Environmental Preferences: Theory and Practice of the Contingent Valuation Method in the US, EU, and Developing Countries.* New York: Oxford University Press.

Boxall, Peter C., Jeffrey Englin, and Wiktor L. Adamowicz. 2003. "Valuing Aboriginal Artifacts: A Combined Revealed-Stated Preference Approach." *Journal of Environmental Economics and Management* 45(2): 213–30.

Boardman, Anthony E., David H. Greenberg, Aidan R. Vining, and David L. Weimer. 2006. *Cost-Benefit Analysis: Concepts and Practice,* 3rd ed. Upper Saddle River, NJ: Prentice Hall.

Card, David. 2001. "Estimating the Return to Schooling: Progress on Some Persistent Econometric Problems." *Econometrica* 69(5): 1127–60.

Carson, Richard. 2008. *Contingent Valuation: A Comprehensive Bibliography and History.* Northampton, MA: Edward Elgar.

Caulkins, Jonathan P., Rosalie Liccardo Pacula, Susan Paddock, and James Chiesa. 2002. *School-Based Drug Prevention: What Kind of Drug Use Does It Prevent?* Santa Monica, CA: RAND.

Cohen, Mark A.. 1988. "Pain, Suffering, and Jury Awards: A Study of the Cost of Crime to Victims." *Law and Society Review* 22(3): 537–56.

Cohen, Mark A., Roland T. Rust, Sara Steen, and Simon T. Tidd. 2004. "Willingness-to-Pay for Crime Control Programs." *Criminology* 42(1): 89–109.

Currie, Janet. 2001. "Early Childhood Education Programs." *Journal of Economic Perspectives* 15(2): 213–38.

Dahlby, Bev. 1998. "Progressive Taxation and the Social Marginal Cost of Public Funds." *Journal of Public Economics* 67(1): 105–22.

David, Robert K.. 1963. "Recreation Planning as an Economic Problem." *Natural Resources Journal* 3(2): 239–49.

Davies, Jim. 2003. "Empirical Evidence on Human Capital Externalities." *Economic Policy Institute Working Paper 2003–5*. London: University of Western Ontario.

Dee, Thomas S. 2004. "Are There Civic Returns to Education?" *Journal of Public Economics* 88(9–10): 1607–720.

Dickie, Mark, and Victoria L. Messman. 2004. "Parental Altruism and the Value of Avoiding Acute Illness: Are Kids Worth More than Parents?" *Journal of Environmental Economics and Management* 48(3): 1146–74.

Diener, Alan, Bernie O'Brien, and Amiram Gafni. 1998. "Health Care Contingent Valuation Studies: A Review and Classification of the Literature." *Health Economics* 7(4): 313–26.

Drummond, F. Michael, Mark J. Sculpher, George W. Torrance, Bernie J. O'Brien, and Greg L. Soddart. 2005. *"Methods for the Evaluation of Health Care Programmes*, 3rd ed. New York: Oxford University Press.

Eckstein, Otto. 1961. "A Survey of the Theory of Public Expenditure Criteria. In *Public Finances: Needs, Sources and Utilization*, ed. James M. Buchanan. Princeton, NJ: Princeton University Press.

Engle, Pär Jason, and David L. Weimer. 2005. "Enhancing Criminal Sentencing Options in Wisconsin: The State and County Correctional Partnership." *La Follette Policy Report* 15(1): 15–18.

Frohlich, Norman, Joe A. Oppenheimer, and Cheryl L. Eavey. 1987. "Choices of Principles of Distributive Justice in Experimental Groups." *American Journal of Political Science* 31(3): 606–36.

Gold, Marthe R., Joanna E. Siegel, Louise B. Russell, and Milton C. Weinstein. 1996. *Cost-Effectiveness in Health and Medicine*. New York: Oxford University Press.

Greenberg, David H., and Abigail Davis. 2007. "Evaluation of the New Deal for Disabled People: The Cost and Cost-Benefit Analyses." Research Report 431. Leeds, UK: Department of Work and Pensions.

Greenberg, David H., Charles Michalopoulos, and Philip Robbins. 2004. "What Happens to the Effects of Government-Funded Training Programs over Time?" *Journal of Human Resources* 39(1): 277–93.

Greenberg, David H., and Philip Robbins. 2008. "Incorporating Nonmarket Time into Benefit-Cost Analyses of Social Programs: An Application to the Self-Sufficiency Project." *Journal of Public Economics* 92(3–4): 766–94.

Greenberg, David H., and Mark Shroder. 2004. *Digest of Social Experiments*, 3rd ed. Washington, DC: Urban Institute Press.

Haab, Timothy C., and Kenneth E. McConnell. 2003. *Valuing Environmental and Natural Resources: The Economics of Non-Market Valuation*. Northampton, MA: Edward Elgar.

Hahn, Robert W., and Cass R. Sunstein. 2002. "A New Executive Order for Improving Federal Regulation? Deeper and Wider Cost-Benefit Analysis." *University of Pennsylvania Law Review* 150(5): 1489–552.

Hammett, Theodore M., Mary Patricia Harmon, and William Rhodes. 2002. "The Burden of Infectious Disease among Inmates of and Releasees from US Correctional Facilities, 1997." *American Journal of Public Health* 92(11): 1789–94.

Harberger, Arnold C. 1978. "On the Use of Distributional Weights in Social Cost-Benefit Analysis." *Journal of Political Economy* 86(2): S87–S120.

Harvey, Carol, Michael J. Camasso, and Radha Jagannathan. 2000. "Evaluating Welfare Reform Waivers under Section 1115." *Journal of Economic Perspectives* 14(4): 165–88.

Harwood, Henrick J., Douglas Fountain, and Gina Livermore. 1999. "Economic Cost of Alcohol and Drug Abuse in 1992: A Report." *Addiction* 94(5): 631–47.

Haveman, Robert. 1965. *Water Resources Investment and the Public Interest*. Nashville, TN: Vanderbilt University Press.

Haveman, Robert, and Barbara Wolfe. 1984. "Schooling and Economic Well-Being: The Role of Nonmarket Effects." *Journal of Human Resources* 19(3): 377–407.

Hayward, Mark D., William Grady, and John O. Billy. 1992. "The Influence of Socioeconomic Status on Adolescent Pregnancy." *Social Science Quarterly* 73(4): 750–72.

Johnson, Bruce K., and John C. Whitehead. 2000. "Value of Public Goods from Sports Stadiums: The CVM Approach." *Contemporary Economic Policy* 18(1): 48–58.

Kopp, Raymond J., Paul R. Portney, and V. Kerry Smith. 1990. "The Economics of Natural Resource Damages after *Ohio v. U.S. Department of the Interior*." *Environmental Law Reporter* 20(4): 10,127–10,131.

Lam, David, and Suzanne Duryea. 1999. "Effects of Schooling on Fertility, Labor Supply, and Investments in Children, with Evidence from Brazil." *Journal of Human Resources* 34(1): 160–92.

Ludwig, Jens, and Philip J. Cook. 2001. "The Benefits of Reducing Gun Violence: Evidence from Contingent-Valuation Survey Data." *Journal of Risk and Uncertainty* 22(3): 207–26.

Laux, Fritz L. 2000. "Addiction as a Market Failure: Using Rational Addiction Results to Justify Tobacco Regulation." *Journal of Health Economics* 19(4): 421–37.

Lynch, Allen K., and David W. Rasmussen. 2001. "Measuring the Impact of Crime on House Prices." *Applied Economics* 33(15): 1981–89.

Manning, Willard G., Joseph P. Newhouse, Naihua Duan, Emmitt B. Keeler, and Arleen Leibowitz. 1987. "Health Insurance and the Demand for Medical Care: Evidence from a Randomized Experiment." *American Economic Review* 77(3): 251–77.

Miller, Ted R., Mark A. Cohen, and Brian Wiersema. 1996. *Victim Costs and Consequences: A New Look*. Washington, DC: National Institute of Justice.

Moore, Tim. 2007. "Working Estimates of the Social Costs per Gram and per User for Cannabis, Cocaine, Opiates and Amphetamines." *Drug Policy Modelling Program Monograph Series* No. 14. Sydney: National Drug and Alcohol Research Centre.

Mukamel, Dana B., Heather Taffet Gold, and Nancy M. Bennett. 2001. "Cost Utility of Public Clinics to Increase Pneumococcal Vaccines in the Elderly." *American Journal of Preventive Medicine* 21(1): 29–34.

Nicholson, Sean, Mark V. Pauly, Daniel Polsky, Claire Sharda, Helena Szek, and Marc L. Berger. 2006. "Measuring the Effects of Workloss on Productivity with Team Production." *Health Economics* 15(2): 111–23.

Nyman, John A. 2007. "American Health Policy: Cracks in the Foundation." *Journal of Health Politics, Policy and Law* 32(5): 759–83.

Olsen, Jan Abel. 1994. "Production Gains: Should They Count in Health Care Evaluations?" *Scottish Journal of Political Economy* 41(1): 69–84.

Olsen, Jan Abel, and Jeff Richardson. 1999. "Production Gains from Health Care: What Should Be Included in Cost-Effectiveness Analyses?" *Social Science and Medicine* 49(1): 17–26.

Persky, Joseph. 2001. "Retrospectives: Cost-Benefit Analysis and the Classical Creed." *Journal of Economic Perspectives* 15(4): 199–208.

Rajkumar, Andrew S., and Michael T. French. 1997. "Drug Abuse, Crime Costs, and the Economic Benefits of Treatment." *Journal of Quantitative Criminology* 13(3): 291–323.

Ridker, Ronald G. 1967. *Economic Costs of Air Pollution*. New York: Praeger.

Schochet, Peter Z., Sheena McConnell, and John Burghardt. 2003. *National Job Corps Study: Findings Using Administrative Earnings Records Data*. Report 8140-840. Princeton, NJ: Mathematica Policy Research.

Slemrod, Joel, and Shlomo Yitzhaki. 2001. "Integrating Expenditure and Tax Deductions: The

Marginal Cost of Funds and the Marginal Benefit of Projects." *National Tax Journal* 54(2): 189–201.

Snow, Arthur, and Ronald S. Warren, Jr. 1996. "The Marginal Welfare of Public Funds: Theory and Estimates." *Journal of Public Economics* 61(2): 289–305.

State of Washington. 2006. *Legislative Budget Notes 2005–07 and 2006 Supplement*. Olympia: Legislative Information Center.

Steiner, Peter. 1974. "Public Expenditure Budgeting. In *The Economics of Public Finance*, eds. Alan S. Blinder, Robert M. Solow, George F. Break, Peter O. Steiner, and Dick Netzer. Washington, DC: Brookings Institution Press.

Viscusi, W. Kip. 1993. "The Value of Risks to Life and Health." *Journal of Economic Literature* 31(4): 1912–46.

Viscusi, W. Kip, and Joseph Aldy. 2003. "The Value of Statistical Life: A Critical Review of Market Estimates." *Journal of Risk and Uncertainty* 27(1): 5–76.

Weimer, David L., and Aidan R. Vining. 2005. *Policy Analysis: Concepts and Practice*, 4th ed. Upper Saddle River, NJ: Prentice Hall.

Weimer, David L., Aidan R. Vining, and Randall K. Thomas. 2008. "Cost-Benefit Analysis Involving Addictive Goods: Using Contingent Valuation to Estimate Willingness to Pay in Smoking Cessation." *Health Economics* (forthcoming). www.lafollette.wisc.edu/publications/workingpapers/#2006–012.

Weinstein, Milton C., Joanna E. Siegel, Alan M. Garber, Joseph Lipscomb, Bryan R. Luce, Willard G. Manning, Jr., and George Torrance. 1997. "Productivity Costs, Time Costs and Health-Related Quality of Life: A Response to the Erasmus Group." *Health Economics* 6(5): 505–10.

Weisbrod, Burton A. 1968. "Income Redistribution Effects and Cost-Benefit Analysis." In *Problems in Public Expenditure Analysis*, ed. S. B. Chase. Washington, DC: Brookings Institution Press.

———. 1981. "Benefit-Cost Analysis of a Controlled Experiment: Treating the Mentally Ill." *Journal of Human Resources* 16(4): 523–48.

Wolfe, Barbara, and Robert Haveman. 2001. "Accounting for the Social and Non-Market Benefits of Education. In *The Contribution of Human and Social Capital to Sustained Economic Growth and Well Being*, ed. John F. Helliwell. Vancouver: University of British Columbia Press.

Contributors

Clive R. Belfield is an associate professor of economics at Queens College, City University of New York. He has published widely in the field of the economics of education. His most recent publications include editorship of a special issue of the *Economics of Education Review* on the economics of early childhood education and a book, coedited with Professor Henry Levin, *The Price We Pay: Economic and Social Consequences* (Brookings Institution Press, 2007).

Jeffrey A. Butts is a research fellow with Chapin Hall at the University of Chicago. Previously he was the director of the Program on Youth Justice at the Urban Institute in Washington, DC. He has conducted research on a wide range of juvenile justice topics, including the effectiveness of teen courts and juvenile drug courts, the methods used by state agencies to anticipate changing juvenile corrections populations, and new strategies for measuring disproportionate minority contact in juvenile justice.

Jonathan P. Caulkins is a professor of operations research and public policy at Carnegie Mellon University's Qatar Campus and Heinz School of Public Policy. He specializes in mathematical modeling and systems analysis of social policy decision problems with a particular focus on issues pertaining to drugs, crime, violence, and prevention—work that won the David Kershaw Award from the Association of Public Policy Analysis and Management. He was codirector of RAND's Drug Policy Research Center (1994–1996), and the founding director of RAND's Pittsburgh office (1999–2001).

Lance Freeman is an associate professor in the urban planning program at Columbia University. His research focuses on affordable housing, gentrification, ethnic and racial stratification in housing markets, and the relationship between the built environment and well-being. He has published several articles in refereed journals on issues related to neighborhood change, urban poverty, housing policy, urban sprawl, and residential segregation and authored *There Goes the Hood: Views of Gentrification from the Ground Up* (Temple University Press, 2006).

David Greenberg is a professor of economics, emeritus, at the University of Maryland, Baltimore County. His major research areas have been employment and training programs, social experiments, and cost-benefit analysis. He is the coauthor of *The Digest of Social Experiments*, 3rd ed. (Urban Institute, 2004), *Welfare to Work: New Labour and the U.S. Experience* (Ashgate, 2005), and *Cost-Benefit Analysis: Concepts and Practice*, 3rd ed. (Pearson Prentice Hall, 2006).

Robert Lerman is a professor of economics at American University, a senior fellow at the Urban Institute, and a research fellow of the Institute for the Study of Labor (IZA) in Bonn, Germany. An expert on youth employment, welfare programs, skill development, and family structure, he was one of the first scholars to examine the economic determinants of unwed fatherhood and to propose a youth apprenticeship strategy in the United States. His most recent publication is "Are Skills the Answer? Reforming the Education and Training System in the United States," in *A Future of Good Jobs? America's Challenge in the Global Economy* (Upjohn Institute, 2008).

John K. Roman is a senior research associate in the Justice Policy Center at the Urban Institute where his research focuses on evaluations of innovative crime control policies and programs. He is currently directing studies of the demand for community-based interventions with drug-involved arrestees, the use of DNA in burglary investigations, and the cost of the death penalty. His research includes studies of drug courts, the age of juvenile jurisdiction, prisoner reentry, and cost-benefit methodology. He is the coeditor of *Juvenile Drug Courts and Teen Substance Abuse* and a forthcoming volume on cost-benefit analysis and crime control policies.

Mark S. Salzer is an associate professor in the Department of Psychiatry at the University of Pennsylvania and a research psychologist in the VISN 4 Mental Illness Research, Education, and Clinical Center at the Philadelphia VA Medical Center. He is the principal investigator and director of the University of Pennsylvania Collaborative on Community Integration of Individuals with Psychiatric Disabilities, a rehabilitation research and training center funded by the National Institute on Disability and Rehabilitation Research (NIDRR).

Nathan Tefft is an assistant professor at Bates College in the Department of Economics. His research interests are broadly related to health economics with recent focus on mental health issues and the effects of soft drink taxes on consumption and obesity. He is currently a predoctoral trainee supported by the National Institute of Mental Health.

David J. Vanness is an assistant professor of population health sciences at the University of Wisconsin School of Medicine and Public Health. He previously was a senior associate consultant in the Division of Health Care Policy and Research at the Mayo Clinic in Rochester, Minnesota. He conducts methodological and applied research in health economics, focusing on medical decision making and the cost-effectiveness of health care programs.

Aidan R. Vining is the CNABS Professor of Business and Government Relations in the Faculty of Business Administration, Simon Fraser University. He teaches and researches in the areas of public policy, policy analysis, and business strategy. His recent articles have appeared in the *Journal of Public Administration Research and Theory*, the *Journal of Policy Analysis and Management*, and *Health Economics*. He is the coauthor of *Policy Analysis; Concepts and Practice*, 4th ed. (Pearson Prentice Hall, 2005) and *Cost-Benefit Analysis: Concepts and Practice*, 3rd ed. (Pearson Prentice Hall, 2006).

Christy Visher is a professor of sociology and criminal justice at the University of Delaware. Her research interests focus on communities and crime, criminal careers, substance use, and the evaluation of strategies for crime control and prevention. She recently completed a multisite longitudinal study of over 1,500 men and women released from prison. She is also co-principal investigator of the Multi-Site Evaluation of the Serious and Violent Offender Reentry Initiative, an examination of state and local prisoner reentry programs funded by the federal government.

David L. Weimer is a professor of political science and public affairs at the University of Wisconsin–Madison. His recent research has been in the areas of environmental and health policy. He is the coauthor of *Policy Analysis: Concepts and Practice*, 4th ed. (Pearson Prentice Hall, 2005) and *Cost-Benefit Analysis: Concepts and Practice*, 3rd ed. (Pearson Prentice Hall, 2006). In 2006 he served as president of the Association for Public Policy Analysis and Management.

Michael Wiseman is a research professor of public policy, public administration, and economics at the George Washington University and visiting scholar in the Office of Policy of the U.S. Social Security Administration. His research interests include public assistance policy, performance management in social assistance administration, program evaluation, and comparative social policy analysis. He is a research affiliate of the National Poverty Center at the University of Michigan and the Institute for Research on Poverty at the University of Wisconsin–Madison.

Barbara Wolfe is a professor of public affairs, economics, and population health sciences and a faculty affiliate of the Institute for Research on Poverty at the University of Wisconsin–Madison. Her research focuses broadly on poverty and health issues. Her recent work addresses the effects of welfare reform, economics of disability, the relationship between wealth and health, racial disparities in health, and intergenerational determinants of success in young adults. She is a member of the Institute of Medicine and vice chair of the National Academy of Sciences/Institute of Medicine Board on Children, Youth and Families.

Index

A+ Accountability Program, 40
Abecedarian Early Childhood Intervention, 19, 37, 223, 228
addiction, drug. *See* illicit substance abuse interventions
Administration for Children and Families (ACF), 164
Agency for Healthcare Research and Quality, U.S., 51
Aid to Families with Dependent Children (AFDC), 167, 196–98, 201–2, 206–9, 243
Akron, University of, 113
alcohol abuse, 53, 94, 263–64
Americans with Disabilities Act (ADA), 58, 68, 71
Annie E. Casey Foundation, 116
Aos, Steve, 25, 106, 134, 139, 235–38
Army Corps of Engineers, U.S., 250
Arrestee Drug Abuse Monitoring (ADAM) project, 135
Aspen Institute, 173
Assertive Community Treatment (ACT), 70, 75–76
Australia, 231, 263
avoided cost method, 10–12

Ballard, Charles, 253
Barnett, Steven, 228
Barrett, Barbara, 75
Baum, Erica, 206
Bazelon Center, 71
Becker, Gary, 49
Belenko, Steven, 90, 94, 234
Belfield, Clive R., 31–43, 223, 228–29
benefit-cost ratios, 13
Big Brothers/Big Sisters, 108, 265
Bitler, Marianne, 21–22
Borman, Geoffrey D., 38, 40

Borum, John, 71
Brewer, Dominic, 36
Brookings Institution, 189
Browning, Edgar, 168
Buchmueller, Thomas, 57
Butts, Jeffrey A., 103–21, 235–36

Caldwell, Michael, 236
California
  earnings and TANF benefits in, 192
  Greater Avenues for Independence (GAIN) program, 208–9
  Proposition 36, 94–95
California Peninsula Academies, 229
Cameron, Jacqui, 93
Canada
  Earnings Supplement Project (ESP), 170–71
  Self-Sufficiency Project (SSP), 209–10, 215
Career Academy model, 174–75
Carneiro, Pedro, 31, 33, 39
Carolina Abecedarian Project. *See* Abecedarian Early Childhood Intervention
Carter, Jimmy, 178
Cartwright, William, 234
Caulkins, Jonathan P., 83–97, 106, 232–33, 263
CBA. *See* cost-benefit analysis
CBT. *See* cognitive-behavioral psychotherapy
CEA. *See* cost-effectiveness analysis
Cebulla, Andreas, 206, 208, 243
Center for Budget and Policy Priorities, 189
Center for Employment Opportunities, 139
Center for Mental Health Services, 72, 78–79
Centers for Disease Control and Prevention (CDC), 51–52
Chalamat, Maturot, 77
Chandler, Sara, 86
Chicago Child-Parent Center Program (CPC), 18–19, 37, 223, 228

children
early investments in (see early childhood
interventions)
immunization of, 52–53
juvenile crime (see juvenile crime interventions)
child support, 165, 180
Chisolm, Dan, 74
Chriqui, Jamie, 96
Clark, Robin, 76
Clarke, Philip M., 11, 231
Clinical Antipsychotic Trials of Intervention
Effectiveness (CATIE), 69
Clinton, Bill, 251
Coggeshall, Mark, 139
cognitive-behavioral (CBT) psychotherapy,
69–70, 75, 133–34
Cohen, Mark, 105, 260–61
Commonwealth Fund National Scorecard,
50, 56
Community Work Experience Program,
197
contingent valuation (CV)
acceptance of, growing, 259–60
altruist value, use in estimating, 260
costs of crime, use in estimating, 105, 261
environmental damages, use in estimating,
131, 251
intangible effects, use of in estimating, 214
monetization, as a method of, 10, 12–13
Cooper, Harris, 38
COSP. See mental health, consumer-operated
services program
cost-benefit analysis (CBA)
agenda for future research (see social policy,
future application of CBA to)
in democratic societies, 1–2, 13–14
distributionally weighted, 258
of early childhood interventions, 25–27, 221,
223, 228
of education, 33–34, 228–30
environmental issues/policies, application
to, 251
government demand for, 250–51
of health-care interventions, 50–51, 53,
58–59, 221, 230–31
of housing assistance programs, 156–58,
238–40

of illicit substance abuse interventions,
88–89, 91–92, 94–97, 232–35
integrity of and experimental vs. nonexperimental data, 249–50
of juvenile crime interventions, 104–6,
118–21, 235–37
of labor market interventions, 176–81,
240–43, 255
of mental health interventions, 73–79,
231–32
of prisoner reentry programs, 129–31, 144,
237–38
in program evaluation, 4–6
social policy, agenda for future application
to (see social policy, future application of
CBA to)
social policy, overview of application to,
14–15, 219–23, 224–27t.
social policy, underdevelopment for evaluation of, 14–15
steps involved in, 6–14
uncertainty in, sensitivity analysis and, 13,
265–67
valuation (see contingent valuation; monetization; shadow prices; valuation)
of welfare-to-work programs (see
welfare-to-work and work-incentive programs, CBA of)
cost-effectiveness analysis (CEA)
of Britain's welfare-to-work and employment
programs, 213
early childhood interventions, applied to,
25–27
health-care interventions, applied to, 50–56,
59, 221, 230–31
illicit substance abuse interventions, applied
to, 90–91, 93
mental health interventions, applied to,
75–79
return on investment studies and, 84
Crane, Barry, 86
criminal behavior
drug abuse (see illicit substance abuse interventions)
estimating cost of, 105, 119, 260–62
estimating savings from avoided, 262–63
juvenile (see juvenile crime interventions)
Culhane, Dennis, 76, 232

Cullen, Julie, 39
Currie, Janet, 21–22, 153, 239
CV. *See* contingent valuation

Daley, Marilyn, 234
Davies, Jim, 256
Davis, Abigail, 212
Dee, Thomas, 40, 256
Deficit Reduction Act of 2005 (DEFRA), 193
DeParle, Jason, 188
Dickie, Mark, 260
disabilities
    Britain's New Deal for Disabled People
        (NDDP), 211–12
    mental (*see* mental health)
    Social Security Disability Insurance (SSDI),
        194–95, 242
    Supplemental Security Income (SSI),
        193–95, 242–43
discounting, real social discount rate, 13
distributional concerns
    improvements in the circumstances of the
        disadvantaged, valuation of, 258–60
    redistributive policies and efficiency, 2–3
Dowling, N. Moritza, 38
Drake, Elizabeth, 237–38
drug abuse and addiction. *See* illicit substance
    abuse interventions
Duncan, Greg, 179
DWP. *See* United Kingdom, Department for
    Work and Pensions

early childhood interventions (ECIs), 17–18,
    27–28
    CBAs and CEAs of, 25–27, 221, 223, 228
    childhood immunization, 52–53
    health care programs, 23–24
    home visit programs, 19–21
    juvenile crime and, 106
    nutrition programs, 21–22
    prenatal care for low birth weight, 52
    preschool programs, 18–19, 37, 41–42, 223,
        228
    shadow price of IQ points for CBA of,
        257–58
    structure of schooling, changing the, 22–23
    success, promising, 22–25
    successful, 18–22

Early Head Start, 19, 38
Early Intervention Initiative (EII), 194–95
Early Training Project, 19
Earned Income Tax Credit (EITC), 167–71,
    178–81, 188–90, 192, 202, 240–41
Earnings Supplement Project (ESP), 170–71
ECIs. *See* early childhood interventions
education
    adult correctional programming, 132
    CBAs of policies/programs in, 33–34,
        228–30
    charter schools, 39
    class size, 35–36
    community colleges, 175
    economic analysis of, 32–34, 42–43
    exit-based exams and accountability frame-
        works, 40
    grade retention, 38
    investment in, analysis of potential (*see* edu-
        cation, investment in)
    job training programs, 171–75, 180–81
    peer tutoring, 38–39
    preschool programs, 18–19, 37, 41–42, 223,
        228
    psychoeducation, 70, 76
    school-based drug abuse prevention pro-
        grams, 87–89
    school choice and competition, 39
    school size, 37, 41
    shadow prices for schooling, 256–57
    significance of, CBA applications and, 27
    special, 41
    structure of schooling, programs changing
        the, 22–23
    summer school, 38
    teacher quality/teacher salary increases, 35
    vouchers, 39
    Washington State Institute for Public Policy
        study of K-12 policies, 230
    whole-school reform, 40–41
education, investment in
    perspectives for evaluating, 32
    potentially desirable, 34–41
    priorities for exploring, 41–42
    private advantages of, 31–32
    programs that are potentially desirable,
        37–39
    reforms that are potentially desirable, 39–41

efficiency
  definition of, 1
  nonefficiency social values and, 2–4
  program evaluation, as a factor in, 5–6
  underrepresentation in representative de-
    mocracies, 1–2
Eibner, Christine, 94
EIDD. *See* Employment Intervention for the
    Disabled Dependent demonstration
Eight Americas Study, 49–50
EII. *See* Early Intervention Initiative
Eissa, Nada, 168
EITC. *See* Earned Income Tax Credit
Employee Retirement Income Security Act
    (ERISA), 58
employment
  assistance programs for people with mental
    disabilities, 75
  prisoner reentry programs and, 138–39, 165
  supported for people with mental disabili-
    ties, 71, 77
  See also labor markets; welfare-to-work
    policies
Employment Intervention for the Disabled
    Dependent (EIDD) demonstration, 193–95
environmental policy, 131, 251
equity
  educational investments based on, 34
  efficiency and, relationship between, 2–4, 34
  health, disparities experienced by the disad-
    vantaged regarding, 49–50
  policy analysis and, 5
European Union, Open Method of Coordina-
    tion, 192

Family Support Act of 1988, 196
Farrington, David, 237
Fass, Simon, 236
Fighting Back initiative, 89–90
Figlio, David, 40
Financial Intermediation and Strategic Sup-
    port (FISS) demonstration, 187–91
First Things First program, 40–41, 229
Fisher, Deborah A., 105
FISS. *See* financial intermediation and strate-
    gic support demonstration
Fleming, Michael, 53, 235
food stamp program, 167, 189–90, 192, 197

Ford Foundation, 198
Fountain, Douglas, 91, 263
Freeman, Lance, 151–59, 238–40
French, Michael, 90, 234, 261
Friedman, Lee, 237
functional family therapy (FFT), 106–7

GAIN. *See* Greater Avenues for Independence
    program
Galster, George, 155
Garces, Erica, 38
general equilibrium analysis, 10–11
Gennetian, Lisa, 198
Gerstein, Dean, 91
Gianfrancesco, Frank, 74
Giannarelli, Linda, 191
Good Behavior Game, 90
Grady, Meghan, 74
Gramlich, Ned, 106
Greater Avenues for Independence (GAIN)
    program, 208–9
Greenberg, David, 205–15, 240, 243, 249
Greenwood, Peter, 106, 235–36
Grogger, Jeffrey, 188
Grossman, Michael, 49–50

Haby, Michelle, 73
Hadley, Jack, 56
Hall, Chapin, 118
Hall, Wayne, 96, 234
H&R Block, Inc., 188–91, 242
Hanushek, Eric, 31–33, 35, 40, 42
Harkness, Joseph, 153, 239
Harwood, Henrick, 91, 234, 263
Haskins, Ron, 206
Haveman, Robert, 256
Hawaii's Opportunities for Probation with
    Enforcement (HOPE), 95
Hawken, Angela, 91, 95
Head Start, 38
health
  alcohol abuse, screening and intervention
    for, 53
  breast cancer screening, 55–56
  CBAs and CEAs of policies/programs target-
    ing, 50–51, 53, 58–59, 221, 230–31
  cervical cancer screening, 55
  childhood immunization, 52–53

Chlamydia screening, 51–52
colorectal cancer screening, 54
disparities experienced by the disadvantaged
    regarding, 49–50
early childhood interventions, impact of,
    23–24, 27
health care insurance, expanding access to,
    56–58
home visit programs (for pregnant women
    or mothers of infants), 19–21
as human capital, 49–51
income and, relationship of, 49–50
interventions perceived to be net beneficial,
    51–56
lost labor, estimating the cost of, 255
mental (*see* mental health)
nutrition programs (for young children),
    21–22
Oregon Health Plan, 58–59
political resistance to use of CEA, 59
prenatal care for low birth weight, 52
RAND Health Insurance Experiment, 250
smoking, screening and intervention for,
    53–54
substandard housing and, 151–53
Health and Human Services, U.S. Department
    of, 50, 193, 197–98
Health Care Financing Administration, 58
Healthy Families, 24
Healthy Kids (HK) program, 24
Healthy People 2010 (U.S. Department of
    Health and Human Services), 50, 56
Heckman, James, 31–33
Hewes, Gina M., 40
High/Scope Perry Preschool program. *See*
    Perry Preschool Program
Hissong, Rod, 111
Honey, E., 51
Hong, Guanglei, 38
housing
    affordability of, future research on, 159
    affordability of, human capital development
        and, 151–53, 158–59
    assistance programs, possible impacts of,
        152–53, 155–56
    CBAs of assistance programs for, 156–58,
        238–40
    human capital and, 151, 158–59

the literature on human capital development
    and, 153–56
Moving to Opportunity (MTO) experimen-
    tal program, 154, 158
securing during prisoner reentry, 133
supported for those with mental illnesses,
    70–71, 76–77, 232
Houston Parent-Child Development Center,
    20
Howell, Rene, 52
Hoynes, Hillary, 168
human capital
    health as, 49–51 (*see also* health)
    housing and, 151 (*see also* housing)
    poverty deconcentration programs and, 155
    process of, cumulative and reinforcing, 18

illicit substance abuse interventions
    CBAs and CEAs of, 88–97, 232–35
    coerced abstinence, 95
    drug and DWI-DUI courts, 94, 108, 112–15
    drug testing programs, 93
    harm reduction programs, 92–93
    in-prison and postrelease, 135–37
    integrative efforts, 93–95
    legalization and decriminalization, 95–96
    prevention programs, 87–90
    school-based drug abuse prevention pro-
        grams, 87–89, 106
    social costs of illicit drug consumption, de-
        veloping shadow prices for CBA of, 263–64
    studies of, issues confronting, 83–85, 96–97
    supply control studies, 83–87
    treatment-in-lieu-of-incarceration policies,
        94–95
    treatment programs, 90–92
    types of programs, 83
impacts of social interventions/policy
    difficulties of assessing, 14–15, 219–21
    identifying and measuring, 8
    net present value and present value equiva-
        lents, 13
    projections of future, 8, 14
    using CBA to assess (*see* cost-benefit analysis
        (CBA))
    valuation of (*see* contingent valuation; mon-
        etization; shadow prices; valuation)
    See also specific policy areas

income, adequacy of, 163–64. *See also* labor
  markets
Indian Alcohol and Substance Abuse Demon-
  stration Programs, 83
Individual Placement and Support, 77
Individual Retirement Accounts (IRAs),
  188–89
Infant Health Development Project, 20
Insell, Thomas, 67
Institute of Medicine, 52, 56

Jacob, Brian, 39, 40
JDAI. *See* Juvenile Detention Alternatives
  Initiative
JDCs. *See* juvenile crime interventions, juve-
  nile drug courts
Job Corps, 172–73, 177, 241–42, 255
job markets. *See* labor markets
Job Opportunities and Basic Skills (JOBS)
  program, 196–97
Job Training Partnership Act (JTPA), 172
Johnson, Byron, 137
Johnston, Susan, 76
Jones, Kristine, 77
juvenile crime interventions
  areas for new research, 108–18
  CBAs of, 104–6, 118–21, 235–37
  the economic perspective on, 103, 121
  functional family therapy (FFT), 106–7
  Juvenile Detention Alternatives Initiative
    (JDAI), 116–17
  juvenile drug courts (JDCs), 108, 112–15
  mentoring programs, 108–10
  multidimensional treatment foster care, 106
  multisystemic therapy (MST), 106–7, 114
  new program models, search for, 106–8
  Reclaiming Futures initiative, 117–18
  research agenda for, 118–20
  research on, existing, 104–6
  systemic reform of the juvenile justice sys-
    tem, 108, 115–18
  teen courts, 108, 110–12
  youth in the juvenile justice system, maxi-
    mizing social investment in, 103–4
Juvenile Detention Alternatives Initiative
  (JDAI), 116–17
Juvenile Justice and Delinquency Prevention,
  Office of, 110

Karoly, Lynn, 25
King, Joanna, 96
Kleiman, Mark, 91, 95–96, 233
Krueger, Alan, 36
Kuziemko, Ilyiana, 37, 86

La Bodega de Familia, 140
labor markets
  African American young men in, 163, 178
  apprenticeships, proposal for expanding,
    180–81
  CBAs of policies/programs providing work
    incentives, 176–81, 240–43, 255 (*see also*
    welfare-to-work and work-incentive pro-
    grams, CBA of)
  the Earned Income Tax Credit and, 167–71,
    178–81, 188, 192, 240–41
  employer wage subsidy programs, 175–76,
    241
  employment and earnings, programs and
    policies to increase, 163–66, 181–82
  employment services of prisoner reentry
    programs, 138–39, 165
  job training programs, 171–75, 180–81
  model demonstration and evaluation of
    work-based antipoverty strategy, proposal
    for, 179–80
  noncustodial parents, mitigating work disin-
    centives of, 180
  productivity assessment for CBAs, 254–55
  welfare-to-work policies (*see* welfare-to-work
    policies)
  work-conditioned benefits and work-related
    subsidies, 166–71
Landenberger, Nana A., 134
Larson, David, 137
Laub, John, 139
Lerman, Robert, 163–82, 240–41
Levin, Henry, 33, 229
Levitt, Steven, 39, 86
Lewin Group, 53
Liebman, Jeffrey, 168
Lieu, Tracy A., 53
Lipsey, Mark, 134
Lise, Jeremy, 210
Livermore, Gina, 91, 263
Loeb, Susanna, 35
Logan, T. K., 235

Long, David, 241
Ludwig, Jens, 38

MacArthur Foundation, 249
MacCoun, Robert, 93, 96
Malpezzi, Stephen, 239
Manpower Demonstration Research Corporation (MDRC), 196, 198–99, 208, 210
marginal excess tax burden (METB), 253–54
Marlowe, Douglas, 141
Maryland Reentry Partnership initiative, 132, 143, 238
Masse, Leonard, 228
Mathematica Policy Research, 241
Mazerolle, Lorraine, 94
McCollister, Kathryn, 234
McDougall, Cynthia, 236
MDRC. *See* Manpower Demonstration Research Corporation
Mead, Lawrence, 188
Medi-Cal, 24
mental health
  Assertive Community Treatment (ACT), 70, 75–76
  case management approaches, 75–76
  CBAs of policies/programs targeting, 73–79, 231–32
  clubhouse programs, 72–73, 78
  community- *vs.* institutional-based care, 71–73, 76–78
  consumer-operated services program (COSP), 72–73, 78
  cost-related analyses needed for, 78–79
  costs of serious mental illnesses, 67
  crisis intervention teams (CIT), 72, 78
  deinstitutionalization, 71
  drop-in centers, 73, 78
  involuntary outpatient commitment, 71, 78
  jail diversion programs, 72, 78
  peer support interventions, 72, 78
  policies and interventions lacking universal acceptance, 71–73
  policy areas needing CBA, 73–77
  promising policies needing more research, 77–78
  psychiatric advanced directives (PADs), 72, 78
  psychoeducation, 70, 76

psychopharmalogical interventions, 69, 73–75
psychotherapy, 69–70, 74–75
socially desirable interventions, 69–71
socially desirable outcomes, 68–69
supported education, 73, 78
supported employment, 71, 77
supported housing, 70–71, 76–77
Messman, Victoria, 260
Meyer, Bruce, 168
MFIP. *See* Minnesota Family Investment Program
Michalopoulos, Charles, 210
Miller, Cynthia, 198
Miller, Douglas, 38
Miller, Marna, 237–38
Miller, Ted, 105, 260–61
Minnesota Family Investment Program (MFIP)
  CBA of, 199–201
  evaluation of, 197–98
  limitations of, 201–2
  outcomes of, 198–99
  significance of, 187, 196
  as welfare experiment, 196–97
Minor, Kevin, 111
Mistral Security, Inc., 83
monetization
  in CBA of social policy, overview of, 222, 226–27t.
  costs of crime, difficulties regarding, 84, 119
  methods of, 9–13
  selection bias based on the ease of, 220
  See also contingent valuation; shadow prices; valuation
Monte Carlo analysis, 13, 266
Moore, Timothy, 93, 263
Mosteller, Fred, 35
Moving to Opportunity (MTO) experimental program, 154, 158
MST. *See* juvenile crime interventions, multisystemic therapy
Murray, Christopher, 49
Mushkin, Selma, 49

National Commission on Prevention Priorities (NCPP), 51–56
National Drug Control Strategy of 2004, 113

National Evaluation of Welfare-to-Work
    Strategies, 196
National Health and Nutrition Examination
    Survey (NHANES), 22
National Institute of Justice, 83, 260
National Institute of Mental Health, 69
National Institute on Alcohol Abuse and
    Alcoholism, 53
National Longitudinal Survey of Youth, 52
National Oceanic and Atmospheric Adminis-
    tration, U.S., 259
National Research Council (NRC), 86, 91,
    233
National School Lunch Program (NSLP), 22
NCPP. See National Commission on Preven-
    tion Priorities
NDDP. See New Deal for Disabled People
net present value, 13
Nets to Ladders, 189
Neumann, Peter, 59, 221
Neumark, David, 33, 39
New America Foundation, 189
New Deal for Disabled People (NDDP),
    211–12
New Hope project, 169–70, 178–79
New Jersey
    Juvenile Detention Alternatives Initiative,
        participation in, 117
    negative income tax experiment, 191, 196
New Jobs Tax Credit (NJTC), 175–76, 241
Newman, Sandra, 153, 239
New York City
    supported housing program in, 76–77, 232
    supported work experiment in, 237–38
Nicholson, Sean, 255
NJTC. See New Jobs Tax Credit
Nontoxic Drug Detection and Identification
    Aerosol Technology, 83
NRC. See National Research Council
Nurse Family Partnership, 20

Office of National Drug Control Policy, 89
Olsen, Edgar, 156
Onesta, Inc., 189
opportunity costs
    of public expenditures, 252–54
    in social surplus analysis, 9–11
    of volunteer time, 264–65

Opportunity to Succeed program (OPTS),
    139–40
Oregon Health Plan, 58–59
Oxford House, 133

Pacula, Rosalie, 96, 234
Page, Marianne, 35
Parents' Fair Share, 171
Partnership for a Drug Free America, 89
Patapsis, Nicholas, 90
Perry Preschool Program, 19, 34, 37, 221, 223,
    228
Personal Responsibility and Work Oppor-
    tunity Reconciliation Act (PRWORA) of
    1996, 167, 195–96
Pesa, Jacqueline, 74
Petralia, John, 71
Phelps, Edmund, 176
Pi, Chung-Ron, 236
Pitts, Timothy, 137
policy analysis
    cost-benefit analysis (see cost-benefit anal-
        ysis)
    definition/description of, 5
    retrospective and prospective distinguished,
        7
politics
    normatively attractive policies and, 2–3
    selection bias in application of CBA due to,
        220
Pollack, Harold, 92–93
poverty deconcentration programs, 155
Prais, Stephen, 36
preschool programs, 18–19, 34, 37, 41–42,
    223, 228
present value equivalents, converting to, 13
President's New Freedom Commission on
    Mental Health report, 68
Preventive Services Task Force, U.S.
    (USPSTF), 51–56
prisoners, reentry programs for. See reentry
    programs for prisoners
productivity assessment, 254–55
program evaluation
    cost-benefit analysis and, 4–6
    policy analysis, CBA, and, 5
Project CARE, 20
Project Greenlight, 140–41

Project Rio, 139
Project STAR, 35–36
psychotherapy, 69–70, 74–75, 133–34
Public Health Service Panel on Cost-
    Effectiveness in Health and Medicine, U.S.,
    50

race, health conditions and, 55–56
Rajkumar, Andrew, 261
RAND
    Drug Policy Research Center, 85–86, 88
    Health Insurance Experiment, 250
rational choice theory, 105
Raudenbush, Stephen, 38
Raymond, Margaret, 40
Reagan, Ronald, 251
real social discount rate, 13
Reclaiming Futures initiative, 117–18
Reclaiming Futures Model, 118
reentry programs for prisoners
    areas for further investigation, 141–43
    CBAs of, 129–31, 144, 237–38
    cognitive-behavioral therapy, 133–34
    community-justice partnership model,
        137
    employment services and job counseling,
        138–39, 165
    faith-based, 137–38
    features associated with better outcomes,
        143–44
    housing, securing of, 133
    in-prison education, 132
    limitations of current research and evalua-
        tion, 140–41
    marriage and family support, 139–40
    mentoring, 137–38
    postrelease, 132–40
    pre-release (in-prison), 131–32
    purposes of, 127–29
    substance abuse treatment, 135–37
Reuter, Peter, 96
Reynolds, Arthur, 228
Rhine, Edward, 141
Ridgely, Susan, 71
Rigter, Henk, 93
Ritter, Alison, 93
Robert Wood Johnson Foundation, 89, 117
Robins, Philip, 210

Roman, John K., 103–21, 127–44, 235–38
Rose, Heather, 32
Rosenbaum, Dan, 168
Rosenheck, Robert, 77
Rothbard, Aileen, 74, 77
Rouse, Cecilia, 40

Safer Foundation, 139
Salzer, Mark S., 67–79, 231
Sampson, Robert, 139
Satcher, David, 51
Saver's Credit, 188
Schochet, Peter, 241, 255
School Breakfast Program (SBP), 22
schooling. *See* education
Seattle-Denver income maintenance experi-
    ment, 196
Sectoral Employment Development Learning
    Project (SEDLP), 173–74
Self-Sufficiency Project (SSP), 169, 209–10,
    215
sensitivity analysis, 13, 265–67
shadow prices
    contingent valuation and, 13
    for the costs of crime, 105, 260–62
    for distributional improvements from social
        policy, 258–60
    estimates of commonly encountered, use of,
        6, 15
    of government expenditures, 253–54
    in illicit substance abuse interventions, 84
    of IQ points, 257–58
    necessity of for CBA, 14
    for schooling, 256–57
    selection bias and availability of, 220
    social costs of illicit drug consumption,
        263–64
    of volunteer time, 264–65
    See also contingent valuation; monetization;
        valuation
Sharkey, David, 158
Shone, Laura, 57
Shoven, John, 253
Shroder, Mark, 156, 249
Simons, Robert, 158
Smith, Jared, 198
smoking, 53–54
social capital, 25

social policy
    CBA applied to, 14–15, 219–23, 224–27t.
        (*see also* cost-benefit analysis (CBA))
    CBA applied to future (*see* social policy,
        future application of CBA to)
    equity-efficiency relationship and, 2–4
    goals and requirements of, 1
    impacts of (*see* impacts of social interven-
        tions/policy)
    improvement in the circumstances of the
        disadvantaged, valuation of, 258–60
    program evaluation, policy analysis, and
        CBA applied to, 4–6 (*see also* policy anal-
        ysis; program evaluation)
    targeting of, 2
    See also specific policy areas
social policy, future application of CBA to
    benefits of avoided crime, estimating avoided
        marginal costs of, 262–63
    costs of crime, updated shadow prices for,
        260–62
    distributional values, shadow prices for,
        258–60
    illicit drug consumption, estimating social
        costs of, 263–64
    IQ points, shadow prices for, 257–58
    Monte Carlo analyses, handling uncertainty
        with, 265–67
    opportunity cost of public expenditures,
        consideration of, 252–54
    productivity assessment in, 254–55
    schooling, shadow prices for, 256–57
    by state and local governments, 251–52
    valuation, use of nonexperimental data and
        emphasis on, 249–50
    volunteer time, valuation of, 264–65
Social Security Administration, 193–95
Social Security Advisory Board, 194
Social Security Disability Insurance (SSDI),
    194–95, 242
social surplus analysis, 9–11
Southern Maine, University of, 114
Special Supplemental Nutrition Program for
    Women, Infants, and Children (WIC),
    21–22, 52
Spitzer, Elliott, 189
SSDI. *See* Social Security Disability Insurance
SSI. *See* Supplemental Security Income

Stahl, Stephen, 74
STAR (Student Teacher Achievement Ratio)
    program, 23, 229
State Children's Health Insurance Program
    (SCHIP), 57, 189
Stern, David, 229
substance abuse and addiction
    alcohol, 53
    drugs (*see* illicit substance abuse interven-
        tions)
    in-prison and postrelease programs address-
        ing, 135–37
Substance Abuse Mental Health Services Ad-
    ministration (SAMHSA), 70, 79
Success for All, 40
Supplemental Security Income (SSI), 193–95,
    242–43
Supreme Court, United States, Olmstead deci-
    sion, 68, 71
Szanton, Peter, 206

TANF. *See* Temporary Assistance for Needy
    Families
Targeted Jobs Tax Credit (TJTC), 175–76,
    241
tax policy
    Earned Income Tax Credit (EITC), 167–71,
        178–81, 188–90, 192, 202, 240–41
    employer wage subsidies through, 175–76
    marginal excess tax burden (METB), 253–54
    negative income tax, 191–92
    saving encouraged through, 188
tax preparation services, 188–90
Tefft, Nathan, 17–28, 38, 223
Temple, Judy, 228
Temporary Assistance for Needy Families
    (TANF)
    AFDC, as replacement for, 196, 198
    the earned income tax credit, tax preparers,
        and, 188–89
    state choices regarding, the Transitional
        Incentives Package demonstration and,
        187, 191–92
    Supplemental Security Income (SSI) and,
        193–95
    welfare-to-work programs under, CBAs of,
        206
Ticket to Work, 194

TIP. *See* Transitional Incentives Package demonstration
TJTC. *See* Targeted Jobs Tax Credit
tobacco use, 53–54
Transitional Incentives Package (TIP) demonstration, 191–92, 201
Turner, Bengt, 239

uncertainty in parameters of CBA, sensitivity analysis and, 13, 265–67
unemployment, rates of, 163. *See also* labor markets
United Kingdom
  Department for Work and Pensions (DWP), 212–13
  New Deal for Disabled People (NDDP), 211–12
Upjohn Institute, 174
Urban Institute, 111, 118, 173
USPSTF. *See* Preventive Services Task Force, U.S.

valuation
  avoided cost method, 10–12
  contingent (*see* contingent valuation)
  general equilibrium analysis, 10–11
  hedonic methods, 10, 12
  monetization (*see* monetization)
  shadow prices (*see* shadow prices)
  social surplus analysis, 9–11
  travel cost method, 10–11
  of volunteer time, 264–65
Vanness, David J., 49–59, 230–31
Vining, Aidan R., 1–15, 219–44, 249–67
Visher, Christy, 127–44, 237
Vos, Theo, 73
Vytlacil, Eric, 31–32

wages, adequacy of, 163–64. *See also* income; labor markets
Wang, Ruey-Hua, 74
Washington State Institute for Public Policy (WSIPP), 230, 236–37, 251–52, 265, 267
Weimer, David L., 1–15, 219–44, 249–67
Weisbrod, Burton, 232, 255
welfare
  the earned income tax credit and, 188, 192, 202

experimentation with, 195–96 (*see also* Minnesota Family Investment Program)
welfare-to-work and work-incentive programs, CBA of
  Department for Work and Pensions (Britain), 212–13
  employment and earnings, programs and policies to increase, 176–81
  further research to improve, 214–15
  Greater Avenues for Independence (GAIN) program (California), 208–9
  meta-analysis of, 206–8
  Minnesota Family Investment Program, 199–201
  New Deal for Disabled People (Britain), 211–12
  overview of, 242–43
  reasons for, 205
  samples of, 208
  Self-Sufficiency Project (Canada), 209–10, 215
welfare-to-work policies
  building human capital through, 187
  Employment Intervention for the Disabled Dependent (EIDD) demonstration, 193–95
  evaluations of, 197–202 (*see also* welfare-to-work and work-incentive programs, CBA of)
  Financial Intermediation and Strategic Support (FISS) demonstration, 187–91
  human capital *vs.* job attachment approach to, 209
  Minnesota Family Investment Program (*see* Minnesota Family Investment Program)
  program activities, 205–6
  Transitional Incentives Package (TIP) demonstration, 191–92, 201
Welfare-to-Work Tax Credit, 176, 241
Welsh, Brandon, 237
Western, Bruce, 130
Whalley, John, 253
WIC. *See* Women, Infants, and Children program
Wiersema, Brian, 260–61
Winterfield, Laura, 139
Wiseman, Michael, 187–202, 240, 242
Wolfe, Barbara, 17–28, 38, 223, 256

Women, Infants, and Children (WIC) program
    prenatal care and maternal nutrition, 52
    Supplemental Nutrition Program, 21–22
work. *See* labor markets
Work Opportunity Tax Credit, 175, 241

World Health Organization, 67
WSIPP. *See* Washington State Institute for
    Public Policy

Yellowitz, Aaron, 153, 239